CW00666635

# A TIDY
# LITTLE WAR

# A TIDY LITTLE WAR

## THE BRITISH INVASION
## OF EGYPT 1882

# WILLIAM WRIGHT

SPELLMOUNT

*For the ladies – Gladys who will never read it,*
*Emma who will and Krisztina who made it happen.*

First published 2009

Spellmount
The History Press
The Mill, Brimscombe Port
Stroud, Gloucestershire, GL5 2QG
www.thehistorypress.co.uk

© William Wright, 2009

The right of William Wright to be identified as the Author
of this work has been asserted in accordance with the
Copyrights, Designs and Patents Act 1988.

All rights reserved. No part of this book may be reprinted
or reproduced or utilised in any form or by any electronic,
mechanical or other means, now known or hereafter invented,
including photocopying and recording, or in any information
storage or retrieval system, without the permission in writing
from the Publishers.

British Library Cataloguing in Publication Data.
A catalogue record for this book is available from the British Library.

ISBN 978 0 7524 5090 2

Typesetting and origination by The History Press
Printed in Great Britain

# Contents

Preface                                          6
Prologue                                        10
    1 Mutiny                                    15
    2 Riot                                      38
    3 Bombardment                               61
    4 Invasion                                 103
    5 Kafr Dawar                               137
    6 Ismailia                                 158
    7 Mahsama                                  175
    8 Kassassin I                              191
    9 Kassassin II                             206
   10 Tel-el-Kebir                             223
   11 Trial                                    259
Epilogue                                       280
Notes                                          288
Select Bibliography                            307
Index                                          316

# Preface

A few minutes before dawn on 13 September 1882 a British army launched itself in a surprise attack on a heavily fortified Egyptian camp at Tel-el-Kebir. The resounding victory won here gave Great Britain control of Egypt for more than seven decades.

This book is the first attempt to tell the story of that war in any detail since the Official History was published in 1887. The author of that work, Colonel John Maurice, called it a 'military' history, with little political or naval background, so it could be argued that this book is the first to give an overview of the whole campaign. I have tried, wherever possible, to use the words of those who were actually involved – statesman, sailors and soldiers – in an attempt to add flesh to the bones of Maurice's pithy and rather dry text.

Why has the Egyptian War been largely ignored while lesser campaigns of the period have been written about in detail? In the past half-century, for instance, there have been at least three full accounts of the short Transvaal War 1881, a fine full-length study of the 2nd Afghan War 1878–80 and frequent accounts of the Sudan campaigns 1884–85, while hardly a month seems to go by without another book appearing on the Zulu War 1879.

Events that happen quickly and end successfully, are usually of less interest than those which take longer or seem fraught with difficulties. General Sir Garnet Wolseley, the victor of Tel-el-Kebir, called it his tidiest little campaign, and so it seems at first glance – a slick operation that was over in less than two months. A huge admirer of the general and one of his staff officers during the war, Colonel Maurice made sure in his short narrative of barely 100 pages, that his Chief's view of things predominated.

On close examination and after more than a century, the Egyptian War is far more interesting than a cursory glance first tells us. For a start its six battles were no mere walkovers but tough and bloody affairs which on at least three occasions the Egyptians had a fair chance of winning. Twice they caught the British general with his pants down – literally! Warfare is often a gamble and Wolseley was a lucky player, yet at Mahsama he almost over-played his hand; in private letters and diaries he was honest to admit that his careful strategy could be compromised at any moment by the enemy and things often did not go to plan. I have tried to show that the background, development and actual campaigning in 1882 was much more complex, fraught with difficulties and minor disasters, and altogether a more near run thing than Wolseley's later bombast, varnished by Maurice, have led us to believe.

The campaign also began with the Royal Navy's only battle of any size between the close of the Crimean War and the start of the First World War. The Bombardment of Alexandria by Admiral Seymour's fleet was also not so one-sided as it might appear; it was here that the Egyptian gunners first showed their prowess as excellent marksmen and won the respect of their adversaries, while the British actually only effectively destroyed two enemy forts and almost ran out of ammunition.

The campaign was the only major combined services operation in 60 years of the *Pax Britannica*. The Royal Navy fought a bombardment, conveyed a whole army, helped to seize the Suez Canal in a complex night operation and provided a Naval Brigade which saw service in all the battles on land. Beauchamp Seymour, who got into the thick of things in two of these actions, was a fascinating old salt who sadly left no autobiography and precious little is known about him; by sifting through his papers at the National Maritime Museum I hope he now comes alive for the reader. A better man than I may one day do him the justice he deserves and write a full biography.

Looking at documents in various collections has helped me try and get an idea of what was going on in the minds of Seymour at Alexandria, Northbrook at the Admiralty and various politicians in Whitehall. I especially wanted to discover if some skulduggery or plot was at work to draw Britain into Egypt by the hawks in Gladstone's administration. I have tried to show how events developed; other historians have and will continue to view matters differently. My general feeling is that Seymour acted more prudently that I first thought, in fact, prudence was part of the problem after the bombardment when he singularly refused to stop the fires and wanton destruction until he got clear orders to do so. In this sense he must be held partly responsible for the chaos.

Wolseley based his plans on information collected by the Intelligence Department's network of spies. Much has been made of his 'secret' move to Ismailia; I have tried to show how several people were in the know. Nothing went quite the way Sir Garnet first envisaged things and information almost leaked out.

The Egyptian commanders can be accused of being over cautious, of refusing to commit their troops to an attack, since they knew their poorly trained raw recruits might panic and run at any moment. But when the British clashed with regiments like the Egyptian Guards, or the Sudanese, or came into conflict with enemy artillery they had a stiff fight on their hands. Before the 2nd Battle of Kassassin the Egyptians marched into position through the night and almost surprised the British camp. Yet this night march has been completely forgotten while that of Wolseley *four days later* is celebrated as a rare feat in the annals of warfare. The British war dead were moderately few, but the wounded at Tel-el-Kebir alone exceeded the combined wounded in all battles of the Zulu War. It was no mere walkover.

This book is primarily a history for English-speaking readers. I am no Arabic scholar and must pay a huge debt to the late German historian, Alexander Scholch, whose fine study of the Arabist Movement, first published in Germany in 1972, with an English edition nine years later, remains the definitive work. Scholch barely touched on the conduct of the war itself and the same is true of the American academic, Juan Cole, who added much to our knowledge of the social structure and philosophy of the nationalists in his 1993 book.

There is a goldmine of biographies and autobiographies by statesman, sailors and soldiers who served in the campaign. These all proved most useful. Fifteen years ago the military writer Donald Featherstone gave us a short but excellent account with superb battle plans in the Osprey campaign series. More recently Spink and Son Ltd published a new compilation of the despatches, casualty figures and awards by Peter Duckers that I found very helpful.

Various libraries and collections were consulted and can be found in the bibliography. I must especially thank two librarians. At Hove the indefatigable Zoe Lobowiecka showed me around the Wolseley Collection and dragged down various scrapbooks from the attic. When I found, with great sadness, that the Egyptian War section of Lord Wolseley's unpublished autobiography was (rather mysteriously) missing she mitigated my misery by telling me she had just heard that some of his diaries had surfaced at a library in Scotland. A quick phone call put me in touch with Aileen Anderson at the Low Parks Museum in Hamilton who confirmed they had several of his personal diaries. The 1882 diary turned out to be extremely interesting and I must thank Aileen and her colleagues not only for their help and enthusiasm but also the excellent cups of tea during the three days I spent with them.

I have already referred to Admiral Seymour's papers at the National Maritime Museum. Several diaries and letters were also examined at the National Army Museum. I was particularly pleased to find that the papers of General Sir Herbert Macpherson turned out to be nothing of the sort but a set of captured Egyptian Army telegrams from Tel-el-Kebir. These were helpful in fleshing out the actions of Arabi after the battle. A friend, Mr Peter Metcalfe, was kind enough to allow me to see his collection of letters by officers of the Coldstream Guards. I was also able to draw on the letters in my possession of Colonel Robert Rogers who commanded the 20th Punjab Native Infantry in the campaign, along with copious notes in books once owned by Sir Charles Dilke and General Sir George Willis.

A final word on spelling; to the irritation of Arab scholars and linguists I have retained the style in most cases best known by the British in the 1880s – thus 'Tel-el-Kebir' and not 'Tal-al-Kabir' and so on. 'Arabi' Pasha should, in pronunciation and spelling, be more correctly shown as 'Ourabi' and I thought long and hard about this but one thing swayed my judgment: I possess the first letter the great patriot ever wrote in English. It was sent eighteen months into his exile from Colombo to an English lawyer. In a firm and flowery hand it is signed clearly 'Ahmed Arabi the Egyptian'. It seems hardly right to argue with one of the main characters in my narrative. So I won't.

I ask the reader to forgive any lapses of style and hope that the events of 1882 might seem by the end of the book to have been worth the effort in staying the course with me.

William J. Wright
Budapest

# Prologue

*We are all Europeans now!*
Khedive Ismail

The loud rumble of cannon fire could be heard all across Cairo. People stopped their usual chores to listen and then digest what the gun salute meant for each of them. It was the hot afternoon of 26 June 1879. Earlier that day the Khedive Ismail, ruler of Egypt, but a vassal of the Ottoman Sultanate in Constantinople, had received the news he had dreaded for so long: a strange telegram addressed to 'Ismail Pasha, ex-Khedive of Egypt'. The gist of this message was that he should pack his bags immediately. The new Egyptian ruler would be his eldest son, Prince Tewfik.

Sixty-eight years earlier the dynasty to which Ismail and Tewfik were heirs had been audaciously created by their ancestor, Muhammad Ali, after his skilfully planned and bloody massacre of the Mameluke princes who had ruled Egypt for centuries. The small one-time tobacco merchant from Macedonia now proved that he was just as intelligent and perceptive as he was cunning and ruthless. By the time of his death in 1849, at the ripe old age of 80, Muhammad Ali had fathered 95 children and found time to transform his country along European lines. A huge admirer of Napoleon, he had enlisted the French to advise him on everything from growing cotton to constructing canals to control the annual Nile floods.

Abbas, who succeeded Muhammad Ali, was described by Flaubert as 'a moron, almost a mental case'. His reactionary views were in deliberate contrast to his grandfather yet, as Scholch has noted, the Egyptian peasants – the fellahin – found his rule comparatively benign since he 'did not wage wars, he did not build or dig canals and he did not constantly raise new taxes'.

Next, in 1854, came Said Pasha. A roly-poly pudding of a ruler, stout, genial, generous, but also easily excitable and thoroughly spoiled. It was this lover of French food, wine and culture, who agreed to permit Ferdinand de Lesseps to start work on his canal across the isthmus of Suez.

This massive project dragged on past Said's death until 1869 by which time Ismail Pasha was on the throne. A remarkable man, the new Viceroy combined a grand vision and high ideals with low cunning and unscrupulous behaviour. His detractors squarely lay the largest share of the blame for the debt crisis and the chain of events it precipitated at his door. In this they are probably correct. Yet his dream of an Egyptian empire, his military forays into Abyssinia, Somalia and the Sudan, the completion of the Suez Canal, construction of hundreds of miles of railway track and telegraph lines, the erection of more than 100 bridges, 15 light-houses, 64 sugar mills and 1,250,000 acres of land reclaimed from the desert, the improvement in customs, postal services and judicial procedure, the increase in elementary schools from 185 in 1863 to 4,685 just twelve years later (including the first state-run one for girls in the Ottoman Empire), all help explain why the Khedive Ismail still has his admirers. To them he will always seem badly maligned and a scapegoat for the Europeans who wanted his country.

In appearance the Egyptian ruler was short and stout, though not so fat as Said, and he tended to waddle when he walked. Usually wearing a black frock-coat known as a 'stambouli', and with a tarboosh on his head, visitors noted his dark brown bushy eyebrows and reddish beard. Some were made nervous by the way his right eye seemed smaller and half closed while the left tended to behave independently and fix on whoever was speaking. Generally in good humour, Ismail made witty conversation in slow, deliberate, well-modulated French, often sipping his favourite wine, Haut-Saternes. 'But it was in the private interview that he excelled,' notes Peter Mansfield, 'for he had a prodigious memory, and the gift of convincing even the most sceptical that he was supremely interested in their their lives and welfare'.

Many in his service adored him. One ex-Confederate soldier who spent ten years in the Egyptian Army wrote that Ismail was a man 'of sleepless energy and wonderful ability … sincere in his desire to pay his honest debts.'[1] Others found the Viceroy to be, by turns, kindly, generous, affectionate, cunning and incorrigible. One opponent called him 'an astute and superficial cynic', and although it was true, there was more to Ismail than mere cynicism. Charm was the chief weapon in his armoury and in a later age he would have made a superb public relations man. His major stunts, such as the lavish celebrations staged for the Suez Canal opening were, in Ismail's eyes, simply ways of endorsing the image of a progressive Egypt. They won him backing in his attempts to break away from Ottoman control and impressed future and current creditors with his wealth. Such displays, noted John Marlowe, who wrote a history of the debt crisis, served a purpose 'for as long as, and no longer than, he was able to pay his debts'. European bankers and officials were willing to turn a blind eye to

Ismail's mis-government, his oppression of the fellahin and wild extravagances just so long as he seemed solvent.

On his visits to London and Paris the Viceroy was first hailed as an enlightened ruler. At the Suez Canal opening ceremony he told his visitors: 'We are all Europeans now!' One of his best coups designed to impress European public opinion was the creation of a Chamber of Notables. This was lauded as a major step towards turning Egypt into a constitutional monarchy. 'In fact', wrote Marlowe, 'the Council had no legislative power and possessed neither the desire nor the means to exercise any control over, or even to criticise, Ismail's despotic acts.'

The bankers who were lending the Viceroy money at high interest, the contractors supervising his extensive engineering works, the European residents benefitting from his largesse, all basked in Ismail's geniality and generosity while carefully maintaining 'a conspiracy of silence' over his misrule. His image was to tarnish gradually. Before the end of the 1860s two women writing in different countries had castigated Ismail and his new Egypt. Olympe Adouard denounced him in France as a blood-sucking savage who seized whatever estates he wanted, used forced labour, and even treated his wives brutally. Lady Lucie Duff-Gordon, an aristocratic Scot who chose to live in Upper Egypt for health reasons, wrote in 1865: 'Egypt is one vast plantation there the master works his slaves without even feeding them.'[2] Two years later the situation was even worse: 'The fellahin can no longer eat bread ... taxation makes life almost impossible.'[3]

Superficially at least some of Ismail's excesses – bribes that totalled £50,000 in a single day, the construction and furnishing of new palaces (four in Cairo alone) – make him seem a mere playboy. But he was no silly debauchee. Every day the Viceroy worked like a businessman in his simply furnished office, seeing financiers, discussing and approving schemes, dreaming up his public relations entertainments and as time went on, worrying where he could procure the next massive loan. Most nights he found time to give a banquet. Where, for a few precious hours, he and his guests would enjoy the best French wines and fabulous food served off silver plate. He would take his cigars and cognac on the terrace and then it would be back to his office until midnight. This he did '13 hours a day for 300 days a year, a cross between a delinquent prince and a diligent clerk'.[4]

There is no doubt that in all his dealings Ismail thought of himself as a clever, sophisticated and wily manipulator. Unfortunately, for both him and the Egyptians, his financial speculations were terrible and the much sharper European bankers and merchants 'managed to ensure that every one of Ismail's major achievements contributed to their own enrichment'. As his debts mounted, the Khedive, as he was now styled, was to become involved in a risky game of high stakes diplomacy with the European Powers, especially Great Britain and France. Frequently he tried to play one country off against the other. In the end this skulduggery was his own undoing.

It was Said who organised the first Egyptian loan — a modest one of 60 million francs. But Ismail took this borrowing to undreamed of heights. Colossal loans meant that by 1875 he had no option but to sell Egypt's only remaining unpledged assets — its 177,000 Suez Canal shares worth approximately £3,500,000. Forewarned that the Egyptian ruler was disposing of this ripe plum, the British Prime Minister, Benjamin Disraeli, moved swiftly to snatch it up. Parliament was not sitting at the time and the only way Disraeli could obtain the shares was by a bank loan. According to the oft-quoted legend, Monty Corry, his private secretary, waited outside the Cabinet room for a pre-arranged signal from his master. Finally the door opened and the Prime Minister simply said 'Yes!' It was the word Corry had been waiting to hear. He rushed to the home of Baron Lionel de Rothschild, head of the British wing of the famous banking firm and told him Disraeli needed £4 million (about £400 million in modern terms). 'When?' asked Rothschild. 'Tomorrow' replied Corry. Slowly the banker peeled a grape before asking, 'What is your security?' 'The British Government' responded the young civil servant. Rothschild's eyes lit up. 'You shall have it!' was the answer. Next day, 24 November 1875, Disraeli wrote excitedly to Queen Victoria of his Suez Canal coup: 'It is settled; you have it, Madam. The French Government have been out-generalled.'[5]

With the Suez Canal now under their control and many millions owed to their banks, Britain and France began putting the squeeze on Ismail. Other European countries with vested interests in Egypt, such as the Germans and Italians, added their support. Ismail used all his wiles and skills to delay his creditors. It was, noted Marlowe, 'a virtuoso performance, a classic example, of the ingenuity of a bankrupt in keeping his creditors at bay.' Slowly but steadily some financial reforms were enacted; Britain and France set up a 'Dual Control' of the Egyptian Government with the intention of getting back all monies owed to their citizens and financial institutions while doing the best they could to return the country to solvency.

The Khedive fought back. He procrastinated, fired, re-instated, then fired again various officials and ministries. It was all to no avail. Far away, in the gloomy Topkapi Palace, Sultan Abdul Hamid had been watching events with mounting distaste. He viewed Ismail as a foreign stooge whose clownish behaviour had led to the humiliating necessity of granting official European participation in the running of not just a large Ottoman province but the most important of them all.

Hence Ismail's rude deposition. He spent four days packing, everything from Aubusson carpets to 22 of his best dinner services, though the rejected harem ladies ran amok and smashed furniture and mirrors to the tune of £8,000. On 30 June, just four days after being de-throned, Ismail and his wives set sail on the Royal yacht, along with as much treasure as he could stash aboard. Ships in the harbour at Alexandria gave him a cheery salute as he set out for Naples and a comfortable exile of sixteen years. An eventful reign was over and Egypt was on the brink of a new era.

# Mutiny

*We are not slaves and shall never from this day forth be inherited*
Ahmed Arabi

Honeymoons are by their nature unique affairs, short, sweet, and never to be repeated.

So it was for the first few months of the new Khedive's reign. Tewfik had decided that stability was vital and it required him not to antagonise the Europeans. A short-lived ministry under traditionalist Cherif Pasha resigned in August, and charming old Riaz Pasha returned from exile to form a government, taking for himself the Finance and Interior Ministries.

That summer the spirit of change was everywhere in Egypt. The Khedive proclaimed 17 July a patriotic feast day; notables from all over the country were invited to Tewfik's palace near Alexandria to be received by him, watch parades and a grand firework display. Decrees now prohibited the use of the whip and placed the army and courts on a new legal basis. A good harvest, improved and fair tax collection controlled by the European Commissioners, a drop in the rates of interest that money-lenders could charge and an increase in the price of land — all were substantial improvements for the fellahin.

The ordinary Egyptians, it seems, were as fascinated with their new ruler as he was by them. It was a land which, under Ismail, had changed dramatically. Telegraph lines now snaked across the desert to all towns and most villages, railway tracks and bridges dotted the landscape, especially in Lower Egypt, where hundreds of thousands of reclaimed acres were under cultivation.

The biggest changes were in the cities of Cairo and Alexandria, one the centre of government, the other of commerce. Cairo in particular had been remodelled by Ismail into almost two cities; the citadel still stood on its hill, but a new quarter had arisen to the west of Esbekiah Square laid out to a French design with straight streets and roundabouts. Initially the buildings had been residential, but soon banks, consulates, hotels, restaurants and clubs followed. Gas lighting adorned the new European quarter by 1870. A year previously a white wooden opera house was opened; Ismail had commissioned a new opera from Verdi but the great Italian composer was not in a creative mood and 'Rigoletto' was the debut attraction. Two years later, on Christmas Eve 1871, courtiers and soldiers, diplomats and pashas, all squeezed into the building to see the premiere of 'Aida' (sadly without the maestro who could not abide long sea voyages).

Shepheard's Hotel, on the corner of Esbekiah Square, was the centre of European life in Cairo and the most famous hotel in the Middle East. Entered by a flight of carpeted steps, visitors found themselves on a celebrated terrace where Europeans-only could survey the bustling panorama of oriental life passing in the street below. The hotel's public rooms were made even more fascinating to Westerners by a profusion of flowering greenery and an exotic garden where weary travellers could relax beneath shady palms. The building was demolished to make way for a new Shepheard's Hotel in 1890 but, years later, old soldiers would wistfully recall that first hostelry as 'one huge club ... And fun and flirtation was the first rule',[1] a great place for conversation or lounging about on the blue divans in the cool stone corridors or the long cane chairs festooned with plump cushions on the wide verandah. Dinner each night was a sparkling candlelit affair, the guests all in evening dress, the room noisy with laughter and banter, while smartly dressed Arab waiters scurried about the huge, high-ceilinged restaurant, its white-washed walls decorated with bright frescoes. At night a wealthy gentleman could enjoy a whisky and soda on the marble terrace of Shepheard's, see an opera or play, then try to wine and dine the young actresses of the Comedie Francaise, or a chorus girl, in one of the French, Greek or Italian cafes in the neighbouring streets, many with orchestras or bands in their lantern-lit gardens.

A building boom began in the mid 1860s and lasted for more than a decade. Cairo was one colossal building site; the beanfields and desolate country near the railway station were replaced by bijou villas and small shops. By 1877 a traveller alighting from a train found the old style donkey transport replaced by an omnibus or carriage direct to Shepheard's. Already several thousand tourists were arriving in Cairo each year. This band of sightseers, eager to experience the mysterious fleshpots of Arabian Nights fantasy, started in 1860 when Thomas J. Cook sent the first 32 ladies and gentlemen of the Victorian middle classes to the city.

In 1870 Brigadier-General William Loring, recently a divisional commander in the Army of the Confederacy, arrived in Cairo on a second visit to take up his duties as Inspector-General of the Egyptian Army. Waxing lyrical he wrote:

The plains were golden with rich harvests and dotted with elegant villas, embowered with roses. On one side, in full view, stood the Mokuttum Hills, the citadel on their slope … But, leaving these familiar scenes, one is impressed by the stately beauty of the new city immediately alongside of it with its comfortable hotels and commodious mansions, its broad avenues tastefully planted with costly shade trees and skirted by modern cottages surrounded by parterres of flowers, shrubs and trees.[2]

Loring was one of about 50 former Union and Confederate officers who entered Khedival service in the early 1870s at a time when Ismail was thinking seriously of breaking away from Ottoman control. The Americans were useful recruits since he knew that soldiers from European countries could not be trusted to give their full allegiance to a fledgling Egypt. The Civil War veterans were collected by Thaddeus Mott, a Union colonel, with the blessing of General Sherman. They kept their American pay rates and agreed to fight any enemy of Egypt except the United States. Quickly Mott brought to Cairo three generals, nine colonels, two majors, a doctor and a professor of geology. All but four of the bunch had fought for the South.

The most important one of them, who soon replaced Mott as the Khedive's favourite, was Colonel Charles Pomeroy Stone. A West Pointer, and veteran of the Mexican War, with greying hair and a neat imperial beard, not unlike a slimmer Napoleon III, Stone was a general by 1860, in charge of the defence of Washington, and credited with being the first soldier of the Union's volunteer army, but had argued with Edwin Stanton, Lincoln's Secretary of War and been demoted. In 1870 Stone was appointed Chief of Staff of the Egyptian Army. In that capacity he would faithfully serve first Ismail and then Tewfik for thirteen years.

Stone Pasha's task to reform the Egyptian Army was immense. He had to deal not just with a Turko-Circassian officer class who resented his interference, along with the usual problems caused by inefficiency and corruption, but a disparate collection of Americans under his command. They ranged from penniless alcoholics, like General Henry Hopkins Sibley; devil-may-care mercenaries such as Colonel Henry McIver who, at the age of sixteen, had almost been killed by a tulwar blow to his skull as a John Company ensign during the Indian Mutiny, but went on to fight under 17 other flags; religious fanatics like Major Cameron, who tried to poison other officers; and hot blooded youngsters such as Captain James Morgan.

A proud Southerner, Morgan had the temperament and good looks of someone born to get into trouble. On his first night in Cairo, for instance, he found his hotel too stuffy and went around opening all the doors and windows, to the fury of more seasoned travellers who knew this was an open invitation to dust and mosquitoes. More than once his pride and hot Louisiana temper led Morgan into fights. Flirting one day with a Royal princess in her carriage led to a chase by two guards waving scimitars. A fine horseman, with a splendid arab bay called 'Napoleon' (an unwanted gift from Ismail to Empress Eugenie), he only eluded his pursuers in true 'Wild West' style by jumping a double gate across a railway line in the path of an oncoming train. One night at the theatre the Prefect of Police, Ali Bey, ordered Morgan to fetch him a glass of water. The American, who was only a junior officer, carefully filled the glass, then threw it in the Egyptian's face and slapped him for good measure. A furious Ali Bey rushed over to the royal box and told the Khedive who replied: 'serves you right. I did not bring Americans here to wait on you … Go and ask his pardon.' Which the Prefect, no doubt smarting from the double humiliation, was forced to do.[3]

With his innate ability to offend almost everybody during his stay in Egypt it is not surprising that Morgan also managed to argue with the colonel of one of the infantry regiments. Inspecting Ahmed Arabi's regiment at the Abbasieh Barracks, the American was suspicious of the number of men who suddenly desired to pray; their weapons, uniforms and equipment thus going unin-spected. Morgan felt this was a ruse by lazy soldiers and so recorded all their weapons as unfit for service. When the Minister of War reprimanded Colonel Arabi he defended his men and accused the American of being prejudiced against Muslims. Then, to make matters worse, Morgan made a surprise inspec-tion the next morning and took away several rifles from praying soldiers which were found to be 'disgracefully out of order'. Unfortunately the incident only served to embarrass the Minister of War. It was decided to let the foreigner cool his heels by the coast and so Morgan was sent to inspect ancient cannon.

In his memoirs Morgan is full of praise for General Stone who he describes as 'a born manipulator of men', handling his troublesome Americans like 'so many naughty children'. Eventually by 1879 only Stone was left, but not before General Sherman had made a visit and been impressed by the efforts of his countrymen to improve Egypt's coastal defences and develop a general staff along modern lines. Ismail was so grateful to Sherman that he presented him with a bag of diamonds worth $60,000 and a special Act of Congress had to be passed to let him take the gems home untaxed.[4]

The task of Egyptian army reform was complicated by the country's social structure. Power rested with the Turco-Circassians and native Egyptians were only admitted to the lower ranks. By 1882 the population of Egypt was about 7,000,000 and less than 100,000 of these were Turco-Circassians. It is true that by this period Arabic was more likely to be spoken than Turkish or French, but other than this they lived apart from native Egyptians and despised them, while owning one quarter of all land. The duties of this elite were rather odd since they changed frequently. 'A pasha might, in the course of one or two years' wrote Scholch, 'be appointed to successive posts as Prefect of Police of the capital, Wakil (Under-Secretary of State) in the Finance Ministry, murdir of a province, president of a tribunal, and finally a commander in the army. The provinces might have up to five different governors in one year.'⁵ Such rule had one clear advantage for the Khedive – no position of power was allowed to become a rival power base. Politically the Turco-Circassians divided into two groups. Those, like Nubar, who demanded closer economic and diplomatic ties with Europe, cemented by autocratic Cabinet rule, and a pro-Ottoman group led by Cherif Pasha, wanting close ties with the Porte and less Western interference.

Reforms begun by Muhammad Ali soon needed more men than could be found among the sons of the Turco-Circassian elite. This meant that native Egyptians were also sent on missions to Europe and to the new state schools. But while they became the technicians or scientific experts, all decision-making roles stayed with Turco-Circassians. Long wars had also seen a necessity for Egyptians to enter the lower officer ranks. Their numbers rose and fell under the whims of different Viceroys and created a vast reservoir of resentment. In his autobiography Arabi Pasha expressed it well:

> I remained lieutenant-colonel for nineteen years; I had to look on as junior officers, who had been under me in the time of Said Pasha and Ismail Pasha, were promoted above me. Some of them rose to the rank of colonel, some to that of brigadier-general and division-general, and not because they knew more than I did, or because of special skills, or because they had been particularly courageous in battle, but because they were Mamelukes or Mameluke's sons of the Khedive's family. The Khedive bestowed on them ranks, decorations, beautiful slaves, extensive and fertile lands, and spacious houses, he gave them gifts of money and precious jewels sucked from the blood of the poor Egyptians and the sweat of their brows.⁶

Those Egyptians who for whatever reasons, were prosperous in the towns and villages, such as the local sheikhs, had high social prestige among their own people. The new Khedive continued the tradition of his ancestors by showering them with minor honours – a personal visit here, a small role in the provincial administration there – to keep them loyal. It worked surprisingly well.

Religion and religious fanaticism, until about 1879, played little part in Egyptian politics. The holders of the important religious positions, such as the Grand Mufti of Cairo, depended on the Khedive for their appointments and to keep them in line he dispensed liberal gifts of property. Occasionally in the provinces of Upper Egypt Sufi fanaticism would rear its head, such as the rebellion of Sayyid Ahmed at-Tib in 1865 at Girga, but soldiers and cannon always ended such rebellion efficiently and ruthlessly. The Nubar-Wilson Ministry changed things by stirring up a wasps nest of clerics opposed to reform. Ulama and religious students were suffering from savage financial cutbacks. Both Nubar and Riaz were denounced as the friends of Christians. Fundamentalist Muslims began to unite.

In the countryside the fellahin lived a life wedded to the land, its rhythms dictated by the seasons and the rise and fall of the Nile. Scholch described things well:

> The existence of the village depended on the Nile's uncertain blessings,but it was further put into question by the inevitable demands from Cairo. If the river spared it, the village looked towards the representatives of the the mighty: how much tax would be demanded of the inhabitants of the village; how many men for the army; how many ... to dig canals which did not irrigate the fields of their own village or to work on the estates of the ruler.[7]

Several other distinct communities were vital to town and country life. About 500,000 Copts lived mainly in Middle and Upper Egypt. In most villages the local clerk was a Copt. By 1880 many of these clerks had lost their jobs to French speaking Syrians and others preferred by European officials. This was creating resentment, not just among the Copts, but also among villagers who disliked the European style bookkeeping methods of the foreigners.

There were about 20,000 Jews in Egypt in 1880, mostly concentrated in Cairo and Alexandria as craftsmen, small shopkeepers and money-changers. It was possible for Armenians such as Nubar to enter the ranks of the elite, but Syrians never did so, although the first important Egyptian newspapers were published by Syrian Christians. Finally, on the fringes of society, were the nomadic Arabs of the desert, the Bedouin. In 1882 they numbered about 500,000 and were 'an incompletely integrated society', with marginal respect for the Khedive and none at all for most others.

By far the most influential group in the country were the Europeans. The 1882 census put their number at 90,886 persons – just 1.34 per cent of the population. More than half lived in Alexandria, with a further 21,650 in Cairo and 7,000 at Port Said. Less than 2,000 lived in Middle or Upper Egypt. Some 37,000 Greeks represented the biggest national group and few contemporary observers have a good word to say about them. Not because they were, in many cases, law-abiding shop-keepers and publicans, but the role they played as money-lenders. They seemed to figure in most fights, brawls and riots. This ill-feeling is hardly surprising when one considers that by 1882 the fellahin of Lower Egypt owed almost £4,000,000 in interest on their debts, a larger sum than the official land tax.

At the start of 1882, 6,118 British subjects resided in Egypt. Some were directly employed by the Khedive, such as Baron de Kusel, Comptroller-General of Customs, and Frederick George, Chief Engineer of the Telegraph Service, while others such as Edward Malet were on diplomatic assignments. The majority were based at Alexandria where they controlled most of the foreign trade. On the whole they were quiet, hard-working and law-abiding. The richer ones could enjoy the raffish lifestyle seen in Cairo, but even a modest clerk at Alexandria was able to sip an Italian coffee in the Place Muhammad Ali after a day's work, or escape occasionally to the delta to shoot quail and snipe. Almost all of them thought they were infinitely superior to those around them, that God had given them the ability to rule native peoples and the vast chunks of red on any map proved it. Only the French were perhaps their equals in arrogance and the policy makers of the Quai d'Orsay tried to match British influence every step of the way.

The treaties granted by Muhammad Ali to Europeans gave them freedom of travel, the right to be tried by consular courts, immunity from Ottoman taxes and the presence of a consular official at any arrest or search of their premises. In 1876 Nubar Pasha tried to bring all of them under Egyptian jurisdiction by setting up what were called 'Mixed Tribunals'. He was only partly successful and the Mixed Tribunals were especially unfair to peasant debtors sued by Europeans, since the proceedings took place in a language unknown to them, presided over by mainly European judges and based on legal concepts Muslims often found alien. The fellahin often felt themselves to be foreigners in their own country.

Not surprisingly, voices started to be raised against these injustices. Chief among them was that of Jemal el-Din al-Afghani, a fanatical Persian Sufi demagogue (though in Egypt he claimed to be a Sunni Afghan), who arrived in Cairo in 1871 after being exiled from Constantinople. During his travels in Afghanistan and India he had developed a fierce hatred of the British and imperialism in general. In May 1879 Jemal el-Din joined many others calling for a national anti-European alliance to combat foreign influence in Egypt. For a time Ismail, and then Tewfik, had been his patrons, but by the summer of 1879 this strident anti-European message was making the Egyptian ruler nervous. Without warning, Jemal el-Din was arrested and made to leave the country. His disciples, initially unmolested, continued disseminating anti-Western propaganda via radical newspapers.

About this time a group of intellectual young Syrians living in Egypt formed the '*Union de la Jeunesse Egyptienne*' and began demanding constitutional rule.

Installed as chief minister, tough old Riaz Pasha was no lover of radicals. In his youth he had been made to perform dances for homosexual Abbas, but was 'now a fragile little man of 50 with a wizened face and a harsh, high-pitched voice'.[8] In the late summer and autumn of 1879 he cracked down on all forms of dissent. Newspapers and journals received a warning and the most inflammatory were banned altogether. Parliamentary democracy was not something Riaz felt Egypt could handle. The newspaper of *La Jeune Egypt* was banned, along with the very different journals of Jemal el-Din's followers, and radicals were advised to go into exile.

In protest at these actions a group of politicians and notables formed the Helwan Society. They opposed Tewfik's acceptance of British and French control over that section of the budget mortgaged to foreign credit and wanted Egyptians to administer debt repayment themselves. Leaders of the Helwan Society included old school Ottoman traditionalists like Cherif Pasha and his friend, Shahin Pasha, staunch opponent of all things European. Later the group would make extravagant claims that they were the first real political party in Egypt, but Scholch concluded that

> ... the term political party cannot be applied to any Egyptian political group at the time ... there appeared at different times different groupings with different intents and aims. To serve them all up together as the 'National Party' would make it impossible to understand the events of that time.[9]

While on the surface Egyptians seemed happy with things generally, and even the *London Times* correspondent called it 'the best administration which Egypt has enjoyed', storm clouds were on the horizon. The first of these – and the first date which can be said to have led inexorably to the British invasion – was the appointment, on 18 August 1879 , of a new Minister of War. The man chosen was a 40-year-old pure blooded Circassian named Osman Rifky. He was told by Tewfik to reorganize the army and impose a strict discipline. Rifky saw this as a chance to return the army to strong Circassian roots and reduce the number of native Egyptian officers. Arabi Pasha later called Rifky 'a Turk of the old school, who hated the fellahin'.[10] He was not alone in these views and Loring Pasha called him 'a notorious scoundrel'. Another American, General Dye, a plain-speaking man and no friend of Loring, was even more blunt; after the disastrous 1875 expedition into Abyssinia he thought Osman Rifky should not have been decorated, but shot.

That Spring a General Election in Britain had swept the Gladstone back into power; Queen Victoria was aghast at having to accept him as her Prime Minister for a second term. A patrician cabinet was formed with the plum jobs of Foreign Secretary, Colonial Secretary and Secretary of State for India going to Lords Granville, Kimberley and Hartington. No one seemed to want the War Office while recent disasters were still front page news and it was reluctantly filled by the 52-year-old MP for Pontefract – Hugh Childers.

At the same time that changes were taking place in the Egyptian and British governments, events were about to push into the spotlight two Englishmen who would play key roles in the drama of the next 20 months. The first of these was Edward Malet, the new British Consul-General, who took up his duties in November 1879. Handsome and suave, Malet had been educated at Eton and followed his father, Sir Alexander Malet, into the well-mannered world of embassies and diplomatic intrigue. He dreamed one day of being ambassador in Berlin and eclipsing his father's old posting at Frankfurt where 16-year-old Edward started his career. On his arrival in Cairo, after a stint at Constantinople, where he had been embassy secretary, the 'placid, cold moon-like' man was soon disliked by colleagues and it created a sensation when he made his first joke. Years later a colleague, who had known him since his teens, praised Malet's discretion, but concluded he lacked imagination,

> … nor any power of dealing on his own responsibility with occasions requiring strong action and prompt decision … Personally he was amiable, without being attractive and he had retained a certain boyishness of mind which in his unofficial moments was very apparent. His industry was great and his conduct irreproachable … He always preferred his work, however little interesting, to any form of amusement, and even when on leave would spend his spare afternoons copying despatches.[11]

Peter Mansfield has noted how Malet's private letters 'reveal an extraordinary lack of inner self-assurance combined with a powerful ambition'.[12] His Egyptian despatches would be marred by a lack of critical judgment. Warned by statesmen like Lord Salisbury against any move that could encourage armed intervention in Egypt he still chose to ignore good advice. Initially he would support the army officers and try to steer nationalistic opinion down a European path. When events moved away from this route he would resort to misleading remarks to create an exaggerated picture in his despatches.

If Malet was to be the often hated mouthpiece and figurehead of British interference in Egyptian affairs then his *éminence grise* was Auckland Colvin. Later Malet would deny he was ever under Colvin's spell but the denials and excuses seem lame. An Anglo-Indian, Colvin was appointed to replace Baring as Controller when the latter was made Financial Secretary to the Government of India. He comes across as a tough, no nonsense man, dismissive of orientals as 'mere children in deceit'. Like Malet he was cautiously optimistic about Arabi and the nationalists, but once he had decided they must go he stuck firmly to that view. He was in a unique position to influence British public opinion since he was the Cairo correspondent of the *Pall Mall Gazette*, mouthpiece of Liberal opinion and Gladstone's favourite journal.

In some ways Malet and Colvin made an odd couple. The former was terribly sensitive to criticism and displayed neurotic tendencies while the latter was as steady as a rock. Somewhat oddly, Malet later described his mentor as 'not a man of many words, nor had he a suave and all-embracing manner, but there was something about him which was attractive *to those whom it did not repel'*.[13] (Author's italics).

In Cairo it was all change in the army as Osman Rifky began appointing Circassians to colonelcies over the heads of senior and more competent Egyptians. He followed this with a recruitment law that limited active service to four years. This Act horrified native Egyptian officers because they knew soldiers from poor families could not reach officer rank by merit in so short a time. In January 1881, 40-year-old Abd-el Al Hilmi, commander of the 6th (Sudanese) Infantry Regiment heard that he was to be replaced by a much older Turco-Circassian officer. The same news was also received by Lt-Colonel Ahmed Abdul Ghaffar of the Cavalry Regiment. At a banquet on the evening of 16 January Colonel Ahmed Arabi (Urabi) of the 4th Infantry Regiment heard with alarm that he too, as a popular Egyptian commander, along with his friend, Colonel Ali Fehmy of the 1st Regiment of Guards, might also be dismissed. In his memoirs Arabi says that he had already avoided assassination attempts and his mood was jittery. Arriving home he found Al Hilmi and Fehmy waiting for him. A noisy and brash officer, Al Hilmi's blood was up and he wanted to go to the war minister's house and arrest or murder him. Arabi replied: 'No, let us petition the Prime Minister, and then, if he refuses, the Khedive.' His friends asked him to draw up the document. In it Arabi pointed out that nearly all native Egyptian officers had been dismissed from active service and there was not one non-Egyptian on the temporary retirement list. Osman Rifky, the petition concluded, must go and in future, military merit alone should decide who was worthy of promotion. All three officers then signed the document and it was delivered to the government the next day.

Riaz Pasha was no friend of Osman Rifky and did not want to see the three colonels dismissed so he let the matter drift. When it finally came up for discussion at a Council of Ministers meeting on 30 January an indignant Rifky argued for immediate punishment. The Khedive, who always had a soft spot for the Guards, swore they would be loyal to the throne. After much talk it was agreed to lure the three officers to the War Ministry on a pretext, then arrest and swiftly court martial them. Hearing on 1 February that they should meet with Rifky at the Ministry made a suspicious Arabi recall the old story of the Mamelukes in the citadel. 'We were on our guard,' he wrote later, 'and made preparations necessary for our rescue.'[14]

Sure enough, when the three colonels entered the building as ordered they were seized, disarmed, insulted by several Circassians and put in custody. A court-martial, under the presidency of Stone Pasha hastily got under way. At the same time three Circassian officers set out to take command of their regiments. When Colonel Basmi, tried to take over the Guards he was promptly arrested by Major Muhammad Abaid, a young officer exceedingly loyal to Colonel Fehmy. A battalion of Guards now took up a position facing the Abdin Palace, while two other battalions surrounded the War Mininstry. About noon, on a pre-arranged signal, one battalion charged the building. There was no serious fighting, but some splendid scuffles, as tables and chairs were overturned and the Circassians inside fled for their lives. Osman Rifky only got away by jumping out of a window. To whoops and cheers the three colonels were carried shoulder-high out of the building to the Abdin Barracks. Sitting largely alone in a wrecked room General Stone tried to carry on with his ghost court-martial until someone pointed out everyone had left the building.

The scene at Abdin was repeated at the 6th Infantry barracks near Turah, south of Cairo, where Major Khadr Khadr locked up six officers hostile to Colonel Al Hilmi, left a company to watch over the prisoners and set off with the rest of the Sudanese for the city. Only in Arabi's own regiment did a transfer of command take place but, as Scholch remarked: 'Even then the regiment did not march against the rebellious soldiers.' At the Abdin Barracks, after the troops had calmed down, Colonel Arabi thanked them and pointed out that their opposition had been legitimate. All they wanted, he told his deliverers, was justice and quality. He then wrote a letter to Baron de Ring, the French Consul, blaming Osman Rifky squarely for all that had happened and asking for the support of the European Powers. All three colonels signed this letter, while colleagues went and delivered a similar message to Raphael Borg, the British Vice-Consul.

Baron de Ring, along with Malet, rushed to see the Khedive. The mood of the meeting was bleak. Surrounded by his ministers and several generals Tewfik received a catalogue of bad news: not one single company of soldiers was willing to support him, the garrison of the citadel had gone over to the mutineers, attempts to prevent the Sudanese reaching Cairo had been in vain and the Circasians commanding Arabi's regiment said it was proving difficult to keep the men confined to barracks. General Stone hopped around with impatience, his neat imperial bristling, and offered to take what Europeans he could find along with a volunteer company of Circassians and attack the Abdin Barracks. It was a suggestion that made Tewfik shudder and he firmly rejected it.

If no resistance could be offered then it was necessary to negotiate. This was the joint view of the British and French consuls. Malet personally thought the arrest plot had been 'stupid'. Nursing dreams of revenge the Khedive accepted the diplomatic solution; Osman Rifky was dismissed and Mahmud Sami el-Barudi, a distinguished courtier from an old Circassian family, became the new War Minister. Up to that time he had little or no acquaintance with Ahmed Arabi but things would change dramatically in the coming months and Mahmud Sami was destined to be one of the intellectual powerhouses of the nationalist movement. He and Arabi would make a grand team – much to the distress of the British Consul-General. A good deal of Malet's antagonism towards the Egyptian officers and the nationalist movement generally, described by him as 'a cancerous growth', seems to have been wrapped up in a dislike of Sami. He wrote 20 years later:

> To me he was, I confess, very antipathetic. I did not like looking at him. He had small shifty eyes set in pink and white eyelids. Some people become thoroughly uncomfortable if there is a cat in the room. I fancy that the feeling they experience is much the same as what I felt when Sami Pasha was about.'[15]

In the barracks soldiers greeted the news of Rifky's dismissal with cheers followed by shouts honouring the Khedive. The men, fearing for Arabi's safety, would not let him go home that night. It was not until next day that he discovered his wife had given birth on the previous evening to a baby girl. Shortly after the delivery she had heard of her husband's release and so named the child 'Bushra', meaning 'Happy Message'.

The next 20 months were to be ones of great upheaval in Egypt. The hero of the times, at least in the eyes of the army rank and file, native-born officers, and vast numbers of ordinary Egyptians, was the unassuming commander of the 4th Infantry, Colonel Ahmed Arabi. Son of a village sheikh, Arabi was born at Horiyeh near Zagazig in 1841. His education began at the local mosque-school but an elder brother taught him to do sums. He went away to Cairo for further studies but in 1854, when Said Pasha was trying to get more sons of village notables into the army, Ahmed, now 'a tall, well-grown lad', gave up his education for the life of a soldier. The fact that he could read, write and do arithmetic now proved useful and an officer relative in his unit helped him gain the post of quartermaster of the 7th Co., 4th Battalion of the 1st Infantry Regiment.

In 1857 he was made an officer. His superiors were so impressed with the young man that in a rapid series of promotions over the next three years he was a lieutenant-colonel by the tender age of 20. The American, General Dye, said Arabi would have made a good soldier in any army, and a duly impressed Said took him to Medina as his adjutant in 1861.

Later Arabi insisted that it was in the desert that Said Pasha prophesied the Egyptian nationalist movement. It was during this period that Arabi read the first non-religious book that impressed him – an Arabic *Life of Napoleon*. The book had belonged to Said who threw it dismissively on the ground with the words: 'see how your countrymen let themselves be beaten!' Arabi picked it up and read all that night. 'Then I told Said Pasha that I had read it and that I saw that the French had been victorious because they were better drilled and organized, and that we could do as well in Egypt if we tried.'[16]

Active service in the Russo-Turkish War eluded him but during the Abyssinian campaign Arabi was in charge of the transport service between Massowa and the army. Mistakes made in this disastrous conflict, by Turco-Circassians like Ratib Pasha and Americans such as Loring, along with the poor treatment meted out to the Egyptian rank and file, haunted him. Officers and men alike were in arrears of pay and Arabi started to pay close attention to the grievances voiced by his troops. Later he wrote that 'it was then I began to interest myself in politics'.[17]

What happened next is sketchy but Arabi seems to have started to get a name for himself among the top brass as the complaining type. This led to his discharge from the Army on charges of corruption, but these accusations were almost certainly trumped up (Arabi always lived off his Army pay, and his home and personal lifestyle, scrutinised upon his arrest in 1882, were found to be extremely modest). He was unemployed for a time, then got a job in the civil service. During this lean spell Arabi returned to attending lectures at the El Azhar Mosque in Cairo and gained a reputation for eloquence.

Marriage to a slave girl from the Royal harem, a happy union by all accounts, led to reinstatement in the army with his former rank. After the February 1879 fracas Arabi was accused of being a ringleader, but he hotly denied it, and he was separated from his regiment. By this time his hatred of Ismail was intense, as he freely admitted in his autobiography:

> I proposed that we should ... depose Ismail Pasha. It would have been the best solution of the case, as the Consuls would have been glad to get rid of Ismail in any way, and it would have saved after complications as well as the fifteen millions Ismail took away with him ... The deposition of Ismail lifted a heavy load

from our shoulders and all the world rejoiced, but it would have been better if we had done it ourselves as we could then have got rid of the whole family of Muhammad Ali, who were none of them, except Said, fit to rule, and we could have proclaimed a republic.[18]

This, then, was the colonel who emerged into the spotlight in 1881, a nationalist whose ideas were still developing, a non-intellectual who had slogged a quarter-century in the service of his country and became increasingly disgusted by most what he had seen. The events of February 1881, not surprisingly left him with little trust in the words of Tewfik or his ministers, but Arabi was no wild revolutionary. He had pledged his sword to the Ottoman Empire and fully accepted the Sultan as his Master under God. Perhaps it was an excellent knowledge of the Koran that made him seem so self-assured to his comrades; already some called him 'Sheikh Arabi', and as he increasingly became their spokesman and his fame grew, coupled with a genuine aura of humility and sanctity, men would call him 'El Wahid' – 'The Only One'.

Europeans who met him were initially ready to write the colonel off as a peasant – 'tall, heavy-limbed, slow-moving, dull-eyed, with a dreamy look on his plain features'. He failed to impress Malet who called him 'a presentable-looking officer of the peasant type, thick-set, burly ... but clumsy in his gait. It was easy to see that in the elasticity of youth he had probably been good-looking and, possibly, smart.'[19] One of the best descriptions comes from Alexander Broadley, the London barrister who would defend Arabi at his trial. At first in a cell he saw just a tall bear of a man, 'considerably over six feet in height and broad in proportion', with a sullen look on his dull face, not made better by a large, flat nose and thick lips. Noticing his guests Arabi smiled, and 'the change in his expression is so wonderful that would hardly recognise him as the same man. His eyes are full of intelligence and his smile is peculiarly attractive.'[20]

It seems that Arabi's political philosophy largely emanated from what he saw in the world around him; his modest library examined in 1882 revealed no Rousseau, no John Stuart Mill. His thoughts were simple and somewhat naive. Europeans who conversed with Arabi often describe him as a 'dreamer'. Seven months before the war for instance, the Austro-Hungarian Consul found that instead of talking revolution Arabi bored him with humanitarian and philosophical thoughts about a vague 'brotherhood of nations'.

Some of those who rushed to support Arabi in the weeks and months of 1881–82 probably had their own hidden agendas and saw him as a convenient stepping-stone to power. Others warmed to his dignity, honesty and moral courage. To the fellahin he championed in the months between the February

1881 mutiny and his downfall in September 1882, it did not matter that Arabi was not a brilliant military thinker or a great revolutionary – he was the first of their kind in centuries to be an inspiration. Arabi was special to ordinary Egyptians, notes Peter Mansfield: 'because he remained part of them and could understand and express their grievances in terms they could understand'. In this lay the core of Arabi's meteoric rise and appeal.

Sweeping reforms followed the mutiny but under the surface things were not good. Tewfik, thirsting to get even, said that he would weed the rebels out of his army 'slowly and unobtrusively', but Malet and Ring warned him on the same day against this course of action. During a private talk with the Royal tutor, Alfred Butler, the Khedive was even more blunt and confided he was thinking of appointing a new Cabinet 'to shoot the mutineers'. In public of course, Tewfik was all smiles and handshakes. He told Ali Fehmy to tell his comrades: 'you three are soldiers. With me you make four.' Unfortunately the insecurity of the colonels and their growing band of dissidents manifested itself in more distrust, hostility and insubordination. A persecution mania gripped the group who saw spies and assassins lurking everywhere. In his autobiography Arabi lists thirteen plots against him in the months up to September. Riaz continued to be sympathetic but he got so irritated by such paranoia that he reprimanded two of the colonels on 21 April in the presence of Mahmud Sami; if he believed every rumour he heard, said the old statesmen, he would never go outside his house. But the rumours kept proliferating. When Riaz and Sami heard talk that the Khedive was thinking of asking for military help from Constantinople they hurried to see Tewfik and delicately advised him against carrying out any policy without the support of the Council of Ministers.

In April the Egyptian army officers submitted a long petition of reforms. This led to a military commission recommending that the army be increased to 18,000 men. Already that spring the rank and file had seen their dull diet of bans and lentils augmented with rice, cake, meat and vegetables, and the Sudanese their special beer. Soldiers pay was also hugely increased, especially the lower and middle ranks, by almost 100 per cent in some cases.

During the summer months of 1881, two events – one internal and the other external – had given fresh impetus to nationalist sentiment in the army. Within Egypt a group of wealthy notables, including several Helwan Society supporters, allied themselves with the officers. They hoped by this ploy to advance their own power or, at the very least, to topple the pro-European government. The main British supporter of Egyptian nationalism, Wilfred Blunt, later said that Arabi allowed himself to become the chief mouthpiece of nationalist rhetoric at this time for very definite reasons. He regarded it, wrote Blunt: 'as giving him and his military friends a security against reprisals by the Khedive and his Ministers. He told me this repeatedly during the summer.' If Blunt was telling the truth, and it does not sound like some of his crazier talk, then at this stage Arabi was no fiery revolutionary. The colonel simply saw the nationalists as an insurance policy that would help his push through army reforms in the face of Turco-Circassian objections.

It was an external event that more than any other single factor, drove Arabi towards hardline nationalism, an event which, after the Joint Note of January 1882 would convince him that the European Powers were not to be trusted and wished to occupy his country. It took place some 1,000 miles along the North African coast at Tunis. Here, at about 4pm on the rainy afternoon of 12 May, amid the faded damask finery of a salon in an Italianate palace, frail old Muhammad es-Sadok, the Bey of Tunis, was told by the French General Breart that he had a maximum of four hours only in which to consider and sign a treaty permitting a French resident and permanent French Army in Tunisia. Just one month earlier, as part of a scheme hatched up by Baron Alphonse de Courcel at the Quai d'Orsay to regenerate France overseas, and given spin by President Gambetta, a *casus belli* in the shape of the Kroumirs, a marauding hill tribe on the Algerian-Tunisian frontier, had seen the Chamber of Deputies vote 5 million francs to stop the raiders. The French Government's fine words that 'it is as allies that we plan to enter and operate on Tunisian territory',[21] was news to the Bey who had not been consulted. Just one hour after Breart presented his ultimatum the Bey looked from a window on the French army camped outside, their artillery trained on his palace, and accepted the inevitable. Holding back his tears he signed with a trembling hand in Arabic a document in French that he could not read, and for which he was not even offered a written translation. In all but name it made Tunisia a French protectorate.

The little war by which France seized Tunisia shocked all Egyptians. If Arabi Pasha, with whom the incident made a searing impression, had known what lay behind it he would have been even more horrified. The ugly truth was that three years earlier, at the Congress of Berlin, as part of a deal orchestrated by Disraeli, Salisbury and Bismarck, the trio had chosen Cyprus as the base in the Near East from which Britain could guard the Suez Canal and the Dardanelle Straits. The Sultan had been obliged to relinquish Cyprus to Britain and a *quid pro quo* had to be found to appease the French. It is rumoured that Lord Salisbury suggested Tunisia with the words: 'you cannot leave Carthage in the hands of the barbarians'.[22] The agreement was kept strictly secret and the French bided their time, watching Queen Victoria's red soldiers get a bloody nose in Zululand and humiliated by the Boers of the Transvaal. It was Baron de Courcel who proposed the French now carve out their own African empire while there was still time. His scheme inspired, as one author wrote, President Gambetta's 'ardent patriotism, his love of action, his wide-ranging intelligence, his idealism', or possibly appealed to his fondness for financial intrigue and the huge sums to be made out of Tunisian government stocks. Either way, the deal was done, and Tunisia's fate was sealed.[23]

With the French occupation of Tunisia on his mind Arabi Bey heard on 6 September that the Cairo Prefect of Police had been replaced by a Turco-Circassian loyal to the Khedive. The rebel officers, each day more nervous of losing their jobs and possibly their lives, realised that a showdown with the Khedive could not be delayed much longer. Then it was announced that the pro-Arabist 3rd Infantry Regiment at Cairo was to exchange barracks with the 5th Infantry from Alexandria, a corps with several pro-government officers in its ranks. To heighten their feelings of paranoia came a rumour that the mullah of the El Azhar mosque had issued a fatwa on Khedival instructions that made the rebellious actions of the colonels punishable by death. Arabi was convinced that an assassin was shadowing him sent by the new Prefect of Police and so, at a meeting on 8 September it was decided to try next day to see the Khedive and demand fair treatment.

As the sun rose above the minarets of Cairo on the morning of 9 September 1881 few would have guessed that the day would be any different from hundreds of other hot summer days. Before nightfall, however, the actions of Colonel Ahmed Arabi, already winning him fame in his homeland, would introduce the idealistic officer to the politicians of Britain, France and a host of other countries. That morning Arabi sent a letter to the War Minister in which he described the planned transfer of the 3rd Infantry Regiment as:

> Intended to disperse the military power with a view of revenge upon us, and as we cannot deliver ourselves up to death, we hereby give notice to your Excellency that all the regiments will assemble today … in the Abdin Square for deciding this question … No regiment will march in obedience to the orders given by your Excellency until ample security be given for the lives and interests of ourselves and our relatives.[24]

A letter warning of the demonstration was also sent to the British Consul. It pointed out that the army officers were acting in self-defence against the threat and persecution they had suffered since 1 February, and that the subjects of friendly countries had nothing to fear.

A loose cannon in Arabi's plans was Ali Fehmy and his Guards Regiment. Stationed during the summer at the Abdin Palace, Colonel Fehmy and his men had been feted by Tewfik. The regiment was 'special', claimed Tewfik, and in any confrontation with mutineers he hoped the Guards would stay loyal to him. No one knew for sure if Fehmy and his men would stand by the Khedive or whether the Abdin demonstration might end in bloodshed.

Hastily Tewfik summoned his advisors. The new French Consul had not reached Egypt and Malet was also away on leave. The senior British Government official in Egypt was Charles Cookson, the Vice-Consul, who arrived at the Ismailieh Palace, but went away to telegraph London. Not that Tewfik lacked advice. Riaz Pasha confirmed the 5th Infantry and the Guards Regiments would stay loyal, and the 3rd Infantry in the citadel might do the same. Stone Pasha and Auckland Colvin urged the Khedive to summon the loyal regiments to the palace, and then 'with all the military police available, to put himself at their head, and, when Arabi Bey arrived, personally to arrest him'. Tewfik replied to this that Arabi would have cavalry and artillery, in addition to infantry, and they might open fire. Colvin told him 'they would not dare to, and that if he had the courage to take the initiative, and to expose himself personally, he might succeed in overcoming the mutineers. Otherwise he was lost.'[25]

All the indications seemed to support what Colvin, backed by Stone, was urging and so Tewfik decided to make a stand. We should pause, just for a moment, to examine this young man. 'Amiable' and 'good-natured' are two expressions that turn up in numerous accounts of him. A third is 'weak'. He was thought of as weak when, as a teenager, he only got as far Vienna before obeying a command of his father to return home, weak in dealing with the Arabists, weak in letting Britain take control of his country and, after the occupation, weak in his later relationship with the imperious Lord Cromer. But was he so weak? Tewfik managed to ride out the stormy sea of Egyptian politics in 1881–82 giving tacit encouragement to the nationalists when it seemed wise to do so, later swerving his allegiance to the British when it was obvious they would win. He seems to have had a clear philosophy in life – survival at all costs, for himself and for the dynasty. Even in conversations Cromer later said that the idea 'he was a mere tool in my hands is wholly untrue … I used to discuss matters with him. When any difference of opinion occurred, I yielded to him quite as often – indeed I think more often – than he yielded to me.' Perhaps, it seems hard to believe 'Over-Baring' giving way on much of importance, but there is obviously a grain of truth in his remarks.[26]

In his early thirties, with an oval face, bearded and dark-haired, Tewfik little resembled his father, although about the same height and, like Ismail, compactly built. He alone of the ex-Khedive's sons had not been educated in Europe. There seems to be some confusion as to whether he had a purely Arabic education, but General Loring says in his memoirs that Tewfik spoke, in addition to Arabic, fluent French, Turkish and some English (he spoke with Wolseley in fractured English). Cromer says the Khedive 'rarely if ever read a book', but looked at the newspapers and was no intellectual fool, 'fairly quick in mastering any facts which were explained to him, and in picking up the thread of an argument'.[27] One of his chief supporters, Colvin, praised Tewfik's 'calm … very present and abiding sense of humour which carried with it the power of looking at matters personal to himself from the point of view of a disinterested spectator', and, above all else, his determination that 'as he had no wish to be swallowed up by any Power, he aimed at being friendly with all'.[28] Happily married to one of his cousins, the Khedive was an indulgent and loving father. His subjects respected him for this along with a reputation for being a pious Muslim.

The problem with Tewfik was that while perfectly respectable in a dull, mediocre way, there was no spark of greatness or integrity about him. One of his toughest critics, Wilfred Blunt, thought he was an intriguer of the worst kind. His instinct for survival and slippery actions certainly made the Khedive seem two-faced at times. John Marlowe concluded that Tewfik was inspired

> … by a quite natural determination to keep his throne at all costs. He wanted to be certain of not committing himself to the losing side … he probably wanted to avert foreign intervention if possible … He then, outwardly at all events, threw in his lot with Arabi, and refused to accept the protection of the British fleet … He therefore remained the titular head of state right up to and during the bombardment, with Arabi acting on his orders.

Around mid-afternoon on 9 September, a fleet of carriage hurried the Khedive, his ministers and advisors to the Abdin Barracks. The Guards Regiment was put on parade and swore oaths of loyalty to its sovereign. Under Ali Fehmy's orders the men started barricading the palace doors and windows, bayonets were fixed, and the men took up defensive positions. Next Tewfik led his entourage at a trot through the bustling streets of the old city and up to the citadel. Here the soldiers also promised their loyalty, but it was also discovered that just prior to the party's arrival, men had been signalling to Arabi's regiment at the Abbasieh Barracks. Tewfik then announced his intention of going to Abbasieh. Colvin and Stone were aghast. It was already 3.30pm. They urged the Khedive to reconsider and return straight to the Abdin Palace with loyal soldiers from the citadel but he would not listen. So the carriages set off again, this time for Abbasieh, only to find after 30 minutes of hot and dusty riding that Arabi had already marched into the city at the head of his regiment.

If Colvin's account is to be believed Tewfik now got extremely nervous. The Khedive led his little convoy on a long detour into the city and slunk into the Abdin Palace via a side entrance to avoid meeting the soldiers massing in the square. Jumping out of his carriage, Colvin raced after Tewfik and told him bluntly that he must not remain inside the building but face the mutineers outside. None of the Khedive's other advisors had a clue what action to take except General Stone who, with customary martial zeal, urged everyone in the palace to stand and fight. Abhorring violence, and seeing the senselessness of such an action, Tewfik had little option but accept Colvin's advice.

Looking every inch a Monarch, the gold on his dress uniform glittering in the late afternoon sunshine, and with a tarboosh on his head, Tewfik stepped outside. The sight that met his eyes must indeed have been frightening. Drawn up in rank and facing the Abdin Palace, light bouncing off its white wooden and stucco neo-classical facade, were 2,500 soldiers and 18 cannon. They stretched in neat lines across the broad square modelled by French architects on the *Champs de Mars* in Paris. The 1st Cavalry Regiment had been the first to arrive and taken up a position facing the west entrance. The Field Artillery had then formed up alongside the cavalry, while Arabi positioned his 4th Infantry in the centre. Colonel Arabi summoned Colonel Fehmy and ordered him to take up a position in front of the Abdin. There seems to have been no dispute as to who was in charge, or the rightness of Arabi to give orders, and the latter must have sighed with relief when he saw the Guards trooping out of the palace and joining the other soldiers in the square. Further calamity was also averted when Colonel Al Hilmi arrived with his Sudanese and the 3rd Infantry from the citadel. The commander of the latter regiment had skulked off, but on hearing this news, the energetic Al Hilmi had marched straight to the fortress and turned the soldiers there to his cause. At the last minute the special constabulary arrived and joined the rest. Four of the seven regiments were without their commanding officers and all were under strength but it was still a formidable display of power.

Arabi Pasha was sitting on a horse talking with a group of fellow officers in the centre of the square when the Khedive began walking towards him. Colvin followed behind the Egyptian ruler at a short but respectful distance. Further back walked Stone Pasha and a few other staff officers and courtiers. To stiffen Tewfik's resolve Colvin told him: 'when Arabi Bey presents himself, tell him to give you his sword and to give them the order to disperse'.[29] Before the Khedive had a chance to do this Arabi seized the moment and rode forward.

Quickly Tewfik told him to dismount. He did so and walked on with a few officers and a guard of honour with fixed bayonets. A short distance from the Khedive the group halted. Arabi then presented his sword with a smart salute. Under his breath Colvin urged Tewfik with the words 'now is your moment'. The Khedive, at his wits end, whispered, 'we are between four fires', then, seeming to accept his fate, said stoically 'we shall be killed'. In a louder voice he told the colonel to sheath his sword. Arabi obeyed instantly. The Khedive then asked what the demonstration was all about?

Confidently Arabi made three demands: removal of the Riaz Government, convocation of the Chamber of Delegates and an increase in army strength to 18,000 men. Tewfik is supposed to have said coldly: 'I am the Khedive of the country and I shall do as like', to which his nemesis replied, 'we are not slaves and we shall never from this day forth be inherited.'[30] Some accounts say that Arabi replied to Tewfik with a verse from the Koran saying: 'The ruler is he who is just; he who is not is no longer ruler.'[31] In his memoirs Arabi says that he remained outside, but most scholars accept that he followed the Khedive into the palace. That Tewfik went inside is not disputed and he could not be seen arguing or agreeing to any demands in full view of the army and the growing crowd of onlookers who now peered into the square from every nearby rooftop and window.

Auckland Colvin's role in the negotiations remains open to interpretation. There is an oft-repeated tale that he advised the Khedive to shoot Arabi on the spot. This legend seems to have started with Wilfred Blunt who loathed Colvin, was not present at the event, and whose reporting of gossip he recorded as fact. It is possible that the Anglo-Indian official said something harsh when the Khedive first arrived at the Abdin Palace or his words may have been embellished by whoever told Blunt the story. What would have been the point of urging a parley, with the Khedive in the centre of things, if Colvin knew it might end in bloodshed? Arabi put it very tactfully when he later wrote: 'If the Khedive had shot me the guns would have fired on him, and there would have been bad work.' Most accounts refer to Colvin as chief negotiator, but Arabi strongly denied this, and emphatically stated in his memoirs that he did not even see the Englishman in the square. This is hard to reconcile with Colvin's statement to HM Govt that he stayed talking outside the building for an hour after Tewfik went inside and until Charles Cookson arrived to continue the negotiations. Twenty-two years after the incident Blunt asked the Grand Mufti, who had been present, to give his account and he stated that 'as Colvin knew no Arabic he probably was not noticed by Arabi. It was Cookson who did the talking.'[32]

It seems then that Colvin's account is as suspect as anything written by Blunt; it was in his interest to build up his part in the affair and it did indeed help him win a knighthood. Blunt once told Lord Granville that Colvin knew no Arabic, and on being questioned about the matter Malet was forced to defend his friend saying he understood 'the substance of what passes in Council, though when the Ministers speak rapidly he may not understand ever word!'[33] Cookson makes clear in his account of the meeting that while Colvin talked to Arabi in the square it was for far less than one hour. It was the British Vice-Consul who became chief negotiator, assisted by Colvin and Bolaslawski, acting Austro-Hungarian Consul. At first the Europeans made veiled threats of intervention by the Sultan, or their own Governments, but Arabi would not budge in his demands. Then they suggested the mutineers go home until the Sultan had given his views. To this Arabi replied stoically that the army would stay where they were until the answer came. The Khedive's authority would not be recognised, he added, until the arrival of the Sultan's messenger.

As dusk fell within the Abdin Palace Tewfik and his officials realised they would have to reach a compromise. Eventually it was agreed that the Riaz Ministry could be dismissed immediately but the other demands must wait on a ruling from Abdul Hamid II in Constantinople. To everyone's relief Colonel Arabi agreed at once, provided no member of the Royal Family entered the government, no Turco-Circassian be made Minister of War and that a new chief minister be appointed on the spot. This last point was a stumbling block until Cherif Pasha's name was raised. Outside in the square the soldiers greeted all the news with shouts of 'Long live the Khedive!' Tewfik appeared on a balcony to more cheers and according to one eyewitness, Arabi and some of the officers even kissed the Khedive's hand before smartly marching their soldiers away in perfect formation.

Arabi and his supporters were elated that night, the Khedive vowed revenge for his humiliation, and the tranquility of the country seemed to rest with one man – Cherif Pasha. A British journalist who knew him once jokingly remarked that Cherif was 'willing to accept any proposition rather than spare a precious half-hour away from his billiard table'.[34] The old statesman was quite unenthusiastic about returning to power 'as the candidate of a rebellious army … He gave it to be understood that he did not want to ruin his good name and risk his political prestige.' Meetings between Cherif and Arabi on 10 and 11 September did not go well.

A group of about 150 pro-nationalist landowners and sheikhs, led by Sultan Pasha (a benevolent and wealthy old landowner from Upper Egypt) now sent a deputation to see Cherif Pasha. They saw the army mutiny as a golden chance to secure a constitution and so promised to provide a written guarantee that the army would be obedient. Sure enough, next day, 13 September, they placed the document in Cherif's hands and the deal was done.

The future looked hopeful. That same week, Auckland Colvin was writing benevolently to London that 'all is being done in an orderly and even exemplary manner ... I do not think it is at all my duty to oppose myself to the popular movement, but to try rather to guide and give it a definite shape.'[35] Blunt later wrote, with fine purple prose, that 'Throughout Egypt a cry of jubilation arose such as for hundreds of years had not been heard upon the Nile, and it is literally true that in the streets of Cairo men stopped each other, though strangers, to embrace and rejoice together.'[36] One month later Colvin had a meeting with Arabi and convinced himself that everything was going to be fine and the situation could be controlled. He told Malet that Ahmed Arabi 'produced a most favourable impression ... He disclaimed all hostility to foreigners, saying that what the Egyptians knew of liberty, and much that they had gained of it, was due to foreigners.' Summing up their discussion Colvin concluded: 'The impression left on my mind was Arabi, who spoke with great moderation, calmness and conciliation, is sincere and resolute but not a practical man.'[37]

Events were now to move swiftly. Opinions and alliances would alter dramatically. Within three months Cherif, Colvin and Malet would be totally opposed to Arabi, within seven months the fleets of two great nations would threaten Egypt and one month later the streets of Alexandria would run red with blood.

# 2

# Riot

*No sooner they saw a European they struck him until they saw him dead. I counted*
*fourteen of such scenes.*
Alessandro Vernoni

Paris on 10 November 1881 saw the fall of a short-lived government under
Jules Ferry, with power returning to that champion of French imperialism,
conqueror of Tunisia and detester of all things German – Leon Gambetta.

Vigour was to be the stamp of his government, decided Gambetta; in Egypt
this would mean an insistence on absolute equality with the British and no
concessions to the nationalists. There seems little doubt that Gambetta had
decided to make Egypt his next North African conquest. If he had to share the
spoils with Great Britain then so be it, the Egyptian bird was ready for plucking
and there seemed to be plenty of meat on the carcase to share; if only he could
goad HM Govt into a more warlike staunch.

The trouble was that Gladstone and his Liberal colleagues had no desire to
get embroiled in yet another war. They had problems enough to clear up in
India and South Africa following three major wars in the year-and-a-half alone.
The Prime Minister urged for a 'minimum of interference' in Egyptian affairs, a
policy endorsed by his loyal, modest and suave Foreign Secretary, Lord Granville.
A patrician Whig of 66 years, the 2nd Earl Granville, known affectionately by
his friends as 'Puss', was a cautious man. In private he would sometimes say that
he was 'dawdling'. The 'dawdling policy', explained Cromer, 'or to put the case
in another way, the policy of having no policy at all, is often very good diplomacy, particularly when it is carried out by a man of Lord Granville's singular
tact, quickness and diplomatic experience.'[1]

In Cairo, where Colvin thought he could shape the nationalists to his whims,
a less sanguine Malet reported to the Foreign Secretary on 25 September
1881 that he was 'rather alarmed at the Pan-Islamic spirit which appears to be
endeavouring to spread in the country and I sincerely hope that Cherif Pasha
will stop it. We owe that to the French in Tunis. I find a deep-rooted feeling

here that we intend to play the same game in Egypt.' A fortnight later the Consul-General told Granville that:

> the programme of Arabi is now pretty clear, and consists in the liberation of Egypt from European control, and a Constitution. Whether he has the perseverance and the intelligence to carry on this propaganda until he forces our armed intervention, time only can show. I have no doubt, however, that if we did threaten armed interference he would show fight, at all events till troops appeared.[2]

Later Malet would claim that he had always viewed an Anglo-French invasion 'with absolute dread', because in his view it would lead to animosity between the two powers. During the late autumn he had enough on his plate already. A rumpus erupted when General Stone was caught trying to buy a stock of hand grenades for use in any future confrontations with the nationalists. It was clear, thought the British Consul-General, that 'at the bottom of the Khedive's heart the only desire is a return to the iron rule of his father'.[3]

While Colvin and Malet tried to watch events from the shadows of the British Consulate, and Tewfik sulked in his private apartments at the Ismailieh Palace, an extraordinary meeting took place on 12 December. The Englishman destined to become Arabi's most loyal foreign friend and advisor at last met his champion. History has recorded how Wilfred Scawen Blunt found 'El Wahid' to be the living embodiment of a new Egyptian national identity. One wonders what Ahmed Arabi saw in the heavily bearded 41-year-old aristocrat from Sussex?

In an age of high imperialism Blunt was to be the square cog determined to spike the wheel. He came from a wealthy background and had friends in high places but his natural inclination was to be the champion of the underdog – in Egypt, India and Ireland. Incredibly handsome, highly sexed, with numerous affairs and mistresses along the way, Blunt gave up a diplomatic career – including living with the Malet family in Frankfurt – to woo and marry Lady Annabella King-Noel, grand-daughter of the poet Byron. In the English countryside the pair created the finest Arabian stud farm in Europe. Both lovers of the Orient, they travelled together everywhere, crossing the Sinai on camels, living with the Bedouin, sailing up the Euphrates, and learning along the way to speak Arabic fluently. Anne Blunt was as tough and only a little less outspoken than her husband. Wilfred adored her.

At Newbuildings Place, their pre-Raphaelite furnished home in Sussex, the Blunts liked to hold dinner parties and ardently discuss political matters. It is difficult, from a gap of more than one century, to fully realise this airy, rich and exclusive world. Most surprising of all is how incestuous it was. Blunt knew

Edward Malet intimately, having worked closely with him in the 1860s, while he and Lord Hartington had shared the same mistress – Catherine Walters, the famous courtesan known as 'Skittles'. Eddy Hamilton, the Prime Minister's private secretary, was a friend from his youth and Lord Lytton, Viceroy of India, a favourite relation.

The Blunts visited India for the first time in 1879 to stay with the Lyttons. It was a period when Wilfred's growing sense of anger at the way his countrymen ruled others was beginning to dominate his life. A hatred of what he perceived as British arrogance, coupled with a desire to fight injustice, would soon mark him out as a man with a mission. This singular loathing of British imperialism left Blunt with no middle ground. Passionate and idealistic, he saw complex political problems only in black and white. In his arguments he was inclined to exaggerate and, many opponents claimed, to lie. In his famous book *The Secret History Of The English Occupation Of Egypt*, written 25 years after the event, Blunt made many claims that seem to be based on hearsay or spite. In the *Dictionary Of National Biography* P. C. Elgood castigated him: 'His discretion is questionable, his judgment superficial; he records gossip as fact and allows prejudice to colour his narration.'

Despite his many weaknesses it is all too easy to dismiss Wilfred Blunt, as Evelyn Baring did, as 'an enthusiast who dreamt dreams of an Arab Utopia' and 'had no political training of any value'. Peter Mansfield notes that Blunt 'understood why Arabi was a hero to the mass of Egyptians. He knew that his power was not based on intimidation and that Egyptian resentment of European control was not merely a manifestation of "Muslim fanaticism".' In Whitehall corridors Blunt tried to make those in power understand the mood of the new Egyptian leaders and in the British Press he championed the cause of Arab nationalism with a total disregard for the loathing many others felt towards him.

Speaking with his English admirer, Arabi said the army would hold the balance of power only so long as it took the Chamber of Notables to speak for the people. Interference by the Porte in Egypt's internal affairs would not be permitted but the Sultan's role as supreme ruler would be honoured. The European commissioners, Arabi went on, had played a useful role in restoring his country's finances but they ought not to try and obstruct reform or support Turco-Circassian rule. Duly impressed by all he saw and heard, Blunt, apparently with Malet'a tacit agreement, helped to draft the 'Programme of the National Party of Egypt' and at the suggestion of his friend, Sir William Gregory, a former Liberal MP (but against Sir Edward's advice) sent a copy to *The Times* for publication.

During the last three months of 1881 officers loyal to Arabi and the nation-alists were put in charge of all Egyptian regiments. This move mortified the Khedive who complained privately that he could no longer trust any of the officer corps apart from the general staff and Stone Pasha.

On a political front Cherif Pasha was stealthily following his own agenda. The Chamber of Notables assembled in December and demanded to be allowed to vote on that part of the budget not directly assigned to the service of the Debt. According to John Marlowe:

> A concession in this direction would have cemented the alliance between Cherif and the Notables, would have encouraged the Notables in their opposition to the Army, and would have provided the Dual Control with a basis on which to build up a permanent alternative to Khedival absolutism.

Arabi's dreams, Cherif's carefully laid plans and Malet's good intentions were all dashed by the Joint Note of 6 January 1882. This document, personally drafted by Gambetta, had started to take shape in his mind in early December when he told the British ambassador, Lord Lyons, that the convocation of the Egyptian Chamber 'made him uneasy'. The delegates might be moderate and support the Khedive, or they might find common cause with the army and wish to dethrone him. In the face of these problems, claimed Gambetta, it would be best if Britain and France showed a united front to help strengthen Tewfik's authority. The two allies, he declared, 'should consider the matter in common, in order to be prepared for united and immediate action in case of need'.[4]

'Puss' must have sighed when he read Lord Lyons account of the meeting. Carefully Granville drafted a reply agreeing with Gambetta, but adding the whole matter 'requires careful consideration'. It was a dawdling ploy. He had no wish to see Britain drawn into Egypt's difficulties any further (personally, as a last resort, he was in favour of restoring Turkish control).

On the other side of the Channel the French premier was not so easily fobbed off. On 24 December he wrote proposing that 'the two Governments should instruct their representatives at Cairo to convey collectively to Tewfik Pasha assurances of the sympathy and support of France and England, and to encourage His Highness to maintain his proper authority.'[5] After reading this document Granville immediately informed Malet and asked for his opinion. Sir Edward saw no dangers in the proposal and intimated it might even prove helpful. The draft note from Paris, which was to be sent to the British and French consuls, landed on Granville's desk on 2 January. He read it, informed the Cabinet, and added his approval, but told Gambetta that HM Govt 'must not be considered as committing themselves thereby to any particular mode of action, if any action shall be found necessary'.

Gladstone, like Granville, had no wish to get more involved in the muddy waters of Egyptian politics and two days later the Prime Minister made clear these views to his Foreign Secretary: '"Egypt for the Egyptians" is the sentiment to which I would wish to give scope: and could it prevail it would I think be the best, the only good solution of the "Egyptian Question".'[6]

Gambetta's Note also made several members of the Cabinet uneasy; especially the old Radical, John Bright, who sympathised with the nationalists, but the general consensus was that it was essential to act in concert with France and maintain an alliance. The Joint Note was a bluff which HM Govt 'hoped would sober Arabi and the nationalists and bring them to respect the Khedive's authority and Europe's financial rights'.[7]

A legend has it that HM Govt agreed to the Joint Note in return for a lucrative trading agreement from the French. In his account of events leading up to the war Blunt is adamant that this is what happened. He accused Charles Dilke, Granville's deputy at the Foreign Office, of some dirty international dealings, though he hotly denied these accusations. I have in my possession Dilke's own copy of Blunt's book and on several pages he has scrawled in pencil 'No' and 'This is lunacy!' He later wrote to Blunt asking for his side of the story to be published in later editions. Not satisfied with the author's reply, Dilke wrote a letter to the *Manchester Guardian*, published on 27 June 1907, in which he claimed he did not know about the Joint Note until after it was sent (he was also not in the Cabinet at that date).

One thing is sure about the Joint Note – it was an horrific diplomatic blunder. On this all parties could agree afterwards. Baring called it a 'mistake', Blunt 'a most mischievous document', while one authority has described it as 'a calculated slap in the face to Cherif Pasha and the Notables'.[8] Gladstone's official biographer, writing at the time in the *Fortnightly Review*, summed it up very well:

At Cairo the Note fell like a bombshell. Nobody there had expected any such declaration and nobody was aware of any reason why it should have been launched. What was felt was that so serious a step on such delicate ground could not have been adopted without deliberate calculation nor without some grave intention. The note was, therefore, taken to mean that the Sultan was to be thrust still further in the background; that the Khedive was to become more plainly the puppet of England and France; and that Egypt would sooner or later in some shape or other be made to share the fate of Tunis. The general effect was, therefore, mischievous in the highest degree. The Khedive was encouraged in his opposition to the sentiments of His Chamber. The military, national, or popular party was alarmed.

The Sultan was irritated. The other European Powers were made uneasy. Every element of disturbance was roused into activity.[9]

In a vain attempt to cushion the Note's effects Malet asked an embarrassed Blunt, who was still in Cairo, to explain to Arabi that it meant simply 'that the English Government would not permit any interference of the Sultan with Egypt, and would not allow the Khedive to go back from his promises or molest the Parliament.' Arabi was not fooled. 'Sir Edward Malet must really think us children who do not know the meaning of words ... it is the language of menace' was his sharp reply. If the British and French invaded, he added, 'every man and child in Egypt will fight them'.[10]

Cables flooded into the Foreign Office including one from Sultan Abdul Hamid who felt it had been 'improper' that no talks had taken place with him. Realizing the damage done, a perplexed Granville suggested sending an 'explanatory telegram' to defuse some of the anger but the French Premier would not agree. The Egyptians, declared Gambetta arrogantly, 'had only to listen to the advice of the two Powers and be silent'.[11]

In the Chamber of Notables the Note caused a stiffening of nationalist opinion. 'What a blunder' was Cherif Pasha's reaction when he read it. The old politician still thought that he could overawe the Chamber and control the Arabists. The Note had arrived, unfortunately, at a critical time while the Chamber was drafting an organic law meant to define the power of the legislature. With one kick the Joint Note upset this constitutional apple-cart. Cherif was nonplussed; he saw it as a totally unjustified but probably unintentional threat of invasion. The Arabists would calm down and fall in line behind him. 'The Egyptians are children and must be treated like children', he declared to Blunt, adding 'it is I who created the National Party, and they will find that they cannot get on without me. These peasants want guidance.'[12]

Always sensitive to criticism, Malet was horrified to find that the Chamber now looked upon him as an arch-traitor who had lured them on to obtain an excuse for intervention. He was so upset that he even wrote to Lord Lyons in Paris asking his opinion on whether he should resign. 'I wonder what could induce Gambetta to propose and Lord Granville to accept such a firebrand document as the dual Note?' he asked Lyons. Ignoring the fact that Granville had consulted him in advance, a depressed Consul-General deplored the fact that 'now all our influence is gone, and we have massed opposition to face'. Four days later, alarmed the way things were heading, Granville wrote privately to his man in Cairo: 'It is important that you should know what I think, but pray keep it for your private information. I am dead against intervention, single or double.'[13]

On the urging of Malet and Colvin a meeting was arranged on 19 January at the home of Muhammad Abdu, editor of the nationalist's official newspaper. Leading delegates were told by Wilfred Blunt, who had agreed to act as go-between, that the British diplomats wanted a compromise but the meeting was a waste of time. During January, as the nationalists dug in their heels, Auckland Colvin's earlier sympathetic mood changed to one of hostility. By the end of the month he told Blunt that he had thought the nationalists:

> ... amenable to reason, but he found them quite impracticable and would do his best to ruin them if they came into office. He said that he had changed his mind about intervention too; that he believed it now to be necessary and inevitable, and that he would *spare no pains to bring it about*.[14] [Author's italics]

Colvin was true to his word. In his despatches to the *Pall Mall Gazette* he began warning the British public that Egypt was 'rapidly approaching a state of affairs which differs little, if at all, from anarchy'.[15] Malet was getting increasingly agitated. In a letter to his mother on 23 January he said:

> I shall be very sorry if it comes to war when I think how easily it might have been avoided, but we are walking in a dangerous road and may not be able to turn back in time with honour. Cherif Pasha is highly incensed with his Chamber. The Chamber is furious with England and France. Cherif and the Khedive are not on good terms, so that altogether I have too much on my hands.[16]

Gradually, as the days of January passed, Gladstone and his Cabinet colleagues became increasingly wary of Gambetta's motives, and their desire not to be dragged into a war by France intensified. Gladstone and Granville wanted to adroitly sidestep the Egyptian business by consulting with the other European Powers or handing the problem over to the Porte. Kimberley at the Colonial Office saw problems everywhere; Childers at the War Office was agreeable to intervention as a last resort; Hartington was one of only two (the other was Harcourt) in the Cabinet who wanted joint Anglo-French action to 'restore the Control and the bondholders rights, and to keep up the Liberal alliance'.[17]

In France the ministry of Gambetta was tottering. Always playing for high stakes, he demanded a crucial vote on 26 January on electoral reforms, but lost. His resignation followed immediately and, to the relief of HM Govt, was succeeded by the 'white mouse' of French politics, Charles de Freycinet. Timidity came naturally to Freycinet who quickly agreed that there was no need for immediate action on Egyptian affairs. He ruled out the use of force though the French Government had no clear ideas how to proceed. Writing privately, Lord Granville lost no time in telling Malet that: 'It is satisfactory that Freycinet is strongly against English or French single or joint occupation.'[18]

Meanwhile in Cairo the Joint Note had set new wheels in motion. The nationalists knew nothing of the new French premier or the cool letters about Egypt passing between him and London. On 2 February a deputation from the Chamber went to see Cherif and asked him to support their demands. He bluntly refused. The delegates asked him to resign. He refused this also but it was to no avail. Even the Khedive had to accept the return as premier of Mahmud Sami. On 4 February he formed his mainly nationalist government and among those taking up portfolios was Ahmed Arabi as Minister of War and the Navy. Pushed aside, left feeling humiliated and bitter, Cherif Pasha would remain a strong opponent of the Arabists, feeding gossip and information – disinformation – to Malet in order to discredit the regime. The rise of the nationalists naturally alarmed thousands of Europeans living in Egypt.

That Spring they complained of a rapidly deteriorating situation. Peasants once so friendly, grew abusive and Muslim fanaticism seemed to be on the rise. In despatch after despatch Malet painted a picture of a sabre-rattling army and a nationalist rabble running amok. But while most Turco-Circassians had been made to give up administrative posts to native-born Egyptians the positions of Europeans in government employ remained unchanged. Even when the Finance Minister planned a commission to investigate the Customs Office no European lost his job. When, on 22 February, the American Consul held a banquet to celebrate George Washington's birthday, the new Prime Minister made a speech praising Republican heroes such as Washington, Lafayette and Garibaldi while Arabi told a visitor from the United States that he 'had come to honour the memory of a man who had freed his country from the yoke of foreigners'.[19] Republican and nationalist rhetoric was kept in check; when one officer and a sheikh spoke violently against foreigners at a public meeting in Alexandria the governor had them arrested and, with the cooperation of the organizers, the pair were made to apologise to the French Consul.

Before leaving Egypt that February an emotional Blunt made a farewell visit to Ahmed Arabi. The new Minister laid out for his English friend some of the reforms intended by the new government. These included a re-distribution of water rights, the founding of an agricultural bank under government control, more schools for all children, girls as well as boys (though Arabi did not particularly like this idea), the final eradication of slavery and better military defences.

Improvements to the coastal defences had already figured in a sniping attack on the nationalists by Malet, (as if to imply this was a bellicose or dangerous act and ignoring its legitimacy). Throughout February and March he warned London several times that the fellahin were now insubordinate and the government unstable.

Back home in England, Wilfred Blunt worked hard to form an Egyptian lobby in Parliament and contacted his old friend, Eddy Hamilton, the GOM's private secretary. He was told that the Prime Minister did not object to his involvement in Egyptian affairs and would see him personally for a discussion. Blunt's hopes ran high on 10 March when he met a 'volubly hostile' Dilke and a typically suave Granville who tried to steer the talk away from Egypt and around to Arab stallions. The Foreign Secretary asked if the Egyptians would give up their demands to control their own finances? 'No' replied Blunt truthfully. 'Then I look upon their case as hopeless' said Granville. According to Blunt he added: 'It must end by their being put down by force.'[20]

Finally, in a fast 40 minute meeting on 22 March, Wilfred met Gladstone who proved that he was not just a grand but also a very slippery old man. Blunt, alone in the presence of this paragon of Liberal values, became convinced that the Egyptian nationalists had nothing to fear. The hoodwinking was not really Gladstone's fault; the man he was talking to had a tendency to hear what he wanted to hear, and he desperately wanted to leave the meeting in an upbeat mood. The Prime Minister really only sent felicitations to the Egyptian nationalists and made no promises (later it would all be a source of much bitterness on Blunt's part).

Wherever one turned and whoever one spoke to in Cairo that March the army seemed to be on people's lips. Malet complained that 'the country will soon be governed by nothing but officers'.[21] With his War Minister powers Arabi was busy pensioning off more than 500 Circassian officers and replacing them with native Egyptians. No longer a mere colonel, Ahmed Arabi was now a brigadier-general (along with four comrades). It was the first time native-born Egyptians had held this rank since the creation of the army by Muhammad Ali. Yet, despite the gloomy warnings of a military dictatorship predicted by the likes of Malet, Colvin and Cookson, there was another picture. Turco-Circassians were in some cases, also promoted (a Turk, Khalil Kamil, was given command of the new 7th Infantry Regiment, while another Turk, Hussein Mazhar, was appointed C-in-C of the Field and Coast Artillery). Things were not perfect and Arabi made mistakes, including some promotions that were not warranted by ability. In some country districts the troops, under new and weak commanders, stole from local people, and carried on a trade in illegal firearms. With the shoe now on the other foot, nineteen officers – Circassians, Turks, Albanians and Persians – quit the 1st Infantry, all disgusted at being passed over for promotion.

In early March a poison attempt on Al Hilmi, one of Arabi's newly appointed brigadiers, was found to have been conceived in the Khedive's entourage. The paranoid Arabi began once again to fear for his life. For a time he moved to live in the heavily guarded Abdin Barracks and drank water only from a locked container. A month later a Circassian officer confessed to General Tulbah Ismat, another of Arabi's appointees (and soon to be his son-in-law), that there was a conspiracy to liquidate Arabi and the other generals. Arrests quickly followed and a plot was uncovered that stretched all the way back to the ex-Khedive Ismail. Sly as ever, it transpired that the old ruler was planning a last ditch attempt to win back his throne. The plot was doomed to failure. In a show trial, 40 officers, including the former War Minister, Osman Rifky, were reduced to the ranks and exiled to the hot wastes of the Sudan.

Since the previous September Tewfik had watched power slip further and further from his hands. Now all he wanted to do was retire to his palace by the sea at Alexandria and wait for the European Powers to end his 'nightmare'. It seemed increasingly likely that this would happen; on 21 April the Foreign Secretary told Malet that the French

> ... are getting alarmed at the prospect of disorder. They have pressed us hard to agree to a change of Khedives ... We have put down our foot and objected entirely ... they would not object to a naval demonstration and a mission of English troops from India ... How far do you believe forcible intervention can be avoided? I detest the very thought of it.[22]

Political skulduggery was already going on in Constantinople where Tewfik had told his representative, Thabit Pasha, to blacken the Sami administration in the eyes of the Sultan. He was told to say that the nationalists wanted to cut links with the Porte and were undermining not only the political but even the religious position of the Sultan with talk that Ahmed Arabi was descended from the Prophet. Several of the Circassian officers had also begged Abdul Hamid to intervene. Rapidly gaining a reputation for cunning the Sultan, later to be known to the world as 'Abdul the Damned', was not fooled by Thabit Pasha. Sources much closer to his throne convinced him that Tewfik was a fool. Given half a chance Abdul Hamid intended to depose him and appoint Halim as his successor but, for the present, he decided to play the Khedive and the Arabists off against one another. In letters to Tewfik he invited him to stage a coup d'etat and kick the nationalists into the Nile while, writing at the same time to Arabi and stressing that he did not care who ruled Egypt just so long as that was person was loyal to him and the Ottoman Empire. He prayed that Arabi would save Egypt from the fate of Tunisia but warned also of giving England or France any pretext for invasion.

Next day Malet was writing to London in his greasiest diplomatic jargon:

> The Egyptian government was bent upon diminishing the Anglo-French protection, and that, as a matter of fact, our influence is daily decreasing. It will not be possible for us to regain our ascendancy until the military supremacy which at present weighs upon the country is broken ... Some complications of an acute nature must supervene before any satisfactory solution to the Egyptian question can be attained, and that it would be wiser to hasten it than to endeavour to retard it.[23]

It is with such language as this that wars are whipped up by diplomats. Only a few days earlier the German Consul had reported a rather different picture; he noted that the Sami Government was continuing to pay interest on the debt, the Caisse was even showing a surplus, foreigners' rights and treaty obligations stayed in force and the Mixed Court were functioning as normal. In view of this kind of report one wonders what sort of tinted spectacles Malet and Colvin were wearing to view Egyptian affairs?

Gambetta stirred up the state of Egypt with his Note. Now it was the turn of his successor to push events towards armed confrontation – not that timid Freycinet fully realised the effect of his actions when, on 11 May, he suggested that a joint Anglo-French fleet should be sent to Alexandria to encourage the Egyptians to come to their senses. Granville was wary of the proposal and agreed to send two ironclads simply to 'protect the life and property of Europeans'. Having lobbied vainly for weeks to get the French to agree to an Anglo-French-Turkish Commission, he concluded that 'such a demonstration could hardly in itself be a sufficient remedy or safeguard for the present condition of affairs, but that it might be useful as a moral support to the three commissioners if it were decided to send them'. Four days later the two countries told the other European powers of their intentions and Granville continued to push the French to support his idea of using Turkish troops to land and restore order. The French, reminding themselves of recent Turkish atrocities in the Balkans, rejected the idea completely.[24]

The bickering between the Khedive and his minsters lasted six days before the British and French Consuls told Tewfik to make peace so that they could, via him, inform Egypt of the naval demonstration. Any joy he may have felt at this news was spoiled by a vinegary telegram from Abdul Hamid expressing displeasure at his weak acceptance of the European demands. On the night of 15 May, at a late meeting, Khedive and Council decided to bury the hatchet. While this meeting was taking place, across the city in the Abdin Barracks a group of hardline Arabist officers swore a solemn oath to 'stand together and defy any attempts at intervention'.[25]

No one could predict what might happen when the fleet arrived. Privately, in a letter home, Malet wrote: 'we are in for the end now, and it is high time that it should come.' He had warned HM Govt for weeks about the dangers posed by the nationalists, and personally told Arabi Pasha of the Anglo-French warships, who typically replied that 'he was glad that the fleet was coming, as the officers could come up to Cairo to see the sights, and also because a good deal of money would be spent in Alexandria.'[31] Quite sensible comments and hardly those of a nationalist fanatic.[26]

Five days later, 20 May, the joint Anglo-French naval force steamed into view. The build-up had begun two weeks earlier when the British Commander-in-Chief in the Mediterranean, Vice-Admiral Sir Frederick Beauchamp Seymour, had sailed from Malta with four ironclads, two gunboats and a despatch vessel to hold exercises off Corfu. When London and Paris sanctioned the joint fleet Seymour learned he was to rendezvous with his French opposite number, Rear-Admiral Conrad, off Crete on 15 May. A secret despatch warned Seymour the 'Government wishes to keep on best terms with Turks and other Powers'. That same day came direct orders to 'Communicate with Consul-General on your arrival at Alexandria, and in concert with him prepare to cooperate with the naval force of France to support Viceroy and protect British subjects and Europeans, landing force if required for latter object', though he was warned 'not to leave protection of ship's guns without instructions from home'.[27]

Ships of many nations were a common sight at Alexandria but these new arrivals and the threat they carried was something altogether different. Compromise now went out the window as the respective factions hardened their positions. Inflamed by a popular press and nationalist agitators the Egyptians got more excited daily. Arabi was inundated with letters and more than 50 petitions from citizens groups pledging him their support. The newspapers accused Tewfik of being unworthy of office, having sided with Christians, and Arabi was proclaimed protector of the faith and asked to defend the homeland and its religion from the infidels.

In secret communications the Sultan was advising the Sami Ministry on how best to resist the European threat. Abdul Hamid was also laying the groundwork for his personal favourite as Viceroy – Tewfik's great-uncle, Prince Halim. It was hardly surprising that on 23 May the Council of Ministers made clear they would reject any interference by foreign powers in Egypt's domestic affairs and recognised only one authority – the Ottoman Sultanate. In secret letters Arabi was corresponding with Abdul Hamid; he blamed Egypt's ills on its incompetent ruler, who had put all his affairs in the hands of the British consul, who was 'the dominating force in Egyptian affairs'. Britain's aim, he went on, was 'to reduce Egypt to a dependency like India' and rumours that European lives were in danger was 'a lie; they were safe'. The Egyptian general told his supreme ruler that he would lead his people in any fight for freedom, 'as well as preserving their status as Ottoman subjects'. He even agreed to support Halim as the new Khedive (although personally disliking him).[28]

Feeling the fleet at his back Malet now felt strong anough to try another showdown. In alliance with Sienkiewicz he sent a second Joint Note on 25 May formally demanding that Arabi 'must leave Egypt for the time being',[29] Generals Fehmy and Al Hilmi should quietly go to the homes, and the Government resign. To Malet's surprise, and for the second time in less than a fortnight, the Goverment collapsed the next day. Sultan Pasha rushed to the palace and warned the Khedive that unless he reinstated Arabi the army might rise and kill him. Tewfik refused to budge. That evening the ulemas and other religious leaders, including the Chief Rabbi, begged the Khedive to back down before blood was shed. The mood at the palace was tense; the colonel commanding the Khedival Guard even told the ruler that units had been doubled to stop him leaving and if he tried to go out for an evening drive they would open fire. One bright spark illuminated an otherwise awful day – Tewfik got news that the Sultan was ready to send an official from Constantinople to reassert his rights and keep Egypt firmly within the Ottoman Empire. Due to the urgency of the situation this official was ready to leave immediately for Cairo.

Bitter and humiliated, the Khedive bowed at last to pressure, and signed a decree reinstating Arabi as Minister of War. Next day he formally requested the Porte send an Imperial Commissioner. On the streets of Cairo and Alexandria it seemed, for a brief time, that the tension had evaporated. The threat of civil rebellion, a military takeover or – perish the thought – a foreign invasion, had all been prevented.

On his flagship HMS *Invincible*, Admiral Seymour watched with growing unease as labourers and soldiers built up earthworks just abreast of his ship.

He cabled the Admiralty: 'Alexandria is apparently controlled this morning by military party … I think an increase of force desirable. There is much panic at Cairo and some here. I would suggest dispatch of Her Majesty's ships *Alexandra, Monarch* and gun-boat.' The Admiralty did not at this stage send *Alexandra* but HMS *Monarch*, along with the gunboats HMS *Cygnet* and *Coquette* now joined Seymour's growing little armada. In London no one was quite sure how to proceed; on 3 June the Admiralty planners cabled Seymour: 'If instructed to forbid armament of earthworks, can you enforce that threat, and at what risk, military and political? Give your opinion of situation? Do you wish for reinforcements?' The admiral's reply was a cautious one: 'Could enforce threat as things are at present, but effect on foreign population would probably be disastrous.' Pressed for more details that same day he added: 'Under these circumstances and necessary long notice to foreigners, without which I do not think France would co-operate, and that three batteries will probably be armed tonight, my opinion is that we must take our chance.'[30]

The British Admiralty, starting to fear that an invasion of Egypt was now a distinct possibility, had a whole mess of logistical problems to solve. Almost the entire Mediterranean Fleet was now concentrated off Greece, Turkey or Egypt. The nearest troops were stationed in Malta, also the Fleet's home port, but if war broke out there were no ships to take them to the theatre of operations. A major redeployment was necessary and on 31 May Rear-Admiral Sir William Dowell was given immediate orders to lead his Channel Squadron from Devonport to Gibralter. The ships arrived there one week later and pressed on immediately to Malta.

Through his telescope Seymour could see the Egyptians working feverishly on improving the ancient forts that lined the harbour. New earthworks were filling the gaps in the waterfront defences daily. Batteries of Krupp field guns and heavier ordnance, including Armstrong cannon of British manufacture, seemed to be arriving daily. On 3 June he cabled: 'Batteries, apparently for mortars going up fast. Matters becoming serious.'[31] Next day he asked permission to move the rest of his fleet into Egyptian waters. Not wanting to exacerbate the situation the Admiralty agreed but added a caution that the ships had to be kept out of sight of the shore. Within a few days HMS *Alexandra, Temeraire, Superb* and *Inflexible* had set course for Egypt. The delighted sailors' high hopes of seeing action were dashed when, on arrival near Alexandria, the ironclads were put under sail to preserve coal or simply allowed to drift without even a sight of land.

During the first week of June tensions in Cairo, and especially Alexandria, started to rise significantly again. The presence of the Anglo-French ships, though still few in number, understandably inflamed patriotic Egyptians. On 5 June more steamed into view when the French ironclad *Alma* arrived and was soon followed by a sister ship, the *Thetis*.

'Everybody in Egypt, from the highest to the lowest, felt instinctively that something was about to happen',[32] wrote Walter Goodall, a young merchant with Government connections, based in Cairo. His sentiments were echoed by Samuel de Kusel, an Englishmen who was Controller-General of the Egyptian Customs Service; in April he had decided the situation was serious enough to send his family out of the country. 'Yet when the climax came', he wrote later, 'it came almost as a surprise … Men and women live on the sides of an active volcano … blissfully hopeful that if there should be an eruption it will go downwards.'[33] On 26 and 27 May, when the soldiers and police of Alexandria had staged their noisy demonstration in support of Arabi Pasha, a rumour ran through the European community that cartridges were being handed out to the troops to be used against them. It took a few days to squash this nonsense, but by 6 June Vice-Consul Cookson could report that 'a perfect calm reigns in the city'. It was broken the next day, according to Carmelo Polidano, a Maltese coffee shop owner, by about 1,000 Arabs attacking some 30 Greeks with sticks. An Egyptian officer tried to get his soldiers to break up the riot but they joined in on the side of the locals. Polidano and some 100 worried Maltese went to see Cookson for advice. He tried to play down the incident and told the Maltese that, if the same happened to them, they had a right to defend themselves.

Riots were nothing new in Egypt. Conflicts had erupted in Alexandria three times between 1865 and 1871 as local citizens fought Italians, Greeks and French. Suez had seen a major disturbance between Muslims and Christians in 1858 and violence erupted no less than three times in the 1870s as Maltese and Greeks brawled with Nubians and Hijaz pilgrims. There had been one major riot inland, at Tanta in 1872, but otherwise they seem to have been restricted to port towns. Clashes between Westerners and the more conservatively religious, anti-European inhabitants of Suez and Port Said, especially where pilgrims en route to and from the holy cities of Islam came into contact with foreigners is hardly surprising. Friction also existed in rough places like the Alexandria waterfront: Italian sailors loathed Egyptian donkey-boys; Greek shopkeepers disliked Nubian guards; orthodox Greeks spat at pious Muslims; and Maltese port workers hated local customs house employees. These were old rivalries based on ancient prejudices.

Sunday 11 June 1882 began like so many other gloriously hot Spring days in Alexandria. Cafes and restaurants in the wide Rue des Soeurs and broad Place

Muhammad Ali opened their doors, laid out their tables and did business as normal. The rich – with time and leisure on the hands – set off in their carriages to enjoy the beach and cooling sea breezes at nearby Ramleh. Later in the day they could drive back to the public gardens on the Mahmoudieh Canal and watch a military band concert.

One of those setting out that morning was Richard Molyneux, the *Invincible's* captain, who had been invited ashore to enjoy a seaside luncheon by Kusel Bey and his friend James Morice, Inspector-General of Coastguards. The noisy quay was packed with porters, merchants, fishermen, beggars and foreigners. Narrow streets ran off it lined with small shops and stalls. In one of these avenues, running parallel to the waterfront and close to the harbour, was the British Consulate, a small, white-washed villa no different from many others in the city apart from a guard of smartly-dressed janissaries outside and a gated side entrance for coaches. Progressing inland, the streets and boulevards became increasingly grand until they spilled into the Place Muhammad Ali, the city's central piazza, dominated by a colossal statue of the old ruler. Laid out with an oval pond and a central green lawn, shaded by trees, this cheerful rectangle was the central hub of the city. Alexandria lived and breathed trade, from its shops and fine town houses, many owned by European merchants, down to its long waterfront, the solidly built and British designed quays and breakwaters ending at the Fort Pharos lighthouse where, at least from the sea, the city presented a first thrilling impression of the East for newly arrived visitors.

A good-natured rivalry existed between Alexandrians and Cairenes. The port city was rainy and grey in winter and stiflingly hot in summer. Cairo, on the other hand, had a drier, less humid climate. One was full of merchants and the other of government officials. Cairenes liked to say that Alexandria was too cosmopolitan and thoroughly mercantile, like another Genoa or Marseilles, whereas their city, despite numerous changes, still had an Oriental stamp. Those who spent their lives working in Alexandria disagreed. 'It was the first place in the world', wrote Samuel de Kusel, 'to me wonderful and sublime'.[34]

At the same time that Kusel and his friends were settling down to some excellent fish, washed down by wine, at Ramleh a young English tourist, Frank Scudamore, sat dozing in the warm sunshine that flooded through the glass-roofed hall of the Hotel Abbat, a stone's throw from the Place Muhammad Ali. On the previous night a tour guide had taken Scudamore to see the city's fleshpots where he had been entranced by the sights and smells – robed Bedouin from the desert, ever armed and dangerous, good natured crowds of city Arabs, dens thick with the smoke of hashish and opium, happy people dancing the frenzied zikka while those watching puffed away at their pipes. Now it was 2.30pm and Scudamore was quite content to have a lazy Sunday afternoon. It was then that the distant sound of firing reached his ears. Curious, he rose and wandered out into the blazing sunshine. The Place was wholly deserted at this siesta hour apart from one or two sentries sheltering under the trees. The Englishman could tell that the gunfire came from a street lying at right angles to the square called the Sikka Sabah Benat (the Street of the Seven Sisters). Guessing the noise probably meant a big native wedding or circumcision procession he decided to amble over and take a look.

Lunch over at Ramleh, Kusel decided to show his naval guest around the city. They set off in an open carriage with Morice Bey and a companion following behind. Arriving at the public gardens on the outskirts of Alexandria they were all astonished to find the place eerily deserted. Instead of the normal Sunday afternoon throng of carriages they saw only one other in sight. This contained a young naval officer in full uniform and two of his friends. The officer, James Pibworth, engineer of *Superb*, and two other pals from the ship, were also intent on seeing the town. Kusel and his companions got out and stretched their legs but could not fathom why so fashionable a place seemed empty. Watching the Pibworth group set off made the others decide to ride into the centre and see if something had happened. By the edge of the gardens a harem carriage suddenly drove past heading out of Alexandria. The Englishmen stopped it and asked the Arab driver if there was any news. He replied that a big fight had broken out between natives and Europeans and several people were dead. Captain Molyneux requested that under the circumstances it would be wisest if he rejoined his ship. With Giovanni, the Italian coachman, cracking his whip and 'Bessie', a sprightly mare from the Khedival stables trotting along quickly, Kusel and Molyneux in one carriage, and Morice in another raced into town. On the way they passed many small groups of Arabs who cursed the rich-looking foreigner in his stambouli frockcoat and tarboosh, and his lighter-skinned naval companion in British uniform and white pith helmet. 'The faster the better', someone shouted, 'you are only going to your death!'[35]

Frank Scudamore in the Place Muhammad Ali had not gone very far in the direction of the clamour when the square suddenly seemed to start filling up with people. The noise was so great that at first he could not comprehend what was going on. All were screaming curses against Christians and the majority seemed stoned or high on drugs. Many carried the clear spoils of pillage; one Arab clutched an immense pile of straw hats, two Bedouin dragged a great bale of silks and velvets, 'several which had fallen, and were making an ever-lengthening trail of bright colours in the dust', another staggered under the weight of a huge candlelabra. In amazement Scudamore saw several of the mob start to smash up the bandstand in the square, breaking apart the cafe tables and chairs, ripping up the iron railings. Soon he was surrounded by blue-gowned fellahin

> … brandishing heavy ironwood clubs; Bedouin from the desert, in coarse white-hooded cloaks of camels' hair, armed with long brass-bound guns; butchers and slaughters, with bare, blood-stained arms and breasts, and with reeking cleavers in their hands; semi-nude and grimy coal-porters from the docks; and a host of other, the scum of the native quarters.[36]

The mob seemed to swell and move over Scudamore, who stood in 'bewildered surprise', for no more than half a minute before a brawny Egyptian threw a piece of ragged table frame at him. It struck his knee so hard that he dropped to the ground in pain. The Egyptian next brought a chunk of wood down on the Englishman's head but as he staggered, the blow was deflected to his right shoulder and upper arm, ripping open the flesh. While his assailant staggered back for a moment, Scudamore got to his feet and decided to make a run for it. At the edge of the square the 23-year-old jumped the low chain fence that ran around the central reservation and spurted off down a side street. His pursuer, with thoughts and eyes squarely on the hated foreigner, lacked the same coordination and tripped over the railings and crashed to the ground. Scudamore was lucky, at the bottom of his street were a cordon of armed Greeks, Maltese and Italians. They bandaged his wound and led him to safety.

Totally oblivious to all these horrors, Kusel and Molyneux reached the city's Rosetta Gate where some soldiers were lounging around. The men were at ease, with piled arms, their officers sitting by the roadside smoking. Kusel gave them a salaam. All returned the salute and he decided the riot, if that was what it was, might not be so serious after all.

He was wrong. All down the long Avenue Rosetta houses and shops were closed and barricaded. From balconies filled with desperate men and women came voices urging them not to go any further. 'Bessie' kept up her pace and suddenly Kusel and Molyneux found themselves in the Place Muhammad Ali and a kind of hell. Screaming groups of Arabs were everywhere butchering any Europeans they could find. Trying to push on to the harbour Molyneux stood up to look ahead and saw Pibworth's carriage surrounded by a large crowd armed with knives and sticks. In the melee the 32-year-old engineer was stabbed to death. Mad with rage, one of his friends, a petty officer from *Superb*, went after the chief attacker, ramming his walking stick so fiercely into the man's mouth that it came out behind his ear and killed him. Stunned by such brutality the crowd paused for a few moments, while the petty officer got away.

It seemed as if reaching the jetty would be impossible so Kusel wisely told Giovanni to head for the safety of the British Consulate. Rearing and plunging, 'Bessie' fought her way through the mob and kept the attackers at a distance. The gatekeeper luckily recognised Kusel, (and Morice Bey had managed to catch them up in his carriage), so all the Englishmen were relieved to get inside the gates. The building they entered was a scene of 'indescribable confusion, women and children crowded everywhere, weeping and terrified'. Mr Calvert, deputy to Cookson, had collapsed with stress and shortly afterwards the Vice-Consul himself was brought in with blood streaming from a head wound.

Things had been normal until about 1pm when a fight started near a coffee house called the Cafe Crystal in the Rue des Soeurs. The true facts will never be known but it seems a Maltese started beating a donkey-boy who, according to one eyewitness, was stoned on hashish. The boy retaliated by knifing and killing his adversary. A bunch of Europeans, mainly Greeks, rushed to help the dying Maltese and in fury turned on the young Arab who they murdered. The American Consul that

> As the news spread, the crowd increased and became turbulent, but it was not until the Greeks and Maltese had commenced firing from their windows and flat house-tops upon the unarmed natives, and some of their number were had been killed and others wounded, that they were aroused to violent acts of vengeance.[37]

Summoned by the police to try and calm the mob, Charles Cookson went to the station in the Rue des Soeurs with the governor of Alexandria, Omar Lufti, and the sub-prefect of police. The trio thought they had been successful. Things seemed to quieten down somewhat and Cookson set off back to the Consulate. Along the way he was hit by a stone. No sooner did he step out of his carriage then a messenger walked up to summon him to a meeting of all the consuls at the same police station. Cookson must have been furious. Without stopping for an instant he jumped back again in his open carriage with one janissary as driver and headed back into the city. Ninety yards from the police station, at a spot near the great square where four roads met, Cookson and his coachman ran into a shower of stones that halted the carriage. Quickly the pair were surrounded by a nasty mob. When the British Vice-Consul stood up a large native ran to the back of the coach and knocked him to the ground with one blow from a quarterstaff. The janissary was also pulled from his perch and severely beaten. Somehow Cookson got dizzily to his feet, blood streaming down his face, and with the mob still hitting him stumbled onto the police station. He noticed, as he crawled along, that a guard of soldiers outside the building 'did not move a step to protect me'.[38] It had been a fool's errand. The meeting had already been abandoned as too dangerous and the Italian Consul had also been attacked crossing the square. Around 6pm a shattered Vice-Consul, his clothes and face still spattered with dried blood, was brought back to the Consulate by a circuitous route. His wounds, as the doctor reported, were quite serious, 'head severely cut several places; lost deal blood; one finger broken; both hands much injured; body full of bruises.'[39]

Many Egyptians died from sniper fire; tobacco grinder Ahmed Hussein and cobbler Ali Salamah were just two of many. At some point two policemen were killed and these murders encouraged the rest of the police and soldiers to support the mob. Many European witnesses remembered the police as the worst perpetrators. When the governor ordered them to disperse the mob several policemen began cursing him for trying to help the 'Christian dogs'. The rioting gradually extended itself along the Rue des Soeurs and into the Place Muhammad Ali (where Frank Scudamore had got caught up in it). From balconies, windows and rooftops the Europeans kept up a spasmodic fire which was returned by the soldiers, police and the mob. Bedouin were also seen in the crowd using their traditional long muskets to shoot passing foreigners. Caught in the crossfire were Lieutenant Seymour Fortescue of *Superb* and some friends. He thought the police were pretty random in their firing, 'but it struck us all that for choice they went for the Europeans'. He and his party were able to get off a main street into a monastery school where they crouched and waited behind a locked door.[40]

Across the city many Europeans met the stuff of nightmares. Several of them appealed to the police for protection but were bayoneted on the spot. Watching from a balcony Fillippo Lais was horrified to see a mob approach a 5-year-old Maltese child and club it to death. Gardello Biagio, a young fireman from the P&O ship *Tanjore* was captured by Arabs on his way to the harbour and saw a soldier slice off the head of his friend, Guiseppe Chiavalin. Even the tiny shoe-blacking boys who worked in the Place Muhammad Ali were seen to gleefully beat out the brains of Europeans lying wounded on the pavement.

Some Europeans had lucky escapes. Surrounded by a large crowd, Frederico Panzetta was badly beaten and heard someone say, 'he is a Christian, we must kill him', but shots fired from balconies distracted the crowd long enough for him to escape. Another mob pursued Riccardo Attard into his home, beat up his wife and threw him out of window, but the couple somehow survived. Arriving back at the harbour after an early afternoon boat trip to see the ironclads,

Alessandro Vernoni walked through the customs house to find three bloody Europeans lying in the street. His long journey to get home that day meant sneaking down the Via Franca where: 'I saw eight groups of Arabs, and in the midst each of which group I saw a Christian on the ground beaten', and crossing the Place Muhammad Ali where the crowd 'ran from one direction to another. No sooner they saw a European they struck him until they saw him dead. I counted fourteen of such scenes.'[41]

By 5.30pm the portion of the Rue des Soeurs where the riot began 'was almost deserted, the ground being strewn with debris of wood and glass, and the windows shattered, many of them by bullets'. Close to the great square witnesses saw a well-dressed European, his black clothes torn and covered with blood, rush backwards and forwards as if distracted. Near the corner of the Rue des Soeurs a crowd gathered around the man and started to hit him with clubs and sticks. Whenever he tried to escape two laughing policemen would push him back into the mob. Nearby, in the same street, were three Europeans lying dead in a heap, one had 'a bullet-hole in his head, another was stabbed through the chest, and another with his skull fractured was lying on his face with his shoes and stockings off'. In the centre of the town all manner of things – brandy, flour, linen and household objects – littered the streets, and amid the city's finest mansions and shops looting became the order of the night. One soldier walked down a street with a glass chandelier balanced on his head and an Arab was even seen riding away on a toy horse.[42]

The European dead and injured numbered just a few British fatalities including George Strackett, the Admiral's manservant, and Alfred Home, the servant of Seymour's flag-lieutenant, Hedworth Lambton. Most had been murdered near the harbour. It was here that two Mancunians, Robert Dobson and Reginald Richardson, employed together in the cotton good trade tried to help friends at the Eastern Telegraph Company on the marina, who were fighting to prevent the shore end of the submarine cable from being destroyed by a mob. In the melee both young men were killed.

The worst attack on a British subject was the murder of Herbert Ribton, a civil engineer and missionary. That afternoon – like Signor Vernoni – he had taken his young daughter and two friends to view the fleet. On landing they found the city gate shut by the customs pier but were allowed to enter the city via the police station. It was their misfortune to go into the street just as a howling mob came into view. The police, their bayonet fixed, looked on and did nothing as Ribton and his companions were bludgeoned to death. Three times he tried to rise and save his little girl. While she screamed in terror the rioters smashed his face to a bloody pulp and stripped the body. Terrified and badly beaten, the toddler was seized by a soldier, thrown over his back like a sack of rice, and taken off to the native quarter of the city. Hearing the child's screams a wealthy sheikh sent men to investigate, rescued the girl and late that night in Arab disguise she was returned to her grieving mother.

At the British Consulate the tension was palpable. Samuel de Kusel recalled it as 'the longest night I ever remember, the hours simply crawled past'. Egyptian troops had marched down the street in the late afternoon, but as the night wore on everyone grew jittery at the approach of tramping soldiers or the rumble of artillery. The occupants were at least well-armed; during the afternoon they had broken into a nearby gunsmith's shop and helped themselves to his stock of shotguns and revolvers. Mid evening Omar Lufti arrived with an army officer, Colonel Suliman Sami and they warned the foreigners not to fire inadvertently or a mob might storm the building.[43]

Just a few days earlier, by a stroke of luck, a telephone link had been made between the Consulate and *Invincible*. The phone now rang and Admiral Seymour said he was sending a party of sailors and marines to guard the building. He needed someone to volunteer and meet them on the quay. While Cookson and Molyneux were debating this news the governor returned to say that spies had indeed reported British boats being filled with sailors. Lufti warned that if any British tried to land the Egyptian Artillery had orders to blow them out of the water. A massacre with terrible consequences now seemed imminent. Molyneux hastily phoned the admiral who was in agreement that the landing had to be stopped somehow, but the boats had already set off in the darkness for the shore. It was decided that Morice Bey, who had been in the British Navy before entering khedival service should go with two Egyptian officers and try to stop the little flotilla. Enlisting the help of some Greek fishermen, Morice reached the boats just in the nick of time but, he later declared, the face of the officer in command, on being told to return to his ship, was 'most expressive, and his language … was even more so'.[44]

Dawn revealed a city exhausted by rampage. Behind the barred and guarded gates of consulates all over Alexandria, scores of frightened Europeans huddled in groups. The final death toll will never be known. Like many great ports Alexandria had a large transient population and people could vanish at will. Most estimates put the death toll at 50 Europeans, although some accounts claim a figure three times that amount. One witness later spoke of seeing several cartloads of bodies thrown at night into the sea near the western harbour. Forty-four dead Europeans were found in the city's hospitals that day, 37 of them so battered as to be unrecognizable, with a further 36 wounded. Some historians have put the death toll among the local population at around

250. Courts subsequently convicted 291 people of participating in the riots including 50 soldiers and 29 policemen, while 9 women were also among those found guilty of looting and 10 more for buying goods known to have been stolen.

A Commission of Inquiry set up to decide who was responsible for the riot, or if it had been planned in advance, fell apart with recriminations on all sides. The European community, naturally enough, blamed it all on Arabi and sympathisers. This was and is a convenient explanation but the facts do not add up. The general had vowed to keep order and as historian Juan Cole remarks, 'to forment a riot would have been to shoot himself in the foot'.[45] Tewfik was also accused of instigating it as a means of ending his problems. This theory has a lot to commend it but no really hard evidence has turned up to convict him. Wilfred Blunt was one of those who blamed the Khedive and argued that Omar Lufti had been told to orchestrate it. He absolved Colonel Sami who 'sent troops at 5 o'clock, armed on his responsibility, and quelled the riot'.

The real truth will never be known for sure. Years later, writing in *Secret History Of The English Occupation Of Egypt*, Blunt also implied that the English diplomats were not free of blame. Did Cookson not connive at arming the Maltese a few days before the riot? In his copy of Blunt's book Sir Charles Dilke has written sarcastically beside Cookson's name: 'I suppose he meant to kill himself. He nearly did.'

The presence of the Anglo-French fleet was a slap in the face to most Egyptians. Tensions in the city were at flashpoint. It took very little on 11 June 1882 to ignite these elements into a combustible mixture with evil results.

# 3

# Bombardment

*Well done Gippy!*
Alexander Bruce Tulloch

Less than four months before the Alexandria Riots occurred, natives living along the banks of the Sweetwater Canal near Tel-el-Kebir saw a curious sight: a balding Englishman with a strange accent who claimed to be on a casual duck-shooting expedition. But observant Arabs, and these included at least one young sheikh the Englishman encountered, noticed he had more on his mind than sport – frequently the stranger missed birds within easy range and could be seen pacing out distances and entering things in a notebook. The foreigner was clearly mad, they decided, for he tried to shoot snipe by day and then went out to pot ducks by starlight. It was of course, all a hoax. The Englishman was not English and his shooting, though a fine diversion, was not what he was about. Alexander Bruce Tulloch was his name, he was a Scot and a British War Office spy.

To the frightened European residents of Cairo and Alexandria war seemed inevitable. The day after the riots a second exodus from Egypt got under way as terrified foreigners made for the coast and the safety of any ship available to take them out of harm's way. Some boatmen made a fortune asking exorbitant prices as they ferried people out to the ships. In the first week alone 14,000 Europeans – almost one sixth of all non-Egyptians in the country – hastily packed their belongings and fled, while 6,000 more crowded around the harbour at Alexandria awaiting transport. Each day more shops and offices closed in the two cities as business people decided that the risk of war and death was too close for comfort. Within a few days this exodus had an economic backlash as thousands of native employees found themselves without jobs or pay (it was estimated the number exceeded 30,000 Egyptians in Alexandria alone).

Walter Goodall in Cairo wondered how long he should stick it out. 'All public works were at an end', he wrote of the dismal capital, 'hotels were barricaded, and, with one or two exceptions, abandoned, the shops were mostly closed, the restaurateurs had put up their shutters. Had it not been for the occasional carts full of luggage, always full in going to the station, always returning empty, the streets of Cairo would have been deserted.' The only regular locals to be seen were the donkey-boys, now sleeping on the street corners, and their donkeys, probably grateful for the unexpected rest. Government offices and the central post office were open but the only busy place was the railway station:

> To be sure of tickets the panic-stricken beings crowded to the waiting rooms and entrance to the station over night, slept beside their goods, fought for their tickets at the right time, and by dint of energy, squeezed themselves into the train if possible. Those who failed in this sat upon the carriage buffers or the plank steps.[1]

With shops, cafes and offices shut, and soldiers patrolling the streets, the Khedive got a far from ecstatic welcome when he visited Alexandria on 13 June in the company of Dervish Pasha, the old warrior sent as the Sultan's envoy. In the harbour Tewfik could see the British and French ironclads now crowded with refugees. Three hundred extra persons swarmed over *Invincible*, and 280 more did the same on *Monarch*, with similarly large numbers on all the other warships. Seymour appointed Commander Lord Charles Beresford of *Condor*, and Lieutenant W. Morrison of despatch vessel HMS *Helicon* to oversee the embarkation of refugees and the chartering of merchant ships to deliver them to several ports around the Mediterranean.

On 14 June Lord Granville received telegrams from both his Consul and Consul-General. The injured Charles Cookson, steadily recovering from his injuries, wrote:

> Great panic yesterday in consequence rumour landing from British and French fleet. I have contradicted it as publicly as possible. A large number of Bedouins reported outside Alexandria, intention unknown, probably for plunder … General flight of Europeans continues. Ships' accommodation quite inadequate, and am begging authorities, if absolutely necessary, to charter vessels for conveyance of British subjects.[2]

Malet wrote in a similar vein that 300 British had taken refuge on an English steamer in the harbour and another 400 on board a merchant ship. He had arrived in Alexandria and been offered a berth on *Helicon* but Cookson, among others, was aghast that this might be interpreted as a signal that naval hostilities were about to begin. So, to prevent causing alarm, Malet had agreed to stay at a nearby hotel.

On the ironclads, after weeks of inactivity, the sudden arrival of hundreds of civilians of all ages, along with mountains of luggage, was treated as a mildly irritating lark by the officers and men. On *Monarch* one of the youngest offic-ers, Cadet B. M. Chambers, later recalled that for a few days the ship was in chaos: 'Our chest-room, the only place we had to dress, was invaded by troops of laughing girls, whilst snotties caught undressing would hide behind the chests.' His most vivid memory was of a small child who decided one night to gaze down the wardroom hatch on the officers at dinner and fell head first, five or six feet, into the soup tureen just as it was being ladled out by the smartly dressed mess president, a major of marines. The child was unharmed, while the major, splattered all over with soup, let rip some very 'sultry' language.[3]

The Khedive and his advisors also found themselves in a mess. The Sultan's envoy wanted to try and mediate with the army officers but Tewfik said it would be a waste of time. He begged Abdul Hamid to send Ottoman troops and restore his rights by force. When the Sultan made clear that this was not going to happen Tewfik began to swing round to the idea that perhaps it might be best to appease the Arabists. They would hardly dare depose him if he was conciliatory, and if the Europeans were not going to invade, then it might be for the best to cosy up to them. A coalition ministry was formed under an old Circassian called Raghib Pasha who assumed the dual roles of Prime Minister and Foreign Minister. Arabi took the War Ministry and Ahmed Rashid, a Tewfik nominee, handled internal affairs. The Council of Minsters was asked to draft a set of laws that would finally make clear 'the rights of rulers and subjects of all classes', along with the future role of the administrative and judicial branches of the government. The Khedive returned to Alexandria on 20 June, but this time his entry was a triumphal one to cheering crowds. The reason was that sitting beside him in an open landau was Ahmed Arabi. During this obvious public relations stunt the pair announced a general amnesty for all those involved in recent events (with the exception of the 11 June riots).[4]

Dervish Pasha, feeling that with a new government in place his task was over, cabled the Porte for permission to return home but the Sultan insisted he must stay longer in Egypt and convince Arabi, on whom Abdul Hamid had just bestowed the Grand Ribbon of the Medjidie Order, to return with him to Constantinople. Ahmed Arabi was far too suspicious of Ottoman intentions to fall for such an attempt to remove him from the political scene, though Dervish kept trying this ruse as late as 7 July before finally boarding his yacht and sailing home.

In the immediate aftermath of the riots, stuck in a hotel in the heart of Alexandria, Consul-General Malet began to wobble again in his staunch attitude against the nationalists. He warned Seymour against any action likely to inflame the situation and telegraphed London that in the event of more disturbances the Admiral would be able to land only 1,000 men, while his French counterpart, Admiral Conrad, refused to land men under any circumstances. 'The 1,000 would be useless' wrote Malet on 14 June, 'as their presence would turn the garrison against the Europeans and a general massacre would probably ensue'. The diplomat who had urged intervention as the best course was now telling HM Govt that 'the fleet is a menace likely to lead to disturbance and not a protection'.[5] Meantime Lord Northbrook at the Admiralty asked Seymour 'if another outbreak should occur, what protection you could give to British subjects?' The Admiral bluntly replied on 16 June that 'Under most urgent circumstances, I would endeavour to hold beach of new port, near Consular residence ... but if weather as it is at present impossible on account on account of surf and sea-room ... our landing would entail most grave consequences.' It was not encouraging news for the mandarins of Whitehall.[6]

The Liberal Government in June 1882 was having a distinctly bad month. Violence much closer to home had left their Irish policy in tatters. One month earlier, on Saturday 6 May, the streets of Dublin had been bedecked with bunting to honour the returning Lord Lieutenant, Earl Spencer, and his Chief Secretary, the diligent 45-year-old Lord Frederick Cavendish, second son of the Duke of Devonshire. Early that evening Spencer looked out of a window of the Viceregal Lodge in the middle of Phoenix Park, where he was expecting Cavendish and his permanent Under-Secretary, Thomas Burke, for dinner and saw what he thought was a scuffle among men on the pavement. The Earl turned away, but what he had witnessed, much to his later horror, was the murder of his guests. Burke, a tough Catholic, was the object of an attack by four terrorists calling themselves the 'Irish Invincibles'. They had no idea who Cavendish was but killed him anyway. The two civil servants stood no chance as their assailants slashed with razor-sharp surgical knives. Burke's throat was cut and Cavendish stabbed many times around the heart.

The mighty Cavendish family were inconsolable over Lord Frederick's murder. One of the most affected was his elder brother, Spencer Compton, Marquess of Hartington, leader of the Whig branch of the Liberal party in Parliament. Only three years separated the two brothers who had grown up together. There can be little doubt that Lord Frederick's death at the hands of extreme nationalists hardened Hartington's resolve that Arabi and his clique should not get the upper hand in Egypt.

In the following weeks Hartington – known as 'Harty-Tarty' by his friends – would gradually push through his Palmerstonian principles. A lofty grandee, heir to the huge Devonshire estates, with four stately homes and a rent roll of £180,000 a year, he liked to affect a boredom with politics and claimed to have no ambitions. Some thought him the most eligible, and certainly the richest bachelor in the country, but he had a secret lover. This was the very beautiful German-born Louise, Duchess of Manchester, with whom he carried on a clandestine affair for more than 30 years. The social historian, Ronald Pearsall, wrote thus of Hartington:

> Described by contemporaries as a 'heavy swell' … he had the 'haw hawy' type of voice ridiculed by Punch. He dressed badly in, ill-fitting tails, which did not close behind him as he walked, and his lemon-coloured trousers were notorious. It was averred that his incredible rudeness and gaucherie were a cover for shyness, and it was reported that he said that the happiest day of his life was when his pig took first prize at an agricultural show.[7]

There was however, a serious side to Hartington and a friend noted that he 'ponders longer over State problems; the bent of his mind is slowly critical and very slowly constructive'.[8] Hartington's wish to adopt a more bellicose line towards Egypt grew out of his impatience with Granville and Gladstone. 'Has Arabi Pasha given in, or has M. De Freycinet been persuaded to get out of bed?', he wrote to the Foreign Secretary on 27 May, 'I wonder whether any human being, (out of Downing Street) would believe that not a word has been said in the Cabinet about Egypt for a fortnight, and I suppose will not be for another week – if then.' Three days later he moaned again: 'Unless the French keep their word to us and are prepared to go in for Turkish intervention at once, we had much better cut ourselves loose from them. What is the use of such Allies?'[9]

The 'Alexandria Massacres', in all their calamity and horror, allowed the British Press a field day in sensational journalism. From the Conservative benches Lord Salisbury thundered that Gladstone's 'pacifism' had led to British subjects being 'butchered under the very guns of the Fleet which had never budged an inch to save them'.[10] The reports coming out of Egypt now swung several Cabinet colleagues to line up behind Hartington. They included Kimberley, Northbrook and Dilke, all clamouring for effective measures to protect the Suez Canal. On 20 June Hartington warned that unless some expedition was sent to Egypt it was likely several Cabinet ministers might resign. A Turkish expedition was preferable but it was probably not going to happen fast enough and the Sultan might make a bargain with Arabi. In that case an Anglo-French expedition had to be sent, though Hartington favoured Britain doing it alone. 'The sooner we are prepared to act the better' he told his colleagues.[11]

In recent years a theory has been expounded by anti-imperialist historians that the British had long lusted after Egypt and been waiting for an excuse to grab it. Unfortunately this ignores the fact that as late as June 1882, when the British were offered Egypt on a plate, they turned it down. It happened on the 23rd of that month, just after a conference opened in Constantinople to discuss the Egyptian Problem. The Sultan's private secretary, Reshid Pasha called on Lord Dufferin, British Ambassador to the Porte and explained that his master, possessed by a fear and loathing of France, wanted to know if HM Govt would sign a bilateral treaty whereby Britain would get the exclusive control and administration of Egypt, with the Porte retaining absolute suzerainty? Dufferin could scarcely believe his own ears. Why was Abdul Hamid, who had denounced the Joint Note and opposed the Anglo-French fleet, now offering the British a free hand in part of his empire? He was immediately suspicious, perhaps the Sultan hoped to drive a wedge into the Anglo-French alliance, or maybe had resigned himself to the fact that a European invasion was the best answer to Egypt's ills, yet found a French one, with its memories of Tunis, more distasteful than a British occupation? Despite the pleas of Reshid, Lord Dufferin turned the offer down flat, commenting that 'if the Sultan were to hand over Egypt to us as a gift, with all Europe consenting, I doubt whether the British Government would accept such a burden and responsibility.' Sure enough, when he informed London both Gladstone and Granville thought it an absurd idea. It was going to take a war and several thousand deaths to thrust Egypt into the lion's paws.[12]

To mollify Hartington and his clique Gladstone agreed to send two battalions of troops to the Mediterranean and asked Childers and Northbrook to examine the best ways of protecting the Suez Canal with the French. This brought forth a reply from Ferdinand de Lesseps that his Canal was quite safe and the biggest danger, in fact, was the threat of foreign intervention. Gladstone and Granville both agreed with this assessment and urged their Cabinet colleagues to wait and see what might be decided at the Constantinople Conference.

By 23 June Seymour was reporting that most British subjects who wished to leave Egypt had done so and those who remained were determined to stay. Miracles had been achieved by Beresford and Morrison in chartering ships and getting the refugees away. Impatient and impetuous, it was the kind of work that suited a man like Beresford. When the problem of cooking facilities for so many people became acute he came up with the bright idea of sawing wooden barrels in half and lighting coal fires inside the tubs. It sounded crazy but somehow worked and after each meal the fires were either doused or the barrels thrown away to be replaced by new ones. Life also had its amusing side, according to Beresford:

> In the course of this work there fell to me a task rarely included, even among the infinite variety of the duties of a naval officer, my working-party was stowing refugees in the hold of a collier when a coloured lady was taken ill. She said 'Baby, he come, sare, directly, sare, myself, sare.' And so it was. We rigged up a screen and my coxswain and I performed the office of midwives thus trust upon us, and all went well.[13]

Towards the end of June Walter Goodall decided that he too should join the throng in Alexandria. The journey from the capital by train was an anxious one, especially at Tanta, where a mob had killed Europeans earlier that month (there were several small-scale riots and ugly incidents following the Alexandria riots, but Arabi Pasha always managed to restore order quickly and provide trains for the fleeing foreigners). At the Alexandria railway station Goodall had to run a gauntlet as scared Europeans were jeered and jostled by the locals. Luckily for him he had secured a berth on the P&O ship *Tanjore* which was soon to be full of influencial people including Cartwright, the acting British Consul, and Auckland Colvin, who stayed in charge of affairs until the last minute. Poor Cookson had been sent back to England for a well deserved rest. His deputy, elderly Mr Calvert, was still in a state of shock and most of the consular clerks in Cairo and Alexandria had already quit their posts.

The strangest departure was that of Malet, who was suddenly taken ill by a mysterious fever on 17 June and left Egypt ten days later. Even in his memoirs, as the Consul-General recounts the incident, it seems rather suspicious: 'It was only after steaming out of the harbour that I began to feel my strength returning.'[14] Twenty-five years later, on reading Blunt's book, Malet came to the dramatic conclusion that he had been poisoned. The whole thing may have been psychosymatic stress, but it is also odd how little enthusiasm Malet demonstrated in getting to the centre of action anyway; he was told to join the Khedive at the coast by Granville on 13 June and his clear prevarication made the usually cool Foreign Secretary telegraph that 'Her Majesty's Government remain of the opinion that your proper place is where the Khedive may be.' A day before the mystery illness struck Malet wrote to his mother that 'I am worked off my legs, but am perfectly well ... I cannot say what may happen from one hour to another, but I am sure that I shall pull through. My colleagues are badly scared. A panic is a very catching thing, and here it has become an epidemic.'[15]

While most Europeans were leaving Egypt, one man returned. This was the duck-hunting spy of a few months earlier. Major Tulloch of the Welsh Regiment had made a confidential report as a result of his Egyptian trip and it was widely circulated among the top brass following the riots. When he went to see the First Naval Lord, Sir Astley Cooper Key, to explain in detail his plan for a proposed landing at Ramleh, he was told: 'you had better go down to the War Office at once; we have applied for you to be attached for duty with the Commander-in-Chief of the Mediterranean Fleet.'[16] On seeing Childers, a surprised Tulloch was told that he had less than six hours to prepare himself and catch the boat-train. Quickly wiring his wife in the country to send up his batman with a blue patrol jacket, sword, revolver and some underclothes, a harassed but excited Tulloch raced off to the Opera Arcade to buy toothbrushes, shirts and collars, just in case the servant did not arrive in time. Luckily all went well and three days later, via a Brindisi crossing, the major, still dressed in city civvies, black hat and carrying a rolled umbrella, stood before Admiral Seymour on the deck of *Invincible*.

Tulloch was given a comfortable berth on the ship and set to work to find out as much information on Arabi as possible, Egyptian troops movements and the condition of the Alexandria defences. On 22 June he informed the War Office that 'Forts can be silenced but further operations impossible without troops: 4,000 necessary to blockade Alexandria until fire of ships and want of water causes surrender: 3,000 requested to guard Canal.'[17] A day later he warned: 'Egyptians have three small vessels filled for explosion in the Canal', and on 1 July cabled: 'The military at Alexandria and the forts are now upwards of 10,000. The recruits or reserve are coming in steadily. Arabi now gives out that he is mightily inspired by the Prophet.'[18]

Bright, energetic and extremely egotistical, it is difficult from a distance of more than twelve decades, to fully evaluate what Tulloch wrote. Like most intelligence gathering that is based on assumptions, with few hard facts, it seems a mix of the real and the exaggerated. Later Wolseley would complain that Tulloch inflated the strength of the Egyptian army. Certainly, his advice to London that Arabi was simply an 'ignorant fanatic with some crude ideas about liberty', was wide of the mark.[19] Though middle-aged Tulloch still revelled in dressing up as an Arab and going on shore to procure information. These hazardous missions were part of the man's courageous nature. He was also an honourable one. During the sacking of the Summer Palace at Peking in 1860 he had looted a fortune in jade but did the rare thing of giving it all up honestly to the prize committee so that the proceeds could be shared with the rest of the troops.

The spying work was full of danger; on one occasion while in disguise Tulloch got lost on the quayside and asked directions of an Egyptian officer who mistook him for a distinguished sheikh and led the major into one of Arabi's meetings. One morning, writing on board *Invincible*, Tulloch looked up to see a sandy-haired, blue eyed 'tall, thin subaltern of engineers named Kitchener ... he had got a few days leave from his general at Cyprus, and as he could speak Arabic, had come to see if he could be of any use to me. "Certainly", I replied, "I hope you will be able to stay with me".'[20] It was to be the young Herbert Kitchener's first taste of Egypt – a land destined to be the fulcrum of his extraordinary rise to power over the next sixteen years. He had spent the past three years working on a dull scientific land survey of Cyprus, went to Egypt in civilian clothes and failed to inform the island's High Commissioner. When General Biddulph found out where his young subaltern had gone during a week's leave of absence he was furious. A string of angry telegrams to Tulloch followed, but the major was delighted, even for a few days, to have an assistant who spoke fluent Turkish and Arabic. Disguised as a Levantine official, accompanied by Kitchener in civilian dress, Tulloch took a a train ride to gather information on the feasibility of an advance on Cairo from Alexandria. By now the Arabists were well aware of Tulloch's spying activities and on the lookout for him. The two British officers got back safely but Tulloch noted that exactly a week later, on the same stretch of line, a light-skinned Syrian was dragged off a train under the impression he was a spy and had his throat cut on the platform. Tulloch had several lucky scrapes. On one occasion a little Arab boy watched him in disguise and then burst out laughing. Asking for backsheesh, the child grinned at the spy and said, 'I see you, Damietta', a reminder of the duck-hunting trip.

During the last days of June, HM Govt still clung to the hope that the Turks would intervene. 'There is a streak of light in Egyptian matters', Granville wrote, 'it is quite on the cards that the Sultan will send troops after all'.[21] Even Hartington was hopeful that the Constantinople Conference would turn up trumps. The Cabinet agreed on 1 July to demand reparations for the Alexandria riots, but would decide on Egyptian policy only after the Conference 'had dealt with, or refused to deal with the problem'.

What made the entire Cabinet nervous was the French. There was anxiety that Freycinet and his colleagues would come to some sly accord with Arabi and the Khedive. These suspicions increased after 24 June when they refused to join the British in protecting the Suez Canal. If, by some master-stroke, France increased its influence in Egypt ministers feared that it would be impossible for Britain to regain its position without military intervention.

On 27 June Seymour sent a long letter to the Admiralty outlining the current state of affairs: the British consular staff in Egypt had almost entirely left the country and Malet was departing that day; the Khedive was in residence at his Ras-el-Tin Palace overlooking the harbour and Arabi was staying at the nearby Arsenal; the Egyptian commander, Toulba Pasha, had with him about 9,000 men quartered in several barracks and forts about the city; the situation was quiet but 'the majority of shops are closed and nearly all mercantile transactions have ceased'.[22] Less than 200 Britons were left in the country, a quarter of whom were based in Cairo and mainly employed on the railways. Despite the mood of the people the French Consul and his staff remained working in their building near the Place Muhammad Ali and this attitude was repeated at the Austro-Hungarian, Danish and German consulates. At the harbour, still busy with departing foreigners and merchant vessels, the quays were filling up with a rapidly growing armada of visiting warships. Austrian, German, Greek, Italian and Russian cruisers, frigates and ironclads had arrived and dropped anchor, as if to see an impending show, including the USS *Lancaster*, bearing the flag of Rear-Admiral Nicholson.

America had been placed in a quandary on 15 June when its Consul and his staff deserted their posts and fled to Europe. The State Department sent an urgent request for help to the most distinguished citizen they could find in Egypt to assist them. This was Colonel Charles Chaille-Long, onetime officer in the Egyptian army, explorer of Uganda and assistant to the great Charles Gordon. Undoubtedly brave and tenacious, Chaille-Long was also a lying braggart with a love-hate attitude towards the British who, he felt, had failed to give him his due credit for such achievements as the discovery of Lake Kioga (which he called Lake Hussein). 'Readers of his books and articles got the impression that Perfidious Albion lurked behind every bush he passed' notes his biographer.[23]

Fresh instructions arrived for Admiral Seymour on 3 July:

> Prevent any attempt to bar channel into port. If work is resumed on earthworks, or fresh guns mounted, inform Military Commander that you have orders to prevent it, and if not immediately discontinued, destroy earthworks and silence batteries if they open fire, having given sufficient notice to population, shipping and men-of-war.[24]

It was clearest indicator Seymour had so far been given that events were slipping towards war and the burden for engaging the enemy was falling on his shoulders.

The orders came from Northbrook as First Lord of the Admiralty, but the fine detail was worked out by Admiral Key. It was once said of the admiral, famously unable to delegate anything, that he 'was never happier than when absorbed in administrative work, completely encased in a comforting cocoon of trivia'.[25] Three years earlier, in a minor scandal, he had married the daughter of an Italian dancing-master. Thirty-six years junior to her husband the new Lady Key immediately became pregnant and officers joked in private that her acquaintance was 'the Key to promotion!' But her husband was no fool. As early as the 1860s Key had argued that masts and sails would be redundant within a few years. It would be wrong to under-estimate his importance in laying Admiralty plans for a possible Egyptian War and it was to be his analytical mind and grasp of technical matters that helped Northbrook reach his decisions.

On 4 July the Admiralty warned Seymour that before commencing any bombardment he must invite the participation of the French ships. 'The following to be kept secret', continued the cipher, 'we do not know the orders of given by French Government to their Admiral, but you are not to postpone acting on your instructions because French decline to join you'. Seymour replied with his latest news: 'Two additional guns placed in Pharos Castle last night. Parapet of battery facing sea front was also strengthened.'[26] The French position was made clear the next evening when Lord Lyons in Paris was told that Admiral Conrad had been given instructions not to assist the British. The French Government, went on to say M. de Freycinet, 'considered that this would be an act of offensive hostility against Egypt in which they could not take part without violating the Constitution, which prohibits their making war without the consent of the Chambers.'[27]

In London, where the Cabinet debated this latest news, opinions seemed to centre around Seymour's right to issue an ultimatum. This matter became even more important the next day when the Sultan made it clear that no Ottoman troops would be sent to Egypt. A major concern was the security of the Suez Canal; if Alexandria was bombarded would the Arabists retaliate by trying to seize it? Despite the assurances of Lesseps that it was a neutral entity, Northbrook and Hartington urged a British invasion to protect the Canal and the rights of the bondholders. Gladstone, Granville, and the old radical, John Bright, 'now stood alone against the rest of the Cabinet in supporting a let-alone policy'. Bright argued the case for non-intervention with some logic. 'Surely, if the attack on the port endangers the Canal,' he pointed out, 'the attack should not be made'. In a spirit of Cabinet solidarity Puss was willing to go as far as bombardment, but the Grand Old Man dithered and when asked on 7 July to call a Cabinet meeting so that Seymour might be given new orders he blustered, 'Hurried and frequent Cabinets create much stir. I do not understand what fresh order Beauchamp Seymour could have.'[28]

The tension at Alexandria was becoming unbearable and the stress on the British admiral very considerable. On 6 July he warned Toulba Pasha that unless warlike preparations were discontinued it would be his duty to open fire on the defences. On the 8th came a simple but clear telegram from London: 'Are you sure of facts?' 'Yes' was Seymour's unequivocal one word reply.[29]

Facts? Well, there were some obvious ones, but the times were now less and less attuned to them as media-hype, human moods, opinions and emotions took over in that horrible malaise that precedes any outbreak of war. Perhaps if a whole blanket of suspicion could have been laid aside and both sides sat down to some seriously open talks war might have been averted. But this calm view is based on hindsight. One can argue that the Egyptians were perfectly justified, as a sovereign state, in building up their shore defences. What rights did the British have to make threats anyway? But after the riots, with the mood and economic situation in Egypt totally unsettled, who knows what spark might have led the Egyptians to open fire on European ships in their harbour. The possibility also remains that, given time, with their forts rebuilt and off-shore mines laid, they might have decided to nationalize the Canal.

A spin on the facts was obvious to neutral observers like Stone Pasha who told his family that 'Seymour will finally bombard Alexandria; and that if he cannot find a pretext he will make one.' (The general left his wife and daughters in Cairo on 6 July, placed his son aboard *Lancaster* and went to the side of his Khedive). It was Northbrook, in the way of politicians, who came up with the final *casus belli*. He told Gladstone that 'if we want to bring on a fight we can instruct B. Seymour to require the guns to be dismantled. My advisers do not think they will do much harm where they are.'[30] Years later Freycinet admitted that 'our information was not so alarming'.[31] The remaining consuls, fearing for the destruction of the town and its citizens wrote to Seymour and he tried to allay their worries: 'I do not propose and have never expressed the intention of bombarding the town of Alexandria. My operations, if rendered necessary, will be directed against the fortifications.'[32]

War correspondents, a relatively new kind of journalist, were to cover the hostilities in unprecedented numbers and detail. One of the most famous, Frederic Villiers of the *Graphic*, a veteran of the Afghan War, ran into a Scottish storekeeper who supplied the fleet with beef and coal. He told Villiers: 'if you drive to my brother's house overlooking the old harbour, you will see from the balcony what the Arab gunners have been doing during the night'. One of a rare handful of war correspondents who was as good an artist as a writer, Villiers went to the address and with the aid of a telescope sketched cannon that had been dragged into position under the cover of darkness at Fort Silsileh. He quickly returned to Condor and Beresford showed the drawings to Seymour.[33]

The admiral felt the matter needed confirmation. A volunteer was thus required for a spying mission – and quickly. The man selected was Lieutenant Henry Theophilus Smith-Dorrien of *Invincible*; one of a trio of remarkable brothers who were all to serve in the Egyptian War. Henry, along with brother Arthur, had seen action on HMS *Shah* when it bombarded the renegade Peruvian warship *Huascar* in 1877. Then, two years later, Arthur had fought with the naval brigade at Gingindlovo in the Zulu War. He survived without a scratch. Younger brother Horace was similarly fortunate when serving in the army, he was one of only six officers to escape alive from the battlefield of Isandlwana. Now, three years on, each of the trio was destined to play a role in the forthcoming campaign.

Dressed as an Egyptian and with a large basket under his arm Smith-Dorrien set off for shore early on the morning of 9 July. Villiers beef contractor friend had again offered to help and on the way stopped to do business on USS *Lancaster*. As the pair were pushing off one of the American sailors shouted at Henry, 'You dirty-looking ruffian, you want a wash', and turned the deck hose on him. Wet, but feeling that his disguise was a success, a confidently invigorated Smith-Dorrien landed by the old Rosetta Gate and quickly took a carriage to the quarantine station, proceeding on foot within 50 yards of Fort Silsileh. Here he saw working parties of more than 200 men moving two 32-pounders towards slides which seemed to have been recently placed near the sea wall. This news, when conveyed to Seymour, convinced him that the Egyptians had no intention of halting their fortifications and each day new guns were pointing at his ships. 'No doubt about armaments,' he told the Admiralty, 'guns are now being mounted on Fort Silsili [sic]. Shall give foreign Consuls notice at daylight tomorrow (10th) and commence action twenty-four hours after, unless forts on the isthmus and those commanding entrance to the harbour and surrendered.'[34]

'We have got the Grand Old Man into a corner now' said a jubilant Joe Chamberlain, 'and he must fight.' The Prime Minister had finally capitulated to those demanding naval action on 9 July. 'I do not feel the necessity', he wrote, 'but I am willing to defer to your decisions and judgments.' The Irish Arrears Bill filled his mind and he had little real interest in events so far away. Only John Bright still opposed any force being used in Egypt. 'Puss' Granville and other moderates had also swung round to become hawks alongside Hartington because they hoped a bombardment might bring Egypt to its senses and destroy the nationalists without the need for an invasion.[35]

Gladstone now turned some petty wrath on Seymour, because he did not like the Admiral's use of semantics. 'Surrender' of the forts was not what Great

Britain wanted, merely the stoppage of fortifications. 'The Admiral's telegram is bad', muttered the Prime Minister to Granville on 9 July, 'but I am at a loss to understand the meaning of the surrender of any forts? And this without instructions'.[36] Next day, to please his Whitehall masters, the admiral was made to substitute the word 'surrendered' for a precise 'temporarily surrendered for the purposes of disarmament'.[37]

The 24 hour ultimatum was a nasty shock for Charles Stone who considered it 'barbarous'. He, like many others, did not hear the news until the afternoon of the 9th, by which time the last train of the day had left Cairo for Alexandria. Anyone wishing to take refuge on the ships had until noon on the 10th when they had been advised to leave the harbour. Since the daily train left Cairo at 8am and did not arrive until 3pm it was clear to Stone Pasha that he could not get his family to safety. He telegraphed his wife and daughters to trust in the protection of his staff and servants in Cairo. For the rest of his life he never forgave Seymour for not issuing a 48 hour ultimatum.

Around dawn on the morning of Saturday 8 July most of the British warships that had spent several weeks hidden from the sight of land began making for the Outer Harbour of Alexandria. Later in the day HMS *Penelope* arrived direct from Gibralter and Egyptian soldiers in their batteries at the Pharos and Mex forts could at last see the British fleet.

One might have expected that Wilfred Blunt would have been appalled that war now seemed inevitable but this was not the case. All month he had protested to anyone who would listen, including a long letter to *The Times,* that 'mischief' was afoot. By the middle of June he was writing in his diary: 'I am quite worn out … I have not had Egypt, sleeping or waking, out of my head since the crisis began.'[38] In the House of Lords one peer called Wilfred 'another Arabi in a frock coat', Edward Malet's brother had attacked him in *The Times* and Colvin now said he had never been used as a mediator. Blunt felt that Arabi must fight, and when a Liberal friend asked him on 10 July to try and work out a compromise solution, he refused, adding truthfully that the Egyptians 'could not give up their forts honourably'.[39]

On the evening of 9 July the remaining few British consular staff and Colvin, along with several khedival officials, such as Baron de Kusel, took refuge on *Tanjore*. Next morning Seymour sent the Egyptians the long-threatened final ultimatum, noting that:

> as hostile preparations, evidently directed against the squadron under my command, were in progress yesterday at Forts Pharos and Sisileh, I shall carry out the intention expressed to you in my letter of 6th instant, at sunrise tomorrow, the

11th instant, unless previous to that hour you will have temporarily surrendered to me, for the purpose of disarming, the batteries on the isthmus of Ras-el-Tin and the southern shore of the harbour of Alexandria.[40]

The ultimatum was received about 11am at the Ras-el-Tin Palace by a war cabinet that included the Khedive, Arabi Pasha, Dervish Pasha, Raghib Pasha and most of the leading nationalists. Arabi later wrote, just as Wilfred Blunt had predicted, that it was decided 'altogether shameful and dishonourable to remove the guns'.[41] The Khedive wrote the minutes of the meeting in his own handwriting. It was agreed to send a party of four to inform Seymour 'that no new guns were mounted in the forts, and to tell him that he was at liberty to send one of his officers, if he desired it, to test the truth of his statement'.[42] It was a fair offer but the admiral declined. In his view the time for talking was over. He sent back a demand that the forts had to be disarmed – the matter was that simple.

The War Cabinet felt that the British demands were contrary to international law, but decided to try and placate them by dismounting three guns in the Silsileh, Caid Bay and Saleh Forts 'in which work may have been undertaken', an odd remark that implies defence work had been in progress. If the admiral refused to accept this gesture – which he did – then the forts were instructed not to return fire until after the fifth shot and, as the Khedive wrote in his own hand, 'God, the best of judges, will decide between them and us.'[43] Surrounded by his senior officers full of military zeal (and unable to escape even if he wanted to), Tewfik was now quite fired up in his new patriotic role. Even Arabi was taken in by the performance and the way the Khedive said that if it came to war 'he would carry a rifle and be to the front with the troops'.[44]

Orders went out to Seymour's captains on 10 July that: 'the squadron under my command will attack the forts as soon as the twenty-four hours given to neutrals to leave the place have expired, which will be at 5am on the 11th.' Far from viewing the attack as a one-sided affair, Seymour was acutely aware that in any battle between ships and forts the scales were weighed in the latter's favour. He warned his senior officers that: 'it is possible that the work may not be completed under two or three days.'[45]

There had been Seymours in the Navy for as long, it seemed, as there had been ships. Just to confuse matters another Seymour – Captain Edward Seymour of HMS *Iris* – was also serving in Egyptian waters. The two men were not directly related. The captain's father had been a humble country parson but the admiral came from a very aristocratic branch of the family. He could claim direct descent from Jane Seymour, Henry VIII's second wife, and her brother, Thomas Seymour, Lord High Admiral of England. His birth in 1821 was into the privileged world of the higher aristocracy. His father, Colonel Sir Henry Seymour, was himself the son of an admiral – Lord Hugh Seymour. Frederick had an elder brother, Charles, who entered the army and became colonel of the Scots Fusilers Guards before his death at Inkerman in the Crimea (in later life one of the joys of being a sailor was that the admiral could make a poignant visit to his brother's lonely grave).

Frederick, in a tradition of younger sons, and after what must have been a rudimentary education at Eton, entered the navy at the age of twelve where he found himself, regardless of his social position, thrust into the rough and tumble of a sailor's life. Naval education in the 1840s meant working along-side the men on deck and aloft with some bookwork supervised by a warrant officer 'schoolmaster', often in the captain's fore-cabin. After two years the boys hoped to be rated midshipmen by the captain and another four years had to be served before they could take an examination for lieutenant. Seymour earned his lieutenancy in eight years, very good going when the bottleneck of lieutenants caused by the run-down in the active fleet after the Napoleonic Wars meant that fellows without influence never managed to obtain even this rank. 'Interest' – the patronage of individual officers – was vital if a young man hoped to progress in the service. Young Frederick was a classic case. In 1844 he was lucky to be appointed Flag-Lieutenant to his uncle, who just happened to be Sir George Seymour, Commander-in-Chief of the Pacific Squadron. During these years a native chief in the Niger delta wrote to the Admiralty accusing Seymour of getting one of his daughters pregnant (we must assume it was a confusion of Seymours again). Their Lordships replied, much to the admiral's later amusement, that he had never been in that part of the world and if it was a Seymour who was responsible, then the chief had accused the wrong man!

The expansion of Empire, which became a virtual race during Seymour's time in the navy meant, as Robert Massie has noted:

> … dozens of captains, hundreds of officers, thousands of seamen, many of whom
> spent an entire career without ever being in battle. Individual ships saw action,
> and individual seamen and officers won medals – but often for heroism on land,
> as participants in one of the naval brigades landed on unfriendly coasts.[46]

Officers were expected to be brave and most were, their courage reinforced by an almost suicidal arrogance. Determined to quell some Turkish atrocities Captain William Pakenham, a contemporary of Seymour went ashore

> … accompanied by a midshipman and a Turkish interpreter, both very frightened,
> and he was dressed in every refinement of British naval elegance, his buttons

blinding, his beard impeccable, his white collar stiffly starched. The village toughs suspended their atrocities to gather round this incongruous visitor from the sea, fingering the weapons and cursing, and presently Pakenham called for silence. 'Let us begin', he said to the interpreter, 'Tell these ugly bastards that I am not going to tolerate any more of their bestial habits.' Thus spoke the voice of late Victorian England.[47]

Commander Seymour showed his bravery as a volunteer at the taking of Rangoon and Pegu in the Second Burmese War 1852–54. He had used his leave to take part in the fighting which saw him mentioned several times in despatches. His first captaincy followed; this was HMS *Meteor*, a floating battery in the Mediterranean, but Seymour managed to get it into waters off the Crimea to do good service in the Russian War. His next command was more prestigious; HMS *Pelorus* was a handsome sloop of the East Indies and China Station. On 27 June 1860 he led a naval brigade from the ship through a sea of mud to attack a Maori Pah at Puketakaure near New Plymouth. In the ensuing retreat the British lost 29 men killed. Among the wounded was the courageous captain of *Pelorus* who had to be carried off the field of battle.

The 1850s had seen the classic three-deck British man-of-war, the ship of Nelson's navy, made of wood, armed with tiers of cannon firing solid round metal balls and propelled by wind in her sails, start to be replaced by steam engines, funnels and propellers. By 1858 the British had built or converted 32 ships to steam and at the end of the decade HMS *Warrior*, the first ironclad was launched. She was a hybrid with a hull of oak and it was not until 1867 that the Royal Navy declared wood obsolete. Iron was to be used to clad the ships as sail gave way to steam.

Aboard his ship each captain was a god. The historian Peter Padfield has written:

He dispensed the patronage and enjoyed the ceremonial of a monarch … He lived in solitary state in a spacious – sometimes leaky – area under the poop at the after end of the quarterdeck … The doors of this suite, guarded night and day by a Marine sentry, led out onto the quarterdeck by the wheel; one side of the deck was reserved for his exclusive use. Except on urgent matters of duty he was not addressed unless he made the first approach. He did not select his commissioned or warrant officers but he had absolute power over them when aboard, and the rest of the crew … It followed naturally that he could make or break a ship.[48]

Seymour saw several floggings in his career before the practice was finally abolished in 1879. He felt that insurbordination increased in consequence, but told Childers in 1880:

> You know I hate flogging, and during my service as captain I managed to get along without much of it, but then the men knew well enough that I would have resorted to it if driven to do so … It is not the older hands who give the trouble, it is the young fellows between eighteen and twenty two and twenty three; and if I had the power … of making an example or two, I am convinced it would be a mercy in the long run.[49]

By 1882 captains still had many gruelling ways to discipline their crews. A spell in the cells meant no bed or bedding for the first four nights and afterwards only on alternate nights. If a captain felt so inclined he could condemn a crew to seemingly endless drills.

Captains could be eccentric martinets and benign old soaks but it is dangerous, as one naval historian has written, to 'attach a Gilbert-and-Sullivan image of genial and fusty ineffectiveness to the Victorian Navy'.[50] Its characters can come across, though, as truly bizarre. Admiral Kingcome, for instance, liked to strap on a drum and march all over the lower deck beating night quarters. Hatchet-faced Captain 'Sharky' Noel once replied to a cheery good morning welcome by snarling 'this is no time for frivolous compliments'.[51] The epitome of dandyism and eccentricity was Captain Algernon Charles Heneage known throughout the Navy as 'Pompo'. Tall and thin, with an affected German accent modelled on the Prince of Wales, Pompo had an immense ego. He broke two eggs over his long blonde locks every morning and once tried to court-martial a carpenter for entering his cabin without permission (a bad sea was flooding the room and the unfortunate man simply went in to close the scuttles). One officer locked himself up rather than face Heneage's tantrums and refused to come out until the surgeon had diagnosed a 'slight rupture' and got his ticket home.

The late Victorian Navy had an obsession with spit and polish. Ships companies were up before dawn to 'holystone' the decks on hands and knees using blocks of sandstone until the wood shone snow-white, the enamel gleamed spotlessly and the brass and metal surfaces reflected like gold and silver. Captain Heneage would carry out inspections beautifully attired while a servant followed with a dozen pairs of Pompo's favourite white kidskin gloves. 'If one speck of dust appeared on the immaculate gloves he would turn to the Commander waving two fingers. 'Dis is not de dirt of days', he would observe, 'no de dirt of weeks, nor de dirt of months. It is de dirt of ages. Coxswain, gif me a clean pair of gloves.'[52] Lavatory bowls were an obsession and Pompo once spent several minutes staring into one as he disputed a nervous officer's assertion that a small flaw in the glaze was ingrained dirt.

Eccentric though many Victorian officers may have been they were not idiots. Pompo Heneage won the Humane Society's medal for saving a seaman's life after one of HMS *Thunderer*'s guns burst, killing the turret crew in 1879. The grim-faced Gerald Noel insisted on sailing *Temeraire,* one of Seymour's fleet at Alexandria and the last full-masted battleship in the Mediterranean, up to an anchorage in Suda Bay, Crete, against a headwind in 1891; he 'tacked her thirteen times while the rest of the fleet watched, mesmerized'.[53]

Dress on board ship could take all manner of guises depending on the whims of the captain. If he liked gold braid, as Admiral Sir Percy Scott, who served as lieutenant in the Egyptian War, recalled, 'he wore gold braid and all his officers wore gold braid ... Some Captains allowed officers to wear any fancy uniform they liked; others insisted on their wearing a blue frock coat, even on the West Coast of Africa.' Uniformity in naval dress would not become general until the late 1880s. Officers had no greatcoats before 1885 and on watch or duty wore a blue frock coat of thick pilot cloth. Some wore oilskins, even when it was raining, just to keep warm. The number of buttons on frock coats was another uniform distinction sometimes abolished and at other times required. Because of the vagueness of the existing dress regulations each station order book contained various and sometimes conflicting rules dictating everything from the dimensions of collars to the proper tying of cummerbunds.

Tropical uniform for officers, such as that worn at Malta and Alexandria, consisted of a white tunic and trousers, although a frock coat and sword was expected on ceremonial occasions. Ordinary sailors on board ship mostly went barefoot, but several of the modern warships like *Inflexible*, had iron decks and ladders so the wearing of shoes, called 'pursers crabs' became the norm. The lower decks were allowed a great deal of latitude in dress as they made their own clothes. The generic term for all clothing was 'slops' and any loss was said to be 'down on your slop-ticket'. Trousers were expected to be cut tight round the hips and bell-mouthed at the bottom of the leg. The loose leggings were extremely practical when a sailor had to roll them up to scrub a deck or go aloft. Trousers had no pockets, so the men stored articles in the crown of their caps. 'At sail drill when the caps fell off these showered down and sometimes a letter just received by the mail, and still unread, was lost' recalled Captain Willis. Sailors stored bigger items in their 'ditty-boxes' and found time to write a letter home, or read one, on Sundays when a suit with trousers and pea-jacket of blue cloth with horn buttons, adorned by a broad-brimmed sennet hat, was carefully unfolded from the kitbag, where 'it emerged, when worn, ridged creases, about six inches square, like a bird-cage'.[54]

Conditions on ships improved during the 19th century but they were still cramped and unsanitary places. Despite an obsession with cleaning and polishing, every ship still had a goodly compliment of rats that, in some cases, swarmed over the sailors as they slept. Even on *Invincible*, pride of the Royal Navy, rats were a nuisance, falling into the sailors' hammocks, gnawing through pipes, and even stealing the crew's bath-water. Senior officers and the captain slept in cabins but everyone else, including the midshipmen, used hammocks. In the case of the ordinary seamen these were slung less than eighteen inches apart all the way down the forward part of the ship between the guns in unbroken rows.

Social life on board ship for the officers centred around the wardroom where they ate, drank and held parties. Food had little changed since Nelson's day. Breakfast at about 5.30am consisted of a pint of cocoa and the notorious, weevil-infested ships biscuits or 'hard tack', baked so tooth-breakingly tough that snuff boxes were made out of it. Dinner at noon was an endless repetition of salt pork one day and salt beef the next. A thick peas soup was served with the pork, some flour with the beef, and once a week suet and raisins might be offered. Tea at about 4.30pm was the last meal of the day and consisted of a mug of tea without milk and yet more biscuits. But it was possible to supplement this dull diet, especially on tropical cruises, with fresh fruit, fish and meat. Each man was entitled to a gallon of beer a day and his rum ration of a quarter of a pint.

Every crew became a family of sorts and this was especially true if the captain was a kind-hearted man. In the evenings the men usually gathered on the deck in good weather to talk or sing. By the 1880s music hall evenings, performances of amateur theatricals or Gilbert and Sullivan were popular. Crossing the equator was always marked by games as Father Neptune came aboard and buckets of water were freely splashed on his victims. The chief time for high jinks was Christmas Day; the lower deck was dressed with flags and paper chains, fresh roast beef and plum pudding was served, and it was traditional fun to carry the officers round the deck. Often the games got out of hand as the men became blindingly drunk. It was a good time to settle old scores, especially on unpopular officers, who were carried so high that they hit their heads on the beams.

Seymour seems to have been free of the pet eccentricities of many of his contemporaries. One admiral who liked milk took two cows to sea with him, several captains kept exotic pets, though none so bizarre as Lord Charles

Beresford who brought an elephant back home from India with him. The beast lived in a house on the afterdeck 'and fed on branches of trees, bran, biscuits and anything else that came its way. Lord Charles trained him to clew the mainsail by picking up a line and walking along the deck.'[55] Beresford's easy-going captain was HRH Prince Alfred, Duke of Edinburgh, the Queen's naval career minded son. In 1879, when commanding in the Mediterranean, the Prince allowed one of his midshipmen to keep a brown bear called 'Bruin' aboard his flagship (sadly he fell over the side one evening and was drowned).

In 1866 Captain Frederick Seymour was appointed an aide-de-camp to the Queen and for two important years, 1868–70, was private secretary to Hugh Childers as First Lord of the Admiralty. One eminent naval authority, writing of the years 1869–85, signalled them out as 'the dark ages of the Admiralty', a time when the Royal Navy was 'backward in technology and often reactionary in outlook'.[56] But a whole host of ideas were under discussion in this stagnant period. It was a period of transition and Seymour, judged against the captains and admirals of the age, was actually a progressive thinker. He was a close friend of Admiral Sir Geoffrey Phipps Hornby, the Royal Navy's chief expert on tactics and he also supported Admiral Philip Colomb with his Signal Book reforms. Both men were considered at the forefront of change in the 1870s. It is interesting that Seymour, although commanding the only large-scale naval action between the Crimean and First World Wars, was not a believer in long-range naval gunnery. Accurate range-finding in 1882 was still technically difficult and the elevation of guns could not be sensibly calibrated (even had ranges been available), while the powder remained chemically erratic.

Ironclads were often built at this time with rams at the prow. Opponents argued that it was very difficult to ram an unwilling victim and rammers usually came off worse than rammees, but Seymour, a disciple of the new, steam-powered, ironclad navy, commented: 'Two-thirds of the fighting in all future battles at sea, rely upon it, will be done with the ram … Why it is simply preposterous to suppose that the enemy is going to make a target of your protected centre just to suit your convenience.'[57] While at the Admiralty he supported Childers in his quest to cut costs and increase naval efficiency. Attempts to reduce the overseas squadrons were only partly successful but the pair managed to fix a retirement age and dismiss all officers then above it, thus improving the chances for younger officers. Pensions were increased and finally bore some relation to the cost of living and pay of serving officers.

Promotion to Rear-Admiral led four years later to command of the Channel Fleet. This was followed four years later by the job of Commander-in-Chief of the Mediterranean Fleet. If one is searching for clear evidence that Beauchamp

Seymour was considered no second-rate sailor by the best of his contemporaries it is the compact that Phipps Hornby tried to create in 1876. Guessing that in the near future he, or Cooper Key, or Seymour, would be offered the seat of First Naval Lord, Phipps wrote to the others suggesting that each refuse office 'unless they were granted the beginnings of a naval staff. This was the most determined attempt yet made to force reform in the Admiralty.'[58]

Malta, base of the Royal Navy's Mediterranean Fleet, was the favourite posting of most officers and crews. The sparkling waters 'served as a maritime adventure playground to which the British had, to all intents and purposes, monopoly rights'.[59] Cruises were a round of political and social programmes punctuated with sessions of slick manoeuvres. The officers in their smart white uniforms could enjoy at Valetta a whirl of regattas, polo, cricket, picnics, dinner parties and balls. The ordinary bluejackets had the three Ps – 'pubs, priests and prostitutes'. It was possible to see 50 ships of the line in the Grand Harbour, anchored in rows, hulls painted black, superstructures white and funnels buff yellow. Special friendships grew up between some ships' crews but the rivalries were more legendary; the men of HMS *Colussus,* for instance, were bitter foes of the men on Seymour's flagship, *Alexandra* and had to be prevented from going on shore at the same time 'for fear of battle, murder and sudden death'.

Crowds would gather every Monday morning to see competitive sail drill performed by the crews. Admiral Seymour especially adored watching it:

At one moment the fleet would be silent and immobile, the men frozen on deck. At the flagship's signal, the fleet erupted into life. Men swarmed aloft, darting along the yards, shifting lines and moving sails with astonishing speed. Time was at stake, not life, and with the ship's reputation to make, men took extraordinary risks so that for a while it was necessary after each drill to make the signal 'Report number of killed and injured.'[60]

In the same way it was traditional, when a ship sailed for home out of Valetta Grand Harbour, that a man would be standing erect on the top of each mast. Balanced precariously 200 feet above the deck, the men would even 'strip off their shirts and wave them'.[61]

It was during his time at Malta, as centre of a heady social world, that according to Robert Massie, Admiral Seymour got his nickname of 'the Swell of the Ocean'. Seymour was a big man in every sense of the word, the very essence of what the Victorians expected their sailors to look like – burly, bearded and with a jolly twinkle in his eye. A great *bon viveur,* there was nothing the admiral liked better than a banquet, some gossip and a good champagne. A confirmed bachelor, his chief recreation seems to have been attending wine auctions and adding to his fine cellar. A relative noted that 'Sir Beauchamp belonged to that old school of men who settled steadily down to their wine after dinner and looked upon tobacco as an abomination.'[62] A year after the war, a journalist attempting a quick sketch described him as 'the most dandified member of the Peerage. He is never met abroad in the streets, be it winter or summer, wet or sunshine, aithout a pair of spotless lavender-coloured gloves on his hands.'[63] Admiral Seymour also had a particular way of walking, the result of a lifetime spent pacing the deck in the face of a gale, a rolling gait, not unlike a swelling sea, slow, deliberate and ponderous.

Criticisms of the admiral seem always to echo a comment made by Admiral Bacon, the biographer of Jacky Fisher, who admitted that his hero's old chief, while entertaining a high opinion of the young man, had 'a far higher opinion of his own importance and was also very pompous'.[64] Bacon was only a junior officer in 1882 so his comments must be taken with a pinch of salt. Garnet Wolseley, not an easy man to please, held the admiral in high esteem, while Archibald Alison, who was in command of the troops prior to Wolseley's arrival, later wrote that his official relations with Seymour 'were one of the bright spots of my life'. In sharp contrast to Bacon's pompous officer, the war correspondent, Frederic Villiers, first encountered the admiral on the quarter-deck of *Invincible* working with his shirt-sleeves rolled up and perspiring under a solar tope:

> The weather was exceedingly hot and he was continually lifting his helmet and mopping his forehead with a voluminous coloured kerchief. After pleasantly greeting me, he said, 'Your colleague, Mr Cameron, is also on one of my ships and is coming to dine with me this evening; will you join us?' I replied that I would do so with pleasure. There was a hearty bluffness about the Admiral that was irresistible. He was rather thickset, of medium height, and he had a face that reminded me of the skipper in Millais' famous picture 'The North-West Passage' – strong, genial, but one that could turn into a sternness most imposing and emphatic.[65]

Seymour seems to have had a good sense of fun; he was willing to be the butt of several of Jacky Fisher's practical jokes, including being thrown off a set onto his backside on one occasion when the latter man was steering *Inflexible*'s steam-powered barge. There was also a place in the admiral's affections for even the most junior of his officers; in October 1881 cadets Chambers and Wemyss, the two newest and smallest 15-year-olds under his command, were invited to join

Seymour and his flag-lieutenant, Hedworth Lambton, for breakfast. Both were very kind and 'tried to make us at home' recalled Chambers in his memoirs, but 'we were too awed by such a multitude of gold stripes to be anything but tongue-tied'.[66]

A later generation might raise an eyebrow at a man who liked wearing lavender coloured gloves, spent his time almost exclusively in the company of other men and invited teens to breakfast, but no hint of scandal ever surfaced in Seymour's life. If he was a closet homosexual he kept it very well hidden. It seems, like so many other Victorian officers (such as Generals Gordon and Kitchener), that he was able to sublimate his sex drive, and a life spent mostly at sea in different parts of the world did not make it easy to find the perfect mate for marriage.

The Egyptian War was not Seymour's first visit to Alexandria. He had made a short inspection of the harbour three years previously during a cruise that also took in Constantinople. 'I had a interview with the Sultan, who, I am happy to say, did not offer me either a horse or a diamond snuff-box,' he wrote to his old friend, Hugh Childers, 'my object in visiting Alexandria was to see the improvements in the harbour works which have been made since 1872 and very complete they are; but to make them perfect, there should be a further expenditure of from £370,000 to £420,000.' It seems ironical, in hindsight, that Seymour was now in command of a fleet ordered to destroy those same fortifications.[67]

Alexandria sits on a tongue of land almost cut off from the mainland by Lakes Aboukir and Mareotis. The city had two harbours on either side of this narrow strip of land. The New Harbour to the east of the town, was a small crescent shaped marina, while to the west was the Old Harbour, a sheltered bay enclosed by a breakwater stretching south-west for nearly three-quarters of a mile. The total length of the harbour area was between five and six nautical miles and its average width was one-and-a-quarter. The breakwater had been completed in 1874. Where the line of loose rocks ended and the crescent of land began the white Eunostos lighthouse signalled to mariners its greeting of safe return. Close by stood the Ras-el-Tin Palace, a handsome building with a large and shady garden of green palms.

Between the end of the breakwater, as it curved south towards the shore, 2,300 yards away, was a space with three channels of water for big ships; the northern Corvette Pass had a depth of 18 feet, the central Borghaz Pass was about 22 feet and the southern Marabout Pass some 24 feet.

The coastline was low, but during the Napoleonic Wars and in the reign of Muhammad Ali a long series of forts had been built to guard over 13 miles of shoreline. The addition of some smaller shore batteries meant that the Egyptians had fifteen major defensive positions. Despite efforts to strengthen them the forts were all practically obsolete, their soft limestone masonry mixed with poor quality sand and the barracks simply constructed. The magazines were described by an officer who visited Forts Ada and Mex after the bombardment as 'ingeniously designed man-traps', with almost no ventilation or lighting, metal floors and tall lightning conductors, 'and seem frequently to have been devised with a deliberate view to ready combustion'.[68]

The area furthest from shore, beyond the breakwater, where most of Seymour's fleet was anchored, was known as the Outer Harbour, the area inside the breakwater was the Inner Harbour. Guarding the New Harbour, but also commanding an angle of the Outer Harbour, was Fort Pharos, its six heavy guns being the only Egyptian ones with proper protection. Not far away and closer to the palace was Fort Ada with five heavy guns. Twenty-six modern cannon guarded the shore nearby along what were called the Ras-el-Tins lines. It was these modern guns, mostly 7- to 10-inch Armstrongs that most worried Seymour. Looking to shore in the opposite direction the chain of forts ran round to Fort Adjemi where construction work was in progress. Opposite this, in the channel, was a small island called Marabout which had the strongest single fort and three more heavy guns. About halfway between the Old Harbour and Fort Adjemi on the mainland was Fort Mex, the largest of the defences, encircled by deep, wide ditch and surrounded by palms. Mex commanded the Corvette and Borghaz Passes and the Egyptians had planned to arm it with ten more heavy guns, but so far only five were in position. The Egyptian defences, then, were quite considerable, a total of 44 modern rifled guns that could be brought to bear on the British warships (not counting the ones in Forts Adjemi and Silsileh, which were never engaged), along with more than 200 smooth bores and mortars (of which about half were to be fired during the fight).

In contrast to the previous day, which had seen a stream of visitors to the Khedive, on the afternoon of the 10th things grew horribly quiet at the Ras-el-Tin Palace. Only five Western officials remained with Tewfik – his ever loyal Stone Pasha and four Italians (his physician, master-of-ceremonies, private secretary and one admiral). Charles Stone was no doubt thinking much of the time about his family in Cairo and cursing Admiral Seymour for preventing their departure from the capital by train.

That afternoon the band on *Invincible* gave a musical salute as the ironclads from the other navies sailed out of the Inner Harbour along with *Tanjore* filled with celebrities. Aboard the P&O ship, at ten shillings and sixpence a head, and also scattered across the fleet, were a number of war correspondents destined to ensure that the Bombardment of Alexandria would be the first fully reported naval action in British history. There was stout, bespectacled Melton Prior of the *Illustrated London News*, who sketched away in the British square at Ulundi in 1879, just as he had done at Amoaful in the Ashanti War five years previously. Frank la Poer Power, a 23-year-old Irish ex-soldier of fortune, who was a gifted artist, was there for the *Times*, along with Moberley Bell, the newspaper's regular Egyptian correspondent. Bennet Burleigh of the Central News Agency had fought for the Confederacy in the American Civil War and twice been condemned to death. Trimly bearded John Cameron of the *Standard* had been in the thick of the fight with the Boers on Majuba Hill in the previous year and was now thirsting to see more action. Hilary Skinner represented the *Daily News*; John Merry Le Sage the *Daily Telegraph*; resourceful Captain Fitzgerald of the *Manchester Guardian*, much to the delight of his editor, had got an interview with Arabi Pasha on the previous day; and everyone knew the two men from the *Graphic* illustrated newspaper – Charles E. Fripp, a skinny 28-year-old who had covered the Zulu War and stocky 31-year-old Frederic Villiers, a notorious snob, fresh from the Balkan Wars, but a man with 'a bright sense of humour and a fund of boyish enthusiasm'.

On board his flagship, the USS *Lancaster*, Rear-Admiral Nicholson sent a message to Charles Chaille-Long warning him to notify 'all persons who are desirous of and entitled to the protection of the American flag to repair on board the ships under my command'.[69] Less than 50 persons, mainly missionaries and their families, were strictly entitled to American protection, but the admiral had already offered sanctuary to around 800 refugees. Chaille-Long got two Levantines and a pair of old French Army friends away and was just leaving the consulate when Ali, his faithful janissary, told him that a party of Hungarian girls were stranded in the Austro-Hungarian Consulate. He managed to get this group out to the ships, along with a final trainload of refugees, before American marines arrived from the ships to insist, on Nicholson's orders, that he close the consulate without more delay. At sundown, as Chaille-Long settled aboard the USS *Quinnebaug* he watched with sadness and stupefaction as dapper Admiral Conrad and his French ships passed, saluted and steamed off to the safety of Port Said.

At Alexandria, battle orders to the British captains were distributed on the afternoon of the 10th. Seymour's plan was that the fleet would attack after the men had breakfasted the next morning. His force in two unequal divisions, would attack simultaneously, on a signal shot fired into the newly erected earthworks near Fort Ada. The admiral intended to lead the attack himself in *Invincible*, with *Monarch* and *Penelope* in support, against the Mex lines from the Inner Harbour, while *Alexandra, Sultan* and *Superb*, outside the breakwater, would bring their guns to bear on the Ras-el-Tin lines and Lighthouse Fort before moving east to attack Fort Pharos and, if possible, Fort Silsileh. HMS *Inflexible* and *Temeraire* were to support both divisions with long range fire. The gun vessels were not to get involved until Fort Mex had been silenced sufficiently for them to assist the inshore squadron. The despatch vessel *Helicon* and the gunboat *Condor* were to act as repeating vessels. Naval historian Colin White has castigated Seymour's general orders as 'a most vague and uncertain document', an opinion that echoes Sir William Clowes, who thought that by attacking all the forts at once the admiral missed the opportunity of concentrating his combined firepower on each one in turn and so demolishing the enemy more effectively. It seems that Seymour had considered this option and concluded that such an attack would take longer. He gambled, correctly as it turned out, that a general bombardment might achieve the same victory in less time.[70]

As the afternoon wore on, the ships struck their upper masts, sent down top gallant and Royal yards and prepared for the morrow. On *Condor,* an excited Villiers watched fascinated as the sailors got out all available canvas and draped it over the inward side of the ship's bulwarks, slung hammocks round the wheel to protect the men and steering gear from flying splinters, lowered the topmast, ran in the bowspit and put canvas round the gatling gun in the maintop. The smaller craft took down all their yards but the ironclads only the upper ones.

On previous nights, big searchlights had been switched on to check the activity of the Egyptians. The first time this was done Egyptian working parties, 'as thick as bees on the parapets', were so transfixed by the powerful lights that they had thought them a new weapon of war and stood transfixed like rabbits in the glare. A few officers had even waved their swords and complained the British behaviour was unsporting. Once used to the brightness, however, the troops went on repairing the forts. But there was no moon that night and the fleet lay in inky blackness.[71]

Admiral Seymour ate and drank with his usual gusto, but probably not as jovially as Lord Charles Beresford, who had invited the captains of some of the American, French and German ships to dinner. The meal was served on the deck of *Condor*, with everyone looking splendid in their best uniforms. The American captain, according to Villiers, exclaimed: 'Well, Beresford, I guess I should like to be waltzing round with you tomorrow dropping a shell in here and there.' The French captain was quite melancholy. He parted from his host with the words: 'Monsieur le Capitaine, it is the fault of my government; but if I am not with you in body, I shall be with you in spirit. Adieu!' Before lights out Beresford assembled the entire crew of 100 men and spoke to them from the bridge explaining that their job in the battle would be to 'nurse' their 'bigger sisters' if they got into trouble. Groans resounded across the deck to this news. 'But, if an opportunity should occur', concluded Beresford with a smile, 'the *Condor* is to take advantage of it and prove her guns ... Now, my lads, if you rely on me to find the opportunity, I will rely on you to make the most of it.'[72]

There was 'little sleep that night' on *Condor*, wrote Villiers later; some of the crew passed the dark hours playing the fiddle and he was awake long before dawn, when the hissing of steam and rattle of coal told him the engineers were stoking up the boilers. On *Sultan*, in contrast, Lieutenant George Mostyn Field was fast asleep until 4am. He had been busy for several days readying the ship for battle and 'the night before going into action I took a complete holiday and for the first time since the day of commission ... went to bed early and slept soundly'.[73]

Under cover of darkness Admiral Seymour had steamed in *Invincible* to a position close to *Penelope* at about 10.10pm and dropped anchor some 1,000 yards from Fort Mex leaving the heavier draught *Monarch* about 500 yards further out. The ships had wire hawsers on their cables to act as springs so they could fire a secure broadside at the forts. In his orders the admiral had given his captains discretion as to whether they anchored for the attack or kept under way. The rest of the fleet manoeuvred silently into position. Cadet Chambers on *Monarch* recalled that the navigator of *Invincible* 'was cracked up tremendously, whilst we drew at least another foot, and in that shallow water every inch counted'.[74]

The fifteen ships of the attacking fleet, which formed the nucleus of the 43 vessels commanded by Seymour in Egyptian waters during June and July 1882, were as varied as the men who commanded them. Three of the captains at the bombardment – Beresford, Fisher and Wilson – were to become among the most celebrated naval figures of the Edwardian Age, while Lambton, Flag-Lieutenant to Seymour, would be a hero at the Siege of Ladysmith, leading a naval brigade. Lieutenant John Jellicoe of HMS *Agincourt*, and Lieutenant Reginald Bacon of HMS *Northumberland,* both famous admirals of the First World War, served in the Egyptian campaign.

HMS *Penelope*, the closest ship to shore, was also the smallest ironclad in the battle; she weighed only 4,470 tons, almost two-thirds less than *Inflexible*, had four 9-ton guns and was commanded by the aristocratic Captain St George D'Arcy Irvine. *Invincible* was to be Seymour's flagship during the bombardment.

This should have been *Alexandra*, but the admiral transferred to the smaller ship because its shallow draught enabled it to get closer to shore. The ship fired ahead two 12-ton guns, and five on a broadside, weighed 6,010 tons and had a crew of 450 officers and men under the command of the youthful-looking Richard Molyneux, who had taken charge of the consulate during the Alexandria Riots. Completing the inner squadron was *Monarch,* weighing 8,320 tons and carrying seven guns, four of which were 25-tonners; in her forecastle were mounted two 12-ton guns and in her poop one of 9 tons. Cadet Chambers considered the ship 'even for those days an archaic anomaly. Her four 25-ton guns were as nearly useless as could be. Her speed was at best 12 knots and her armour protection negligible.' *Monarch's* captain, Henry Fairfax, was 'a quiet and rather nervous man, but he had the faculty inherent in so many men of his type of rising to an emergency'.[75]

In the Outer Harbour sat one ship that already brushed with destiny. *Alexandra* had flown the flag of Rear-Admiral Hornby during the Russo-Turkish crisis of 1878 and led his six ships through the Dardanelle Straits to Constantinople. She was a two-decker ironclad of 9,490 tons firing ahead two 25-ton guns and two 18-ton guns and, on the broadside, one 25-ton and five 18-ton guns. The ship's crew of 671 officers and men were under the command of vandyke-bearded Captain Charles Hotham. He, like the admiral, had served in the Maori Wars and been wounded in action. A kindly man, Hotham had welcomed the war correspomdent Melton Prior aboard for a ringside view of the battle. HMS *Sultan* was an inferior *Alexandra*, firing ahead two 12-ton guns and, on the broadside, four 18-ton and two 12-ton guns. She weighed 9,290 tons and had a crew of 400 under Captain Walter Hunt-Grubbe. He was one of a trio of captains in the action who had been wounded on land, in his case at Amoaful in the Ashanti War. His Gunnery Lieutenant on 11 July 1882, George Field, noted that Hunt-Grubbe 'seemed to think we were in for a good row, evidently to his intense delight … I did not believe it myself'.[76] HMS *Superb* was the same size as *Sultan* and, like her, fully rigged. She had been built on the Thames for the Turkish Navy in 1878, but acquired by Britain after the war scare of that year. Under the command of Captain Thomas Warde, with a crew of 620 officers and men, *Superb* could fire a broadside of eight 18-ton guns.

Two strange ships completed Seymour's main fleet. The first of these was *Temeraire*. She had been launched only six years earlier and had a unique design combining a central battery with barbettes fore and aft, each holding a 25-ton gun on a disappearing carriage that made the cannon bob down out of sight by the force of the recoil. The ship was also fully rigged and additionally armed with three 25-ton guns looking to the front, and three 25-ton and two 18-tonners on the broadside. She carried Whitehead and Harvey torpedoes and a ram that projected eight feet from her bow. A compliment of 534 officers and men under Captain Henry Nicholson crewed the ship.

*Inflexible*, and its remarkable captain, John Fisher, have had whole books written about them. She was the Royal Navy's latest man-of-war, the pride and joy of countless inventors and the largest ship in the service. In essence she was a double-screw ironclad with armour 16 to 24 inches thick and armed with four monster guns of 81 tons each worked by hydraulic pressure. These goliaths were mounted in two turrets, so that they could all be fired ahead or through a limited arc on either broadside. She was the first battleship to have submerged torpedo tubes and compound armour and, in keeping with latest naval theory, had a powerful ram on her bow. The ship was full of gadgetry, like ballast tanks to reduce rolling and electric light, 'both of which were doubtful in operation and even dangerous'. Despite powerful engines she was also fully rigged, a quant anomaly of the period, but *Inflexible's* 11,400 tons meant, as Fisher wrote, 'The sails had so much effect upon her in a gale of wind as a fly would have on a hippopotamus in producing any movement.'[77] Below decks the ship had poor ventilation and so many narrow passageways and compartments that 'men used to lose their way altogether amidst the mazes of this iron labyrinth, and knew not what deck they were on, what compartments they were in, or whether they were walking forward or aft'.[78] This problem was solved when Captain Fisher painted bulkheads and passages in different colours and added a direction code with arrows and signals.

Short and stocky, with a rounded, boyish face, full lips and slightly exotic almond-shaped eyes, John Arbuthnot Fisher was destined to become the greatest admiral since Nelson. He had first seen action at the capture of the Peiho Forts in China at the age of nineteen. In 1882 he was 41 years old and had been a captain for six years, a meteoric rise for a man 'who owed nothing to family, wealth or social position, and everything to merit, force of character and sheer persistence'.[79] Already he had shown himself to be 'one of the finest brains in the Navy, with an inexhaustible capacity for hard work'.[80] Fisher could be charming when it suited him but was getting a reputation for plain speaking that bordered on downright rudeness. 'I have had to fight like hell and fighting like hell has made me what I am', he would tell listeners. He was determined to reform the Royal Navy at any cost.[81] His blunt language, even by 1882, was making him enemies but opponents he declared, were 'pre-historic admirals', 'mandarins' and 'fossils'. Admiral Seymour liked the tough-talking young captain and watched over his career, encouraging his work on torpedo defence in the 1870s, and the handling of *Inflexible*, the Royal Navy's mightiest battleship.

It had been 22 years since Jacky Fisher had last seen action and, until a week before the bombardment, he thought the chances of seeing any more in Egypt were remote. 'You must not be the least bit anxious,' he told his wife, 'I feel sure the Egyptians will not fight … there is not the slightest prospect of my landing with the men, the more's the pity.' He had little doubts as to the ability of the Egyptian gunners either: 'They have not fired a shot for 25 years from a single gun here, so you may suppose how indifferent their practice will be.'[82]

Assisting the ironclads were the gunboats *Beacon*, *Bittern*, *Condor*, *Cygnet* and *Decoy*, and the paddle despatch vessel, *Helicon*. Of these six ships it was *Condor*, and its celebrated commander, Lord Charles William de la Poer Beresford, who was to be the best remembered and see the stiffest fighting. In time, Lord Charles and his pet bulldog would come to epitomise the late Victorian Navy – 'John Bull at Sea'. He would also have a legendary spat with Fisher, one standing for all that was traditional in the Royal Navy, the other for all that was forward-thinking. But that was in the future. In 1882 the 36-year-old Beresford, second son of the Marquess of Waterford, was still well liked enough by his future nemesis. 'I wish Beresford was here' Fisher gossiped to Seymour from Cannes a few months before the bombardment, 'all the young ladies are asking for him and saying what a pity he married and I notice they call him "Charlie".'[83] Full of energy, Beresford was not just a sailor, but also a MP who spoke in Parliament whenever he had time. He was a friend of the Royal Family and such a keen huntsman that it was rumoured he had a large tattoo of the Waterford Hunt in full cry down his back. By middle age, riding accidents would result in a broken chest bone, pelvis, right leg, right hand, one collarbone three times, the other once, and his nose in three places.

In many ways Beresford and Fisher were similar; both took care of the men under their command and were adored by them, both cocked a snoop at authority and were not shy of publicity. Jacky Fisher's chief weakness was his colossal ego, while Charlie B was torn by an over-weening vanity. But while Beresford loved the London Scene, the hunt and lots of escapades, Fisher was obsessively career-orientated. The two men in time came to represent totally different views of the Royal Navy, yet both adored ships and the sea, and believed mightily that they were serving the finest institution and finest race in the world.

The ships going into battle on 11 July 1882 would be the last British fleet to fire muzzle-loading guns, the last to be wreathed in the smoke and smells of Nelson's day. The eight ironclads mounted a total of 77 rifled guns, but since five of them were broadside ships, only 43 could be brought to bear at any one time. Machine guns completed these arsenals at sea; these fairly new innovations were either Gatlings, with a vertical feed case and ten barrels capable of firing more than ten rounds a second or its heavier rival, the two or four barrelled Nordenfeldt.

The bombardment would also be the last occasion when an underwater threat did not hamper the Royal Navy. The Egyptians had intended to lay torpedo mines but circumstances prevented them. Kusel Bey, in charge of customs, had impounded some weeks earlier a mine-laying device ordered from America by General Stone and acting on his own initiative (and clearly exceeding his authority), had the weapon dismantled and secretly sent to Seymour. It was also known by Tulloch that there was a large store of torpedo mines in Fort Mex and boats had been got ready by the Egyptians to be sunk laden with rocks in the Corvette Pass. It is clear that if the British and French ships had arrived a month or so later than they did, say in August, then the Alexandria defences would have been much more difficult, if not impossible, to breach or overcome.

The sun rose early on 11 July as the men of the fleet started to eat their breakfasts. On *Monarch* the hot plates of the galley had been dismantled to make improvised shelters for the machine guns so Chambers and his companions had to make do with a cup of cocoa and a little biscuit. The men on *Sultan* had slept on deck, their hammocks being used to cushion the ship, and Lieutenant Field joined the rest of the crew for a hurried breakfast. About 5am the bugle call 'Quarters for Action' sounded around the fleet. Each man rushed to his station. On *Invincible* the men were already stripped to the waist when Seymour, Molyneux and Lambton took up their positions on the hammock-barricaded bridge. It was about this time that a boat with three Egyptian officers bumped against the side of the ship. The trio claimed to have had a miserable night crawling about in the darkness looking for the flagship. They brought a final proposal from their commanders, but Seymour politely rejected it, pointing out that the time for talking had passed. The dejected Egyptians were made to row hastily for the shore.

The great turrets on *Monarch* with their 25-ton guns, half as broad as they were long, now began swinging backwards and forwards. Cadet Chambers felt distinctly uncomfortable and could not stop himself thinking that as soon as the first shot was fired an enemy shell might burst through the ship's side and 'all would become a scene of blood and destruction'. The men had stripped to the waist, while Chambers and his colleagues wore singlets with blue serge jackets and trousers. Time seemed to hang in the air as the occasional shouts of officers in the sighting hoods altering their ranges wafted over the ships.

As the minutes ticked down to the deadline a torpedo boat depot ship, HMS *Hecla*, hove into sight and took up a position out of range to the north of the offshore squadron. She was commanded by a tall, bearded, taciturn 40-year-old Norfolkman, Arthur Knyvet Wilson, known by the sobriquet, 'Old 'Ard 'Art'. Three days earlier the admiral had ordered *Hecla* and a sister ship, HMS *Achilles*, to leave the Channel Fleet at Malta and join him. Wilson, who had pushed his crew, was delighted to get to Alexandria in time for the battle ahead of the heavier *Achilles* (though Seymour might have preferred the bigger ship). Now *Hecla* was to have a ringside view of the bombardment.

In the Outer Harbour the offshore squadron of *Alexandra, Sultan* and *Superb* formed line of battle and steamed in towards the batteries stretching from Ras-el-Tin to Pharos. Lieutenant Field, on *Sultan*, felt nervous seeing the surgeons taking off their coats and setting out tables, pillows, mattresses and instruments to treat the wounded. A grim thought flashed through his mind that 'soon it might be one's own turn to be laid out and carved up on that horrible-looking table.'[84] He decided to go down to the main battery, in his capacity as gunnery officer and make a little speech to give his men some courage. It was so well received, and did Field some good himself to say it, that he went on through the vessel giving each sailor he met a few words of encouragement.

On *Alexandra* a 'remarkable silence seemed to pervade the whole ship' as the minutes ticked down to 7am.[85] Then came the Admiral's signal, 'Fire one shot'. The sailors, stripped down to jerseys and trousers as in Nelson's day, rushed to load and fire a 25-tonner, all eyes following the shell as it screamed towards the recently armed hospital battery at Ras-el-Tin. This was followed by a signal to the whole fleet, 'Attack the enemy's batteries'.

The morning's stillness ended abruptly in a deafening roar as the ships executed the order. *Sultan* fired the second shot with a heavy roll of her great guns. High columns of smoke began to rise as the ironclads launched their cannonade, each ship quivering with the concussion of its firepower. The boom from the fleet blended in the air with a loud rumbling, 'like that of a distant train', as *Inflexible*'s monster shells screamed towards the shore. All around was the drumming and tap-tapping of the Gatling and Nordenfeldt guns firing from the decks and masts.

The first salvo from *Inflexible* blew Captain Fisher's cap off and almost deafened him. The ship was busy engaging the Lighthouse and Mex Forts. Very quickly the Egyptian gunners had the ship's range and within 15 minutes shells were bursting all over the vessel and passing between the masts. About this time a glancing shot hit *Inflexible* on the port side near the waterline causing a leak in the breadroom above the armoured deck. Not long afterwards a 10-inch Palliser shell, fired from a 40-pounder gun in the Lighthouse battery, screamed into the ship below the upper deck. The blast killed the ship's carpenter instantly, seriously wounded an officer and injured two men. The projectile, rather curiously, was turned around as it entered the great iron ship and continued on its way base first, stamping the word 'Palliser' onto a beam before ending its journey.

Within seconds of *Alexandra's* opening shot the Egyptian ramparts were swarming with activity. On the torpedo boat *Hecla* which steamed around just beyond the range of the furthest shots, Captain Wilson had a 'perfect view' of the battle. He thought the Egyptians 'showed a great deal of pluck. Until their heavy guns were actually capsized or disabled they made a very good fight of it'.[96] His words are echoed by Alexander Tulloch on *Invincible*:

> It was wonderful to see how well the Gippies stuck to their guns; more than once I saw one of our shells go square and fair into an embrasure. 'That gun is finished' I thought. Not a bit of it! Back came the answer in due course. The answer was so quick in one case that I could not help jumping onto the top-rail and, holding on with one hand to a stay, giving a cheer, 'Well done, Gippy!'[87]

Plucky little *Penelope,* being the closest ship to shore, got a heavy plastering. Most of it came from a 40-pounder Armstrong gun which the Egyptians had cleverly camouflaged in an ordinary house. The ship was struck by three shots above the waterline on her starboard side without any effect, but one other entered her via the thin plating, causing many splinters, a second shell burst in the wardroom and admiral's storeroom, a third hit the starboard gangway and a fourth smashed a gun, wounding ten sailors and ripping up the deck. A fifth shot did damage to the main yardarm, whilst several others 'carried away ropes of all descriptions'. In his report after the battle Seymour wrote that 'it was only by a narrow escape that the shot which entered abaft the narrow plating did not go down among the engines, there being nothing to stop it.'[88]

A kind of holiday mood prevailed among the sailors for the first hour or so of the engagement. Some men squatted to watch the action, cheering and applauding every well-aimed shot of their gunners and jeering the misses with choice comments. Crews also cheered loudly each time a ship near them scored a direct hit. The concussion of the big guns was followed every so often by the rushing roar of the Hales war rockets, each one causing a long trail of smoke as it whizzed haphazardly towards the shoreline.

On *Sultan* the gunners worked steadily and silently and Lieutenant Field felt very proud of his men. But until the initial excitement of the battle had worn off it was difficult to get them to aim accurately. Field felt odd inside to 'actually find oneself with full leave and licence to indulge in the natural instinct to kill and destroy'.[89] The gun crews carried out his orders implicitly and after an hour or so, 'settled down to the most workmanlike style of action'. HMS *Sultan, Superb* and *Alexandra* had decided to steam past the shore batteries at Ras-el-Tin but after two circuits it became clear that their fire lost in accuracy. To make matters worse for the first hour the morning sun shone brightly in the eyes of the British gunners. About 9am the three ships anchored off the Lighthouse Fort and their firing improved. This was no mean feat, since as the morning wore on, thick smoke hung all around them in a heavy pall, so that the forts could only be glimpsed in outline.

Smoke was also a problem for Admiral Seymour and Captain Molyneux on *Invincible* where it lay thick upon the gun decks. Accurate fire was only made possible thanks to Midshipman Ernest Hardy, manning his 1-inch crank-operated Nordenfeldt gun in the maintop, who reported the result of each shot. He was joined by Major Tulloch where the pair, without any protection, had a clear view of the forts. Looking down at the deck below Tulloch was amused to see two ex-naval friends who had smuggled themselves onto the ship 'lying down comfortably behind the mast'.[90] Staring to shore he watched as the Egyptians put up a pretty accurate fire, their shells hitting the water and shooting under the surface to strike the ship just below the waterline. During four hours of firing the major reckoned *Invincible* was hit about 40 times but luckily the force of the projectiles were spent. He teased young Hardy each time the boy ducked, but the last laugh was on him when 'a thing like a railway train' – in reality a shell from an 18-ton gun – whizzed past his head. No direct hits were made on the flagship but its crew had a scary moment when a live shell landed on the deck. Fortunately its fuse had fallen out and a sailor quickly tossed it overboard.

It was another shell, very much alive and fizzing, that saw the only Victoria Cross to be won in the battle. It was 28 years since a VC – the first one ever awarded – was given to a sailor for an act of shipboard valour, though 40 had been won by the Royal Navy on land. It was about 8am on *Alexandra* and Assistant Paymaster Maxwell was walking up the starboard side of the half-deck when a shell hit the portside, whizzed through a cabin and onto the deck, struck the engine room hatchway narrowly missing some officers, bounced backwards against the rifle racks and rolled over to the starboard side under Maxwell's feet. Not far off men were hauling up powder for the gunners. Maxwell gave the shell a kick, thinking it was spent, but as it rolled across the deck he saw to his horror that the fuse was fizzing. 'I shouted out to prevent the powdermen and others from coming up the ladder', he wrote later, but very calmly one of the old gunners, white-haired Israel Harding, 'rushed up, seized the shell, and taking some water from a tub standing near, threw it on the burning fuse and afterwards placed the shell in a tub of water'.[91] Next day Harding was promoted to master gunner and recommended for the Victoria Cross, (he almost didn't get it because Lord John Hay at the Admiralty thought Harding had shown 'some courage', but saw 'nothing praiseworthy in putting a shell in a tub of water', until someone pointed out that the first ever award for a VC in 1854 went to Midshipman Lucas for an identical act of gallantry).[92] Had the shell exploded on *Alexandra* it would have caused severe damage and many casualties.

Melton Prior burst on deck just in time to see Harding's brave act. It came at the climax of a fairly hot time for the celebrated journalist. At the start of the bombardment he had stood near the men working the Nordenfeldt machine gun on *Alexandra*'s poopdeck, but Captain Hotham, fearful for his visitor's life, ordered him to the ship's conning-tower. Few civilians had seen as much action as Prior – it was his eighth campaign in less than a decade – but he admitted later that being in his first sea battle made him 'squeamish' since 'on shore you can get away from a battery heavily engaged', he wrote, 'but on board ship there is no retreating'.[93] Prior now watched as one Egyptian shell rebounded off the water, passed through the ship's funnel and exploded with a tremendous crash into *Alexandra*'s steam launch. Rushing over he saw one man had been killed and several others injured, while Captain Hotham was enveloped in a cloud of sparks and smoke. Back in the conning-tower, the captain had another close shave when a shell ricocheted off the waves and made him jump as it passed between his legs.

The smile on Prior's face as he watched the incident soon vanished when a major of marines came up and told him that a shell had smashed through the cabin of Commander Hoskins where his belongings had been placed. Prior was prevented from going to investigate by the intense Egyptian fire. This probably saved his life as another shell passed through the same cabin reducing it to matchwood. The war artist got to view it full of smoke and his sketchbooks destroyed. The major suggested they should grab a quick beer in the wardroom to get the sulphur out of their throats. Prior readily agreed and they were just quaffing a tankard each when a shot crashed through the skylight showering them in splinters of wood and glass. It was at this moment that he dashed out onto the deck just in time to see Harding win his medal.

Once the ships were anchored, Field on *Sultan* found it necessary to change the manner of firing of his guns. Independent firing in succession was replaced by the careful aim and detonation of one gun at a time. Both Field on *Sultan* and Tulloch on *Invincible* noticed that two hours of firing had 'left practically no impression on the forts'. The new gunnery, however, had an immediate impact, 'now gun after gun on shore was being knocked or the gun crews swept away (in which case they were instantly replaced by fresh men and the gun brought again in a most astonishing way)'.[94]

A gun cotton magazine to the rear of Fort Marsa-el-Khanat was exploded by *Monarch*'s fire at about 8.30am. At one point in the bombardment *Monarch* accidentally fired a broadside when passing the line of *Penelope*. The shells screamed across her poop, but fortunately their trajectory was high. 'There goes my commission', exclaimed the astonished officer in *Monarch*'s turret. Field and his men hardly noticed the smaller projectiles whizzing overhead, but as the morning wore on the fire got hotter. One large shell passed under Field's arm, which was luckily raised at the time but it ruined his frock coat. A hot piece of metal from another shell grazed his neck as it sped past. He watched a sailor standing nearby fall wounded onto the deck. In his journal he related his feelings:

> I had been even pitying the unfortunate Egyptian soldiers opposed to us, but now I saw, and so did us all I think, that it was no child's play we were about, but downright grim earnest and that they must go down and the sooner the better. From the time they began to kill and wound our men, the guns were worked in a different spirit to what had been previously. Before it was all good fun and the men rather looked upon it as a fine lark. Now it was thorough earnest determination throughout.[95]

*Sultan* remained undamaged until about 10am when a 10-inch shell smashed into her forecastle, knocking away the short anchor, disabling a Nordenfeldt gun, killing two sailors and wounding five others. It was swiftly followed by another shell that went through the mainmast, its pieces 'making a tremendous clatter as they rattled down inside', while a third shell made a huge rent in the aft funnel, 'big enough to drive a small coach through'.[96]

Further to the west, Beresford and the crew of *Condor* had spent the early part of the bombardment towing *Temeraire* off some shoals. The ironclad moved off to assist *Invincible* and *Penelope* in their attack on Fort Mex. Beresford now noticed that these ships were 'getting pepper' from the guns of Fort Marabout at the western end of the bay. It is possible that Seymour assumed that the Egyptian gunners would be no good at such long distances but the British ships were soon enfiladed. Seeing an 'opportunity' had occurred, Beresford raced *Condor* towards Marabout. He knew his ship had only three guns and one well-aimed shot from the enemy could sink his little vessel. In his autobiography he explained:

> I hoped to be able to dodge the shoals, of which there were many, and get close
> in, when I was quite sure they would fire over us. That is exactly what occurred.
> I got in close and manoeuvered the ship on the angle of the fort, so that the heavy
> guns could hardly bear on me, if I was very careful. The smooth-bores rained
> on us, but only two shots hit, the rest went short or over. One heavy shot struck
> the water above six feet from the ship, wetting everyone on the upper deck with
> spray, and bounded over us in a richochet.[97]

Early in the action the admiral signalled 'Well done, *Condor*'. This was picked up on by Moberley Bell, *The Times* correspondent on board, who telegraphed to London a running commentary, the first time this kind of thing had been done in warfare. The little vessel sped away to shouts of 'Well done, *Condor*' echoing across the bay from the other ships she passed. With admirable tact Seymour also sent a message, 'Well done, *Inflexible*' to Fisher, whose ship was the most damaged, but this accolade, without a Moberley Bell on board to give it legend, was soon forgotten.

In his memoirs Rear-Admiral Chambers insisted that the gunboat *Bittern* gave *Condor* valuable support. No other writer or account seems to substantiate this, yet Chambers was an eyewitness. He was insistent that the glory was not *Condor*'s alone and '*Bittern*'s name should have been joined with hers'.[98]

Fire from the forts seemed to slacken around noon and the British gunners found time to get a little rest. Field noticed that some men on *Sultan* were laying down between their guns, 'some had gone to sleep, some were quietly eating their dinners and others I saw actually having a game of cards (strictly against the ordinary rules of a man-of-war), and this with the roar of action going on, on all sides.' The thirsty men, their throats parched by smoke and sulphur, were given water 'and gallons of lime juice'. The midday sun burned down in a clear blue sky. Steaming at full speed for several hours had also done nothing to make the ships any cooler. 'Down below the men supplying the guns with ammunition were working nearly naked', wrote Field, 'the heat being almost unbearable, for it was no light matter to keep supplying shell of 400 lbs weight all day, in such a temperature.'[99]

A huge explosion at Fort Ada transfixed the fleet around 1.30pm. The magazine had been hit by a lucky shot fired by *Superb*. While officers and men on all the ships gave a huge cheer they saw a 'bright upward burst of flame, and then the dense black column of smoke, dust and stones shooting upwards and spreading outwards like a great pall, followed by the long sullen roar of the explosion.' Egyptians in their white uniforms were seen hurrying out of the fort which 'resembled the crater of a small volcano'.[100]

All morning the Egyptian gunners had stuck grimly to their duties in what must have a living hell of dust, smoke, heat and dangerous fumes, their bodies caked in sweat and blood, wondering all the time if the next shot aimed at their fort would send them to blazes. During the early afternoon the Egyptian fire slackened and Fort Pharos was evacuated. Firing ceased along the Ras-el-Tin lines by mid-afternoon and white flags were hoisted with the exception of one gun (at 5pm it was still firing at ten minute intervals). Aboard *Monarch,* Cadet Chambers watched the shelling of Fort Mex. A barracks lay at the back of it reached via a drawbridge over a deep dry ditch. One of *Monarch*'s shells fell into a storeroom containing several thousand heavy observation mines intended for the harbour. It did not go off, but in a blind panic to get away, the soldiers made for the drawbridge just as a second lucky shell cut one of its supporting chains. Through his telescope Chambers watched in horror as the bridge 'sagged over on its side … I could see the soldiers falling off it into the ditch. They clutched vainly at the timbers whilst a veritable hail of iron mowed them down.'[101]

After a time Fort Mex seemed eerily quiet and deserted. It was decided about 2pm to send a boat ashore and to try and spike the guns. Twelve bluejackets from *Invincible* were selected, with command going to Lieutenant Bradford, the ship's gunnery officer, aided by Lambton, Tulloch and Lieutenant Poore. A hot and dusty Tulloch found the water looked so inviting that near the shore he decided to jump in. He reached the beach out of breath and very wet. The fort was indeed deserted, so Bradford quickly blew up its two biggest guns, while Lambton and Tulloch 'raced off with the hammer and bag of nails to spike the smooth-bores which we did'.[102] The major swam out to fetch the dinghy, but almost immediately it smashed against some rocks and started to sink, so he had another exhausting swim back to shore. Luckily a second boat was available to pick up the party who were all warmly thanked by the admiral before Tulloch tumbled below where he was 'horribly sick' from his intake of sea water.

Further out to sea, on the decks of the foreign warships and on the P&O ship *Tanjore* the bombardment had been observed by a fascinated crowd. 'To a civilian who had never seen warfare the spectacle was magnificent', wrote Baron de Kusel. The dense white smoke around the fleet meant that the onlookers could hear everything and see little but:

> The roar of the broadside, the deep booming of the turret guns and the quick tap-tapping of the Nordenfelt, caused our hearts, I think, to beat a trifle faster.

Occasionally, too, we caught a glimpse of a ship, and many Egyptian shells, which, through the faulty aim of the gunners, passed right over the British ships and went skip-skipping along the sea, throwing up clouds of spray before sinking.[103]

One of the last ships in action was *Monarch*. She obtained permission to proceed close to shore and attack the Windmill Fort. For weeks the ship had anchored under the guns of this battery and the crew saw it as an 'old friend'. The Egyptian gunners, however, quickly got the ship's range and sent an opening shell screaming under the hurricane deck, narrowly missing an officer of marines. Chambers was stationed by the conning tower near the captain when a shell whizzed overhead. Everyone ducked except Captain Fairfax, a veteran of the Crimean War, who just laughed and said, 'No need to duck, gentlemen.' The young cadet noticed that the stammer which usually affected the captain's speech had gone completely. A short time later, Seymour, worried that the ship might take a direct hit, signalled for it to retire.

The 'Ceasefire' was hoisted at 5.30pm. Herbert Kitchener later maintained that *Invincible* fired the last shot, an experimental shell that could only be expended at risk to its gun crew. It hit the upper works of a fort directly on target. Dust and debris rained down. 'But,' Kitchener recalled with amusement, 'when this cleared away, an old woman rushed frantically from an outhouse and chased in some fowls!'[104]

Along the shore most of the forts had smashed and battered ramparts, the lighthouse looked in a sorry state, barracks were in flames, along with the harem of the Ras-el-Tin Palace and several outbuildings. Here and there an occasional gun spat defiance. Lieutenant Field had a snack of cold meat and beer, and went to look at the officers messroom, now a makeshift hospital, 'the wounded being laid on mattresses on the top of, and under the ward-room table, the sick taking possession of the sofas'. Seeing how well the doctors were caring for the men made Field think 'of the awful state of misery' of the Egyptians on shore, 'without the possibility of help or assistance, and was it really necessary to us to kill and destroy all these poor wretches who had only obeyed orders.' The Egyptians, he felt, 'had certainly fought their guns in the most wonderful way', and their courage under fire 'was the theme of admiration and praise of us all.'[105] Their direction had been excellent, he thought, only the gun elevations were weak. He had watched with pride and amazement as the commanding officer of the Lighthouse Fort, in grimy white uniform and red tarboosh, had climbed onto the parapet to shake his fist at the fleet when his last gun was gone. He was a colonel of engineers and, Field was in no doubt, 'a credit to any Service'.

The Royal Navy had fired 3,782 shells from its big guns along with 33,493 bullets from its Gatlings and Nordenfeldts. 'Our shooting was not all that could be desired', wrote Captain Fisher with remarkable (for him) understatement. Only 10 of the 43 guns in the batteries had suffered a direct hit. Commander Goodrich of the American Navy reckoned after examination, that all the forts except Ada and Mex, could have been in operation the next day. Fifty per cent of all British shells fired had malfunctioned, either exploding prematurely, or failing to explode at all. Fuses were to blame. The machine guns had fired 'tons' of bullets but, as Fisher commented, 'The Lord only knows where they went to.'[106]

The bombardment was, most officers thought, 'a great success but it was a great stroke of luck'.[107] The Royal Navy had lost 5 men killed and 28 wounded (one mortally) in the engagement. Egyptian losses are harder to ascertain; officially they had between 100–150 dead and 250–350 wounded. Lieutenant Field wrote that three separate persons counted over 600 bodies in the Ras-el-Tin lines, figures not corroborated, but they are not impossible since the Egyptians probably downplayed their losses to boost local morale.

The bombardment had lasted for so many hours that the ships had been in serious danger of running out of ammunition. *Alexandra*, for instance, had only fifteen shells left. The gunboats had been able to get fresh supplies from *Hecla*, but the rest of the fleet had to wait until the evening of the 12th when HMS *Humber* arrived. If the bombardment had needed to go into a second day, as Seymour had warned, then none of the ironclads would have been able to fire for very long.

Gunnery mistakes were made but the British sailors and ships had fought magnificently. There had been no engine troubles, despite steaming for so long under a fierce sun. The men had operated their guns very well and the armour plating had meant that most Egyptian scores were minor dents.

No less than four major reports were to be written on the performance of the fleet and its gunnery on 11 July 1882: Captain George Clarke of the Royal Engineers made a confidential account on the defences of Alexandria and results of the action; Fisher responded with one that gave more credit to the Royal Navy; Commander Caspar Goodrich wrote a highly elaborate document for the United States Office of Naval Intelligence; and finally, Seymour made his own based on reports from all his captains and the ships' logs. In essence they agreed that gunners needed to be more prac-tised, that earthworks were an excellent shield for a fort's defence, and that the Royal Navy's percussion fuses were hopelessly inefficient and had to be improved.

That night, as the officers and men of Seymour's fleet enjoyed a well-earned rest they saw a terrible sight on shore. A dark sulphurous cloud hung over Alexandria and red tongues of flame began to lick upwards in a lurid light. From the Ras-el-Tin Palace, near the water's edge, buildings could be seen to be ablaze, 'and the flames of other conflagrations rose elsewhere and were beheld with consternation by the unhappy European refugees, who crowded to our ships, and knew that all they possessed on earth was perishing by fire and pillage …'[108]

# 4

# Invasion

*Our first site in Egypt, be it by larceny or be it by emption, will be the almost certain egg of a North African Empire that will grow and grow.*
William Ewart Gladstone

The streets of Alexandria on the morning of the bombardment had seemed, at first, to be even more peaceful than normal. In clear blue skies and a light north-westerly breeze the early sun glinted off the domes and minarets of countless mosques and warmed the yawning soldiers who had spent an uncomfortable night sleeping in doorways and park benches in the Place Muhammad Ali. Military posts were relieved at 6am, as normal, native door-keepers smoked their cigarettes like every other morning and chatted to the women selling milk.

Before the clock on St Catherine's church had finished striking seven the distant boom of *Alexandra*'s opening shot was heard. Just before 8am a shell fell in the Arab quarter causing a panic. Near the arsenal the fire was so hot that Toulba Pasha, who was in charge of the city's military defences, left alongside Arabi Pasha and an escort of cavalry to a more safe position behind Fort Kom-el-Dyk.

By 9am Alexandria seemed a ghost town as the locals locked their doors and prayed for a safe outcome or huddled in the coffee shops debating events. A rumour spread about this time that two ironclads had been sunk and five more were disabled. The joy of this news was short-lived as the fire from the fleet increased. Shells began over-shooting the forts at the rate of about two a minute; one landed on the terrace of a mansion in Rosetta Avenue, another burst spectacularly above the German Consulate and the Rue Copt was enveloped in a cloud of dust when a shell fell on some stables. By lunchtime several buildings had been hit, including a Jewish synagogue and an Anglican church. The destruction was, on the whole, relatively slight, such as the shell which fell into the Franciscan convent, destroying only a couple of walls and injuring no one. Shortly after midday two shells smashed into the khedival schools and swept away several classrooms.

Things began to get ugly for the 1,500 foreigners still left in the city. Most of them were employees of European banks, hotels, consulates and religious institutions scattered across Alexandria. Egyptian soldiers began to cut all the telegraph wires and check that foreigners watching the bombardment from the flat rooftops of their buildings were not sending messages to the ships. A handful of unlucky Europeans were dragged into the streets and set upon by angry locals. Clubbed with the butt ends of rifles, these unfortunates were hustled along by the soldiers and finally thrown, bloody and terrified, into police cells where Arab criminals gleefully beat them up.

The mobs started to get bolder as the afternoon wore on. Egyptians smashed down the doors of the German Hospital and surged in as screaming patients and staff made a rush for the cellars. A senior diplomat fired his revolver and the crowd paused long enough for someone to bring them to their senses. They rushed off clutching the flag that had flown over the building. Another band demanded the Danish Consul give up his flag but he refused. Just as events looked set to turn ugly a shell crashed into the street nearby killing three people and the rioters ran for their lives.

From 10am until late afternoon carts laden with dead Egyptian artillery-men, their bodies stripped and tied together with ropes, clattered through the streets. Officers, many with terrible wounds and blood pouring down their faces, hurried along in carriages, the wounded rank and file in carts, all heading for the main hospital in the Avenue Rosetta. Each arrival was followed by a wailing gaggle of wives, mothers, sisters and children. Next day, when General Stone went to visit his troops, he described the scene at the hospital in a letter to his daughter, as quite awful, 'the wounded were lying on the bare stone floors, covered with blood and dust, gasping for water and some dying for want of proper care, as there were only three doctors there.'[1] Deaths in the city residential districts from the British cannonade were few. Perhaps the worst incident occurred near the Moharrem Bey Gate when a shell exploded instantly killing two officers and six policemen.

When, in late afternoon, the bombardment died down, an exodus of inhabitants streaming out of the city along the banks of the Mahmoudieh Canal, or following the railway line towards Cairo, was only halted by the coming of darkness. No one lit the gas that night and Alexandria 'resembled a vast necropolis'. Fires flared along the water's edge and at the Ras-el-Tin Palace, but deep within the city all was in terrible darkness.

During all this time, one lone Englishman had stuck to his post. This was Mr J. E. Cornish, manager of the Alexandria waterworks. He had refused point-blank to leave the city and prepared an elaborate system of defence for the main water installation including jets of hot steam which could be turned on attackers, sticks of dynamite and as a last resort in the engine-house, a goodly supply of firearms and ammunition. Cornish and his nine European assistants kept the water-pumps going throughout the bombardment so that Alexandrians could get drinking water or douse a fire. Next day he and his team supervised a remarkable act of charity. As the locals left the dust and smoke of their burning city they found two huge jars of water placed at the gates of the waterworks so that everyone could refresh themselves.

Dawn on the morning after the bombardment came with gloomy skies and a haze over the city. Offshore the wind had picked up in the night and the ships in the Outer Harbour rolled in choppy seas. Matters, so far as Seymour was concerned, still lay unresolved. No official surrender had been made and for all he knew the Egyptians might begin firing again. At 10.45am he permitted *Inflexible* and *Temeraire* to fire a few shells at Fort Pharos. Within minutes of this opening salvo a white flag appeared above the parapets. Hedworth Lambton was sent to investigate. He had no sooner stepped aboard the khedival yacht when Toulba Pasha pulled up alongside in a steam launch. Lambton made clear that Forts Mex and Adjemi must be surrendered, and the former temporarily occupied, while the defences of the latter would be destroyed. He promised that no British flag would be flown, but the admiral 'required the peaceful surrender as a guarantee of good faith'.[2] Seeming to play for time, Toulba said he needed to communicate all of this to the Khedive, but that the telegraph was no longer working. He begged for the surrender time to be postponed by one hour to 3pm.

It is clear from despatches that Lambton and Seymour both felt the Egyptians were trying to evacuate as many men as they could during the truce. Arabi, in his memoirs, defended Toulba's actions and pointed out that the small time frame given by the admiral allowed him and other members of the War Cabinet very little opportunity to communicate with Tewfik, who was outside the city at Ramleh. He insisted that the Khedive actually ordered troops to occupy Fort Adjemi and resist any British landing. When Arabi pointed out that any garrison would be cut off from the city and an easy target for the fleet, a furious Tewfik replied, 'Why do you call yourselves soldiers if you cannot prevent the landing of an enemy in our country?'[3]

The short resumption of British firing convinced thousands of natives that the fighting was about to begin in earnest. When it stopped as quickly as it had begun the same frightened souls were convinced that British troops were about to land. This jittery mood was not eased by news that convicts in the Arsenal Gaol had somehow got free and were going on a rampage. During the morning Egyptian infantry began leaving the town, marching in fours, some 1,800 of them swung smartly out of town on the road to Ramleh. Things seemed to change in the afternoon following a visit to the garrison by Colonel Suliman Sami; plunder now became the theme and soldiers began breaking into shops with the same bravado as the lowliest criminals. Fights broke out near the Rosetta and Moharrem Bey Gates between natives laden with belongings and loot – gilt chairs, ornate mirrors, silver cutlery and velvet gowns. Soon the roads were littered by a trail of broken ornaments and other debris.

The hours ticked by; Toulba Pasha returned to the harbour but narrowly missed Lambton who had returned to the fleet. Seymour ordered one shot to be fired at the Mex battery. It resulted in the fast display of another flag of truce. This time Commander Morrison of *Helicon* was sent to investigate. He found the khedival yacht deserted. An eerie silence seemed to have descended on the waterfront. Not a soldier was to be seen and Morrison reported to the admiral that he saw a red glow in the sky above the city centre. The quick descent into night confirmed on the ships everyone's worst fears – the richest part of Alexandria, the European quarter, was in flames.

Arabi Pasha had returned into the city from his meeting with Tewfik at Ramleh in the late afternoon. It was then that he learned that Colonel Suliman Sami, 'wild with rage', intended to burn the city. The general went to see the colonel who denied the charge. Despite several attempts, Arabi was unable to stop large bodies of troops from looting as they retreated from Alexandria. In his opinion the destruction of the city was not due to Sami but the Bedouin who had been waiting, under cover of darkness, to fire and pillage it. The Egyptian leader had a heap of problems – his army was depressed, weary and disaffected and it took him several hours to bring some organization out of the chaos. Finally a camping ground was chosen just beyond the bridge over the Mahmoudieh Canal but due to the vast numbers of refugees, animals and transport on the road it was not until 2am that most of the Alexandria garrison trudged into camp.

Debate has raged ever since as to what extent the British bombardment damaged Alexandria. The admiral's only intended objective had been to destroy the forts. It is clear, however, that his promise prior to the battle that he would not damage the city proved on the day to be incorrect. Several European residents complained afterwards about the loss of property and the hysteria caused by the shelling. One of them, the elderly Swiss merchant, John Ninet, was vociferous in accusing the British of starting the fires that destroyed the European quarter. But Ninet was extremely anti-British and even Scholch, stern critic of the European Powers, called him an 'unreliable' witness. Clearing up the shells a week later was the task of Percy Scott, a young gunnery officer from HMS

*Inconstant*. He was not present at the bombardment, yet declared in his memoirs that 'the town appeared to me to have suffered more from the misses than the forts had from the hits'.[4] Obsessed with the need for British sailors to improve their gunnery training, Scott's remarks must be seen in the context of a jocular reprimand to the Royal Navy.

The question is not whether shells fell on the city, nor how many – probably as high as 30 per cent of those fired may have overshot their targets though many observers put the figure lower – but did those shells cause major damage, or even start the great fire? It is worth remembering that a chief criticism in all official reports of the bombardment is that shells exploded prematurely or failed to explode at all due to poor fuses. Lieutenant Scott also recounts finding a gigantic 16-inch shell outside the door of a bakers's shop but the building had no external damage, 'I wonder how this bloody thing came here; there is no hole anywhere', remarked a sailor to Scott. Gazing up the narrow alley the man's mate declared, 'I suppose it must have made this bloody street!'[5] (It was found to have fallen through the roof of the house, destroying the interior without affecting the walls). The number of arsonists seen running around the city in the four days after the bombardment, the widescale looting and wanton destruction of property in the richer homes (the British Consulate was seen to be unharmed on 13 July and a smoking ruin three days later), all point to dark forces at work that had nothing to do with the fire from Seymour's ships (photographs taken a few days later show the size of the devastation, but the rubble in the streets is mainly the result of explosives used to detonate unsafe buildings and walls).

Incendiaries all through that night, and until order was restored half a week later, used rags soaked in paraffin or gasoline, poured over furniture, along with bedding stuffed in doorways, to create a massive conflagration. More than 140 mansions and apartment buildings were fired in this way.

Not every Egyptian left the city or sympathised with the mob. The staff of the renowned Hotel Abbat had long fled but the doorkeeper stayed on and refused to unlock the doors when pillagers demanded to be let in. Wondering how to scare them away, he suddenly recalled some of the choice expressions he had often heard used by angry tourists. Putting on his best English accent the gatekeeper shouted out, 'You bloody bastards! What the bloody hell do you want?', along with a few more Anglo-Saxon expletives. The effect was magical; the mob, assuming there might be armed Europeans inside, skulked away leaving the hotel undamaged.

Seymour's shells may not have destroyed Alexandria but his failure to land marines or sailors and restore order most certainly contributed to the city's destruction. He had 5,880 men on his ships excluding civilians. Finally, when forced into action by the initiative of the Americans, it required only a few hundred well organised people to end the chaos. The admiral's reticence to occupy the city stemmed, of course, from his realization that such a landing would be viewed by opponents as a pretext to a full-scale British invasion. His orders had been to destroy the forts. There was no mention – yet – of occupying the city. The admiral had been reprimanded by the Prime Minister only a few days previously for exceeding his instructions and he did not intend that it should happen twice. It is also pretty clear that Northbrook, Key and Seymour had all assumed that a bombardment would end Egyptian army opposition or, at the very least, hand them Alexandria on a plate. Rampaging locals led by desert Bedouin and disaffected soldiers were not part of their scenario.

The first foreign troops to land on the Egyptian shore were American marines. Ahead of them went a small reconnoitring party headed by the bumptious temporary consul, Charles Chaile-Long. The captain of the USS *Quinnebaug* refused persmission for him to go ashore but Chaille-Long disobeyed the orders and pressed a passing Greek boatman into service. Just before dawn on 13 July, with a journalist friend in tow, the trio set off for the harbour. They docked by the Ras-el-Tin Palace steps and the Greek rushed off to grab some loot. Double quick Chaille-Long and his companion made their way to Fort Pharos, 'the road being strewn with ghastly bodies, and the debris of flight under heavy fire. In the fort the stench from the dead was stifling.' Expecting at any moment to be shot, the pair hurried over to the marina and customs house where scores of abandoned boats bobbed up and down at the jetty. Floating in the water they saw the bodies of several men, women and children, 'swollen and inflated with gas, black with corruption', mainly Syrian jews slain by the marauders.

Wharves all along the waterfront were on fire with tongues of flame reaching high into the sky. Chaille-Long described the scene:

> The wind would occasionally sweep away the thick curtain of smoke, and finally I saw a number of wretches engaged in their work of pillage and destruction. One of these, his arms filled with booty, came running towards the place where I stood ... As he attempted to pass my hiding-place, I extended my foot, he stumbled. In an instant I was on the fellow's back, my revolver pressed to his head. 'Where are Arabi Pasha and the army?' I asked in Arabic. He told me, after protestations and appeals for mercy, that Arabi had abandoned Alexandria and the army was posted along the Mahmoudieh Canal and towards Kafr-ed-Dawar. Satisfied that the man had told the truth, I gave him a rude punch with my pistol and bade him begone, an invitation he obeyed with alacrity.[6]

With this news Chaille-Long decided to return and see Admiral Nicholson, pausing just long enough to purchase several bottles of Chambertin from the Greek boatman, 'for the modest sum of one franc per bottle, for which the Khedive had doubtless paid forty francs'. The American admiral listened eagerly to his report and agreed immediately that a detachment of sailors and marines should accompany him back to the city, try to extinguish some fires and check the situation at the United States Consulate.[7]

While all this was being organized, and Chaille-Long was enjoying a well-earned bath and some lunch after his adventure, the first Britons had landed and penetrated to the heart of the fiery metropolis. Lieutenant William Forsyth of *Invincible* anchored a steam pinnace at the marina while three brave civilians, all volunteers, explored the burning city. They were led by John Ross, merchant and purveyor to the fleet, a man with a good working knowledge of the harbour district's narrow streets and alleys. With him went two intrepid journalists – John Cameron of the *Standard* and Frederic Villiers of the *Graphic*. The trip sent off in darkness, possibly before Chaille-Long's expedition, Ross insisting that all firearms must be left on the boat (both newsmen disobeyed him). Clinging to the meaner streets, carefully avoiding main avenues, the party aimed to get as far as Place Muhammad Ali. The trek was described by Villiers:

> In the fitful light of distant flames as the burning embers shot skyward, we could see bodies lying here and there outside looted stores, cats mewed piteously for the water, for the mains had burst and all supply had ceased. The rumble of the burning buildings, as they flared and toppled to the ground; the hissing of steam as the melted leaden piping let loose jets of water into the burning debris, and the howls and screams of frightened animals made the night hideous. At last we arrived at our destination and looked upon what was once the famous square.[8]

The great statue of Muhammad Ali still sat on its plinth but round about was 'a whole quadrangle of lurid flame. The trees, once the glory of the square, though set well in the centre were shrivelling in the heat. The sap was hissing into steam and the stems were beginning to split and burn.'[9] Not a soul was to be seen. Suddenly Cameron and Villiers gasped in horror. In the centre of the square could be spied, amid the smoke, a group of mutilated bodies, headless and armless. The war correspondents, hairs rising on their backs, rushed over for a closer inspection and their nervousness gave way to laughter. The 'bodies' turned out to be a bizarre collection of dress-maker's dummies left by some looters.

Returning towards the harbour the trio heard the sound of tramping feet and quickly hid in the shadows. They did not expect to meet Egyptian troops and knew no British soldiers had been authorised to land ashore. To their relief and surprise the marching sounds turned out to be an American detachment, some 160 sailors and marines, under the command of walrus-moustachioed Lieutenant-Commander Caspar Goodrich. Before moving off the Britons advised the Americans to use the English Club – which was still standing near the big square – as their headquarters. Goodrich and his men thanked them politely and plodded on; as they crossed the Place des Consuls the burning roof of the nearby French Consulate caved in with a tremendous crash. The Americans formed an impromptu fire brigade and tried to save as many buildings near their consulate as they could including St Marks Anglican church.

During the morning of 13 July, Admiral Seymour sent landing parties to spike guns in three of the forts. At the same time, Commander Hammill of *Monarch* led 250 sailors and 150 marines in the seizure of the western end of the Ras-el-Tin peninsula, occupying the arsenal and extending to north and south a thin line of sentries. Shortly after noon a few British marines and a Gatling gun crew from *Monarch* pushed a little way into town firing on looters and taking a few as prisoners. 'The work of incendiarism was still going on, and even the women were setting fire to houses with petroleum,' wrote a contemporary historian, 'Walls were tumbling down, and the hot air was opaque with limedust and smoke.'[10]

During the afternoon an aide-de-camp from the Khedive reached Seymour asking if he could guarantee his master's safety? The admiral gave full assurances and at 4pm a visibly relieved Tewfik, accompanied by an escort of cavalry and 50 infantry, arrived back at Ras-el-Tin. It had been a tense 24 hours for the Egyptian ruler. On the previous day troops had surrounded the Royal party at Ramleh. Tewfik, ever suspicious of Arabi's intentions, guessed correctly that this move was a prelude to being forcibly escorted back to Cairo. When questioned about this Arabi denied it, sent an apology to Tewfik, and Toulba Pasha promised to punish the officer in command. Most of these soldiers had been withdrawn on the morning of the 13th but 250 still remained. Determined to get away and not trusting his army leaders, Tewfik's finely-tuned survival instincts did not let him down; jewels from the royal harem were liberally dispensed to the troops to secure their loyalty.

It was a confusing week for patriotic Egyptians. Should they support their natural ruler, the Khedive, or the army under Arabi Pasha? One day their ruler seemed to be at war with the British, and on the next he was at war with his army, who were now 'rebels'. On 11 July the nationalists declared a state of martial law and begun requisitioning mules and horses for the army. The popular press and imans took up the cry for jihad. Then, one day after the Khedive accepted British protection, everything changed again and the martial law decree was lifted.

Arabi Pasha spent 13 July gradually reassembling half of the Alexandria garrison. When he heard that that Tewfik had slipped away he was furious. It was not just a betrayal by the leader of the state but it broke Arabi's deep-seated sense of honour. 'It was not, according to our law, either permissible or fitting for the ruler of a country, to act thus,' he declared, 'and side with a nation that was fighting against us, and which he himself in solemn council decided to resist ... such a man cannot be a Muslim, therefore he ought not to rule over Moslems.'[11] Seizing the initiative, Arabi began to assert his leadership of the anti-invasion forces; on 11 July he had already demanded that the administration of the country be subordinated to to the demands of the army, now he wrote a proclamation, published on 17 July, in which he assumed the burden of defending Egypt. The British were aggressors and the Khedive a traitor: 'English soldiers butchered and shot our soldiers and police who had been left in charge of the city ... The Khedive remains at night with his women afloat amongst the English, and by day returns to the shore to order the unnecessary slaughter of Mahommedans in the streets of Alexandria', ran the colourful propaganda, but such rhetoric ensured in future only Arabi's commands would be obeyed.[12] Army rule would hold sway in Upper and Lower Egypt and violations treated as infringements of martial law.

On the afternoon of 13 July the Admiralty order that Seymour had been waiting for at last arrived; it allowed 'a landing of seamen and marines for police purposes to restore order'. The admiral now put his two most energetic officers to work on shore. It was to be the only time that the pair worked closely together and got along. Overall command of the city and outer defences was given to Fisher of *Inflexible*, his provost-marshal, responsible for restoring order in Alexandria, was Beresford of *Condor*. Fisher would later recall the next two days as 'the most anxious ones I have ever spent'.[13] He had only a small force and worked without sleep for almost the first 60 hours. On the very first night he nearly lost his life inspecting an outpost, when he arrived without warning and a jumpy sentry fired at him close-range with a revolver. A junior officer managed to knock up the man's arm just in time and the bullet whizzed over Fisher's head. He took not the slightest notice, warning the gun crew that an attack might come at any minute. Pointing at a cannon he declared merrily, 'You can't miss 'em. You've only got to put in the ammunition and off it goes.'[14] Then he was off as stealthily as he came.

Establishing order in the city was to be no easy task. One of *The Times* correspondents landed with the second detachment of Royal Marines,

200 strong, accompanied by Auckland Colvin and Admiral Hoskins, the jaunty commander about to take charge of operations at Port Said. Entering Alexandria they found the native quarter untouched. A few Egyptians were encountered wearing white armbands and a handful of soldiers red ones (the newly adopted sign of allegiance to the Khedive). Past smouldering ruins and piles of trash, in single file, pausing occasionally for a wall to fall, they made their way into the heart of the city. In the great square the equestrian statue of Muhammad Ali and the *Palais de Justice* still stood, but all around 'was one long line of fire'. Among the smoke of burning buildings *The Times* man tried to get his bearings but failed. 'In a place which I have seen almost daily for 17 years', he wrote, 'I could not even find out the openings of the familiar streets leading to the markets.'[15] Moving on, the detachment found the British Consulate still safe (it was fired on the night of the 15th) and caught a berber trying to burn down houses near the Coptic church. He was shot on the spot.

The same story was repeated by others who ventured into the smouldering city. Kusel Bey was saddened to see so much death and destruction. When at last he got to his own apartment he found the building standing, but inside everything 'was smashed, the household glass broken to smithereens – not a whole wineglass left; chairs broken, carpets all ripped to ribbons.'[16] Going out to the stables he found them barricaded from within. Shouts and knocks roused Giovanni, his coachman, who had risked death in the city rather than leave 'Bessie', his mare. The Englishman, Italian (and perhaps the horse) had a tearful and joyful reunion.

Plucky little Melton Prior had a reputation for getting in the thick of things. In his autobiography he admitted ordering a Gatling gun crew to shoot down suspected looters. It is clear summary justice prevailed and the bluejackets were inclined to shoot first and ask questions later. One day, near the marina, Prior came across a stumbling band of about 150 Europeans of all ages. They had been scattered across Alexandria in cellars and similar places during the bombardment and fire and, on seeing the British, 'were almost delirious with joy and happiness'.[17] The heroic merchant, John Ross, opened up his store for free to these starving people, a kindness he also bestowed on parties of sailors and marines.

On their first night ashore the various war correspondents had to sleep where they could. Prior and John Cameron curled up on the floor of Mr Ross's shop while all around the two men could hear walls crashing down, roofs tumbling in, occasional gun shots and the sounds of rioters in the streets. Prior recalled it later as 'not an ideal time for slumber', but slept soundly nonetheless.[18]

Determined to impose his authority, stop the looting and put out the fires, Charles Beresford landed on the morning of 14 July, got a horse, guide and escort of about 30 cavalry loyal to the Khedive. What he then witnessed were sights he would never forget:

I never saw anything so awful as the town on that Friday, streets, square and blocks of buildings all on fire, roaring and crackling and tumbling like a hell let loose, Arabs murdering each other for loot under my nose, wretches running about with fire-balls and torches to light up new places, all the main thorough-fares impassable from burning fallen houses, streets with many corpses in them.[19]

Using a chart, Beresford divided up Alexandria, establishing depots and police stations. Seymour was reluctant to exceed his orders and provided only 60 sailors and 70 marines, so Lord Charles got proportions from the foreign warships in the harbour and by nightfall had 620 men spread across the city and 140 more operating in patrols.

In a secret report to the admiral Beresford admitted that the night of 14 July was one of 'great anxiety to myself', as new fires were lit, and several people shot as incendiarists. Next day four more were executed in the act of setting fires by patrols and new corpses found in the streets. Lord Charles now demanded the right to shoot all persons caught firing houses. Those caught looting would be whipped and if found guilty a second time would also be executed. Seymour gave his assent despite strong opposition from Tewfik and Colvin (both of whom felt Egyptians ought first to be tried and then executed by their fellow countrymen).

Beresford soon found that the Greeks were shooting natives 'unnecessarily' and duly cancelled all the foreign patrols apart from 25 American marines. Keeping trigger-happy Europeans in check was difficult but he strove to be correct; any foreigners caught shooting at Arabs without just cause were put in irons and naval patrols were now told to fire over the heads of looters rather than at them. In a spirit of cooperation with the local people Lord Charles even appointed the Egyptian ex-commander of Fort Marabout onto his personal staff.

The shortage of manpower was boosted on 15 July by the arrival of Admiral Dowell and his Channel Squadron. Seymour now began the complete destruction of the guns in Egyptian forts. Smaller cannon were ripped from their carriages while the bigger ones were destroyed with gun-cotton. Stores of gunpowder were also destroyed in a move one naval contemporary called 'wanton and useless destruction', judging the admiral's actions to be 'incomprehensible'. It seems he was again exceeding his orders since a short telegram to him from the Admiralty on the 13th had clearly stated: 'Opposition having ceased, do not dismantle forts or disable guns.'[20] It must be assumed that Seymour feared what might happen if the Egyptians gained control of Alexandria. With so few men under his command and so many shore batteries to defend it was an easier solution to ignore his orders and render the forts useless.

Fires sprang up all over the European quarter again on the night of 16 July and Beresford confessed to the admiral that he was 'dead beat' and he and his men had not seen a bed in 48 hours. That night Bedouins made their most energetic attack so far when 150 of them tried to enter the city by the Gabari gate. All they managed to seize was one donkey before running smack into a twelve-man Gatling gun crew from *Alexandra* under the command of young midshipman Eustace Stacey. The bluejackets considered this kind of action 'as being the best lark in the world'.

Lord Charles asked the admiral for more men but the request was refused. Captain Briscoe of *Tanjore* offered 20 of his crew to help and Beresford accepted them to form a fire brigade. A rumour that 30,000 Egyptians were going to attack the city that night so alarmed him that he hastily drew up a plan to evacuate all foreigners back to the ships using the American marines and two Gatling gun crews to bring up the rear. Several consuls re-embarked for safety's sake but Charles Chaille-Long declined. Instead he had the doors and windows of the American Consulate thickly stuffed with mattresses and pillows. All the Americans spent an anxious night protecting their building but the attack turned out to be, like so many others, another false alarm.

By now Beresford had 70 male prisoners. The khedive wanted all executions to be carried out quietly at night but Lord Charles refused; he felt that after short trials in Arabic and English the offenders found guilty should die publicly and in broad daylight to deter others. Each man was made to dig his own grave in the Place Muhammad Ali before being shot by Royal Marines. On the 16th he delayed some executions when it was found that women and children were in the square. Later that day a native was brought before him still clutching a flaming torch. An incensed Beresford had him shot immediately. When an Egyptian soldier was brought before the provost-marshal on 17 July accused of murdering three people he was duly executed despite a written request from Tewfik that he should be shot at the Ras-el-Tin Palace (presumably as a warning to the troops).

Walter Goodall, the Cairo merchant who had taken refuge on *Tanjore,* recorded his impressions of those destined for execution:

> They are brought from the guard house into the square, close to the round foun-
> tain, tied to a tree with their backs towards a file of marines. A rattle, a puff of

smoke and a miserable cheer from some loafing Levantines looking on. Decent bystanders hiss at this revengeful demonstration, and our men glance angrily in their direction as though they would like to load again and fire at the cowards who could cheer at such a moment. By this time the bodies are buried where they fell, and only a clean yard or two of freshly turned earth shows where that is.

Curious to see a whipping, Goodall found the prisoners to be aged from 15 to 70 years and the sight disgusted him:

> A soldier takes a prisoner, ties him up, back bare and exposed. Another takes in the cat with its short handle. He passes the knotted cords through the fingers of his left hand, gives it a twirl in the air, and brings it down hard upon the shoulders of the culprit; the skin starts up into bright red lines, and a groan escapes from somewhere, whilst the officer says 'One!' The punishment comes to the end of a dozen. The inflictor resigns his whip to a fresh man, who lays on with new vigour upon the blue, swelled, bloody meat that was a human being's back just now.[21]

Putrefying bodies lay in the streets and at the forts. Thanks to the hot sun the sickly sweet stench of death mingled everywhere with the scent of wood-smoke. Cadet Chambers of *Monarch* got permission to go ashore and visit Forts Pharos and Mex. It was not a pretty experience:

> The stench of the gun emplacements was beyond all description, the bodies of the artillerymen, mostly negroes, were lying unburied, except where the fallen masonry had covered them in. The corpses had swollen to an enormous size and the flies were in myriads. Even these were outclassed by the fleas. On coming out of a store-house I noticed that the coat of the man ahead of me was absolutely dark-brown with the repulsive insects, and we brushed them off like dust.[22]

In a daring reconnaissance on 17 July Commander Eustace Maude of *Temeraire*, with four British sailors and four men of the Khedival Guard rode out to within 300 yards of Arabi's lines at Kafr-Dawar. That same day saw the arrival of the troopship *Tamar* with 1,000 Royal Marines from Cyprus, along with HMS *Agincourt* and HMS *Northumberland* from Port Said carrying the 38th (South Staffordshire) Regiment and a battalion of the 60th Rifles. Last, and by no means least, came the despatch vessel *Salamis* with General Sir Archibald Alison and his staff. Two of the ships could not enter the Inner Harbour, 'so our men had to be landed in driblets', as one officer wrote, but by nightfall on 18 July a total of 3,686 British troops were on Egyptian soil.[23] The invasion, for that was what the landings had become, had changed from a purely naval affair to a combined services exercise.

The arrival of a British Army in little more than a week from the date of the bombardment might seem miraculous but it was a mixture of good planning and good luck. Those plans had been laid over a long period of time in the Army Intelligence Department. This branch of the service, which began as the Depot of Military Knowledge, and after 1815 called the Topographical and Statistical Department, existed for much of its history as a map-making office. Deficiencies in army intelligence became apparent during the Franco-Prussian War. Lord Northbrook, then under-secretary to Edward Cardwell, the reforming minister at the War Office, was impressed by the efforts of the two officers responsible for collating intelligence – Captain Evelyn Baring, Royal Artillery and Captain Charles Wilson, Royal Engineers (both men would be wrapped up the affairs of Egypt before, during and after the Egyptian War). With an annual budget of little more than £600 the newly created Intelligence Department was chaperoned into existence by Northbrook on 24 May 1873. Its tiny team (as late as 1886 it consisted of just sixteen officers and six clerks), divided the world into sections and 'scanned the international press for details useful to the Army, and added attaché's reports, the narratives of travellers and articles from military periodicals'.[24]

Considering the numerous small wars fought across the Empire in sun-scorched deserts, pestilential jungles, across snowy wastes and awesome mountains it seems amazing that the Intelligence Department largely got its facts right. True, maps were not always up to date, but the work of the topographers still saved many a soldier from death. Without computers, satellite navigation aids, mobile phones or television, the intelligence men did surprisingly well at trying to prepare the army for war on any continent.

One of the weaknesses of this system was reliance on information volunteered by officers travelling incognito. Budgets rarely allowed payment for such information. One of those who deliberately spied in Egypt as early as November 1881 was Colonel Richard Harrison. A clever Royal Engineers officer, who almost ended up as a scapegoat for the death of the Prince Imperial in Zululand, Harrison was returning to England from South Africa in March 1880 when he noticed the growing unrest. In conversations at the War Office, where he already knew fellow Royal Engineers employed on intelligence duties, he agreed a plan to take his wife with him to allay suspicion and do a little spying in Egypt. At Alexandria and Cairo the couple prowled around on donkeys visiting forts and arsenals, wharves and storehouses. He later wrote:

Soldiers ran at us whenever we came near a fort, but I was able to note the actual position of the works and their state of repair, and I could make a good guess at their armament. My inspections were, of course, accompanied by oral evidence regarding the preparations being made in the country, and the feelings of the people … I also secured some valuable plans of the Suez Canal, and of the subsidiary one that supplies it with fresh water.[25]

Back in London Harrison saw Sir Garnet Wolseley at the War Office and told him that trouble was brewing in Egypt. Wolseley, in turn, promised to instruct the Intelligence Department to investigate further and during the first half of 1882, as information was assembled, he began to formulate his own plans for an Egyptian campaign.

The first mention of Egypt in Wolseley's pocket diary is on 9 January after a meeting at the War Office. 'Affairs in Egypt look as if we may have to send a Force there at any moment', wrote the general. Five days later he wrote pithily, 'Egypt is one everyone's mouth', and on 17 January commented, 'The whole world very much disturbed about our foolish note to the Khedive.'[26]

The next important officer to spy in Egypt was Tulloch whose snipe-shooting trip proved so fruitful between January and March 1882. He had worked for the Intelligence Department ever since 1875 when he wrote a discussion paper on the possibility of an advance on Cairo via the Suez Canal. Watching events with a keen eye, Tulloch gave Wolseley a précis of this document when they met in Portsmouth in 1881. The upshot was a request for Tulloch to visit the War Office and permission for six weeks leave.

One of Tulloch's old friends, a retired admiral, agreed to go with him so that the pair might seem like typical sportsmen. They landed at Port Said and immediately began making observations. Tulloch noticed that easterly gales could reduce Lake Menzaleh, on the west side of the canal, to a muddy swamp. Landing a fleet to the east of Port Said, he concluded, was an impossibility. Journeying on to Cairo, he made friends with an American who knew Stone Pasha. An introduction followed and the Scotsman got permission to inspect the Abdin Barracks. He made a calculation on how many men could be accommodated, minutely inspected the Egyptian rifles and learned that in the dry desert heat, oil was unnecessary on any part of a weapon exposed to air, and could lead to sand clogging the mechanism (it was only after the first Battle of Kassassin that British soldiers implemented Tulloch's notes on oil). In 1857 he had been a young subaltern during the Indian Mutiny, so with memories of Cawnpore and Lucknow, he rambled around Cairo and made notes on the best places where a force of Europeans might hold out until relieved. Posing as a geologist, he was able to locate the proper position for a breaching battery if the citadel had to be stormed. He collected data on Egyptian cannon, ammunition, magazines, factories and forts.

One of his priorities was to try and work out how Alexandria could be captured and an army safely landed there. The west coast where Napoleon had disembarked was too full of forts. The east coast at Abourkir Bay seemed too far off. Tulloch settled on Ramleh; he noted that the onshore wind did not usually spring up until the afternoon and that the waterworks hill gave a splendid view of the whole peninsula. He calculated that '3,000 infantry, with half-a-dozen ships field-guns and Nordenfeldts, could hold our position between Ramleh and the lake so strongly that no force of Egyptian troops from Ramleh could turn them out.'[27]

Tel-el-Kebir in the desert near Zagazig was the place where the Egyptians had made fortifications to resist any army attacking from the direction of the Suez Canal. At a lock-keeper's cottage on the Sweetwater Canal the sportsmen-spies found lodgings and Tulloch set off to investigate. He reported that Tel-el-Kebir could be easily taken but the Sudanese soldiers and long-service garrison artillerymen would put up a stiffer fight than normal conscripted fellahin. With some foresight he wrote: 'If defeated, they would lose all their artillery, and it is more probable the fellahin soldiers would avail themselves of such a favourable opportunity of disbanding and returning to their homes.' When he left Egypt the clever spy even got a British official in the telegraph service to keep an eye on goings-on at Tel-el-Kebir, the two men corresponding in a 'sporting-like cipher' in which 'snipe' or 'sand-grouse' meant much more than game birds. Back in Britain he wrote up a report which was printed by the War Office and circulated confidentially to top officials after the Alexandria Riots. It was the major document used by Childers and Wolseley, in their respective political and military capacities, to plan the invasion.

Hugh Childers was a career-politician who did not wish to be Secretary-of-State for War but had a formidable reputation of mastering whatever he was required to do. With a thick white beard and greying hair he looked like a latter-day Old Testament prophet. His weakness was on occasion an arrogant refusal to listen to the advice of others but he had a fierce allegiance to the GOM. 'None ever strove more assiduously than Mr Childers to modernise our out-of-date Army system', wrote Wolseley, who admired him enormously, and summed him up thus: 'Mr Childers was a very keen Army Reformer, but first of all he was a dedicated follower of Mr Gladstone.'[28] One of those politicians who did not court publicity, content simply to get quietly on with the job, Childers is today largely forgotten, but his tenure at the Admiralty and War Office in Gladstone's first two administrations, mark him as an arch reformer.

Born into a partly Jewish family with banking connections, Childers was 55 at the time of the Egyptian War. He had gone to Australia as a young man during the gold rush and returned as Agent-General for the Colony of Victoria with a wife and four children. When the job was cancelled at short notice a relative suggested he stand for Parliament. He had met Gladstone socially and admired him. So it was that he won a by-election at Pontefract and took a Commons seat in January 1860. Financial administration was his forte and he dreamed of one day being Chancellor of the Exchequer but by 1882 this plum had still not dropped in his lap. No one, it seemed, wanted the nasty task of clearing up the Zulu and Afghan war messes, but when asked by Gladstone to take over the War Office a disappointed but loyal Childers confessed to a friend, 'I have got a very heavy task before me, one with an innumerable number of lions in my path, but I do not shirk from either the work or the responsibility.'[29]

The second half of the Afghan War fell within this period including the terrible disaster at Maiwand. A year later Childers had to deal with a crisis in the Transvaal that exploded into a short, sharp war with the Boers. The crowning disaster of Majuba, where General Sir George Colley, a protégé of Wolseley, managed to get killed on the top of a hill and British soldiers had to run for their lives, did nothing to make the War Minister's job an easier one. Despite a tough workload one of his private secretaries at the time found him to be:

> A very pleasant chief, prompt and punctual, very good at figures … He soon became popular with the civil officials … There was not quite the same feeling at first on the military side; they were nearly all political opponents, and there was a curious idea he was an Australian adventurer … they were quite surprised to hear that he belonged to an old Yorkshire family.[30]

We will examine Childers army reforms a little later in the context of his relationship with the Duke of Cambridge and General Wolseley but, in any case, those policies have been well documented. What is less well-known is that he held strong views about the security of the Suez Canal and more than a decade before the Egyptian War, while at the Admiralty in 1870, had written to 'Puss' Granville about the '*immediate* and to my mind, vital concern' that would occur if a single ship was ever sunk in the Canal. 'It may', he wrote, 'prevent all communication by it for months; it is the route both for our Navy, and almost our entire commerce to and from the East.' He urged the Foreign Secretary to think carefully: 'If we are at war, what will be our status with respect to the Canal, and what will be the status of others?'[31]

Again and again the 'protection' or 'security' of the canal seem to be expressions dominating Cabinet talks in 1881–82. Gladstone's Colonial Secretary, Lord Kimberley, for example, placed it as a conduit to India, only a little less important in the scheme of things than India itself. Later he confessed, 'But for India, I feel certain that no Egyptian expedition would ever have taken place.'[32] Childers, who had been to Egypt at least four times in his life, took the safety of the Suez Canal as seriously as Cabinet hawks Dike, Chamberlain and Hartington. It was clearly on the back burner of his mind for more than twelve years. Perhaps it is not surprising then that he consented to another very secret mission that was organised within days of the Alexandria Riots. This was a plan to send a professional spy in the company of a respected scholar to help secure the Suez Canal, in the event of war, by enlisting the help of the Bedouin tribes of the Sinai desert.

Quite who dreamed up the scheme is unclear – Wilfred Blunt thought he gave Northbrook the idea – but it certainly gripped the latter's imagination and he saw it as his baby. To put the plan into practice required someone who was a daring adventurer and orientalist. The Intelligence Department had just the man for the job; William Gill was a 24-year-old captain in the Royal Engineers and a most adept spy. One of the richest officers in the Army, with a private fortune worth millions by today's standards, Gill had started spying in 1878. During the next two years he posed as a tourist in Bulgaria shortly after the end of the Russo-Turkish War, served as an assistant boundary commissioner for the Ottoman-Russian frontiers following the Treaty of Berlin, and wrote a major intelligence assessment on the Chinese Army. Then it was off to Afghanistan. In theory he was a humble survey officer on Major-General Sir Charles Macgregor's staff, but he quickly got mentioned in despatches for good work in an expedition against the Marri tribesmen.

Not long after his recall to London in October 1881, Gill was sent to modern-day Libya. In view of the conquest of Tunisia by the French earlier that summer the Intelligence Department wanted to know the state of things in the desert regions between there and the Egyptian frontier. At Tripoli the young officer failed to get a travel permit but set off anyway. He was caught, arrested and kicked out of the country. Depressed, he returned to London, noting in his diary on 16 June 1882, 'Alas, alas. Spilt milk in huge cans full. It's no use crying over it, but its uncommonly hard to help it.'[33]

Four days later, after a meeting with Northbrook, the young spy was elated to find that he was off again on another dangerous mission. Needing an expert on the Bedouin he recruited Professor Edward Palmer, formerly professor of Arabic at Cambridge, a lonely figure who had lost his wife four years earlier. He seems to have been a classic head-in-the-clouds academic, happiest cataloguing oriental manuscripts, or surveying the Sinai. Latterly he had been trying to make ends meet as a journalist but times were hard. On 24 June Gill met with Palmer and got him to agree to go out to the desert and report on the mood and movements of the tribes. Six days later, using his credentials as a journalist, Palmer set off and by 9 July was in Jaffa. Three days after the Alexandria Bombardment he set off by camel across the desert from Gaza towards Suez. Less than a week later Captain Gill got orders to join Admiral Hoskins at Port Said as his intelligence officer. Unbeknown to most people, the academic and the officer planned to rendezvous in the desert.

It is the role of army intelligence experts to see that their country is prepared for war. Putting those plans into effect and mobilizing an army is an entirely different matter. Six days after the Alexandria Riots the Duke of Cambridge, Commander-in-Chief of the British Army, wrote to Childers to say: 'I am, of course, quite in the dark as to what the Government views or plans as regards Egypt ... I presume that it has occurred to you that some landing of troops may become necessary ... but I have not been called upon to propose or suggest anything.'[34] The War Minister replied that the Cabinet had met the day before, 15 June, and discussed 'the propriety of making some preparation for the possible contingency of having to send a British force'. Anything done must be kept very secret, warned Childers, because if it 'oozed out that any preparations were being made, another outburst of violence might take place'.[35]

A preliminary meeting to discuss Egypt was held at the War Office on 17 June but the first official step took place on 28 June when the Commissariat Department supplied Sir Garnet Wolseley, the Adjutant-General, with details of the various amounts of transport it had available at home, and in Cyprus, Malta and Gibralter, along with the amounts required if a first corps of 24,000 men was sent overseas. Next day Cambridge and Childers agreed that preliminary steps should begin and as much information on all aspects of an invasion be complied. This had to be done 'without attracting attention and without exceptional expenditure'. One day later, 30 June, a committee made up of Navy and War Office officials met to start the detailed planning. Wolseley surprised everyone by showing that, thanks to the work of Tulloch and others, a surprising amount of information on Egypt had already been collected. His speech at the meeting was the basis of a memo on 3 July that clearly outlined the shape of things to come. In Wolseley's opinion it required two divisions of infantry and one cavalry brigade to be sent to Ismailia, 'each regiment of cavalry, battalion of infantry, battalion of artillery and company of engineers should embark with their regimental transport'. Camels and pack animals would have to be imported since the Egyptian Army would obviously requisition those already there. An advance on Cairo would follow the railway line via Zagazig, and so five locomotives, including supplies, and 'at least 10 miles of steel rails' would be needed; Royal Engineers would have to carry out this work and run the trains which would 'enable us to cut down our transport very much'. The sick and wounded would be nursed aboard hospital ships at Ismailia. Wolseley concluded that the Egyptians would make a stand 'somewhere in the neighbourhood of Tel-el-Kebir'. They might also try to hold Cairo, but 'if the Egyptian army is well defeated in the field, any further resistance would be insignificant'.[36]

It was a remarkable document, predicting very well the campaign that was to follow, and demonstrating the genius of a remarkable soldier. 1882 would see Garnet Wolseley's career, at least in the popular imagination, reach its zenith. The supreme master of the colonial 'small war', he had only recently been satirised in *The Pirates Of Penzance* as 'the very model of a modern major-general', (Wolseley liked the compliment so much that he sang the tune at home to his wife and daughter). Slight in build, with prematurely greying closely curled hair and a chestnut moustache, people who met him also recalled his penetrating blue eyes. Actually he was half-blind, but then he had fought on just about every continent and had the wounds to prove it. The premier advocate of army reform was also a mass of contradictions; a snob who was self-made and claimed to hate snobs; a courageous man who feared he would faint at the sight of a flogging; an egotist but not a noisy braggart; and a formal and very smart commander who could turn on his Irish charm like a gas lamp.

Those who worked closest with him, with few exceptions, seem to have adored him. 'The best and most brilliant brain I ever met in the British army', wrote William Butler, who was to be on Wolseley's staff in Egypt, adding he was 'the only man I met in the army on whom command sat so easily and fitly that neither he nor the men he commanded had ever to think about it'.[37] Another one of Wolseley's staff, John Adye, later dedicated his own autobiography to 'the finest soldier I have ever known'. Adye felt that the general's cleverness in the field was the result of 'careful staff work and the elaboration of many details ... he, chief among all the commanders I have known, combined the large ideas of a brilliant imagination with a knowledge of military detail.'[38]

Physical courage was something that Wolseley valued and he had it in spades. Butler wrote of him:

> His body had been mauled and smashed many times. In Burmah a gingall bullet fired within thirty yards of him had torn his thigh into shreds; in the Crimea a shell had smashed his face, and blinded an eye; but no man who rode beside

Wolseley in the thirty years of active life in which I afterwards knew him could ever have imagined that, either in the grip of a horse, or at his glance at a man on a battlefield … I never knew him tired, no matter what might be the fatigue he underwent. I never knew his eye deceived, no matter how short might be the look it gave at a man or a plan.[39]

In his public persona Wolseley was invariably all smiles and charm. Evelyn Wood, one of the circle of gifted officers that he drew around him (and base commander at Alexandria during the Egyptian War), thought his chief characteristics were a 'cheery optimism and his pleasant unpretentious manners'.[40] Unlike many stuffy army types Wolseley and his wife, Louisa, liked to entertain. Writers, such as Henry James and Andrew Lang, were frequent visitors. Lady Elizabeth, Butler's wife and a famous painter of military subjects, said that as a child she had met Charles Dickens and only ever heard one man use the same distinct and hearty laugh – Wolseley. The journalist, Frank Harris, while admitting that the general was 'an excellent host', and 'eminently kind and fair-minded too', dismissed him at the dinner table as 'a lightweight, no power of personality, no depth of insight, an ordinary English gentleman'.[41]

Perhaps it was Wolseley's detached manner, or an effortless superiority at military facts and figures that prevented any deep cult of personality developing around him in, say, the way it did for his rival, Frederick Roberts, an energetic field commander from the recent Afghan War, whose mystique and fame would grow as Wolseley's fell into decline. The poet, Kipling, would soon immortalise Roberts as plucky 'Bobs', but Wolseley had no literary champion. Nor did he care. Few generals ever tried harder to improve the lot of the common soldier but Wolseley, as Joseph Lehman has stated, 'had neither the personality nor the inclination to create legends'.[42]

Not that Wolseley was quite so insensitive to the Press as he made some believe. He gave interviews freely, wrote articles and even ghosted a biography of himself in 1878. Privately he loathed all politicians, distrusted journalists and scorned civilians. It irked him greatly that many considered him an intellectual and, worse, a Liberal! These were insults to a man who once called war correspondents 'those newly invented curses to armies, who eat the rations of fighting men and do no work at all'.[43] Liberals he dismissed as 'churchwardens and parish vestrymen more than Englishmen'.[44] He considered himself 'a Jingo of the Jingoes'.

An innate conservatism in Wolseley's heart did not sit well inside a man who was an arch reformer. George, Duke of Cambridge, his nemesis in the Army, saw an altogether different man. The general was 'that cocksure young bookworm',

that 'radical Cardwellite' and 'reform-mad'. In short, as one of the Duke's dearest friends put it, 'a humbugging, lying, brute!'

All his life Wolseley wanted glory; self-advancement grew out of his need
to compete in an unfair military world where rich fools could command
regiments. Dinner guests, like Frank Harris, noticed 'an ambition altogether
out of proportion to his capacity',[45] but most in Society were forgiving. When
Queen Victoria criticised him Disraeli replied: 'It is quite true that Wolseley is
an egotist and a braggart. So was Nelson … Men of action, when eminently
successful in early life, are generally boastful and full of themselves.'[46]

The publication in the past 40 years of Wolseley's private journals, written
in Ashanti, South Africa, Cyprus and the Sudan, have revealed a man who was
viciously insulting about almost everyone he met, a spleen vented in conceited
and unpleasant remarks. Study of these journals, along with his uncensored letters and recently discovered campaign diaries, show that what was written on a
daily basis by him needs to be read with a pinch of salt. These highly personal
writings were his emotional safety valve, an individual castigated one day, when
the general was in a bad mood, might just as easily be praised on the next.
Adrian Preston, who edited Wolseley's South African and Sudan journals, has
noted that the 'decisive, iron-willed, charming and tactful' general loved by his
staff, 'stands in almost incredible contrast to the apprehensive, querulous, bom-
bastic, vain and uncharitable' man who inhabits many pages of his confidential
writings. Preston observes, quite rightly I think, that Wolseley's barbs 'were an
inverse reflection of the self-control and flattery he exercised' dealing with dull
colonial officials, crafty politicians and stupid soldiers who did not share his
views on army reform. He writes that his:

> … impression of toughness and cheerfulness in the face of despair and defeat,
> unhurried or unharassed by rumours or errors, this radiation of confidence in
> ultimate success, Wolseley deliberately manufactured in the interests of morale
> and policy, but the strain maintaining such a front built up to an intolerable level
> of acrimony and frustration.

The only outlet being to set his thoughts down on paper.[47]

Garnet Joseph Wolseley was born on 4 June 1833 near Dublin, the eldest
child in a family of four sons and three daughters. His father, 'a very poor and
proud' major in the 25th Foot, died when Garnet was only eleven. An aristocratic
private education was out of the question and he had to attend a local day school.
There was never any dispute as to what his intended career would be but without
money to purchase a commission it had to be hoped that the Commander-

in-Chief, the mighty Iron Duke, would accept the son of a valiant officer who had died after more than 30 years service. At fourteen, Wolseley's request for a commission without purchase was ignored by Wellington. This state of affairs continued for five more years, by which time he was working in a land-surveyor's office and wondering if his 'irksome' life would ever end. Within days of joining the Army in 1852 ensign Wolseley transferred from the 12th Foot, a regiment he could not afford to live in, to the 80th Foot. To his great delight the 80th were just about to depart on active service for the East in what became known as the Second Burmese War.

In his first two years in the Army young Garnet would see Cape Town and Calcutta, men who had been tortured to death by Burmese dacoits, lead his first charge and get his first wound. Commanding a small band of men to death or glory was, he wrote later, 'a supremely delightful moment ... The blood seems to boil, the brain to be on fire.' His wound was painful: 'I tried to stop the bleeding with my left hand, and remember well seeing the blood squirting in jets through the fingers of my pipe-clayed gloves.'[48] Astonishingly, the first man he saw killed in action was a Burmese at the burly hands of none other than Frederick Beauchamp Seymour (and the two mens' paths would not cross properly again until thirty years later in Egypt). Wolseley enjoyed the glory of war, but admitted that killing did not excite him, but 'gave me a rather unpleasant sensation'.

On a social level the young officer was soon educated in the often bizarre institution that was the mid-Victorian army. In his first year as a subaltern, for instance, he put some men on a charge for disobeying orders. To his surprise the old colonel did not recommend a court-martial, as prescribed in Queen's Regulations, but simply gave the offenders a tongue lashing and booted them out of his office. It was an army in which men were expected to fight in thick red serge uniforms and heavy helmets through Burmese jungles, Indian plains or Russian winters. Minor infringements of discipline usually resulted in a bloody lashing. 'I am glad to say that I never saw a soldier flogged,' wrote Wolseley years later, 'I did see one hanged without wincing, but I feel I should have broken down at what was known in my soldiering days as a flogging parade.'[49]

The Commander-in-Chief had his office at Horse Guards in Whitehall, but until the Crimean War the British Army was administered by thirteen departments, and any cooperation between them depended on 'the whims and caprices of the departmental heads and clerks'.[50] The heart of the Army lay in the regimental system, officers viewed their regiments as a club, other ranks were comforted by its clan-like atmosphere, and all felt members of 'a hierarchal extended family'. Garnet Wolseley was uncommon in not following a regimental tradition of service. Captain John Adye, who was with him in Egypt, could trace a line of association with the Royal Artillery back to his great-grandfather in 1757. At one time in the 93 Highlanders there were no more than a dozen family names in the whole regiment. Honours won in battle were recalled with pride on regimental days. Many of these had Napoleonic associations, but the rapidly expanding empire was quickly adding new glories. A gallant stand by the 13th Foot at Jellalabad in the First Afghan War was celebrated every 7 April, while each 13 January the 24th Foot remembered how it had been decimated taking a Sikh position at Chillianwallah in 1849.

There were close friendships between several regiments and long-standing feuds. The 17th Lancers and 8th Hussars were on such good terms that officers sometimes combined their numbers and called themselves 'the 25s'. after fighting side by side in Marlborough's wars, and more recently against the Sikhs, the adjutants of the 10th and 29th Foot always referred to each other as 'My dear cousin'. One of the strangest feuds, on the other hand, was between the 24th and 51st Regiments and started one Christmas Day at Aldershot, where the men took to arguing over the respective merits of their regimental plum puddings! The Black Watch and the Rifle Brigade also had an hereditary rivalry. On one occasion, before a famous fistfight in a theatre, a Black Watch private trod heavily on the foot of a Rifle Brigade man. 'You stepped on my foot!' hissed the latter. 'Well', said the Highlander in mock apologetic tones, 'I did mae best tae leap over it, but a Hielan' man is only human. I'm nae a kangaroo!'[51]

Regimental mascots and pets were taken wherever a regiment served. The Royal Welch Fusiliers always kept a goat after Queen Victoria presented it with one from a herd at Windsor in 1844. 'He stood on parade', notes Byron Farwell, 'and even marched to church with the troops'. When the regiment was sent to India, the goat went along, and because of the lavish care it received, many Indians assumed the regiment worshipped it.'[52] The 1st battalion the Gordon Highlanders charged at Tel-el-Kebir with a dog called 'Juno' barking along. Some dogs were regimental mascots and many officers took their dogs with them on campaign or adopted a stray. A cat-lover, Captain Elliott Wood surprised a picquet on the banks of the Mahmoudieh Canal during the Egyptian War by emerging from the water with a kitten on the top of his head! On service in Canada the men of the 88th Foot took such a liking to a pet bear that when it was time to return to Ireland they chloroformed the creature and hid him in a cask on the ship.

Officers needed to be gentlemen because, as the Duke of Wellington observed, 'to compose the officers of a lower class would cause the Army to deteriorate'.[53] It did not matter that men like Wolseley were half-blind and lame, or 'eccentric', (a polite term for various psychiatric problems) like Major-General

Sir Henry Havelock-Allan VC, who turned up unwanted at Tel-el-Kebir, just so long as they did their job. Wolseley's friend, Evelyn Wood VC, had a reputation as the most accident-prone officer in the Army. He once fell off a giraffe and suffered holes through both cheeks and a crushed nose, was wounded in the arm in the Crimea, shot by a nailgun in the Ashanti War, and fractured his spine falling out of a carriage in South Africa, with the added complication that his feet swelled to an enormous size. Usually complaining of various aches and pains, and notoriously half-deaf, an aide once moaned that it was necessary to 'carry a chemist's shop' to treat Wood's ailments.

The most prestigious regiments were the Guards, the 60th Rifles (King's Royal Rifle Corps) and the cavalry. Commission by purchase meant that only the very rich and aristocratic could afford to join these regiments. In 1869 Hugh McCalmont, a Wolseley Ring member, paid £5,125 (equivalent to nearly £500,000 today) for his captaincy in the 9th Lancers. Officers tended to be independently wealthy since it was impossible to live in style on their pay. They had to buy their own uniforms and weapons, provide horses and much of their equipment. In the Mess too each officer had to pay his way. It was here they relaxed; dinner was the highpoint of the social day and 'shop talk', along with sex, women, religion and politics were outlawed, so conversation was mainly restricted to sports of all kinds, but especially hunting, and anything to do with horses. Riding to hounds or steeple-chasing seemed to occupy the thoughts of many officers far more than soldiering during peacetime. Senior generals encouraged this attitude. Evelyn Wood, despite his many bruises, wrote a chapter in his memoirs entitled 'Hunting As Military Training', while Bindon Blood, who also served in the Egyptian War, claimed that field-sports helped 'train eye and hand', giving a man 'the coolness and self-confidence in action that is essential to the soldier'.[54] Sixty years later one officer recalled Army life in the 1880s as 'delightful ... mostly duck shooting and hunting in the winter, and tennis and cricket in the summer'. Lord Gleichen, who joined the elite Grenadier Guards in 1881 recalled, 'We thought ourselves badly used if (except on guard days) we did not find ourselves free by luncheon time.'[55]

There were two military colleges – Sandhurst for the cavalry and infantry and Woolwich for the engineers and artillery. About half of the officer corps came from the ten leading public schools and more than eleven per cent of these had been educated at Eton. There was 'a good deal of drunkenness in those days', recalled Lord Gleichen of Sandhurst in 1880, 'and among a certain set it used to be the correct thing to return from their Saturday and Sunday leave in somewhat advanced state of intoxication'.[56] The Royal

Military Academy at Woolwich, known as 'the Shop', had an austere reputation. Elliott Wood, who passed out in the 1860s, remembered dormitories with beds hinged back against the walls in daytime and breaking the ice in the bathrooms on winter mornings. Officers could also educate themselves further in a two year course at the Staff College, founded in 1858, at Camberley in Surrey. Wolseley was its champion and used 34 of its graduates on his staff in Egypt. The Duke of Cambridge saw things differently and declared 'a man who will stick to his regiment will learn his profession in that regiment much better than in any college'.[57] On one occasion Wolseley remarked to the Duke about an able officer who had just graduated at the Staff College. 'Oh has he,' replied the Duke, 'damned fool then!'[58]

In a regiment, bets, japes and silly wagers were a major part of the fun. This 'cockalorum' sometimes bordered on lunacy. During a few months when the Queen's favourite son, the Duke of Connaught, joined the 7th Hussars his friend Hugh McCalmont ducked when a fellow officer threw an orange at him and the Royal guest got a black eye. A week later McCalmont and two friends took Connaught over Maidstone Weir in a boat that lost its bottom and duly sank as the Royal party swam to shore. Capping this escapade, McCalmont set off a naval maroon rocket one night under a table whilst Connaught was playing whist. The explosion destroyed the table, broke a mirror and some windows and filled the room with thick smoke. Luckily no one was injured (and one suspects Prince Arthur was rather glad to leave the regiment a short time later).

Such high jinks were not restricted to home service. In the spell after Tel-el-Kebir, when Cairo was full of British officers, Captain Andrew Haggard (brother of the novelist Rider Haggard), gave his chum, Lieutenant Chamley Turner, a box full of venomous snakes on the busy terrace of Shepherd's Hotel. With delight Turner dug down in the box and pulled out a clutch of the deadly reptiles, waving them around and shouting, 'Snakes! Oh ripping!' Chairs and tables were overturned as guests ran for their lives. Turner calmly threw the snakes into the street. 'It was only later that he asked if they were poisonous,' notes Haggard's biographer.[59]

Such foolhardy bravery was not uncommon in an army where officers were expected in war to lead from the front. Under withering fire a British officer, mounted or on foot, did not get off his horse or take cover. Tommies tended to forgive tactical blunders by their superiors, but an officer who was lacking in courage was stigmatised by his men and shunned by his comrades.

Garnet Wolseley transferred again, this time into the 90th Regiment, and managed to see plenty of action in the Crimean War, the Indian Mutiny and the 2nd Chinese War, where his luck at getting staff appointments helped him to be noticed by superiors. Back home he fell 'most dreadfully' in love with a Miss Louisa Erskine, a moderately wealthy, well-educated girl whom he called 'Loo'. She was petite, fair-haired, exquisitely proportioned and, some thought, looked a lot like the Empress Eugenie. Her beau, like so many officers in India, had kept a native mistress (a practice so common, and such a good way to learn Hindustani that there was even a term for it – 'buying a native dictionary'). Now Wolseley poured out all his affections on Louisa and the couple were to have a long and extremely affectionate relationship. A mild fetishist, he always remarked on her ears, legs and especially her feet (so much so that he had a cast made of them).

The 1860s saw Wolseley in Canada. He visited America during the Civil War and made no secret of his Confederate sympathies, later declaring Robert E. Lee to be one of the two greatest men he ever met, (the other was Gordon of the Sudan). Clearly a rising star in the army firmament, in 1868 he returned to England while Quartermaster-General in Canada, to marry 'Loo' and take her back with him. A year later his remarkable *Soldier's Pocket-Book For Field Service* was published, a compendium on everything from tactics to caring for elephants, military law to recipes for Irish stew. The book, of course, gave Wolseley his first real chance to promote army reforms. It was widely read and went through several editions. Cocked hats at the Horse Guards took note and feathers were ruffled. By now Wolseley was a colonel, an incredible rise in 18 years based solely on merit. His chest was ablaze with medals but he still yearned to 'become at least known if not famous'.

The chance for an independent command came in 1870 when settlers in the Red River district of Manitoba rose in revolt under the charismatic leadership of Louis Riel. They established a 'Republic of the North-West' at Fort Garry and murdered a minor government official. Hastily Wolseley was told to assemble a force and take charge of an expedition to restore authority. His army of less than 1,000 British troops, supported by Canadians, used trains, steamers, canoes and their feet to cover the 1,200 miles to remote Fort Garry. Not a man went sick or was lost. On arrival they found Riel had already fled, but Wolseley's bloodless little expedition, costing only £100,000, was hugely popular and made him a hero in much of Canada.

This tiny Canadian victory was overshadowed in Europe by the Franco-Prussian War. The speed with which the Prussian eagle brought the French cockerel to its knees shocked the British Army. Warfare, so long the prerogative of gentlemen, had been turned, it seemed, into an exact science. Reform of the Army had been on the back boiler for years, ever since the Crimean War had highlighted many defects, but now it seemed essential, and Gladstone selected

Edward Cardwell, 'a thoughtful and coldly methodical politician', to tackle a host of issues.[60] Around him the War Minister gathered a team of like-minded reformers, led by Lord Northbrook as Under-Secretary, and including Captain Evelyn Baring, Major Robert Biddulph (the same man who was Kitchener's scolding superior in Cyprus in 1882), and the new Assistant Adjutant-General, Garnet Wolseley. This team had their hands full, but set to work abolishing the purchase of commissions and promotions, introducing short-service for soldiers, forming a reserve army, ending flogging in peacetime (it was totally abolished in 1880), withdrawing Imperial troops from self-governing dominions, improving education for the rank and file, instituting a retirement system that gave younger officer a better chance of promotion, moving the Horse Guards staff to the War Office in Pall Mall and bringing the Commander-in-Chief more closely under the control of the War Minister.

The Cardwellites were met head on by the old school of officers to whom all this change was poppycock. They were led by HRH Prince George, Duke of Cambridge, the Queen's cousin, who had commanded the British Army since 1856. Prince George was irascible, deeply conservative, suspicious of anything new and felt that an institution approved by the great Duke of Wellington did not need any tinkering. He deeply resented politicians trying to meddle with his authority. His blimpish looks – stout chest, white mutton-chop whiskers, saggy jowls and pink bald dome – made HRH seem the perfect choleric old soldier. Indeed, his parade-ground speeches were the stuff of legend. In Hyde Park he once told the Grenadiers: 'In all my experience of reviews in England, Ireland or on the Continent of Europe I have never witnessed such a damnable exhibition of incompetence as has been shown by the Grenadier Guards today. When the 'Cease Fire' sounded the 1st Battalion was firing at the Serpentine, the 2nd Battalion was firing at the Marble Arch and God Almighty knows where the 3rd Battalion was firing. I don't!'[61] At Sandhurst on another occasion he marvellously began a speech to the officer cadets with the words, 'You dirty little bastards!'[62]

Prince George was no fool and his opposition to reform sprang from a very deep-rooted love of the Army and its traditions. It was a reaction based on fear that the reformers would undermine or damage an institution he was proud to serve and which had a noble history. The Duke of Cambridge may not have approved of several of Cardwell's reforms but they did much to improve conditions for the ordinary private soldier. They were, however, extremely gradual. The abolition of flogging was a clear enactment but literacy, diet and other social aspects took longer to change. By 1876 there were 150 libraries for the men with 230,000 books, yet in 1882 the vast majority of troops were still illiterate or had the reading skills of an 8-year-old. An infantryman got 1s. 2d.

a day, but stoppages, especially for kit, always reduced this figure. Thankfully, pay could be supplemented, if a man was lucky, by extra duties such as being a cook, officer's servant, a tailor or a groom in the cavalry. The men in 1882 still came from the poorest classes. One recruiting officer in 1879 told a Royal commission that it was not wise for him to ask too many questions about the background or parentage of new soldiers since in London most 'would refer me to a common lodging-house'.

Life for the ordinary soldier revolved around the barrack-room. Each had white-washed walls, bare boards on the floor and some centre tables with forms for sitting. Plates and basins for each man were kept on a shelf hung over the tables. Iron bedsteads were arranged around the walls. Shelves and hooks running around the room allowed the men to hang their knapsacks and store kit and personal keepsakes. Sir William Robertson, who rose from a private to field-marshal, recalled those rooms in his memoirs:

> The brown blankets were seldom or ever washed; clean sheets were issued once a month; and clean straw for the mattresses once every three months … Tablecloths there were none, and plates and basins (paid for by the men) were the only crockery, the basin being used in turn as a coffee-cup, tea-cup, beer-mug, soup-plate, shaving-mug, and receptacle for pipe-clay with which to clean gloves and belts.[63]

Reveille was normally at 6am. The men paraded and ate breakfast at 8am, usually coffee with bread and butter, later in the morning the men drilled, orderly room punishments were meted out and after another parade, dinner was served at 1pm. This varied a little in regiments as some, such as the Royal Irish Rifles, became famous for good cooking and others did not. Basically a man got three-quarters of a pound of low-grade beef or mutton a day and a pound of bread with a small quantity of butter. Everything else, from potatoes to sugar, was provided by means of a compulsory stoppage of three pence a day from each man's pay. There was a mid-afternoon drill, tea at 4pm and then free time until 9.30pm when a roll call was made of each company, followed by guard duty or 'lights out' at 10.15pm. Cavalrymen had a tougher schedule since horses, saddler and stables required extra work. In peacetime the routine became monotonous. 'Idleness is the bane of the soldier', recalled an old sergeant in 1883, 'and the hardest foes to overcome are not always to be found on the field of battle'.[64]

There were hardships. It was not an easy life. Yet for many soldiers who had come into the army from the slums a barracks was more clean and comfortable, while the food, especially the excellent army bread, was regular, free and nourishing.

The ousting of the Liberals 'in a torrent of gin and beer', as Gladstone called it, also halted the reform process for six years and allowed the Army to come to terms with change. Cardwell was given a peerage but his health was permanently damaged by over-work. Wolseley during this period continued on his upward path. In 1874 he was sent to the Gold Coast of West Africa to subdue the powerful Ashanti tribe, his superbly conducted campaign not only achieved all its objectives but won him praise from ordinary folk back home who were thrilled at his exploits against blood-thirsty savages. The growth of a popular press and a new breed of man – the war correspondent – were to make Wolseley famous at last. He returned home to a sheaf of honours including a knighthood and promotion to the rank of major-general. One of his rewards was an audience with his Sovereign. She found Wolseley to be 'a very smart, active, wiry-looking man, full of energy and calm and decided-looking'.[65] He thought Victoria was 'gracious and sympathetic', and he told her 'all sorts of amusing things about the Gold Coast that made her laugh'.[66]

The Colonial Office now requested Sir Garnet's services and he was sent to South Africa in 1875 as Governor of Natal. It was not a job he liked, but set to work anyway overhauling the colony's administration. Four years later he was appointed the first High Commissioner in newly-acquired Cyprus, and barely twelve months later was back in South Africa again to take command after Major-General Lord Chelmsford's forces had been decimated at Isandlwana. Chelmsford managed to defeat the Zulus at Ulundi before Wolseley could supersede him. It simply left Sir Garnet to track down and capture the Zulu King and wage a small local war against the tiny bapedi tribe who were troubling Natal. The general not only predicted the date he would take tea in Chief Sekukuni's hut, but did it after a night march and a fiercely fought battle at dawn.

In 1880, with the Liberals returned to power, reform began anew. It was soon clear that a battle was about to break out between Childers, who objected to the way that Cambridge 'went chattering about the place, refused to behave as a subordinate, and wrote direct to the Queen'[67] and Wolseley, the new QMG, who told his brother, 'I cannot pull with the Duke and we shall have continued rows and he will hate me more than before if indeed that be possible',[68] and HRH who found the new Secretary of State to be 'full of new projects … most prejudicial to the Army and extremely distasteful to myself',[69] while Sir Garnet wrote articles for the radical Press, 'damn his eyes …'

A severe attack of gout did nothing to improve Prince George's temper and in July 1881 he even tried to resign when Childers censured him over the death of some soldiers at a hot Aldershot review. At the same time Cambridge had a few victories. He was able to block Wolseley's bid to become the next Commander-in-Chief, India, along with his plans for a general staff along European lines. It was galling for Sir Garnet to see his career and beliefs dashed by a man 'who knows as much of modern warfare – or indeed of any warfare, as my top boot does'.[70] In the face of stiff opposition from reactionary officers, whom Wolseley called 'Wellington's men', Childers pushed ahead with a reform programme, most controversially the territorial reorganization of regiments including the job of renaming them. according to Lehmann:

> The introduction of the territorial system produced more friction and hard feel-ings than any other major single reform introduced into the British army. To be linked with another battalion, as Cardwell conceived it, was bad enough, but to be permanently wedded with a subsequent loss of historic numbers, traditions and exclusive battle honours won with blood was an intolerable innovation to most soldiers. Even the treasured regimental facings were to be obliterated.[71]

Now Childers began marrying single battalion regiments to one another. It was an amalgamation that worked well in some cases and took decades of acceptance in others. The 43rd and 52nd Regiments, for instance, bonded together as the Oxfordshire and Buckinghamshire Light Infantry, soon known to all as 'the Ox and Bucks', yet even when new identities had been forged one old officer of the 52nd spoke for many when he said, years later, 'I strop my razor fifty-two times and when I come to forty-three I spit.'[72] In the Egyptian War one of the last regiments to arrive for service was the old 63rd Foot or West Suffolk Regiment. It had become, in one of the least successful amalgamations, the 1st Battalion of the Manchester Regiment. 'It would be untrue to pretend that we were pleased at losing our old title', wrote an officer, 'our Lincoln green facings, and our silver fleur-de-lys badge. We had never been to Egypt, and had no interest whatever in our new badge, the Sphinx, and we generally felt aggrieved at the loss of our identity.'[73]

When, in the Spring of 1882, the post of Adjutant-General, second only in the Army to that of Commander-in-Chief, was due to become vacant Childers made it plain that he wanted Wolseley to get the job. Cambridge was aghast and the Queen supported her cousin. Indeed, it was whispered that the Royal Family would have liked to burn him at the stake. When, after he took up the Adjutant-Generalship in April, the Duke found Wolseley, who turned on his charm, to be 'hard-working … decidedly clear-headed and an able administra-tor', tempers at last began to cool.[74]

Such was the state of affairs at the War Office when Wolseley issued his memorandum on 3 July 1882. Next day secret instructions were sent to commanding officers of regiments of cavalry, battalions of infantry and batteries of artillery that might be sent to Egypt. Embarkation details and the numbers of men expected to go on foreign service were included. Many of these arrangements could be done, rather conveniently, under the guise of the forthcoming Army manoeuvres, that were now cancelled. Over the next six days countless committees met, vital details like the number of mules required, the formation of a railway construction company of Engineers, a postal corps, water supply and the regulation of war correspondents, all had to be thrashed out. Wolseley, whose forte was detail, the man the popular press called 'our only general', lived up to a term that had lately been coined. People in the streets were saying that when a job was well done it was 'All Sir Garnet!'

In the days preceding the bombardment, and while HM Govt dithered, the Admiralty refused to consider that a land operation was on the cards. It was with reluctance on 2 July, after pressure from Childers and Wolseley, that Northbrook agreed to the despatch of Sir Archibald Alison to take command of an advance force drawn from the garrisons of Cyprus and Malta. These rapid deployment troops were to 'be ready to seize the Suez Canal twenty-four hours after receiving orders for action.'[75] Four days later Alison set off for Egypt via Cyprus.

At Simla on 6 July, white-haired Sir Donald Stewart, Commander-in-Chief, India, was officially told to furnish a brigade 'for the protection of the Canal from Suez to Ismailia'. The composition of this force had largely been decided at the India Office, but Stewart recommended not sending any Sikhs or Gurkhas because there was no telling when they might be needed at home: 'The Egyptian people are doing their best too to create ill feeling all over the East against the English and this being so we think it desirable to keep our best troops in India.'[76]

In Whitehall the bombardment was met with excitement at the Foreign Office and the Admiralty where Hartington, Northbrook and their fellow hawks gathered to hear the latest news. The Prime Minister was so immersed in his Irish Arrears Bill on 11 July that Hartington complained to Granville that he could not get Gladstone to show any interest whatsoever in Egyptian affairs. By now the Foreign Secretary had decided that troops would have to be sent to settle an 'intolerable' situation. In fact 'Puss' was getting quite bullish and told a colleague next day that it 'is well for a country whose strength is maritime, that naval demonstrations should not be thought to be absolutely without a sting'.[77] He told the Queen a bombardment might settle matters. On 13 July he asked the French to join in further action if Turkey declined. To his delight this brought forth a positive response from Freycinet who called for 'prompt action' if Abdul Hamid procrastinated.

In Constantinople the Ottoman ruler had watched events with misgivings. A complaint was made to HM Govt about the landing of Royal Marines and the 'agitation' it would cause in Egypt. Now Lord Granville rather disingenuously called the bombardment 'an act of self-defence', and declared the destruction of Alexandria was 'the deliberate work of the military party under Arabi Pasha'. The troops, he added, 'had no view of permanent occupation' and were there merely 'as police'.[78]

It was soldiers in the guise of police, and what would follow when General Alison's troops arrived, that precipitated matters in the Cabinet. The Prime Minister, perhaps remembering that exactly five years earlier he had predicted: 'Our first site in Egypt, be it by larceny or be it by emption, will be the almost certain egg of a North African Empire that will grow and grow', refused to budge from his position that Britain was not at war.[79] He would be pushed to a naval 'police action' with France to protect the Suez Canal and no further. Hartington, ever at the fore, demanded on 18 July that: 'We should act with anyone who will act with us; and if need be alone.'[80] It was a view widely supported by the whole Cabinet with the sole exception of John Bright, one of Gladstone's oldest political friends, who resigned.

Arabi meanwhile wrote to Gladstone via Blunt. He did not mince his words:

I repeat again and again that the first blow struck at Egypt by England or her allies will cause blood to flow throughout the breadth of Asia and of Africa. England may rest assured that we are determined to fight, to die martyrs for our country, as has been enjoined on us by our Prophet; or else to conquer, and so live independently.[81]

An exasperated Childers, keenly aware as each day passed, that the military juggernaut had a momentum of its own, wrote to Granville on 19 July demanding some decisions. The Foreign Secretary, could dawdle no longer. He had that same day got a telegram from the Khedive also demanding answers and warning HM Govt to 'take further action without delay' before his entourage left him.[82] At a heated Cabinet session next day it was finally agreed to send Lieutenant-General Sir Garnet Wolseley GCB, with Lieutenant-General Sir John Adye as his chief-of-staff, and an army to Cyprus where 'they will be available for operations in any part of Egypt'. Even the Duke of Cambridge, who was warming slightly to Sir Garnet, admitted to the Queen that he 'was decidedly as able a man for the field as we have got'.[83]

In the House of Commons on 24 July the Liberal Government asked for £2,300,000 to pay for Wolseley's expedition. The cost would be met by raising income tax to three half-pence in the pound. Gladstone, wily as ever, made a masterly speech which flew in the face of much that he knew to be true. An invasion, he argued, was required not to preserve the security of the Suez Canal, but to settle the root cause of Egypt's malaise. 'The seat of the disease is in the interior of Egypt,' he bellowed.[84] It was left to Dilke, Hartington, Chamberlain and other ministers to emphasize that 82 per cent of British trade passed through the Canal and it was the main highway of the Empire.

The motion passed by 275 votes to 19 votes. On the same day, 27 July, Gladstone wrote to the Queen that 'the entire House, with infinitesimal exception, recognises the necessity and justice of the steps now about to be taken'.[85] It had been 75 years since Major-General Fraser's ill-fated expedition landed there, but Britain was about to embark one of the largest armies in its history to crush Arabi Pasha on Egyptian sands.

# 5

# Kafr Dawar

*If harm shall come to my family I will kill Sir Beauchamp Seymour*
Charles Pomeroy Stone

By the eighth day after the bombardment, order of a kind was returning to
Alexandria. Fires still burned in places but they were fast dwindling. The smells
of death and destroyed buildings hung in the air like some dreadful miasma.
The finest homes in the city were now burnt-out shells, their blackened brick
walls and gutted dark interiors spreading, like a loathsome ink blot down a
page, to the water's edge at the marina.

On 17 July Mr Peter Towrest of the Customs Service and a team of 129 men
began pulling down dangerous walls and clearing blocked streets. Much of
this work was done using explosives. Next day a corps of Arab policemen
was formed and on the 20th the job of burying the bodies started. Beresford
thought he had the city pretty ship-shape:

> I had a clear thoroughfare through every street in the town by Monday (24th)
> and all debris from fallen houses piled up on each side and all dangerous walls
> pulled down. These things were generally done by organising large working-par-
> ties of from 100 to 200 hired Arabs. At first collected them at the point of the
> bayonet, and made them work, but I paid them a good wage every evening, and
> the bayonets were unnecessary after the first day, when they found that England
> would pay well.[1]

With his customary energy Beresford collected all the fire-engines he could
find, bought some, requisitioned others and had a bluejacket fire brigade.
'Regular London Fireman Steam Engines we had', seaman Charles Hickman
of *Invincible* wrote in his diary, 'we carried our cutlasses and rifles wherever
we went. Very hot. Houses falling ...' He thought it comical that the fire
station was an abandoned theatre, as 'we are very theatrical you bet'.[2] An Arab
'road brigade' cleared the rubble, while a sanitary committee took charge of

burying the bodies, refuse and remains of loot. Patrolling the streets was now left entirely to British soldiers and marines.

Lord Charles was most proud of the Egyptian courts he set up to try looters. He did his best to make the witness statements impartial, using shorthand writers placed behind separate screens, so there could be no collusion. A guilty verdict meant the death penalty for an offender but, Beresford wrote later, that he tried to get 'the clearest and most uncompromising evidence'.[3]

Installed in a suite at the Ras-el-Tin Palace, 'very cool and pleasant. But its a mass of fleas and dirt', Captain Jacky Fisher was just starting to enjoy life. He confessed that his men had been 'regularly done up when the General (Sir A. Alison) arrived with his troops … I now have command of the city, and the sea-forts of Alexandria, and have also charge of the Khedive and am responsible for his safety.' The admiral had been 'most wonderfully kind to me', and Fisher feared that colleagues would be envious of 'the junior Captain being given the best berth of all; but I must endeavour to deserve his partiality.'[4]

While Fisher enjoyed the splendours of the palace, tough Captain Wilson of *Hecla* had his 'hands full of work' spiking and disabling all the guns in the forts and destroying ammunition. He was annoyed that orders prevented him from blowing up the 'enormous' ammunition dump at the arsenal, 'and I have to carry it half a mile and throw it into the sea'. Wilson made one discovery that suggested the British fleet had been very lucky: 'Yesterday I came across an enormous store of torpedoes which fortunately for us they did not use. Probably they did not know how.' About five miles eastward along the sandy coast from Alexandria lay the sleepy little resort of Ramleh. The railway line and Mahmoudieh Canal followed the shoreline about a mile inland, but just before Ramleh both curved sharply inland towards Cairo. Three miles further in that direction, where the rail track and canal ran side by side through marshland, with shallow Lake Maretois on the western side and rapidly dwindling Lake Abourkir on the other, the Egyptians had constructed defensive positions at a spot called Kafr-Dawar.

Their main defence was an earthwork running 200 yards between the canal and the railway line. It had 18 gun embrasures with eight Krupp guns and one very large one big enough for a monster 15cm gun. A small fort had been built, obviously with the intention of continuing the earthwork, some 400 yards into swampy Lake Mareotis, so that it could flank the main approach. Across the Mahmoudieh Canal the Egyptians had built a massive dam, 120 feet broad at the waterline, with embrasures for three more field guns. In front of the main defensive position, facing the British, were a series of shelter trenches at 200 yard intervals, while a natural hill protected the Egyptian supply lines to the rear.

Rumours suggested that Arabi quickly assembled 30,000 troops at Kafr-Dawar, but the figure seems exaggerated, and a lower estimate by one observer of 15,000 Egyptians by the start of August seems more likely. His defences were nevertheless formidable. A British officer inspecting them later commented, 'Nothing could have been better done.' The lines had been made of mud and chopped straw in traditional fashion, but were extraordinarily tough, and able to withstand heavy artillery fire. The Egyptian right and left flanks were shielded by the two lakes, the ground in front was low and afforded no protection to an enemy, the boggy stretches of water were too shallow for an attacking gunboat or steam launch, while command of the railway line enabled Arabi to bring up fresh supplies, including guns, men and horses, to his rear.

Tewfik and Arabi who, little more than a week before had been on the same side, now fell into personal recriminations as their respective positions hardened. On 17 July the Khedive told his general by telegram that England was not at war with Egypt, the bombardment had been 'a counter-measure in reply to the construction of defences',[5] and that Admiral Seymour was willing to hand over Alexandria to Ottoman troops.[5] He asked Arabi to attend him immediately at the Ras-el-Tin Palace for fresh orders. Ahmed Arabi was not foolish enough to walk into the lion's den. In reply he reminded Tewfik that the two of them had agreed just a week earlier to oppose the British, even if it meant war. While an enemy fleet sat in the harbour at Alexandria, the Egyptian Army would continue to prepare for war and while enemy troops occupied the city he would not visit the Khedive. Cheekily, Arabi suggested to Tewfik that he was willing to meet with any deputation from the ruler that cared to visit him at Kafr-Dawar.

From mosques throughout the land imans called for holy war. 'Truly Allah has attained a Believer's life and possessions so that he may attain Paradise fighting for Allah's religion' (Koran IX: 111) and 'Inflame, O Prophet, the Believers for battle' (Koran VIII:65) were favourite texts.[6] Arabi Pasha had ordered all officials to safeguard the lives of foreigners, but with passions inflamed it was inevitable that outrages would occur. One of the grisliest incidents was at Galioub where a family were taken off a train, tied to the rails and crushed by the engine. General Arabi stamped out the riots swiftly; local officials were dismissed in some cases and transport made available to bring foreign civilians to the coast.

Stone Pasha, fearing for the safety of his family still stuck in Cairo, went to see Admiral Nicholson on the USS *Lancaster* in a vain hope that a rescue be attempted through Egyptian lines, but according to Charles Chaille-Long who was present, the meeting went off badly. The Admiral, he wrote, was 'cold, cynical and unsympathetic, and, indeed, criticized the General severely for having trusted Arabi'. Stone did not disguise his contempt for the British and an admiral whose actions had marooned his wife and daughters in a dangerous city. In front of a group of bystanders the American said loudly: 'If harm shall come to my family, I will kill Sir Beauchamp Seymour.'[7]

General Stone had bid farewell to his wife and daughters in Cairo on 6 July, warning them of his conviction that Seymour would find a pretext to attack Alexandria. Two days later, on the eve of the bombardment, Fanny Stone, his teenage daughter, noted in her diary that Egyptian women were going through the streets wailing and covering their heads in dust. Confusion reigned the next day as the Stones tried desperately to find out if the general was safe, or if they should try and leave Cairo. 'The panic is simply frightful,' wrote Fanny, 'and every hour that we remain increases the danger of trying to escape.'[8]

On 13 July the general's wife, who seems to have been about as strong-willed as her husband, gathered the girls together and lectured them: 'Now I want you to promise me to be patient, to be cheerful, and always brave. Go on with your studies, keep always busy, and trust me to save you, if it is possible, when the worst comes. We have firearms enough in the house to defend ourselves.' Mrs Stone stayed firm in her resolve that she would not move without news from the general. Six of his Egyptian aides came to offer their services and protection. It did not seem to matter to them that the family were Americans. They declared 'Stone Pasha is the Father of the Staff; we will protect you with our lives.'[9]

A few days later the servants started to show disrespect by calling the American women 'dogs of Christians' behind their backs. The redoubtable lady of the house gathered them all together and lambasted them: 'There never lived the Arab who could frighten me. No, not Arabi and all his troops can do it. Go back to your work, you miserable cowards, and the first time you *look* insolent I will have you thrashed.'

On the morning of 18 July, Fanny walked to a little English chapel chaperoned by two of the orderlies. She was astonished when they followed her inside and began to pray. How was it possible, she asked, for devout Muslims to say prayers in a Christian church? 'Why not, my lady?', answered one of them, 'We Muslims can pray anywhere. Do not we all pray to the same good God? Jesus Christ belongs more to us than He does to you. You call him the Son of God, which He was not. He was a great Prophet, and we love and respect Him. We love his blessed mother, too, the Sitta Miriam.'[10] Fanny went off to borrow some books from the church library and when she returned the two Egyptians were examining, with much curiosity, the organ. Happily she told them how it made sacred music. The orderlies begged her to play and so, across Cairo that afternoon the babble of shopkeepers selling spices and sherbet, oranges and dates, blended in the torpid air with the mournful strains of 'Nearer My God To Thee'.

Each day seemed to bring fresh troubles for Mrs Stone and her girls. The servants got so insolent that it was necessary to discharge them, while every night children gathered at the gates of their villa to shout, 'Long Live Arabi!' and 'Death To Christians!' When on 23 July, Mrs Stone realised the family had barely enough cash for one more week's expenses she decided to send Arabi Pasha a letter demanding her husband's July pay. The coterie of aides all thought she was crazy. 'Madam, you will not get a centime. How could you do such an impudent thing?' One of them told her. 'I shall get it,' she replied, 'but I may have to go to Kafr-Dawar before I succeed.' The officer was impressed. 'If all American women are like you,' he replied, 'I would not like to go to war with your men.'

On 25 July, a message at last got through from the general telling his family that he and Fanny's brother were safe. The day was made ever better by the surprise arrival of a letter from Ahmed Arabi himself enclosing £50 of the general's salary. But the situation in Cairo remained extremely volatile. Plucky Mrs Stone, encouraged by her financial success, decided to petition Arabi for permission to join her husband. He agreed, and so on 5 August, the Americans were allowed to leave the capital by a special train for Port Said and four days later the whole family were reunited. 'Oh, what joy to be safe and all together again', wrote Fanny in her diary. Home was now 'an exquisite little palace' at Alexandria that had been partly spared by the rioters. It still had 'enough furniture … to make us very comfortable' and, to Fanny's joy, 'it was very pleasant, on entering this refuge, to pass under the shield of the United States, which is beautifully painted over the doorway.'[11]

The 5th August also saw the first serious engagement between the British and Egyptian Armies. It had been a hectic nineteen days since General Alison had landed, with a very confused start, but order gradually emerged from what seemed chaos. Much of the credit was due to Alison himself who, along with his commanding Royal Engineer, Lieutenant-Colonel John Ardagh, represented two of the sharpest brains in the British Army. The general was universally respected. The men liked the fact that he led from the front and shared their hardships, the officers knew he was cool and clever, even the Duke of Cambridge respected him, which was unusually high praise indeed. Commissioned into the 72nd Foot in 1846, the son of a famous Scottish historian, he had fought bravely in the Crimea, especially before Sebastopol and the attack on the Redan. Here he got noticed by the commander of the Highland Brigade, Major-General Sir Colin Campbell. During the 2nd Relief of Lucknow a cannon ball took away Alison's arm and knocked him off his horse and it took him four years to recover. In 1874 he was selected by the Duke of Cambridge to lead the European brigade in the Ashanti expedition. This did not sit well with Garnet Wolseley who was furious at first, declaring: 'I don't care much for him and I don't think he is the man I want.' He changed his mind when the one-armed Scot proved to be a tough commander under fire. The pair became good friends and Alison came home to a knighthood and promotion; in 1878 he had taken over command of the Intelligence Department at the War Office. He was thus the perfect man to send to Egypt as he knew more about the military situation there than anyone, (not excepting Garnet Wolseley himself), a discreet, shrewd and smart old officer.

Equally bright and cool, with two years more service than Alison in intelligence was John Ardagh. With a long, lugubrious face, hair neatly parted in the middle of his scalp and a large nose, the 41-year-old Irishman was respected for his intelligence, but considered 'something of a mystery' by his colleagues. A workaholic, Ardagh's only hobbies were painting watercolours and, for real relaxation, solving arcane mathematical problems. A decade later Lord Gleichen would work under him at the War Office and recall Ardagh as 'silent, monocle, skinny-necked (he always reminded me of a marabou-stork, I fear), the writer of beautifully-expressed far-seeing memoranda on the most abstruse questions.'[12]

Alison's expedition had got off to a dreadful start. He left London under the assumption that he might have to take charge of the Suez Canal in concert with any attack on Alexandria. Landing at Cyprus on 12 July he found the ironclads and troops all ready but no fresh orders and the uncomfortable news that Seymour had launched a bombardment. An officer on the general's staff concluded that HM Govt 'were, as a matter of economy, employing the Ottoman telegraph line, as being a few pence cheaper than the deep-sea one, and that the Turks were purposely delaying our messages, whilst their experts hammered away endeavouring to decipher them.'[13] There also seems to have been a misunderstanding between the Army and Navy. Alison expected to be under the orders of Seymour but this information had not been conveyed to the admiral. Exasperated, the general decided to press on to Port Said, regardless of fresh orders. Here two surprises awaited him. Despite the fighting that had gone on at Alexandria an Egyptian military band was lined up to meet him at the quayside and its perspiring musicians burst into an ill-tuned discord as he stepped ashore, a fresh order from London told him to return immediately to Cyprus while HM Govt decided if troops should really land in Egypt at all. Alison now demonstrated his clear-headedness. He told his staff that if they had to turn back it was not inappropriate to do this *via* Alexandria. Going at full steam they got there the next morning.

Fresh orders now forbade the disembarkation of troops except for policing purposes. By telegram to the War Office the general pointed out that, in fact, the men were landed and 'events were allowed to take their course'. Headquarters were made opposite the railway station in a house 'so hastily abandoned', wrote a staff officer, 'that all sorts of toilette requisites and boxes of bon-bons were still on the tables'.[14] The next morning, Alison and Ardagh made a careful inspection of the city's defences and decided that gaps in the walls and several of the gates needed urgent repair. Three days later it was seen that the enemy were allowing salt water from Lake Mareotis into the Mahmoudieh Canal. Conservation of fresh drinking water was vital and Ardagh used civilians to help where possible with a commission headed by Seymour and including the redoubtable water-works engineer, John Cornish, to oversee the city's supply.

The busiest soldiers were the 7th Company, Royal Engineers, under Captain Elliott Wood, an energetic 38-year-old excited to be on his first campaign. For the first few days the soldiers worked alongside parties of bluejackets whose energy and cheerfulness impressed everyone they met. Lieutenant William Pigott of *Inflexible*, along with one seaman, got somehow to the top of the Pharos lighthouse and relit the lamp. The building was badly damaged and the pair had to wait for help before they could descend. Fort Kom-el-Dyk, an old Martello tower, so dominated the Egyptian quarter that it was decided to put a couple of field guns on an upper platform. When Brevet Lieutenant-Colonel Montagu Gerard, late Bengal Staff Corps, hastily seconded to Alison's staff, tried to bully a naval officer to do the job he found that the sailors, 'goodness knows how', had already 'bundled the guns of something like three-quarters of a ton up the narrow corkscrew staircase'.[15]

Gerard had just returned to England from a trip to Persia and was paying a call on the Intelligence Department when circumstances found him offered a place on Alison's staff. Now he watched the bluejackets with some amusement, prove to be more than a match for any landlubbers. The air at times, he recalled in his memoirs, was thick with 'blankety-blank' expletives far more blue than anything commonly heard in the army. On one occasion two sailors saw an army officer approaching weighed down with field-glasses, water-bottle, cigar case, torch, sword and medals, all glinting brightly in the sun. 'Bill, who the hell is that?', asked one of them. 'Why, he is the new Colonel', replied his mate. 'Oh, new Colonel is he?' said the first bluejacket, 'Why, he only wants the candles to make him into a regular fucking Christmas tree!' On another occasion an Egyptian major and a Maltese interpreter were stopped by a sailor on duty at the city gates. 'But he is a Bimbashi,' protested the interpreter, referring to the Egyptian's rank, but the bluejacket was unimpressed, declaring bluntly, 'Well, I ain't no orders to pass no blooming bumbaskets through.'[16]

Less than a year previously the 60th Rifles (King's Royal Rifle Corps) had been fighting in the Transvaal under their no-nonsense old colonel, Cromer Ashburnham. It was the first campaign for a cheerful lieutenant, 21 years old, called Percival Marling. A classic 'young blood', getting thrown out of London clubs with his pals and hunting with the Berkeley appealed more to Percy than study, but when he learned he had muffed his Sandhurst entrance he swotted hard to put things right. Two years later he had fought through the rain at Ingogo Hill against the Boers, witnessed the burial of General Colley and seen men killed in action – maturing events indeed for a young man. The 60th landed on 18 July and marched to quarters at the railway station. 'The heat and flies were awful', noted Percy in his diary, but his soldier-servant managed to loot him several comforts including a large baking trough that made a first class bath.[17] Marling and his men arrested several Arabs caught looting over the next few days – one had 17 watches, 21 rings and bracelets on him.

On 24 July General Alison made a successful push to move his base to Ramleh. It seemed for a time that the Egyptians were going to contest this enemy advance, yet despite keeping up a hot fire for more than an hour they did not try to repulse them. On the same day the troopship Malabar arrived with the 46th Regiment (Duke of Cornwall's Light Infantry), a wing of the 35th and a battery of artillery, increasing Alison's little army by 1,108 officers and men. A young Aberdonian, Corporal John Philip, found his excitement at landing in exotic Egypt somewhat lessened by the 'miserable-looking streets' and 'dingy' houses near the waterfront. Philip was shocked by the devastation:

Here were standing the blackened walls of what once had been stately mansions ... Others again were intact so far as outward appearance went, but the streets or grounds in front of them were strewn with furniture, massive glasses, wardrobes, pianos, whole libraries of finely-bound books lay smashed, torn, trampled and utterly destroyed ... I heard several of my comrades remark, 'What a glorious chance of furnishing a house in elaborate and princely style, and all for nothing.'[18]

Ramleh now became the spot where Alison concentrated his troops. The 38th and 60th Regiments, along with the Royal Engineers, occupied a former Egyptian cavalry barracks. It was a 'pretty good' place, thought the easy-going Percival Marling, 'but full of mosquitoes and other objectionable insects and indescribably filthy ... They nearly pulled me out of bed.'[19]

Generally it was agreed that Ramleh and its gentle sea breezes was a delightful spot. It was not a town, or even a real village, but a summer resort created for the European residents of Alexandria. Here, amid the dunes, they had tried to recreate a quasi–Biaritz. Country villas were scattered about with high walls and exotic gardens. Since June they had been deserted by their owners and many had been looted. There were no roads and each house was reached by trudging through the ankle-deep soft sands. A tiny railway station, its fencing and ticket-office designed to resemble a small Swiss chalet, linked the resort with Alexandria. The British soldiers thus found Ramleh oddly exotic, like making war in a seaside spot on Orford Ness or Blakeney Point.

Control of Ramleh meant that Alison had effectively prevented any easy link between Arabi's troops at Kafr-Dawar and the 4,000 Egyptians who still occupied the string of forts around Abourkir Bay. The waterworks at Ramleh pumped fresh water from the Mahmoudieh Canal and it became, along with a nearby tower, the centre of a strongly-entrenched British position. Heavy guns were positioned on the high ground, musketry redoubts thrown up on the flanks, picquets positioned towards Abourkir and by the canal bank in the direction of Arabi's lines. This latter position was soon nicknamed 'Dead Horse Picket' by the men. Other defences guarded the road to Alexandria, the walls of a nearby deserted village were loopholed, and an electric light illuminated the approaches from Kafr-Dawar and Abourkir at night.

Lord Charles Beresford ceased to be provost-marshal at the end of July. One night, riding past Abbat's Hotel with his mounted Egyptians, a friend shouted out, 'There you go, Charlie, swaggering about with an escort at your heels.' Beresford cheerily replied, 'If you had hanged and flogged half as many men as I have, you'd be damned glad to have an escort also.'[20]

After Tel-el-Kebir one private soldier was accused of cowardice. At his court-martial the man was asked why, if he did not intend to fight, had he joined the army? 'Starvation' was his stark one word reply. Little wonder then that so many men, starving and overawed by the recruiting sergeant standing smartly proud and clean outside many a public house accepted the Queen's shilling. The army was not short of men but it had to send 16,416 troops, including staff officers, to Egypt, along with 5,487 horses. The plans called for three cavalry regiments and a complete Household Cavalry Regiment, ten infantry battalions, eight batteries of artillery and finally, Royal Engineers, Commissariat and Transport troops, military police, ordnance men, medical units, railway staff and telegraphists.

Constant daily meetings between the Admiralty and War Office experts were needed to facilitate the smooth transfer of such a mass of men, animals and supplies. Much of the credit was due to Sir William Mends, Director of Transports at the Admiralty, who had begun to hire troop transports on 12 July. Sailing began on 27 July, and was at its peak during the first two weeks of August, though some troops did not leave until 5 September. The busiest port was Southampton. In just three days from 7 August, some 21 per cent of all the soldiers and 36 per cent of all the horses departed from its docks. The pattern was repeated in the Mediterranean where the garrisons of Gibralter and Malta were denuded by 7,592 officers and men, a total of nine infantry battalions, to take part in the Egyptian operations.

The Indian Contingent was very much the baby of Lord Hartington at the India Office. He made it clear in the House of Commons on 31 July that, in view of Arabi's pretensions to be a Hero of Islam, it was important to show that Great Britain could trust her Muslim and Hindu soldiers who were not merely the garrison of India, but 'form part of the forces of the Crown and are able to support the policy of this country … in all cases in which the interests of India are concerned'.[21] There was a precedent for Hartington's decision in that Disraeli had brought Indian troops to Malta, with the intention of having them fight alongside Muslim Turks, during the Russo-Turkish Crisis of 1878. It is also clear that more than two decades after the great rising of 1857 the British were still nervous that Muslim fanatics, especially the Sufi Wahabi sect in the Punjab, might be inspired to jihad by the fate of co-religionists in Egypt. The inclusion of a mixed body of Indian troops was thus an imperial public relations exercise. Almost alone in objecting to an Indian Contingent was the Viceroy, Lord Ripon, who opposed the expedition on financial grounds, declaring it was a tax burden on the Indian peasant 'in which he is not directly interested'.[22]

Wolseley had a low opinion of most Indian soldiers ever since he had seen them under fire in the Mutiny. It is for this reason that he gave them a minor role in his campaign. Even Sir Donald Stewart admitted to his old friend, General Roberts, that the 'native troops will do capitally for Canal work, but it is hardly fair to put too great a strain on them'. There was a high level debate on whether troops from all three presidencies should be sent (Roberts favoured only troops from northern India, Stewart disagreed), and many of the best regiments were exhausted and under-strength after the lengthy Afghan War. Eventually it was agreed to send a mixed force of two British infantry battalions from India with three Bengal-Bombay infantry battalions, three regiments of Bengal cavalry and Madras sappers and miners (6,930 troops in total), under the command of Colonel Sir Herbert Macpherson VC (with the local rank of major-general). The son of a soldier, he had a reputation as a tough commander. He had fought in the night battle of Kooshab in the Persian War in 1856, won his Victoria Cross leading a charge at Lucknow during the Mutiny, and seen active service on both frontiers of India in campaigns against the Hazaris and Lushais. More recently, in Afghanistan, his 1st Brigade was credited with winning the 2nd Battle of Charasiah and breaking the enemy in a charge at the Battle of Kandahar.

Any final hopes that the French might participate in an expedition were dashed on 29 July when Freycinet's ministry was heavily defeated in a vote of credit. That same day the Italians, who had been hesitant, made plain they also would not send an army. In Britain the Foreign Secretary was now telling everyone that a war was necessary to protect the Suez Canal. The general about to lead the expedition was clearly told by his war minister that the Royal Navy would look after the Canal, while the Army's main task must be to 're-establish the power of the Khedive'.

To a large extent Wolseley was given a free hand in selecting his commanders and staff officers for the campaign. Problems arose because he had to accept generals chosen to command in the autumn manoevres (now cancelled). Here the difficulties lay with the two divisional generals foisted on him – Sir Edward Hamley and George Willis. The pair had not seen active service since the Crimean War nearly 30 years earlier. Hamley, at least, had an excellent reputation as a teacher at the Staff College and was the author of a military textbook that was something of a classic. Now the desk theorist and lecturer might get a chance to show his mettle in the field. Willis was one of Cambridge's old school to whom good manners and quiet understatement in all things were part of the breeding necessary to be an officer.

Wolseley was notorious for surrounding himself with, in his view, the best men for the job. The Egyptian War was to be his most perfect application of this rule. It applied also to the rank and file as well as his famous 'Ring' of officers. Edward Spiers, author of several books on the late Victorian Army has noted that Sir Garnet favoured, even in the ranks, 'the formation of an elite corps, drawing upon volunteers and strong companies from the home-based battalions and when Parliament called out the Reserve, upon unmarried reservist.'[23]

It was the general's selection of a band of personal favourites among his officers, particularly those on staff duties, which infuriated his critics. It had become apparent during the Ashanti War, where many of the special service officers had also been with him on the Red River Expedition four years earlier, that he nurtured his favourites like exotic blooms in a greenhouse. In Natal, Cyprus and Zululand this 'Ashanti Club', as the Duke of Cambridge sneeringly called it, had developed into a circle of men whose careers and progressive views, championed by their chief, were starting to be noticed throughout the Army. But Wolseley was very selective in admitting officers in to his Ring. 'Each man was studied, polished and fitted like a precious stone', wrote Lehmann, 'he carefully distinguished between fighting leaders and regular staff officers. Each had his speciality.'[24] The power of the Ring was greater than the sum of its parts. Every member succumbed to Sir Garnet's subtle charm, his enthusiasm and praise for a job well done and, above all, the confidence he exuded. Because Wolseley believed in himself, he believed in each man he appointed and they, in turn, felt ready for any task 'the Chief' gave them to do.

Since its formation the 'Garnet Ring' had lost men killed in action, like Colley, while others such as George Greaves, were serving in distant parts of the Empire. One major figure, Henry Brackenbury, wanted so desperately to join the expedition that it cost him his job as intelligence chief in Ireland, but all to no avail. Most of the regulars were luckier: junior staff appointments went to William Butler, an outspoken and perceptive Irishman who usually had a good word to say for the underdog, and Frederick Maurice, a brilliant but absent-minded academic (the former had been with Wolseley since Red River, the latter joined in Ashanti). Fresh from the Transvaal War but with their careers far from enhanced came the notoriously egotistical, unbelievably clumsy Evelyn Wood, and 'arrogant, blimpish' Owen Lanyon, 'goggle-eyed with a monocle, a dropping moustache and hair plastered on his domed head'.[25] Wood was chosen by his old chief to be base commander at Alexandria with the clear intention that this dull posting would take him down a notch or two. Lanyon had been a poor administrator in the Transvaal and now hoped to redeem himself under Wolseley's guidance in Egypt.

The Cavalry Division was peppered with Wolselyites. The commander, Drury Drury-Lowe, had led the 17th Lancers in the Zulu War to universal praise. As its quartermaster-general was Sir Garnet's top protégé, Herbert Stewart, 3rd Dragoon Guards. He had made friends with him in the Sekkukuni Campaign, fought bravely at Majuba in 1881 and been a Boer prisoner for a time. The 1st (British) Cavalry Brigade also included two of the general's favourite fighting soldiers – Baker Russell in command and Hugh McCalmont as his brigade-major. The former, with his immense, stentorian-voice, had been with Wolseley in Ashanti, while the latter, a none-too-bright but courageous warrior, had served the general ever since he hitched passage to Canada and turned up in the camp of the Red River Expedition.

The Wolseley Ring was always ready for new faces to replace those officers who died or got posted overseas. John Adye, son of the general who was now Wolseley's chief-of-staff, was soon to become a junior member, along with Neville Lyttelton, one of Adye Snr's aides (and a relative of Mr Gladstone). Burly, no-nonsense Redvers Buller VC, a friend of Sir Garnet's since Red River days, would rush from his honeymoon in August to take charge of the intelligence department. Also remembered from the Riel Rebellion was another Victoria Cross recipient, Sir John McNeill, who had been second-in-command during the Ashanti War. Command of the 2nd Brigade of the 1st Infantry Division had been reserved by Wolseley for one of his oldest friends: tall and handsome Gerald Graham was another Victoria Cross holder, won leading a ladder party right up to a cannon's mouth in the Crimean War and was, in his estimation, 'the bravest man I ever knew'.[26]

Buller and Wood had both distinguished themselves in the Zulu War. That hard-fought campaign had also seen active service for several of the officers now en route to Egypt: Henry Hallam-Parr had slept on the grisly battlefield of Isandlwana on the night of the massacre surrounded by the mutilated bodies of his friends; Francis Grenfell, a staff officer, was there the next day; William Molyneux and Richard Harrison got caught up in events after the death of the Prince Imperial; Fitzroy Hart, a fighting Irishman, had been with General Pearson's column at Ekowe.

Besides his divisional generals Wolseley's chief annoyance was the way in which the Duke of Cambridge gave command of the Guards Brigade in Willis's 1st Division to the Queen's army-minded son, Prince Arthur, Duke of Connaught and Strathearn. Thankfully, when the Prince of Wales wrote to Wolseley suggesting that he too should come along the idea was flatly vetoed by Her Majesty. For Victoria it was enough to lose Arthur, her favourite boy. 'When I read that my darling precious Arthur is really to go, I quite broke down,' the Queen confided in her Journal, 'It was like a dreadful dream … Still, I would not on any account have him shirk his duty.'[27] Wolseley was well aware of the drama, recriminations and tears that followed the death of Prince Louis Napoleon in Zululand. Bad enough to be saddled with a French Royal but even worse to be stuck with a British one. Now, he had to give a senior command to the Queen's beloved son and yet, somehow, protect him from Egyptian bayonets and bullets.

There were other Royal vexations. Cambridge begged that his playboy son George should go in some capacity. Wolseley, who really had no option, gave him a position as one of his private secretaries. The Duke was delighted. To cap it all Sir Garnet was lumbered with the Duke of Teck, a middle-aged complaining type who was married to Cambridge's hefty sister, Mary. Sir Garnet tried to be polite to all these Royal millstones but, in his letters to his wife, as well as his diary and journal, it would be the bumbling Teck who would be the butt of his sharpest sarcasm.

The regiments, officers and men now prepared to depart. Feelings in the country ran high as a huge wave of patriotic fervour swept over the nation. It was jingoism unadorned, unpretentious and unashamed. One young officer of the late Victorian Army described in his memoirs how 'We learnt to believe that the English were the salt of the earth, and England the first and only country in the world. Thus England became the real and true love of our lives.'[28] Confidence in the Nation's power and impossibility in defeat were as certain to soldiers and civilians alike as night follows day.

Emotional scenes were played out on all the quaysides as the troops set off for Egypt. The Scots Guards, for instance, paraded at 7am on Sunday 29 July while the united bands of the Brigade of Guards played regimental marches. Colonel Knox read a letter from the Queen wishing them every success. The men then reformed into column, the order: 'Battalion, fourth right, quick march' rang out and the 1st Battalion, Scots Guards marched briskly out of Wellington Barracks. Twenty-six-year-old Corporal Henry Porter was astonished to see well-wishers crowded all along the Embankment and Westminster Bridge as the regiment in three steamers proceeded down the Thames. The band on deck played merry airs and when the concert ended with 'God Save The Queen', he said 'it sent a thrill of pride through me'.[29] When the Duke of Connaught came on board at the Docks she wept profusely and her husband was much effected. The Prince of Wales was there too to wish his brother God speed, along with Cambridge, Hartington and many old Scots Guards officers, all of them cheering as the vessels slipped down river towards Gravesend.

The Egyptian War was to be the last campaign in which Victoria's soldiers fought in their traditional scarlet uniforms. The Queen hated the idea of her troops wearing 'khakee' and two years later would tell her private secretary that it was 'hideous, and hopes she may never see it'.[30] In fact 30,000 suits of a grey serge cloth were sent to Egypt but did not arrive until the fighting ceased. The only soldiers, apart from the Indian Contingent, to wear khaki uniforms were the 87th Regiment (1st Battalion, Royal Irish Fusiliers).

Despite the Cardwell-Childers reforms many regiments, such as the Berkshires, fought in Egypt with their old regimental facings. Most infantry had the white Wolseley cork helmet with pagris and brass chin-chain but no spike on top. Exceptions were few but the Highland Light Infantry had a khaki helmet. En route to Africa the men were expected to dye their helmets, pouches and belts with tobacco-juice or tea to get a brown effect. The cavalry got blue goggles and blue veils to wrap around their helmets and let down when flies or the sun were a nuisance. The general effect, as Padre Male noted, was 'grotesque' and 'comical', in practice the goggles were found to be helpful and the veils useless. Mounted infantry wore their own regimental uniforms and the cavalry were dressed basically for home service with modifications. Male described the Life Guards uniform as 'looser and more serviceable ... Puttees, or cloth bindings, around the legs, in place of boots; a roomier tunic of blue, and no heavy steel cuirass; the white helmet plumeless.'[31] Some artillery officers and men had salmon breeches, but most wore traditional blue ones, and jackets of the same colour.

On his back each Tommy carried a waterproof canvas bag known as a 'valise' with straps to a waist belt with two pouches each containing 20 rounds of ammunition, and a ball bag slung below the right hand pouch with a further 30 rounds. Inside his valise each man had a cape for wearing in wet weather (or to wrap around him at night) and mess equipment. A new, longer bayonet, was slung on the left side of the waistbelt. Men complained that the bayonets got stuck between their legs when running and ammunition fell out of the pouches too easily when lying down. Rising from the ground meant a balancing act of fastening the pouch, pushing the bayonet out of the way, and preventing the helmet from falling off.

The soldiers were armed with the Martini-Henry Mark III rifle. Introduced in 1879 it was the most sophisticated weapon given thus far to British infantry, offering a smaller bore, greater range, lower trajectory and quick reloading. It weighed 9 pounds and fired a black powder .45 calibre centre-fire Boxer cartridge of slim rolled brass, with a 480 grains lead slug. Firing from 300 to 1,400 yards tended to be delivered in volleys, usually by section, because officers found it easier to control the rate of fire and prevent the men from wasting their ammunition. The Martini-Henry bullet was vicious, the slug flattening when it hit a victim, splintering bone lengthways. Soldiers complained that the rifle jammed, especially if grit got in the mechanism, and was difficult to keep clean. Its least popular characteristic was a kicking recoil that left the soldiers sore. Rapid firing also made the barrel too hot to touch and there was no safety catch.

Swords and bayonets were to prove very defective in Egypt. The Martini-Henry bayonet was easily bent, while the cavalry sword was castigated as 'too straight and too blunt, so that the enemy had to be out with the point'.[32]

The Field Artillery were equipped with 13 and 16-pounder guns, the Horse Artillery with 9 and 13-pounders and the siege train with 25 and 40-pounders. Much store was set by the new 13-pounder rifled muzzle-loading gun that used a slow-burning powder and thus allowed a longer barrel. In practice the gun's recoil was to make it very unpopular, in contrast to another new invention that was a great success – this was the 2.5in rifled muzzle-loading mountain artillery gun. Famous as the 'screw-gun', because it was made of two steel portions, it was to become a favourite weapon of British gunners for many years to come.

Officers during the campaign had some latitude in dress (but not at the start) as Padre Male explained:

Special regulations with regard to this were tolerably strict, and some who wished to follow their own ideas as to what would be suitable in shape and looseness for the rough knockabout of a desert campaign had to put their ideas in their pocket, and conform strictly to regulation. Scarlet blouses of a Norfolk jacket cut were de rigueur for the Headquarter Staff, together with brown leather gauntlets, and many other little specialities.[33]

Officers were allowed to choose their own make of swords and some carried the new 1880 Mark I pattern Enfield revolver, though favourites were the .45 Mark II Adams and Webley Royal Irish Constabulary models. Each officer had to carry a sword, revolver, 20-pound pouch, field-glasses or telescope, haversack and water bottle. Percival Marling said his haversack contained: 'a towel, soap, pair of socks, cap, flask of whisky, two days rations of biscuits, goggles, cigarette-case, pipe, tobacco, matches, notebook and pencil, two handkerchiefs, and a box of Cockle's pills.'[34] In special circumstances it was not unknown to be outfitted on arrival, such as the Guards Brigade officer who rushed to join his regiment and landed at Alexandria in a morning-coat and top hat.

While the troopships got under way, steamed across the Mediterranean and deposited their assortment of men, horses and equipment on the Alexandria quayside, General Alison was starting to use his troops to probe the Egyptian defences at Kafr-Dawar, with orders to 'Keep Arabi constantly alarmed'. Alison was wise enough to realize that whatever might be Wolseley's final plan it was vital to make Arabi Pasha believe that troops were being concentrated at Ramleh in preparation for an assault on Kafr-Dawar.

The most exciting event of the Ramleh garrison occurred during the last week of July when Jacky Fisher and Arthur Wilson invented an armoured train. It happened on 25 July when Alison asked the pair to test the possibility of an attack on the Egyptian lines via Lake Mareotis. 'No one knew whether there was depth of water enough in the lake or not,' Wilson told his wife in a letter, 'but I offered at once to prepare a raft to carry two Gatling-guns, and to go and see what could be done.'[35] The two naval officers mounted an additional pair of machine guns on the front of a train and set off down the line. Then, while Wilson and his pet dog waded into the lake, Fisher kept up a steady fire on the enemy. Unfortunately the lake turned out to be only ankle-deep. The armoured train, however, seemed such a good idea that its inventors set to work next day armour plating it. With a 16-pounder gun on the front, two 9-pounders at the rear, and a Gatling gun truck in the middle, it was the talk of the camp. General Alison was especially delighted, telling Fisher, 'No light cavalry can equal you for reconnaissance duty.'[36]

Jubilation filled the Egyptian camp when it became known that Admiral Seymour had been captured. Unfortunately all the excitement was misplaced since the British officer taken prisoner was not the burly commander but a young midshipman from *Alexandra* called Dudley de Chair. Travelling with secret despatches from Alexandria to Ramleh, he had got on the wrong rail line and found himself at a place called Mandara. Trying a short cut across the desert he was caught by the enemy, placed under escort and marched through the streets of Cairo, to the delight of crowds of natives and placed in a garden wing of the Abdin Palace. Fanny and Mrs Stone went to see him with a present of books on 2 August. To their surprise the young midshipman 'came forward smiling to meet us', wrote Fanny. Chair had been made prisoner in the quarters of the Khedive's eldest son, his blue naval uniform replaced by an elegant suit of white linen. 'Mama laughingly told him that he looked more like a young English prince at home than a prisoner of war, and he replied that he was called the "guest of Arabi Pasha", and that he had only to express a wish for anything except liberty, and it was gratified if possible.'[37]

At Ramleh during late July outpost duty seemed a dreary affair. Lieutenant Marling found things enlivened one night by some of the Naval Brigade who acquired a goat, tied it to their Gatling gun and tried to feed the animal with tinned milk, as one bluejacket explained, 'so as to 'ave fresh milk for breakfast tomorrow morning'. When the sailors were called away it was left to Marling's men at daybreak to discover it was a billygoat. 'So they ate him', he noted laconically in his diary.[38]

Bedouins attacked a detachment of the 38th on 31 July, so the following night Marling took a patrol two miles into the desert and waited for a chance to surprise the enemy. He was unlucky, but to his right rear some enemy cavalry launched a surprise raid. Four men of the 60th Rifles, caught up in the attack, panicked and ran all the way back to the Ramleh barracks. Here a furious Colonel Ashburnham, disgusted to have cowards in his ranks, threatened to shoot them.

HM Govt, obsessed with fears that the security of the Suez Canal was under threat, permitted Rear-Admiral Sir William Wrighte Hewett VC, Commander-in-Chief of the East Indies Squadron, to bring a portion of his fleet into the Red Sea. On 2 August Hewett landed 450 Royal Marines and occupied Suez on the pretext that it was in danger of falling to the Arabists. The operation went off smoothly but the Porte was not pleased to hear that the admiral had raised the British flag alongside an Egyptian one. 'We are acting in support of Viceroy against rebels', cabled a tetchy Admiralty, 'Do everything in his name, and make it plain that we have not taken possession for ourselves.' Next day Hewtt explained how 'on landing found no Egyptian colour flying. After explaining to Acting-Governor that the British were acting in the interest of, and with the full consent of the Viceroy, hoisted British and Egyptian colours side by side on the same mast, which has had the desired effect of greatly reassuring the people.'[39]

Captain Wilson had in the meantime been experimenting with an idea to mount a 40-pounder gun on the armoured train. 'I first arranged it so that I could hoist the gun out and fire it on the ground alongside the railway, but that took more than an half an hour,' he explained, 'and in case of a reverse there was every chance of being cut off.' He concluded that the big gun could be mounted on the truck itself and fired direct from the train. General Alison came out to watch the experiment and told him, 'It is sure to smash the truck all to pieces.' 'We fired two rounds and nothing happened', wrote Wilson to his wife, 'so he quite altered his opinion and went away delighted'.[40]

Next day, 5 August, Alison finally got to use his three infantry battalions, supported by the armoured train and marines, in a major reconnaissance towards Kafr-Dawar. Its purpose was to weaken and frighten the enemy who had been mounting increasing night attacks on the British outposts. Some of the rank and file were starting to get demoralised and the time seemed ripe to return the favour and put Arabi's troops on their guard. Locals had also reported to the British that Arabi was preparing to move his forces away from Kafr-Dawar.

It was late afternoon before Alison began his advance using four companies each of the South Staffordshires and Duke of Cornwall's Light Infantry on the left, or northern side, while Colonel Tuson brought seven companies of the Royal Marines, with the armoured train and Fisher's 200-strong Naval Brigade on the right, or southern side of the Mahmoudieh Canal. The general accompanied his troops in a second train full of marines that followed behind the armoured one. In support came six companies of the 60th Rifles with one large gun. Their colonel, Cromer Ashburnham, was elderly, hard-drinking, eccentric and damned proud of his regiment. Tough as old boots, he had been at Meerut on that terrible day when the great Indian Mutiny had started, slogged with his men on Roberts' famous march from Kabul to Kandahar, and been praised by General Colley just a year earlier for his bravery at Ingogo. Before setting off for Kafr-Dawar the colonel addressed the regiment: 'Men, we are only going for an afternoon's walk but we may fall in with Mr Araby and his friends, and if we do you will take all orders from me and your captains, and if you should fire, be sure and fire low.'[41] The men marched off, no doubt thinking over their colonel's words of wisdom. At the railway bridge crossing the Canal they moved over to the south side to assist the Royal Marines.

For the first two miles the British moved on without any trouble past small houses and gardens, over irrigation canals and ditches, until at last they came within range of the Egyptian artillery. Trudging along, Corporal Philip of the DOCLI listened to the whizz of the shells and the crash as they struck the ground. 'Very few of them exploded, which was fortunate for us,' he noted, as his mates fell grimly silent, apart from the occasional nervous laugh, as the enemy lines drew closer.[42] Major Fitzroy Hart, an officer with an almost foolhardy approach to warfare already demonstrated in a flagrant disregard for danger against Ashantis, Zulus and Boers, was marching with the Staffordshires and DOCLI when, at about 5.10pm, some Egyptian cavalry were spotted not far away in the garden of a house. A first British shell crashed into them and the horsemen instantly galloped away into the cover of some long grass and trees. 'Directly after bullets began to whizz overhead in great numbers', wrote Hart, 'and it was clear that the enemy's infantry were firing hard at us from the cover in front, and with very bad aim'.[43] Most of the Egyptian snipers were hidden in the tall reeds and palm trees on the south side of the Canal. The 6oth now hurried forward across a sandy plain and into the reeds to dislodge them. Meanwhile on the north side of the Canal the rest of the British infantry kept up a steady fire, though it meant shooting across the front of the advancing King's Royal Rifle Corps. Slowly the Egyptians started to sneak away until the movement became a general one. 'Fix swords – forward' shouted the officer of the leading company, 'The long wavy sword blades glittered in the sunshine, as they were instantly fixed on the muzzles of the short rifles', noted an observer, 'and our men dashed into the charge cheering loudly'.[44] Bugles soon blew as the enemy fled in disarray.

Corporal Philip was irritated, like many of his pals, by one skilled sniper who hid himself in the branches of a palm tree, 'and from this point of vantage he peppered away at us. Regularly his rifle flashed and the solitary bullet whistled amongst us with an annoying sound.' Philip thought the marksman, who was eventually killed, had been responsible for mortally wounding Lieutenant Henry Howard-Vyse of the Mounted Infantry. While bullets whizzed all around, Howard-Vyse's orderly, Private Frederick Corbett, refused to leave his side and cradled the dying young officer's head in his lap. Henry Hallam-Parr, who was in command of the Mounted Infantry, went to their assistance, but Corbett, a 6oth Rifles man, refused to leave saying, 'Please sir, let me stay. I was his servant ever so long.' Hallam-Parr told him to lie low, 'as the bullets were hitting all around us … and I found him there when I was ordered to retire'.[45] Corbett was duly recommended and awarded the Victoria Cross for his bravery. Hallam-Parr, who thought him 'a very nice little chap', subsequently made him his orderly. Possibly the ranker's past held a dark secret. He had enlisted under an assumed name (not that this was so uncommon in the Victorian Army), but just 17 months later he would be found guilty of theft and stripped of his award, the first (but not the last) man to lose the Victoria Cross in this way.

During all this time Captain Wilson kept his big gun firing from the armoured train. He found it 'rather nervous work'. The train was now a veritable fortress. It had, in addition to its forward 40-pounder, an ammunition wagon, a machine-gun truck with one Nordenfeldt and one Gatling, a torpedo truck, a field-gun truck with two 9-pounders and, at the rear, a further Gatling gun. Any weapon that could be directed on the Egyptians was blazing away.

In the twilight, with smoke swirling around the battlefield, things started to go wrong. Colonel De Wilton Thackwell of the 38th, an old soldier who had served in the Crimea and at the Siege of Lucknow, mistook the white house which was the objective of the attack on his side of the Canal for a similar looking but wrong building. Here he halted, but Alison had been aiming for a white house that stood at the Yehalla Junction of the two embankments. An advance to this point would have squeezed the Egyptians in a pincer movement. On their bank the Royal Marines advanced to the correct rendezvous point in a charge that sent the enemy fleeing in all directions. Many fellahin in their white uniforms were shot or drowned trying to cross the Canal.

By now some of the Naval Brigade were on the northern bank and amid the dust and smoke, mistook the Royal Marines on the opposite side of the Canal for blue uniformed Egyptian cavalry. Sailors had already laid a gun and were preparing to fire when Montagu Gerard, who had been staring hard through his binoculars, noticed the enemy were helmets and not fezes. 'For God's sake, hold hard', he cried, 'why those are the marines!' An unabashed sailor replied, 'well, if we can't have a shot at Araby, let's have one at the blooming marines.'[46]

The Egyptian artillery kept up a steady barrage on the armoured train. Luckily no one was seriously hurt. Captain Fisher was supervising the relaying of some track when he stood too close to the 40-pounder and 'was knocked down by the concussion and stunned for some time'.[47] The enemy also fired several rockets at the trucks in an attempt to set them alight. Sitting on a horse quietly making notes all the time was Alison. With him and ready for action is his first land battle in almost 20 years was Beauchamp Seymour, along with Hedworth Lambton, and young Midshipman Hardy who had done such fine work with his Nordenfeldt gun on *Invincible* during the bombardment.

When, at about 6.30pm, the Egyptians started to advance again for a short time, the South Staffordshires moved forward, with a naval 9-pounder and the armoured train in support. In quickly gathering darkness the Royal Marines were told to retire on their side of the Canal and the remainder of the British forces started to fall back on Ramleh. Egyptians in their thousands crowded onto the parapets of Kafr-Dawar to cheer and jeer and the 'infidel dogs'.

The British had lost one officer and three men killed and 27 wounded. Most of the losses had been in the Naval Brigade. It is difficult to be sure of Egyptian losses but they probably sustained about 200 casualties. The problem with such a reconnaissance and withdrawal is that it can all too easily seem like a retreat to the enemy. Egyptian morale was certainly boosted by the action at Kafr-Dawar. From their perspective, they had fought off a British attack, held their position, given the armoured train a very heavy shelling, tactically withdrawn in the face of a highly disciplined enemy, and then met them again in a counter-attack. The British had retired company by company in the face of that attack. Only the coming of darkness had prevented the action from lasting any longer. It was the first time Arabi's men had met the celebrated Tommies in anything resembling a battle and they felt well pleased with the result.

Five days later, 10 August, Sir John Adye arrived at Alexandria with the Duke of Connaught. Down the gang planks came the Brigade of Guards to the loud cheers of the foreign community and long, cold stares from the locals. Adye was able to tell Archibald Alison that the commander-in-chief was just hours away from reaching Egypt. The campaign proper was about to begin.

# 6

# Ismailia

*We were the victims of a rather superfluous practical joke*
William Molyneux

At sea Wolseley was pacing the deck of the *Calabria* and wishing himself on land. He had never wanted to take a long sea voyage but his doctors insisted it was necessary to improve his health. Along with the other major generals he had been entertained at Osborne by the Queen on 28 July. It had all gone off rather well but next day he felt 'very seedy with a fever and swollen face, must have slept in a draught in the train,' he wrote in his pocket diary, but within hours the illness developed into erysipelas.[1]

The original plan had been for the commander and his staff to use the fast overland route to Egypt via Brindisi, then by sea, stopping briefly at Cyprus to inspect the depots. Now, while his staff took the boat-train, he was quietly taken to the Albert Docks on 2 August, 'bundled up as if it were the middle of winter,' and put in a 'sumptuous' cabin.[2] Wolseley was pleased to be on board without attracting attention. Under doctor's orders he felt 'like a clown in a pantomime, my face being covered with white powder' to ease the reddish inflammation.[3] Confined to his cabin and watched over by Herbert Stewart, who insisted accompanying him, the general set sail with most of the officers, men and horses of the elite Household Cavalry. 'What a valuable cargo!' he joked in a letter to his wife.

Even on the first day of the campaign Sir Garnet was missing Louisa. Writing to 'my dearest sandpiper', he admitted that when thinking of her 'my eyes fill unpleasantly … You are such a plucky little woman far more so than I am a man.' Later, on the same day, he wrote again: 'I miss you already so much and I reproach myself with having been so often cross when you were so gentle and so kind – The doctor said I must not work my brain but I might read light literature. I prefer you to any sort of literature.' Next morning he was feeling better and wrote again to his wife that 'I slept soundly in my swing cot … Stewart is too stern: he won't even allow me to read the newspapers for more than a few minutes, and I leave to write this behind his back.' Five days later, off Gibralter, Wolseley could write, 'I am quite well. I write this on deck, having left my cabin for several days and my only dread is that I shall become like a stuffed pig, so great is my appetite and so freely does the doctor cram me with food.'[4]

The *Calabria* was an odd ship. Many of the Household Cavalry horses were quartered in wooden stalls on the upper deck with more below. The captain built Wolseley 'a charming little house' on deck where he was able to convalesce gazing out to sea, thinking of his 'little rumterfoozle', as he called Louisa, and adding touches to his carefully laid plans. The illness had given Sir Garnet an excuse not to have to get involved much with shipboard life and he found companionship with a white terrier that had followed the Life Guards on board, 'an ugly beast but very friendly and affectionate … I hope he may live through the campaign and to march through London at the head of his regiment!'[5]

The sea air and gentle motion of the ship as it ploughed into the warmer waters of the Mediterranean aided the general much in his physical recovery. His sharp brain was constantly running over the finer points of his simple but cleverly worked out plans. It would be a campaign of mainly logistics since there was no certainty the Egyptians would put up much of a fight. The chief ruse would be to lead the enemy into thinking the advance to Cairo would be from Alexandria while, in fact, transferring the base of operations to Ismailia. This scheme placed the British advance in a parallel line with a freshwater canal and a railway line that took a shorter route to the capital. A march up the Nile valley from Alexandria, especially if the Egyptians destroyed the railway, would require an army to traverse numerous irrigation ditches at a time of approaching high Nile waters. The Ismailia route, despite is advantages, was still a hazardous gamble requiring the seizure of a major neutral international waterway and defeating the enemy in the desert in a major battle. If the Egyptians would only stand and fight at Tel-el-Kebir a swift coup de grâce could be administered and the war would end quickly. This conjecture depended very much on ensuring that the various Egyptian garrisons stayed split up and that the Suez Canal be made safe and secure before the enemy could take control, block it or contaminate the freshwater supply of the Sweetwater Canal.

Stuck at sea Wolseley started to fret. He feared that his delay in getting to the front would have an 'injurious' effect on the campaign. 'Northbrook and the Navy', he told Louisa, 'will have been allowed to have their stupid will and to begin upon Ismailia before we are ready'.[6] Four days before leaving England he had heard a rumour – hotly denied – that Northbrook was proposing a move on Ismailia. Such deviation from his plans (and glory) terrified the general. Hastily he wrote to Childers:

> There are good grounds for believing that Arabi is under the impression that our operations upon Cairo will be from Alexandria; and it is very important that he should remain of that opinion. The day you occupy Ismailia you show your hand, and he will at once make every arrangement for meeting you upon the Ismailia–Cairo line. To take your enemy into your confidence is not a wise act.

Fears that an unforseen event might precipitate a hasty occupation of Ismailia continued to vex the general. When Sir John Adye at Alexandria heard that Arabi was moving troops towards Suez and Nefiche and strengthening Tel-el-Kebir he wired the news to Wolseley at Malta, adding that he would make no movement on the eastern side of the Nile Delta unless it was vital for the security of the Canal. His Chief hastily replied: 'Do not move troops to Canal until I arrive.'

Wolseley would have been mortified to know that while he lay sick on 30 July, General Willis had left with the Scots Guards under secret orders 'to go as fast as possible to Ismailia and take possession of it'. In his copy of Shand's *Life of Hamley* (opposite page 85 of the second volume) Willis signed a pencilled note that adds, 'I should have arrived at Ismailia on 10th or 11th of August had I not been ordered to Alexandria by telegram at Malta *owing to Alison's intentions.*' (Author's italics). One must assume that Sir Archibald wished to gather all possible troops for a plan he was formulating to attack the Egyptians at Abourkir Bay, something he wanted to do before Wolseley arrived and which the two generals had never discussed.

A cunning feint at Abourkir was the most secret part of Wolseley's plans but it has become misunderstood over the years. While much was top secret, the principal generals knew, even before they left England, that an advance on Cairo would be via Ismailia. In his campaign diary General Hamley wrote that: 'in all interviews while in London with Sir G. Wolseley and Sir J. Adye'[7] this line of attack was taken for granted. Similarly, the maps sent out by the Intelligence Department to commanders, along with copies of Tulloch's report, all pointed to Tel-el-Kebir as the likely place, strategically and tactically, where the Egyptians would stand and fight. It was in the fine detail, and especially the ruse of a feint at Abourkir, that would contain several surprises.

In the lanes off Malta it was animals, as always, that took Wolseley's mind off things. He liked the look of his new horse, a bay with one speck of white on his forehead and one white fetlock, and decided to call the beast 'Arabi'. 'Everyone has been very nice to me on board', he wrote to his wife, 'and Stewart

Arabi Pasha. An idealist loyal to his Sultan but determined to defend his country's honour, he became the figurehead of the Egyptian Nationalist movement.

Ismail Pasha. His reforms modernised Egypt but colossal loans drawn from European banks allowed creditor nations to take an unhealthy interest in the country.

Tewfik Pasha. Often portrayed as a weak man, he was a realist determined to secure the survival of his dynasty even if it meant acting obsequiously towards the Nationalists.

Ab-el-Al Hilmi. A bear of a man who, alongside his fellow colonels, Arabi and Fehmy, led the Army reformers.

عبد العال حلبي

Ali Fehmy. Intelligent and loyal, he was one of the three colonels who galvanised the Nationalist movement in the Egyptian Army.

علي فهمي

Benjamin Disraeli. His purchase of the Suez Canal outwitted the French but the security of this Imperial lifeline was to become an obsession of subsequent governments.

Sir Garnet J. Wolseley. To his supporters on Army reform and Ring members he was a genius, but others found him to be an egotist with a vicious spleen.

Lord Hartington. The leading Hawk in the Liberal Government, the murder of his favourite brother by Egyptian Nationalists determined his tough stance on Egypt.

Hugh Childers. Intelligent, perceptive and a loyal follower of Gladstone, it was his tight control of affairs at the War Office that enabled Wolseley to win his campaign.

Leon Gambetta. Determined to match the English in Africa, his war with Tunisia made the Egyptian Nationalists distrustful of the European powers, while his Note raised sentiments to fever pitch.

Admiral Sir Beauchamp Seymour. A bachelor with a love of fine food and wine. At Alexandria he led his ships into the largest Royal Navy action fought between the Crimean and First World Wars.

General Sir Edward Hamley. An academic soldier with a high opinion of his abilities, Sir Edward felt humiliated by Wolseley and later took revenge.

General George Willis. An officer of the Old School, Sir George found himself in the thick of things, almost dying from sunstroke in the desert and getting wounded at Tel-el-Kebir.

General Sir H. T. Macpherson. A fighting soldier from India, Sir Herbert's Indian Contingent proved themselves a worthy part of the British force, much to Wolseley's chagrin.

General D. C Drury Lowe. Continuing the success of his cavalry command in the Zulu War, Sir Drury led his men at Kassassin and Tel-el-Kebir and personally took the surrender of Arabi Pasha in Cairo.

Sir John Adye. From a military family, Sir John could trace a line of association with the Royal Artillery back to his great-grandfather. He was a great admirer of Wolseley and dedicated his autobiography to the General.

General Sir Archibald Alison. One of the sharpest brains in the British Army, Sir Archibald was well-respected by all, from his men up to the Duke of Cambridge. In 1878 he took over command of the Intelligence Department at the War Office.

General Sir Evelyn Wood. A friend of Wolseley's, Sir Evelyn had a reputation as the most accident-prone officer in the Army.

General Gerald Graham. Commanded the 2nd Brigade of the 1st Infantry Division. Victoria Cross holder Graham was an old friend of Wolseley who considered him 'the bravest man I ever knew'.

The Military clearing the streets of Alexandia, 11 June 1882.

The Bombardment of Alexandria. It was the last battle fought in the smoke and style of Nelson's day and the first to see modern armour and machine guns.

The British Fleet bombards the forts at Alexandria, 11 July 1882. The Egyptians fought magnificently and died bravely. Their accurate gunnery won them many admirers on the British side.

# THE BOMBARDMENT OF ALEXANDRIA

## "GRAPHIC SPECIAL NUMBER

# THE ILLUSTRATED LONDON NEWS.

REGISTERED AT THE GENERAL POST-OFFICE FOR TRANSMISSION ABROAD.

No. 2255.—VOL. LXXXI.　　　SATURDAY, JULY 22, 1882.　　　WITH TWO SUPPLEMENTS } SIXPENCE. By Post, 6½d.

FIRING ROCKETS ON BOARD H.M.S. MONARCH.

Firing rockets from HMS *Monarch*.

Covering the landing party at Fort Mex from gunboat *Condor*.

Armoured train. The brainchild of Arthur Wilson and Jacky Fisher, the train was put to good use in the first land action at Kafr Dawar.

The ruins of Fort Mex.

Ammunition among the ruins of Fort Mex.

British Marines arresting Arab looters at the custom house gate.

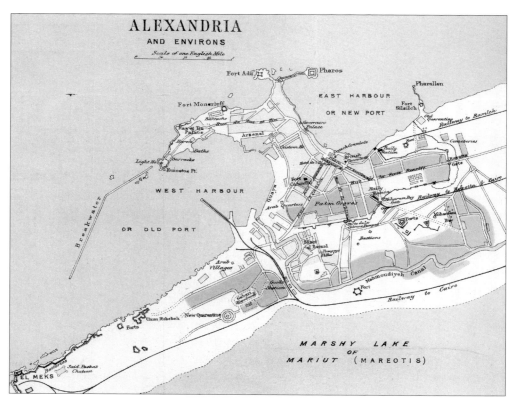

Map of Alexandria.

The execution of a Christian incendiary, Alexandria.

The men of HMS *Invincible* cheering the *Condor* after her attack on Fort Marabout.

Alexandria after destruction. Fires raged throughout the city after Seymour's bombardment. Most were the work of arsonists on the loot. This photograph of Rue Rosette was taken shortly after the British had dynamited the streets and begun clearing the rubble.

A guard–house of soldiers of the line in Cairo.

Bluejackets at Alexandria.

The guards equipped for service in Egypt.

A narrow escape whilst repairing the railway lines near Ramleh.

Royal Marines in the reconnaisance towards Kafr Dawar.

Action near Kafr Dawar.

Illustration highlighting Arabi's position at Kafr–Dawar from the British lines at Ramleh.

An Egyptian shell lands among the General's staff, Mahuta, 24 August.

Royal Marines capture two guns at the Battle of Kassassin.

The mountain battery in action in front of Kassasin, 9 September.

Horse Guards charge the enemy's guns.

Royal Marines rush for water after the battle of Kassassin.

A sketch of two war correspondents.

Soldiers charge at the Battle of Tel-el-Kebir.

The Battle of Teb-el-Kebir. It was vicious hand-to-hand fighting using the bayonet that won the battle. British fatalities were slight compared to Egyptian.

The Bengal Lancers in pursuit of fugitives at the Battle of Tel-el-Kebir.

The Highland Light Infantry in the trenches at Tel-el-Kebir.

The Battle of Tel-el-Kebir.

After the Battle of Tel-el-Kebir.

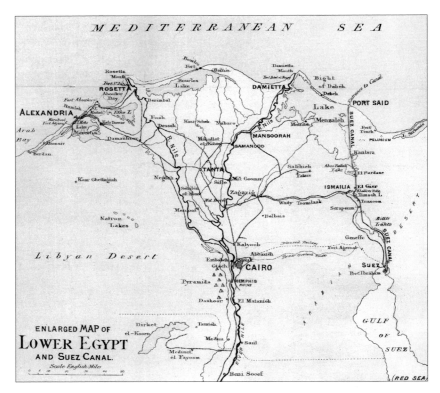

Map of Lower Egypt.

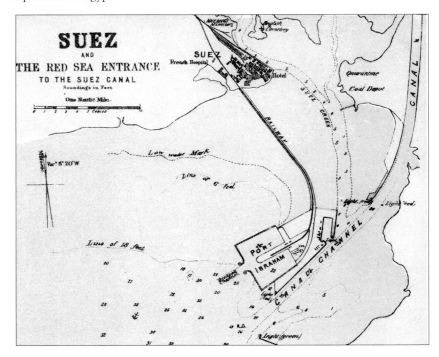

Map showing Suez and the entrance to the Canal.

has been a real brother.' He noted that 'nearly every officer on board has cut his hair as short as a rat. I have had mine clipped so that I cannot part it.'[8]

Next day, as the *Calabria* docked for six hours, Sir Garnet was able to exchange news with Generals Hamley and Wood who were departing for Alexandria ahead of him. The meeting raised all his old fears and left him depressed. His latest worry was that Turkish troops might land in Egypt and Arabi Pasha would surrender to them. 'This will be unfortunate for us politically I think and very unsatisfactory to us as an Army,' he told Louisa, adding miserably, 'I wish from my heart I was at Alexandria. Every day now is of much consequence to me. I hope nothing may be done until I get there.'[9] When he heard of the Kafr-Dawar engagement Sir Garnet began to have severe doubts about Alison's generalship. Though done in good faith to harass the Egyptians into thinking the main British movement on Cairo would be from Alexandria, Wolseley thought the action had been, as recorded by Hamley, 'injudicious and unfortunate … such reconnaissances always in the end wore the appearance of defeat'.[10] In the ten days since the skirmish at Kafr-Dawar the arrival of large numbers of men, horses and supplies had changed the scene at Ramleh so that now, as one observer noted, 'the ground for over a mile square was a scattered mass of white tents'.[11] 'We have got seven generals here and not one of them has the most remote idea what we are going to do,' complained one officer, 'It is to be hoped that Sir Garnet … has the plans in his pocket because we are simply wasting time now, and the worst of it is that Arabi is making the best use of his.'[12]

Wolseley was far from alone in raising his eyebrows at Alison's little 'reconnaissance'. Writing shortly after the war Caspar Goodrich, the American Naval Attache with the British forces, called it 'barren of results', the strength of the enemy being unascertained, 'nor was the position held from which they had been driven. The balance of advantages seems to be negative, valuable lives were sacrificed, and the enemy regained the ground he had lost without suffering severely enough to be seriously affected.'[13] One British officer who also agreed that the engagement 'resulted in nothing' was Major-General Sir Gerald Graham VC who had arrived two days earlier to take command of the 2nd Brigade of the 1st Division. Next day, 6 August, he spoke with Alison and noted in his diary that 'Sir Archibald seems quite satisfied with the reconnaissance and says he found out all he wanted – viz, that Arabi isn't going to retire.'[14] In fact Alison was encouraged enough by the sortie to start making his own plans for an attack on Abourkir Bay.

Meanwhile several minor skirmishes gave the opposing sides a chance to shadow-box. The gentlemen of the Press, desperate for good copy, found it all rather boring. Without a battle to report they made the most of whatever action was at hand. Three days after Alison's engagement a large body of Egyptian cavalry approached the British lines and were fired on, and Bedouins were seen constructing earthworks on the edge of the desert about 2,200 yards from the shore. This was close enough for HMS *Superb* which obligingly shelled them. That night the warship turned its searchlights towards the beaches but 'the chief effect of them was to confuse the British pickets'. Searchlights, noted the same naval authority, were often 'a positive source of danger to their users and their users' friends'.[15]

The Naval Brigade were still active and Lieutenant George Mostyn Field of *Sultan* was now on John Fisher's staff and 'in the saddle all day riding round the different posts, and writing and organizing in the evening'. In his usual direct manner Fisher warned Field that heads of Department would be hung if anything went wrong. The young officer, who had been so busy during the bombardment, found his work was tough but exhilarating: 'We put up a gun, Arabi put up another; we built an earthwork, Arabi promptly built two; we ran an armoured train, as soon as he conveniently could Arabi did the same.'[16]

The quality of life by the sea for the soldiers depended very much on their ability to cope with personal hardship, and their rank. For many Tommies it was their first trip abroad, their first campaign and the hottest climate they had ever experienced. Every activity had to be undertaken wearing thick red serge uniforms. Private Lachlan McLean of the Black Watch wrote home that the heat was 'something fearful, the sand about six inches deep, and the dust so thick that we could not see three paces in front of us'.[17] Sergeant Charles Spriggs, a 35-year-old Scots Guards non-commissioned officer, who had already served 21 years in the regiment, noted that 'we can scarcely get any water and what water we manage is not very good'. Gradually things improved for his regiment when water filters arrived, but on 17 August he still complained that it 'will be a treat when we get a fresh water wash with soap'.[18] Lieutenant Balfour, also in the Scots Guards, disagreed and found Ramleh to be a very healthy place: 'Having the sea close by me, one can get a bath there twice a day, and the fresh breeze off it is very pleasant. We sleep by companies three in a tent, and have our breakfast and lunch there.'[19]

Eighteen-year-old Private John Gordon agreed with Balfour and adored the place:

We had a lot of fun at Ramleh. I learned to swim here. I can never forget the gorgeous fruit we discovered on abandoned villas ... Vines hung heavy with great clusters of rich, white, in fact almost transparent, grapes. And there were figs galore; as we opened them and spread the halves, the delicious juice oozing out, on slices of bread at the same time besmearing our hands, faces and clothes, what a feast![20]

Stuck on outpost duty, around 2.30am on 13 August, Lieutenant the Hon. Eustace Dawnay, 2nd Battalion, Coldstream Guards, decided to pass the time writing a letter home. He and his fellow officers had enjoyed a pleasant voyage out on the SS *Iberia*, annoyed only by a large number of rats, 'which, as there is no cargo, came up to the saloon and our cabins looking for food'. The weather was good and the officers had daily lectures and 'got through a great deal of reading, everyone having a different book on Egypt'. The Coldstreams had arrived at Ramleh on 11 August. 'I have seen better camping grounds for this is nothing but white dust,' wrote Dawnay, 'not a blade of anything green … The Grenadiers and Scots are here too having come in the day before. Here we are a short 2 miles from Arabi's position and which we can see quite plainly from the top of the house I am at the present moment in.' His outpost was on the extreme left of the British lines, about two miles from Ramleh, a place of 'low villas with uniform gardens, the most awful place to lose one's way in'. Already there was talk in camp that a move was soon to take place. Dawnay showed himself to be quite perceptive when he wrote: 'They say our 3 regts shall be moved aboard ship again in a few days and taken somewhere else. I suppose it to be Ismailieh [sic].' He admitted that any guesses as to the course of the war were pure speculation as 'nobody has the slightest idea of what Sir G. W. will do'. Returning to his duties he complained:

> The worst part of this place must be I think the fleas. At present this house is pretty dreadful. I am simply crawling. Nasty but true! I dare say they won't like a sea bath. I mean to have one at the first opportunity. I had a most delicious one yesterday afternoon before arriving on duty.[21]

'Very unwillingly', as Arthur Wilson described it, the Naval Brigade, with the exception of two field-guns and the armoured train, was broken up on 11 August and the sailors returned to their ships. There was still time, however, for Beresford and Wilson to make sure the Royal Navy left Ramleh with a bang. On Saturday 12 August Wilson sent twenty bluejackets and six marines from *Hecla* to assist Lord Charles in the destruction of an immense store of gun-cotton and detonators found in a quarry shed among low hills some two miles inland behind Fort Mex. Five hours into this work, lookouts noticed clouds of dust on the horizon. This turned out to be upwards of 900 Bedouin and 300 enemy cavalry who had probably been alerted by the rising smoke. Quickly Beresford ordered his men to retire towards the shore while a ship's gunner and one bluejacket remained with him to light the a fuze. In his memoirs Charley B. recalled: 'It was a five-minute fuze. The retreating men had been told to count as they ran, and at the end of four minutes, or when they saw us lie down, to halt and lie down.' Seeing his men were on the ground, Lord Charles and the two sailors ran. After about 300 yards they flung themselves onto the sand as the sand about was ripped apart by a huge explosion that burned their cheeks. 'A vast column of yellow smoke, boxes and pieces of paper were whirling high,' recalled Beresford, 'and a strong wind sucked back into the vacuum, almost dragging us along the sand. The enemy were so interested in the spectacle that they gave us time to get back to the boats.'[22]

That night Captain Wilson heard news of the exploit from Lord Charles, but also learned of another vast store of gun-cotton, 'and worse, a large store of mechanical torpedo primers'. Wilson knew the matter was urgent:

> I went down to Mex as soon as it was daylight, roused up Beresford and Colonel Le Grand, who was in charge there, and got two companies of Marines and a 7-pounder gun and rocket, that Beresford had cleverly mounted on country carts, and sent them by an inland road.[23]

All went according to plan at first. Wilson's party destroyed the gun-cotton and the primers were located when suddenly sentries reported seeing Egyptian cavalry. To Wilson's annoyance 'the impatient Marines opened fire too soon, before I could get up and stop them', and Beresford gave a salvo from the hill with his 7-pounder, knocking one or two horsemen to the ground. With enemy skirmishers creeping towards the shore Wilson ended his 'miniature battle' by burning the store of primers and heading fast towards the beach, 'a very interesting day to me, but much more like a sham fight than a real one'.[24]

During the night of 14 August Lieutenant Henry Smith-Dorrien of *Invincible* (who had spied so gallantly just prior to the bombardment), now attempted a repeat performance. In company with Lieutenant Hamilton of *Helicon* he splashed through the waters of Lake Mareotis for 16 miles until the pair were within 300 yards of Arabi's tents. Noticed by a picquet, the officers rushed back into the water as bright lights were turned on in their direction. Smith-Dorrien and Hamilton had to keep still in two feet of water for several hours while Egyptian cavalry, their horses refusing to enter the lake, tried to find them. Eventually the clamour died down and by 7.30am next morning the pair, damp and exhausted, got back to Ramleh.

Early that same morning saw a spirited mounted infantry reconnaissance as Hallam-Parr 'took every available man and horse' to escort Montagu Gerard to spy on the enemy's position. The body of 40 horsemen went closer to the Egyptian lines than during the action on 5 August, halting quietly as Gerard, along with one M.I. officer and four men went one mile nearer to Kafr-Dawar. Soon they all came galloping back pursued by a small body of cavalry. In his memoirs Hallam-Parr described what happened next:

> I advanced to cover them, and, when they were past our flank, retired also. They thought, I suppose, we were bolting. When they got within three hundred yards I suddenly halted, dismounted six men and opened fire. One man fell dead on his horse's neck, and another seemed to fall dead out of his saddle, and the enemy's courage evaporated and they all galloped away to their lines. The first man shot was a Bedouin who had been careering along in front flinging his bernous round him with a fine gesture.[25]

Much of this news was reported to Wolseley on arrival at Alexandria and the most important item – Alison's impertinent little plan to attack the Egyptians at Abourkir Bay – was immediately quashed.

On the political front the general was relieved to find that no Turkish troops had proceeded beyond Crete, although the Sultan was assembling an army there. Abdul Hamid was in a quandary. He feared that an Arabist victory might set off a nationalist chain reaction throughout his sprawling Empire, and knew the British were the only ones who could stop this rot, but 'much as they needed each other, the Ottoman and British Empires could not overcome mutual prejudice and distrust'. The Constantinople Conference was grinding on and Lord Dufferin was still trying to cope with the Sultan's 'erratic negotiating style'. At the end of July the Porte agreed to send a Turkish army 'but insisted foreign troops evacuate the country upon the arrival of Ottoman forces'. There was a genuine British fear that these Muslim soldiers might join Arabi's army and HM Govt remained suspicious of the Sultan's intentions. So, while the Foreign Office demanded precise details of a Turkish expeditionary force Abdul Hamid helped complicate matters by giving his negotiators constantly contradictory instructions.[26]

Sir Edward Malet had returned on 10 August and that day thus saw Admiral Seymour's special powers come to an end. On the morning of the 16th the Consul-General met his military commander. In a letter to Louisa, Sir Garnet grumbled about Malet's title of 'minister plenipotentiary'. An immense ego and distrust of civilians made him complain: 'I think the Govt. should have given the position to me .' Next the general made a call on Seymour, 'whom I knew of old, a very good fellow and with whom I shall get on swimmingly'. Then, in the company of Malet, it was time to see the Khedive and Wolseley dressed for the reception in the blue campaign tunic he wore throughout the campaign, gauntlets, brown boots, large black sun goggles and a solar topee. This formal reception was conducted in

French, not an easy task for Sir Garnet, but he thought it went 'very well', Tewfik seemed 'a nice unassumed fellow', affable and pleasant, and the general invited him to make a visit next day to HMS *Salamis*, his new headquarters.[27]

Wolseley rode back to see Seymour aboard *Helicon,* and over lunch revealed his secret plans while the admiral plied his old comrade with customary good food and wine. Secrecy was essential to prevent the enemy or even politicians from interfering. The full plan, timing of embarkation, and objectives were to be treated as highly classified information. No British generals were to be told, except Sir John Adye. Not even Malet (who was Wolseley's superior in most matters non-military), or Childers at the War Office knew exactly what he was going to do. Time was of the essence. As early as 14 August Admiral Hoskins was telling the Admiralty that

> Port Said is full of spies, by whom, and by the Canal Company, information of all our movements and preparations are forwarded to the rebels: Mr. de Lesseps being in constant personal communication with them and having control of the telegraph wires. He professes ... he will at once sink one or more dredgers in the Canal if we attempt to land troops.[28]

Exactly who knew Wolseley's plan prior to its execution is an interesting point. In a letter home on the 18th he said 'only about three people amongst the soldiers are in the secret'.[29] Next day he wrote to Childers that: 'No one is in the secret beyond the Admirals concerned, one Naval Captain, Adye, my Military Secretary and myself.'[30] Besides Seymour this meant that Admirals Hewett and Hoskins were in the know, along with Adye and Major Swaine, his military secretary. The naval officer was almost certainly Captain Harry Rawson, an old friend of Sir Garnet's from their days in China who was the expedition's Principal Transport Officer. The third soldier referred to in the letter to Louisa was most likely Tulloch, who until the arrival of Redvers Buller, was still in charge of intelligence and currently devising a clever ruse to mislead the war correspondents and Egyptians.

That afternoon, after 'a very hot and extremely dirty drive' Wolseley arrived at Ramleh to find the Duke of Connaught and his staff awaiting him. Connaught was 'burnt as brown as an old saddle' and the two men rode off a little way in the direction of the Egyptian lines where, as Wolseley self-deprecatingly admitted to his wife, 'I did the "Commander-in-Chief" thing, putting on an air as I looked towards the enemy that would have done credit to Napoleon as he was crossing the Alps.' That night aboard ship, Sir Garnet enjoyed one of Admiral Seymour's celebrated dinners – 'a really good dinner, the best I have had since I left England', the meal washed down with 'very good' and 'very cold' champagne.[31]

Wolseley fared better than his staff. Paul Methuen had got them a new chef in Malta and they were looking forward to some fine meals. Sitting down to their first repast, the group, including John Ardagh and William Butler, were 'somewhat disappointed' when a 'very indifferent soup' was followed by the cook's piece de resistance – a dish of sheeps heads, 'their glassy eyes glaring at us from the depths of a large mess tin,' recalled Francis Grenfell.[32]

Knowing that his family would not receive his letters for several days, Wolseley felt secure in writing about his plans, 'or rather for opening the Ball', as he cheerfully described matters on 17 August:

> We leave here on Saturday avowedly for the purpose of landing at Abourkir, and of attacking Arabi's position near there, but really to go down the Canal to seize Ismailia. I expect to have my first skirmish with the enemy next Sunday which I hope may be a successful one.'[33]

The usual assumption is that Wolseley's strategy worked like clockwork. Yet on the same day he admitted in a letter to the Duke of Cambridge that the

> ... plan I drew out on board ship had to be greatly modified, as it was based on the assumption that the Indian Contingent would have been able to co-operate, and that the distance between Port Said and Ismailia could have been done in about six or seven hours. Now I find it cannot be done in safety in less than ten hours.

News that Arabi Pasha had broken up his camp at Nefiche also worried Sir Garnet a great deal:

> This may prevent me from having a satisfactory skirmish with Arabi's people on Monday; it is very provoking because I had hoped with the Household Cavalry to have been able to cut him off from his great position in rear at Tel-el-Kebir.[34]

Next day he wrote home again:

> We start from here tomorrow at noon for Abourkir Bay where the fleet and all the transports carrying the first Division will anchor at 4pm tomorrow to pretend that we intend landing there during the night to attack Arabi's position in front of that place on Sunday morning. Everyone here believes we intend doing so ... and I have completely befoozled the 'Press' gang ... I suppose they will be furious when they find how they came to be taken in, but if I can take them in, I hope to take in Arabi also. On Sunday evening I hope to be at Ismailia although have today heard that a

French ship has been run aground near Lake Timsah – I presume done by Mr Lesseps on purpose to impede our advance ... If on Monday morning the enemy still hold the Nefiche Junction (about two and a half miles west of Ismailia on the Canal) I hope to be able to bag any troops that may be foolish enough to stay there.[35]

Regarding the secrecy of the operation Wolseley told his wife that

It is very amusing that General Hamley who commands the 2nd Division and Generals Alison and Wood who command the two brigades of that Division are under the firm conviction that we mean to attack here on Sunday and that they are to take part in this attack: I am leaving sealed orders to be opened by Hamley at daybreak on Sunday morning in which I tell him the whole thing is a humbug and that my real destination is the Canal.[36]

Throughout the long hours of 17 and 18 August, staff officers, especially those attached to the 2nd Division, sweated in their tents preparing plans for the dis-embarkation at Abourkir Bay and the attack on Kafr-Dawar. Hamley expected Sir Garnet to advance from Abourkir while he led a frontal assault from Ramleh. The commander-in-chief even went through a charade of examining Hamley's carefully thought-out plans and endorsing them. He warned the general not to be surprised if he heard firing at Abourkir on the Saturday evening.

Everyone knew something was about to happen and it was all supposed to be a 'big secret'. Most of the troops, bored by Ramleh, wanted a change of scene, some action and a chance for glory. This mood was strongest among the large party of war correspondents in the camp. One can imagine their sur-prise and suspicion when, on 17 August, the journalists were told that the Press Censor, Colonel Paul Methuen, was lifting restrictions, and they were invited to tell their readers that an attack on Abourkir Bay, site of Nelson's great victory, was in the offing. Major Tulloch, aware that any wires sent to London would be copied en route at Constantinople and relayed back to the Arabists in Cairo, concocted a fake news story and sent it to the *Standard* under the name of its famous war correspondent, John Cameron:

M. de Lesseps, who has the French Government behind him, has settled that the neutrality of the canal shall be rigidly observed. The guard-ships at Port Said and Ismailia are merely for the protection of those towns, as some people fear they might be burnt by the evil disposed. It is now an open secret that whilst the British portion of the force will move from Alexandria and attack Kafr Dewar, the troops coming from India will move from Suez direct on Cairo.[37]

One of the earliest examples of false newspaper reporting designed to mislead an enemy, Tulloch's subterfuge was also hugely successful, alarming Arabi Pasha so much that he ordered all spare railway sleepers to be collected, and had laid fifteen miles of track from Cairo towards Suez. When Tulloch was told he could not cut the marine telegraph cable he sent a man overland to Jaffa and snipped the wires there, effectively stopping all communication between Cairo and Constantinople for the next ten days. Cameron, whose opinion on having his name used without permission is not recorded, rushed to Abourkir in a specially chartered yacht thinking he was onto a scoop.

Later in the campaign, when Wolseley's subterfuge was understood, several newspaper men and officers denied that they had ever been hoodwinked. Melton Prior always insisted he and his colleagues 'had one eye wide open'. Gerald Graham was definitely not fooled and listened with disbelief when Alison told him the 1st Division was to go to Abourkir and disembark while the latter cooperated from Ramleh. 'I can't quite credit this. Is Sir Garnet humbugging Alison?' he wrote in his diary on 17 August. Two days later, before the fleet had even anchored in Abourkir Bay, he wrote, 'supposed bombardment and landing at Abourkir is humbug'.[38] Moberly Bell of *The Times* was not fooled either by an interview he had with Methuen. He sent a telegram to his newspaper in the early hours of 20 August, while the British were seizing Port Said, that said if Sir Garnet's 'stated plan does not come off, it must be assumed that circumstances have compelled him to change it within the last twelve hours'.[39]

The secret plan had, in fact, been revealed to London by Seymour, though to what extent is unknown, but two days after Sir Garnet had told the admiral a telegram arrived from Childers warning him that he had heard a rumour all had been revealed to the Admiralty. Hardly surprisingly, a furious Wolseley wrote to Seymour reproaching him for this 'unworthy' behaviour as 'he had promised he would not telegraph the news home'.[40]

The secrecy was just 'a nuisance' in the opinion of some officers. With his horse already on board a ship Major Molyneux, DAA and QMG of the 1st Division, walked to *Salamis* on the boiling hot afternoon of August 18th to get his final orders. Here he was told to collect them at the Moharrem Bey Gate, and so he trudged another one-and-a-half miles only to discover, along with several others, including Ardagh and the Deputy Adjutant-General, that 'we were the victims of a rather superfluous practical joke ... I cannot believe that the arrival of a lot officers clamouring for orders ... was necessary to confirm Arabi's spies in the belief that Abourkir was our destination and not Port Said.'[41] Back at the quayside Molyneux and his associates found the ships had sailed without them! Cursing loudly they had to arrange a fast boat to catch up with the fleet.

It had been a busy day that started early on the waterfront. Supplies of every conceivable kind littered the quayside while the cries of porters and traders mingled with the neighing of frightened horses being loaded and the shouts of officers as they embarked their men. 'It was first come first served', noted Corporal Philip as men from each battalion fought over carts and drivers to get their regimental baggage from the railway station and onto the ships.[42] During the afternoon of the 17th the troops of General Willis' 1st Division began boarding the seventeen transports. By late afternoon the next day, Wolseley's armada, escorted by eight ironclads, steamed eastwards. The spectacle, thought one observer, was magnificent:

> A red sunset was shining on the sea, and cast far across it the vast outlines of the ironclads and the stately white 'troopers', their sides crowded with red-coats thick as clustering bees ... On every deck the regimental bands filled the air with music; and ship cheered ship as they neared each other.[43]

The enterprise Wolseley and Seymour were now embarked on, depended for its success on a large element of surprise and a great deal of inter-services cooperation. No combined services exercise conducted jointly by the Army and Navy between the Crimean and First World Wars was so large, so potentially hazardous or so successful. The transport arrangements at sea had been worked out by Captain Harry Rawson, whose younger brother, Wyatt, was Sir Garnet's Naval A.D.C. A plump man, but full of energy, Captain Rawson had numerous things to consider, not least of which was that just one vessel running aground or blocking the Canal could spell complete disaster. Admiral Seymour was in overall command of the naval aspects but for Wolseley's plan to work it was vital to simultaneously secure Port Said and Suez. Operations at these places depended on two other admirals – crinkly-haired old warrior William Hewett VC and cool, unsmiling Anthony Hoskins.

A tough old bird, 'Billy' Hewett was one of those rarest of the rare – a man with a clasp to his Victoria Cross. At the Battle of Inkerman when ordered to retire he replied, 'retire be damned – fire!' and turned his one gun against thousands of the enemy. It was said he had 'seen more war service than any other officer in the Navy'. Percy Scott, who served under him as a midshipman, wrote admiringly that Hewett 'did not know the meaning of fear'. Sir William preferred to lead his boys from the front, waving a cutlass, yet at sea, 'handling a ship under sail he was a master sailor'.[44] Vice-Admiral Sir Anthony Hiley Hoskins, known by bluejackets throughout the world as 'Sir Hanthony, Sir Iley, Sir Oskins', had a reputation of being 'unsympathetic and inhuman', though a clever sailor, but this 'stern, strict and even severe' admiral was the right man to capture Port Said.

When the British transports and warships reached Abourkir they struck their topmasts and went through all the preparations for an attack. The war's foremost historian, Frederick Maurice, said that Wolseley tried to persuade Seymour to deceive the enemy by firing a few dummy shells, but in a letter written that same afternoon to Childers it is clear Sir Garnet wanted even tougher action:

> The small boats of the fleet will go in at dark and open fire upon the beach to attract as much attention as possible to that quarter. Naval etiquette prevents the Admiral from opening fire from his big guns upon the forts at very long range, as I wished him to do; but the Navy have some funny notion that if they open fire on a battery they are bound by some peculiar code of honour of their own to fight on until they silence it.[45]

In his diary the general wrote: 'Of course, no admiral (except Billy Hewett) could do anything ... for they anchored too far out for my plan.'

Abourkir Bay was protected by some smaller forts and one Fort Sumter-like monster. The Egyptians stood to their guns but every fort flew a white flag. The Hon. Guy Dawnay, Eustace's brother, had arrived in Alexandria just 48 hours earlier hoping to see the 'show'. His old pal, Paul Methuen, had given him a press pass and he was now aboard *Iberia* surrounded by Coldstream Guard chums as special correspondent for the *St James's Gazette*. Revolver at the ready, Dawnay was expecting 'a warm day's work' to begin at dawn, 'when a naval lieutenant boarded us, and brought us the news that we were to go on to Port Said as soon as it was dark ...' Dawnay was disgusted:'What the object of concealing our intended move may have been, heaven knows. It certainly could not deceive Arabi, except for an hour or two.'[46]

Under the cover of darkness, as the ships weighed anchor at Abourkir and steamed off, things were starting to happen all along the Canal. Under Hoskins direction, at 3.30am seamen and marines from the crews of *Monarch* and *Iris* quietly sneaked ashore and surprised the sleeping garrison of Port Said. Bluejackets now spread out across the narrow isthmus from Lake Menzaleh to the sea. A party under Captain Edward Seymour of *Iris* occupied the Canal Company offices and took possession of the telegraph equipment, much to the disgust of its mainly French employees.

At the same time further down the Canal at Ismailia, 565 officers and men from HMS *Orion, Northumberland, Carysfort* and *Coquette* occupied the European quarter of the town. At the lock gates there was a skirmish with both sides opening fire before all the principal buildings and offices were seized. The Arab quarter was more difficult. Fights broke out and *Carysfort* and *Coquette* each fired five shells at the guardhouses. The bluejackets had to barricade some streets, 'building up sandbag batteries, and making a platform of doors, etc. for the guns to work on, the men working very well,' recorded Lieutenant Pitcairn-Jones of *Carysfort*. Later, two of the ships fired on the railway station at Nefiche, two miles inland, wrecking the line with damaged wagons and putting a neat shell through the station window, accurate shooting that kept the 3,000 strong Egyptian garrison on its toes. 'It was very pretty to watch the shell coming over *us* and bursting over *them*', noted Pitcairn-Jones in his diary. When it was realised that telegrams from Cairo were still arriving at Ismailia asking for information, one was cheekily sent to the War Ministry pointing out that the town was now occupied by 5,000 British troops and that any relieving force would be too late (a polite acknowledgement was received from the Arabists saying that its contents had been passed on to all concerned).[47]

Events were also fast-moving but more bloody near Suez. Egyptian infantry had dug in at Chalouf on the 17th not far from the British lines. Luckily for Hewett he had with him the advance guard of the Indian Contingent in the shape of the 1st Battalion Seaforth Highlanders (late 72nd Foot), freshly arrived from Aden. During the night of 18 August the admiral had the telegraph wires cut between Suez and the first canal station. Next day he prohibited all craft from entering the Canal and at daybreak on the 20th Lt-Colonel Stockwell led the Seaforths in the direction of Chalouf to make a feint attack, while 200 more Highlanders were taken by boat towards Chalouf up the Canal. Stockwell's men had an uneventful march but the other party of sailors and soldiers ran into 600 Egyptians hidden on the banks supported by a small body of cavalry. The official despatches conceal what must have been a massacre. Gatlings from the British gun boats hailed lead at the enemy who, it turned out, were mostly old reservists chained at the ankles to stop them running away. When the firing stopped the British had lost just two soldiers drowned and two seamen wounded, but 168 Egyptians had been slaughtered, including all their officers, and 27 of those taken prisoner were wounded.

During the 20th and into the 21st, Wolseley's ships sailed past Port Said and into the Canal. Major Molyneux thought it was 'a stately sight, and might have done some of the grumblers at home good to see'. Ships of other nations were at anchor waiting to use the Canal. 'The Frenchmen were mute, and so of course were the Turks and Egyptians,' wrote Molyneux, 'but the Italians gave us a cheer, and when we got abreast of the Americans blood proved itself thicker than water, and they gave us such ringing rounds of applause that it seemed as if it would not have taken much to make them join us.'[48] One ship, SS *Catalonia*, ran aground, effectively blocking the waterway for several hours. Three hundred men of the Royal West Kent Regiment had to be transferred across to the gunboat *Beacon*. Also on board was General Earle, in charge of the lines of communication, who ordered Beacon to get him to Ismailia double-quick. His chief staff officer was the one-time spy, Richard Harrison, now impressed as *Beacon* steamed along and some Arabs in a dhow gave them a cheer.

Old Ferdinand De Lesseps was furious that the neutrality of his canal had been broken. There seems to be some confusion among historians and chroniclers whether he met the British at Port Said or Ismailia. It is possible that the Frenchman made his presence felt in both places, though Marling's ship was moored next to Admiral Seymour's at Port Said so he should have had a grandstand view when, around 10am on 20 August, Lesseps' carriage arrived and he went aboard the flagship. For weeks he had been acting as if he owned the Canal and seems to have been terrified that either side might harm his dream-child. Pilots working for the Suez Canal Company had been barred from assisting the British. On *Helicon*, accompanied by his son Victor, the old man proved he was still not lost for words and made it plain that he thought Britain had acted in clear disregard of the Canal's charter to be 'a neutral highway for the ships of all nations.' He could invoke precedents; during the Franco-Prussian and Russo-Turkish Wars its neutrality had never been violated.

The move on Cairo from the direction of the Canal was vital to Wolseley's plan and questions of neutrality had thus to be pushed aside if Arabi was to be quickly defeated. According to one naval authority Beauchamp Seymour listened patiently to Lesseps diatribe before handing him a piece of paper and saying, 'M. De Lesseps, please read that.'[49] It was one of his intercepted telegrams to Arabi stating, 'The English are only a few in numbers; come and drive them into the sea.' When the British departed Port Said at 1pm the Frenchman was 'dancing on the quay, foaming at the mouth, shaking his fist and shouting, "*Sacres Anglais*".'[50] This marvellous picture may or may not be true, but Lesseps certainly did send a telegram to Arabi on 21 August to say 'Make no attempt to intercept *my* Canal. I am there. Not a single soldier shall disembark without being accompanied by a French soldier. I answer for everything.'

There is another story, probably apocryphal, that he stood by the landing-stage at Ismailia and declared: 'No one shall land except over my dead body.' A British tar then gently pushed him aside with the words: 'We don't want any dead bodies about here, sir; all you've got to do is step back a bit.' Next day Swaine, the general's military secretary, met with a 'very civil' Lesseps and a few days later when Wolseley made a call on him he pledged 'eternal friendship for the English', but accused the Navy of having acted brutally towards him.[51]

Many British sailors and soldiers waking up on the 20th looked out to shore at the grimy waterfront that was Port Said. Captain Wilson of *Hecla* was put in charge of strengthening its defences:

> We landed shortly after eight o'clock with all the spades we could lay our hands on, and by ten we were comfortably entrenched, as the sand was easy digging, sentries posted, and the men stretched out; and, if they followed my example, enjoying a very comfortable sleep on the sand, which was almost as soft as a feather bed.[52]

Staring from a ship, Corporal Philip thought Port Said looked 'grimy' and its inhabitants 'rascally'. The journey to Ismailia for the Duke of Cornwall's Light Infantry was without incident. Not so the Coldstream Guards with war correspondent Guy Dawnay on board. It had taken hours to get past the grounded *Catalonia* that morning and then steam slowly along while the sun glared back off the desert on either side and the occasional flock of pelicans or a wavering mirage gleamed across the sands. The ship ahead of them ran aground seven times, so each time they too needed to drop anchor so as to prevent a collision. The delays made Dawnay think of Arabi: 'Why he has made no attempt against the Canal I cannot understand.'[53]

Many officers, including Wolseley, were wondering the same thing. Arabi's mistake would cement a British victory and ensure his downfall. Wilfred Blunt was later told by Sir Garnet that 'if Arabi had blocked the Canal ... we should be still at the present moment on the high seas blockading Egypt'. But the Egyptian commander was not as incompetent as the English Press later made him out to be. Early on he had seen the very real possibility of a British attack via Ismailia and asked the War Council in Cairo for permission to station troops along the entire length of the Suez Canal. This request had been rejected on 22 July because it would have been interpreted as a threat to the Canal's neutrality. Arabi was not even informed that his plan was rejected for three more days. A plea by him for total mobilization utilizing a home guard was similarly rejected. With his strong sense of personal honour and friendship with Lesseps, coupled perhaps with a feeling that the grand old Frenchman could somehow make good his promises, Arabi had written on 4 August that 'the Egyptian Government will not violate that neutrality ... only in the case of the English having committed some act of hostility at Ismailia, Port Said, or some other point of the Canal.' Wolseley was thus able to exploit the decent assurances of a decent man – and topple him. 'Twenty-four hours delay saved us', Sir Garnet later told Blunt. He might have added that it was his enemy's supreme and fatal blunder.[54]

# 7

# Mahsama

*I confess I was very glad when the sunset came*
Reginald Arthur Talbot

Ismailia was a small but pretty town founded some seventeen years earlier as the half-way point along the Suez Canal. It had been laid out on the western shore of Lake Timsah, through which the Canal runs, as a shady, flower-filled oasis after the heat and glare of the desert. Built of stone from quarries on the other side of the lake, with broad macadamised streets in the European quarter, its main boulevard, Quai Muhammad Ali was 40 yards wide and ran along the side of Timsah for more than a mile. The most prestigious building overlooking the waterway was the huge Swiss chalet of the Lesseps family. Not far away was a wooden palace hastily built by Ismail to accommodate guests during the Canal's opening festivities.

Sir Garnet and his staff landed on 21 August and took up residence in the governor's house. The Khedive's palace was quickly converted into a makeshift hospital. One of the first officers to arrive in the advanced guard was the irrepressible Percy Marling who noted in his diary: 'We got to Ismailia and found two of Arabi's trains there. One just got off, but we shot the engine-driver of the rear train and bagged the train. Good bizz!' The KRRC officers were able to order dinner for 22 persons the next night at the Hotel de Paris 'and all the meals for the next day … It was great fun to see the hungry Guards officers prowling about trying to get something to eat, but as we'd ordered it all and were seated there it wasn't much good!!'[1]

The unloading of such a large mass of animals, men and supplies took time. Wolseley tried to be patient but confessed in a letter to his wife that 'it is no easy matter getting an army of about 30,000 men assembled at one point when we have only a canal to depend upon as a means of approach'.[2] 'That day and the next everyone worked as a slave' recalled William Molyneux.[3] The blue expanse of Lake Timsah was filled by craft of all sizes trying to disgorge their cargo at Ismailia's little wooden jetty. Sailors at the quay rolled barrels, carried cases or pushed railway trucks along a line that had been hastily laid down from the shore to the town. Close to the jetty the Hotel des Bains, soon known by all Tommies as 'Baines's' was doing a roaring trade in refreshments. Chaplain Male noticed that around 'a shaded fountain in the centre of the place ... two regiments had taken up their quarters ... Along the lime-tree avenue to the right, from end to end, regiments and batteries had fixed themselves just where a cool shelter could be obtained from the trees.' Most houses and shops had been shut up when the British arrived, the local Arabs having fled, but gradually the tradespeople 'began cautiously to open their stores; and finding that all goods sold were paid for at once, and that they could with impunity demand exorbitant prices, they began to do a roaring trade.' A few locals – Male says they were Greeks and Syrians – tried to steal from the Army supplies piled up on the jetty. Nineteen thieves were caught by the military police and ten were promptly shot in the main square. This summary justice put a swift end to the looting.[4]

Knowing that the Egyptians could threaten Ismailia from Nefiche, Sir Garnet ordered his best fighting general ahead to seize it. From Port Said, where he received his orders on the 20th, Major-General Graham pushed ahead with 600 men of the DCLI and the York and Lancaster Regiments. They got to Ismailia at 10pm, but Graham set off that night and despite severe back pain, slept with his troops on the sand. Next morning at dawn he pushed them on again, many men collapsing in the intense heat, until Nefiche railway station was reached. It was the first terminus across the desert in the direction of Tel-el-Kebir and Cairo. While Graham tried to get a little refreshment an old woman gave him a severe telling-off in Arabic about the shelling.

Vital to Wolseley's advance was the Sweetwater Canal that ran across the desert close to the railway line. It had been built to convey fresh water to the labourers working on the Suez Canal construction, but Sir Garnet's plan required it as a means of sustaining his army as well as a waterway of traffic during the advance. News had just arrived that the water level was shrinking. The Egyptians, it was soon learned, had built a dam and torn up part of the rail track at Magfar, six miles in the direction of Cairo. Wolseley was still concentrating his force at Ismailia but he now knew that he would have to immediately capture the place. Beyond it

> ... the land rose steadily towards Tel-el-Mahuta and it was considered that while the Canal could still be damned above Magfar, it would be far less easy to break down the banks where they were so much higher. Thus to safeguard the water supply, it was necessary to press on to Magfar.[5]

Let us pause here to consider the enemy now facing the British in the desert. For a start Wolseley was not sure how many Egyptians opposed him. He considered the estimates of his own intelligence department, led by Tulloch, to be 'wild' and reckoned that Arabi commanded throughout the country very nearly 100,000 men, and that some 20,000–25,000 of these were real soldiers, 5,000–10,000 armed Bedouin, and about 10,000 new levies. On 15 August, Stone Pasha had told Wolseley that Ahmed Arabi had recalled to the colours 50,000 old soldiers. Egotistical as ever, Sir Garnet was dismissive and told Childers in a letter on 19 August that 'with our two divisions and the Indian contingent, the whole of Egypt assembled at Tel-el-Kebir would be made short work of'.[6]

In his private thoughts and letters Wolseley was far more cautious. Historical hindsight can tell us the Egyptians did not stand a chance of winning but at the time this was not quite so obvious. If they had delayed the British until the season of high Nile, if the Delta had been flooded, if they had stolen a march on Wolseley's army along the Suez Canal, or destroyed the invaders water supply, then the outcome might have been different. It must be remembered that the Egyptians did have certain advantages. They were fighting in defence of their homeland, an event which often galvanises an army; they knew their own terrain and were perfectly acclimatised to it; they were also well-armed with modern weapons. Support from the Bedouin tribes was never guaranteed but these well-mounted nomads, if cleverly employed, could harass an enemy, attack their supply columns and compel the invaders to keep a fighting force extended along the line of communications.

General Arabi actually had about 11,300 regular soldiers, fewer than Wolseley dared hope, though large numbers of veterans, along with fellahin dragged from the villages, were sent to the front (about 45,000 men), but they had 'little cohesion or confidence in one another'.[7] The infantry were dressed in tunics and trousers of rough white cotton. 'Tunics', says Featherstone, 'had low round-fronted standing collars, six buttons in a single row, with badges and buckles all of brass bearing the star and crescent.'[8] Shoes and equipment, including a field-pack with its cooking-pot strapped to it, were black, a grey blanket-roll was thrown round it, wrapped around the body, or worn over the left shoulder. Officers wore trousers and single-breasted frock coats of dark blue, sunlight often reflecting off their rows of eight yellow metal buttons, while shoulder epaulettes of varying types helped denote rank. Both officers and men wore red tarbooshes with a black tassel hanging from the crown. Cavalry were dressed in more or less the same fashion.

The chief weapon of the Egyptian soldier was the Remington 11mm (.433) rolling-block repeater rifle. Made in the USA, it could fire seventeen shots a minute and the Army had a huge supply of them. Remingtons were also given to the cavalry as carbines and as musketoons for the artillery. Due to the climate and dangers of sand clogging the mechanism, oil was never used on these weapons 'which were so rubbed by their owners as to look as though made of silver'.[9] A sword-bayonet was mounted on the right side of the barrel. Egyptian rank and file carried these on their left side in a brass-mounted steel scabbard. Officers carried swords of white-hilted Mameluke design in a black leather and yellow metal scabbard, or three-bar hilted in a plain steel scabbard. The Egyptian irregular cavalry – the Bedouin – fought in their flowing robes and turbans, armed with swords and guns of beautiful and antiquated design.

Ai Fehmy, Arabi's great friend and one of the three colonels who had started the army mutiny against the Khedive, and pivotal in the Abdin Palace demonstration a year earlier, was now the general commanding the Eastern Army based at Tel-el-Kebir. It lay approximately 30 miles across the desert from the British at Ismailia. The Egyptian local commander, who had fallen back from Nefiche to Tel-el-Mahuta, was General Rashid Pasha.

To deal with the problem caused by the threat of the Magfar dam to his water supply, Wolseley ordered an advance in that direction to start at 4am on 24 August. General Drury Lowe with three squadrons of Household Cavalry, a detachment of the 19th Hussars and a small body of Mounted Infantry, supported by the only two guns of Royal Horse Atillery so far disembarked, would march accompanied by Wolseley, General Willis, and some of the staff officers, to join up with Graham at Nefiche. With Graham leading forward, assisted by the York and Lancaster Regiment and Royal Marines already with him at Nefiche, the whole force would move on Magfar. At the same time the DCLI would march from Ismailia to Nefiche and protect the Canal and railway. The march would be through a wilderness of soft sand, a bad terrain for foot soldiers and horses, and the day promised to be scorchingly hot. The regiments were issued with two days' rations but most of the food was carried in the regimental carts. These rickety contraptions would have to follow the army across the desert.

At 4am the cavalry started off along the right side of the railway line. With them, and ahead of the infantry and guns, which stayed close to the railway embankment, rode Wolseley, Willis and several officers. One of these, William Butler, never forgot that first impression of the Egyptian desert:

> ... sand, drifted into motionless waves, heaped in ridges, scooped into valleys, flattened, blown up into curious cones and long yellow banks, the tops of which the winds have cut into fretted patterns as it blew over them. And all so silent, so withered, and yet so fresh; so soft, so beautiful, and yet so terrible.[10]

Not trusting his intelligence reports, Sir Garnet viewed the morning march as a reconnaissance. 'A morning ride', as Butler called it, then back to Ismailia for breakfast. All went like clockwork at first. By 7.30am the cavalry reached a point about halfway between Magfar and the next Egyptian defensive position at Tel-el-Mahuta. In a brief charge the Household Cavalry made short work of outlying Egyptian picquets. The Household Cavalry gave chase but were hampered by some irrigation channels which their horses refused to jump. The horse carrying Colonel Ewart, commanding the 2nd Life Guards, stumbled at one of these ditches, and a mounted trooper and his charger following close behind 'jumped right on his back, and the whole four fell over sideways into the water, Colonel Ewart being between the horses. He lost his sword and had an uncommonly narrow escape from drowning.' Pursuing a small party of Egyptians, Major Fitzroy Hart was impressed by the courage of his enemies on foot:

> Poor fellows, they were quite blown, but they kept close together as the cavalry came up, and would not surrender, even to our very superior numbers. They even fired a volley at us, but without hurt ... and one of them took a deliberate shot at me, but his bullet whistled high over my head. At last they were encircled and taken, but before it had been necessary to fire at one of them, who was about to fire at us again. The shot wounded him in the hand, and then all laid down their arms. [11]

Through an interpreter the Egyptians explained that their stiff resistance was because they had been told the British habitually killed all prisoners. One Life Guardsman, separated from his troop during the charge and on broken ground, had his horse shot from under him by an Egyptian officer. Dizzily trying to rise from the ground the officer rushed at him and gave the trooper a heavy cut across his right arm. Swiftly the Life Guardsman drew his heavy sabre and with one mighty blow cut his opponent completely in two.

A few prisoners were taken. They spoke of a second dam, 3,000 yards ahead, near hilly Tel-el-Mahuta. A large body of cavalry and infantry were supposed to be guarding the place. It sounded rather ominous. Wolseley's breakfast jaunt was turning into a major engagement. The Magfar dam was found to be about 70 feet wide and 'a model of efficiency from the enemy's point of view', formed of 'alternate layers of strong reeds and sand which had become so solidly compressed below water-level that no tools could make much of an impression on it'.[12] In addition it contained telegraph posts, tied together with wire, and was anchored in position by lines of piles.[13] If the Tel-el-Mahuta dam was just as strong then it was vital to seize it as early as possible.

At 8.30am Lieutenant Childers, one of Sir Garnet's aides (and coincidentally a son of the War Mininster, who had two sons serving in Egypt) set off with orders for the Guards Brigade and all available cavalry and artillery to leave at once for the front. The Duke of Cornwall's Light Infantry at Nefiche were also ordered to hasten forward. These men were in shirt sleeves, squatting on the sand, endeavouring to eat their hard regulation biscuits and waiting for coffee, when the bugles sounded 'Assembly'. In a 'maddening charge' the soldiers grabbed their rifles, jackets and kit. Riding along urging them on with a cheery word, Lt-Colonel Richardson led a forced march under a cruel sun. After almost two hours, with men collapsing from heat exhaustion, there occurred one of those bizarre moments that make warfare so memorable at times. Rounding a ridge of sand hills the regiment found itself in a melon field. Corporal Philip described the next three minutes as 'amusing and ludicrous. Our grey-haired colonel sat on his horse busily eating a melon, which someone had handed up to him. All around him scarlet coats and big green leaves blended in harmonious mixture.' When the order 'Fall In' was given most of the men failed to hear it, 'as most of us were so intently engaged in slicing and eating the delicious fruit'.[14]

While a rider had been sent to hurry up the DCLI at Nefiche, the York and Lancaster Regiment and Royal Marines arrived, led by Gerald Graham. Grimy and sweat-stained, the York and Lancasters took up a position between the Magfar Dam and the railway as the Marines were echeloned further to the right. Beyond them, closer to the enemy and about a mile from the Canal, were the cavalry and mounted infantry. Under the shadow of a sand hill, Lieutenant Hickman carefully positioned his two guns. A short distance away, on another mound, Wolseley, Willis and the Staff officers waited to see events unfold. Command of the troops was given by Sir Garnet to Willis. Thrown into his first battle in more than 25 years, he ordered the men to lie down under any available cover, and not to fire unless ordered to do so.

The British troops were positioned over a series of very sandy low hills with a fast-rising sun beating down ferociously on friend and foe alike, though it was facing the Egyptians and largely behind the invaders. The official historian, Frederick Maurice, described the Egyptian position as 'like that of the upper seats in a lecture theatre', with the British infantry in the position of the lecturer.[15] The cavalry were 'on the same high ground as the enemy's left, threatening and opposing any attempt to extend further round us on that side'. William Butler described the scene thus:

> From where we stood the desert for three thousand yards rose gradually to Tel-el-Mahuta, where some lofty mounds of sand and broken pottery still marked what is supposed to have been the spot at which Pharoah decreed that the Israelites should make bricks without straw. These mounds ended the forward view; they were now

black with figures, while to the right and left of them a long, open line of Arab camel-men and horsemen stretched along the skyline far into the desert on either flank.[16]

Rifle barrels and spears glittered and flashed in the bright sunlight. Above and beyond the ridge black columns of smoke now started to rise in the still, clear desert air. The Egyptians were hurrying up reinforcements by train. It seemed likely that Tel-el-Mahuta would live up to its grim name – 'the hill of the accursed'.

The smoke columns, wrote Butler, 'really changed the plan and purpose of the morning's work. The reconnaissance became a fixed movement.'[17] Wolseley was now to face his greatest gamble in the whole campaign. He had no way of knowing what lay beyond the Tel-el-Mahuta ridge or how many men and guns the Egyptians could throw at his meagre forces. Yet if he could hold off or repulse the enemy, even move on Kassassin, the next major spot towards Tel-el-Kebir, then the war might be shortened by weeks. But it would take four or five hours for reinforcements to arrive and those men would have to trudge through the sands when the sun was at its peak and probably fight a battle as soon as they arrived.

About 9am the Egyptians, estimated at between 7,000–8,000 men, began to advance their cavalry, artillery and infantry but were checked by a steady fire from the York and Lancaster's half-battalion scattered in a well-protected position. After a time the Egyptians gave up this attack while extending and slowly advancing a thin line of men on their left. Here, amid the gravelly flats of the hill tops the British cavalry and mounted infantry kept them at bay for most of the next hour. Hallam-Parr and his men had been having an exciting morning. Near Magfar they had given chase to a party of 50 Bedouins, shooting a few and capturing more than a dozen. Ordered to engage the enemy at 9.30am on the hills, Hallam-Parr cantered forward half his men up a little slope and opened fire. Soon he found himself facing one and a half battalions of Egyptian infantry and 'a good portion' of a whole cavalry regiment. 'I soon had to dismount all my available men – about thirty – and with these we kept the enemy from advancing,' he wrote, 'the Household Cavalry guarding our right flank half a mile to the rear. Our shooting was excellent. Once, seven or eight men fired at nine hundred yards and three men fell in the enemy's ranks.'[18]

It was 9.40am. The day looked destined to be exceptionally hot even for late August. Not a breath of wind stirred. Then, while Wolseley was considering all his options, the Egyptian gunners opened with a well-aimed shell that struck the foot of the hill in front, while a second shot passed just a couple of feet over the general's head and burst among the artillery horses (these Sir Garnet quickly ordered to be withdrawn out of sight). Twenty minutes later, four bronzed rifled muzzle-loaders, worked with such skill and accuracy that the British were quite taken aback, started raining shells in the direction of Wolseley's entourage and his own guns. Luckily for Sir Garnet this barrage made obvious the best aspect of his position as the enemy were clearly silhouetted on high stony ground in front, firing into the sun, as the British infantry lay amid the soft sand dunes and marshland, both of which cushioned them against the shellfire, or buried the projectiles filled with percussion fuzes before exploding.

Sometime after 10am the cavalry and mounted infantry were ordered to fall back because of the additional fire now directed at them by two more Egyptian guns. During this movement Hallam-Parr was hit. He considered the bullet was 'as civil as possible', since it went straight through his right leg, but missed the knee and major bones. 'I was much relieved to find I could stand,' he wrote afterwards, 'I mounted and took the troop a little further back', before going to a dressing-station and a two hour jolting cart journey towards hospital.[19] Despite making light of the injury in his letter, Hallam-Parr's wound was quite serious and by the time he got to Ismailia 'was in a bad way', according to Chaplain Male, who saw him about this time. A short time later, Viscount Melgund, who was attached to the mounted infantry, was also wounded, though less seriously than Hallam-Parr, when a bullet smashed through his hand.

With such a hot enemy fire and mounting casualties Wolseley decided around 10.30am that he should test out his guns. This was a risky business since the enemy would try hard to knock them out and mirages made range-finding very difficult. Hickman was keen to get to work and two rounds of shrapnel from the British guns quickly burst over the Egyptian artillery and infuriated them so much an uneven duel commenced. Gunner Joseph Knowles was struck in the face by a shell fragment early in the fight. The wound was nasty but he refused to seek medical assistance, roughly bandaged himself and went back to firing his gun. He was duly awarded the Distinguished Conduct Medal for his bravery.

Tubby little Melton Prior, also not lacking in courage, decided to get close to the British guns to make a sketch. While he was drawing a shell fell right in front of him, knocking Prior over and covering him in sand:

> My first impulse was to get up and bolt, my second was to do nothing of the kind. What I did was to shake the sand off my clothes, wipe it out of my eyes, pick up my book, lie down again, and go on with my sketch as though nothing had happened. This seemed to tickle Captain Hinckman [sic] very much, for I heard him exclaim, 'Well, that is pretty cool.'[20]

In reality, Prior felt he had made a 'fool' of himself and he later got a 'strong reproof' from Wolseley.

With the sun overhead at noon the British watched with consternation as the Egyptians wheeled a new battery of six Krupps into position and started to rain shells directly on the British front. The midday heat was, recalled Butler, 'simply outrageous … the yellow sand glowed like hot coals'.[21] A squadron of the 1st Life Guards was ordered by Drury Lowe to replace the Mounted Infantry. Dismounting half his men Captain the Hon. Reginald Talbot, commanding the squadron, found it was tough work: 'The men were very steady, firing as ordered, occasional shots. My horse had a lot of work to do, as the Squadron occupied ground enough for a Brigade.'[22]

William Butler was impressed by the way 'the Chief' seemed oblivious to the dangers of his position or the sun overhead, remaining 'cool and cheery, with a kind word for everyone who approached him, an eye for everything that happened on front or flank'.[23] One suspects that Wolseley was using this show of bonhomie to calm his own nerves. All ranks were impressed by their commander's coolness under fire. A conspicuous target, the sun reflected 'like a heliograph' off Sir Garnet' scabbard, while his helmet was clearly distinguishable by a pink scarf tied around it. General Graham thought his old comrade grew more serious around noon. This was hardly surprising since, in addition to extra guns, the Egyptian reinforcements summoned by train were starting to work around the British right and the artillery were dropping well-aimed shells.

In the nick of time, or so it seemed, a party of bluejackets from HMS *Orion* marched in dragging two Gatlings. Quickly the rapid firing guns were placed on either flank to give added protection. Not long after the Duke of Cornwall's light infantry arrived, while the artillery duel was at its height. 'Shell after shell whistled around us and, as they exploded, their jagged fragments flew in all directions' recalled Corporal Philip. Before taking cover the DCLI carried their wounded, some still clutching melons, across the open plain behind the British guns. 'Those brave fellows were stripped to their shirts and trousers, sleeves rolled up, the perspiration streaming from their faces as they loaded and fired like devils let loose', wrote Philip.[24]

As the afternoon wore on increasing numbers of British infantry in their red coats collapsed from the heat and dehydration. But the clock was ticking on Wolseley's side. His opponent, Rashid Pasha, was nervous about committing his troops in a general assault and hung back his men, content to play 'at long bowls with his twelve guns'.[25] The strain on the men of the Royal Horse Artillery must have been immense. Around 2.45pm the Egyptians scored two direct hits in succession, killing two men and wounding several horses. Corporal Philip watched as a tall gunner, (probably Bombardier Ballard) was 'directing his eye along his gun, apparently taking careful aim. While doing so, his head was literally blown to pieces.'[26] For almost five hours Hickman and his men 'engaged six times their own number, firing 280 rounds, a fifth of the ammunition expenditure for the whole of the 1882 Egyptian campaign'.[27]

The artillery duel ceased shortly after 3pm though the Egyptians continued to lob shells especially at the cavalry on the British right flank. In mid-afternoon Wolseley decided to take a closer look at events there and ordered Butler to accompany him. The pair reached the cavalry just as a shell hit and killed a horse nearby. Its trooper was instantly on his feet, shouting, 'Three cheers for the first charger in the Life Guards killed since Waterloo!'[28] Closest to the enemy was Captain Talbot and his Life Guards. Late in the afternoon they were reinforced by some mounted infantry who were placed under his command. Talbot's orders were 'to hold the position, if possible, till after dark ... There was a desultory fire of shell occasionally, waxing hot if we advanced, and long range rifle fire. I confess I was very glad when the sunset came.'[29]

More British cavalry arrived about 5pm in the shape of 350 sabres of the 4th and 7th Dragoon Guards under the command of Sir Baker Russell. At the sight of these reinforcements the Egyptians moved their guns and cavalry slightly further down the hill on their left but quickly stopped. It was the furthest point of their advance that day.

A little after 6pm, with the sun fast setting and gunfire falling away, the weary Guards Brigade started arriving led by the Duke of Connaught. They had left Ismailia shortly before 1pm on what proved to be a gruelling ordeal. 'Hot work it was with sword, revolver, twenty round cartridges and telescope, and the men with 100 rounds, haversacks and bottles,' wrote Lieutenant Balfour, Scots Guards, Sergeant Spriggs found the march, 'very heavy ... the sun very near cooking us alive.'[30] Lieutenant Dawnay of the Coldstreams described the march as 'rather like the retreat from Moscow,' the whole line being 'strewn with men quite beaten ... if it was not that a fight was expected next morning they would not have got through it half as well.'[31]

With the Guards struggling into camp, dusk falling all around, the British advanced to the foot of the Tel-el-Mahuta slope facing the Egyptian batteries and halted. Here Willis formed a camp in a semi-circle facing towards the enemy. His soldiers were exhausted and in desperate need of provisions. Most of the regimental carts had broken down in the deep sand. Five months earlier a report had called for: 'Maltese carts, fitted for two mules, with wheels not less than five feet in diameter', but only the Indian Contingent seem to have paid any attention. The Royal Horse Artillery got only a pint-and-a-half of water that day and the same on the next. Lt-Colonel Coghill, 19th Hussars, recalled that once his horses had eaten the ten pounds of oats and hay brought with them from Ismailia they had nothing to consume but some rushes cut from the banks of the Canal. It was the same for the officers; Major Molyneux drank his fill of the 'pea soup' Canal water and joined the rest of the Staff who 'reposed on the sand with their arms through their bridle reins'.[32] General Graham fell asleep on the ground 'dead tired' after eating a bit of hard biscuit and chocolate. He awoke feeling cold at 1am and managed to get a rug. He seems to have been less fortunate than some of the men. Driver Wickenden and his Horse Artillery pals made 'capital beds by scraping holes in the sand, rolling ourselves in our blankets, with our helmets for pillows, and then raking the sand over us so that we were almost buried'.[33]

Before returning to Ismailia to spend a few brief hours planning the next day's assault, Wolseley went round to each position, thanking the men personally, telling them how brave they had been. Corporal Philip noted that the general stopped about every twelve paces, speaking softly, with the words, 'Men, you have the place of honour; the safety of your comrades, and the glory of your country is in your keeping; you must stand or fall where you now are, even though the whole army of Egypt come against you.'[34] Stirring stuff and typical of Wolseley. By the time the general and his escort got back to Ismailia he had spent more than sixteen hours in the saddle. Old General Willis had collapsed from sunstroke earlier in the day but not Sir Garnet.

Guy Dawnay, who hoped to be a war correspondent, had been told earlier in the day that his application was not acceptable after all. He was, however, given a pass and permission to proceed to the front. It was after dark when he got there, boiled some Canal water, had a cup of cocoa and bedded down near an Arab hut. Dawnay tried to sleep, 'but mosquitoes, ants, inquiring soldiers looking for their regiments or for water, made it almost impossible'.[35] During the night his donkey ran off and at 4am, 'wet through with dew', he got up to search for the Coldstreams.

Regiments were already on the move to reinforce the British position. At 9pm on the 24th the 60th Rifles set off with several other detachments including Horse Artillery. Private Wilson of 'A' Company, KRRC, was not impressed by Colonel Ashburnham who, before setting out, was 'as drunk as a fool and trying to give us a speech'.[36] Chaplain Male wrote that it 'was a pitch dark night ... hot and weird'. The wheels of the big guns slid more than a foot into the sand, while the horses sank fetlock deep at every step. The sand made every step hard work. A staff officer saw sixteen horses being required to pull just one wagon. Lt-Colonel Schreiber, commanding the Royal Artillery, was everywhere shouting: 'Encourage your horses, men! Encourage your horses!' Route of march was a fifteen mile detour around the enemy's left flank, but in the darkness, without stars for guidance, the staff officer leading the column was forced to confess, 'I am sure I don't know where we are.' It was 2.30am and Cromer Ashburnham called a halt for one-and-a-half hours so that every-one could grab some precious rest. Three-and-a-half hours more toil, with the KRRC pushing the guns most of the way, brought them, by good fortune, to the centre of the British position.[37]

Sir Garnet was in an upbeat mood that early morning of 25 August with a plan neatly formulated to

> ... pivot his force with the left fixed on the canal near the dam, by swinging his mounted right in a great arc into the desert, and then bring it down on the canal far to the right so as to cut off the Egyptian retreat. If successful he might bag the entire enemy force, guns and all.[38]

He and his escort arrived at the British camp about 5.30; dawn had broken, and Willis had already drawn up the whole army in attack formation. As the men advanced up the slope towards the long ridge of sandhills, crowned by the Egyptian earthworks, 'hearts beat fast with suppressed excitement', as the troops waited for the expected crackle of rifle fire.[39] None came; 300 yards from the brow of the hill a mounted officer was sent to investigate. He galloped back to say the enemy had fled. The staff around the general gasped in consternation, orders were quickly barked out and gallopers rode pell-mell with news orders to the various corps.

Setting a fast pace to the top of the ridge, Wolseley saw on the far side a long stretch of open desert that opened up all the way to Kassassin, ten miles away. 'The sun was now up and the mists were drawing off from the desert,' wrote Butler, 'several trains were moving along the railway in the valley to our left front; clouds of dust showed that artillery was retiring before us.' Sir Garnet knew immediately what had to be done. Calling Butler to his side he said: 'Gallop to Drury Lowe, tell him to take all his cavalry and Horse Artillery for-ward, and *coutre que coutre* capture one or more of those trains. An engine could be worth a lot of money to me now.' With shells dropping around him, from Egyptian guns on lower ground near the railway, Butler spurred his horse on and delivered his orders.[40]

Now with extra troops and with the Egyptians in retreat Wolseley knew he could win, could hurt the enemy. 'I have never seen him so eager or so bent upon anything in my life', wrote Maurice.[41] The cavalry set off as 'admirably directed' shells fell among them killing some troopers and several horses. Major Bibby, commanding the 7th Dragoon Guards was struck by a bullet in the back that passed clean through his lungs and came out on the other side. Watching from the heights, Wolseley's frustration grew as nothing seemed to happen very quickly. The army, as one officer described it, 'were too beat, owing to the heavy sand, to do much,' while the cavalry horses 'did not appear capable of effective action.'[42] At least the mounted infantry, a corps who owed their existence to Wolseley, seemed in better shape. Galloping up close on their small Cypriot and Egyptian horses to the enemy, the riders dismounted, fired and 'proved very useful'.

Three miles ahead of the rest of the cavalry brigade, due to their point of arrival from Ismailia just minutes before the attack, the 4th Dragoon Guards found themselves almost level with one of the trains as it puffed along at full speed. Before they could seize it, a large body of Egyptian cavalry suddenly approached at a fast gallop. The 4th Dragoons advanced in echelon to meet them but at 40 yards distance the more than 700 Egyptians fired a hurried volley and 'bolted', the left wing of the regiment pursuing them with great effect through the enemy camp at Mahsama. Careering through the camp the British ran smack into seven guns that opened fire. The first shell dropped into the middle of a squadron of dragoons, scattering horses and men, while subsequent Egyptian fire 'was equally accurate'. Three battalions of enemy infantry now moved into the camp supported by artillery. Baker Russell ordered his Brigade-Major, Hugh McCalmont, to gather together some cavalry and clear the enemy in a charge. 'One man fired at me about four yards – I stuck my head behind my horses's neck,' recalled McCalmont, 'well, we killed every man jack of them except one and I saved *his* life. I saw he was unarmed and shouted not to kill him. He was holding on to my leg like grim death.'[43] During the melee a gigantic Life Guardsman called Browning, fighting on foot, received a cut on the wrist from an Egyptian. Chaplain Male later heard Browning tell the story: '"He prodded me in my arm," said our cavalryman, "and got my monkey up." "What did you do then, Browning?" said the listeners, "Why," said he, "I up with my sword and just *halved* him."'[44]

It was a little after 10am when the British infantry reached the camp. During 'Fall Out' the men, as Corporal Philip admitted, 'ransacked every tent'. Many of these were wonderfully decorated inside and out. Clothing, smouldering fires, water tins, Remingtons, sword bayonets and all kinds of equipment and food lay scattered on the ground. Along with the usual loot, the British took possession of seven Krupp field-guns. Between the camp and Mahsama railway station, about a mile away, 'dead, dying and wounded lay in hundreds'. Philip and other soldiers now took pity on the wounded enemy, carrying several 'into the shade of the station house and the trucks or carriages that stood on the line'.[45] Running parallel with the track was the Canal where more Egyptians lay shot and cut down by the cavalry as they had tried to escape.

Patrick O'Riordan, known to all as 'Mike', a cheery sergeant in the Duke of Cornwall's Light Infantry, now won a Distinguished Conduct Medal in a matter of seconds, while the Egyptians tried to jump on the last train as he gathered steam he saw that the coupling of the second carriage was slack. 'Springing from his horse he undid them,' wrote Philip, 'and the engine steamed off, leaving our gallant Mike the capturer of about twenty trucks and carriages (some of them loaded with provisions and ammunition) and some 300 prisoners'.[46]

The sun remained a fierce enemy. In his diary Percival Marling painted a miserable picture of the engagement:

> Both sides ceased firing about 10am, and as our men were nearly dead from want of water, we were ordered to retire some 3 miles to the Canal. We hadn't even a water-cart. The heat was intense, and the sand very deep, and the men fell out all over the place. We reached the Canal bank about 12 noon. One poor fellow, Ebbs, in my company, after we got in, just lay down and died. I'd been carrying his rifle for the last mile or two, as he was rather bad, but I never thought he was so far gone as that.[47]

Marling divided the last of his own water bottle between his soldier-servant and two other men, then rushed down to the Sweetwater Canal 'and drank three great canteens full of the muddiest water I ever tasted in my life. The heat was appalling.' Eight soldiers in his company had collapsed earlier in the day, everyone was seeing mirages and Marling heard several men say, 'There's the bloody water, for Gawd's sake, let us go and get a drop, sir.'[48]

It was just as bad for the cavalry. Every 200–300 yards on the way to the Canal, noted Sergeant Littlejohn of the 4th Dragoon Guards, 'a horse would fall under its rider, who would dismount or extricate himself; if the horse fell on him, take his carbine out of the bucket and leave the poor brute to die 'in its own time'.

That afternoon Wolseley rode back to Ismailia having spent more than a dozen more hours in the saddle. At Mahsama, as the day drew to a close, regiments and individuals had varying degrees of discomfit. The Life Guards were able to seize rice, barley, lentils, biscuits, beans and chopped straw in the enemy camp along with cigarettes and coffee. The men of the 4th Dragoons, who got back to camp about two hours before sundown, had 'nothing cookable or eatable in the Regiment, with the exception of the biscuit we carried with us from Ismailia'.[49] Lieutenant Balfour of the Scots Guards had managed to feast on a little rice and whisky during the day, but admitted that he 'fared better than most'. When, about 4pm, some tinned meat and coffee arrived, 'many men were too hungry to eat,'[50] noted Balfour, though Sergeant Spriggs saw 'a great many men turned very sick through eating so hearty after going without for so long'.[51] That night, another damp and chilly one, most of the officers and men slept again on the sands. One of them was Major Molyneux, who dined on 'some unleavened bread taken out of a dead Egyptian's haversack'.[52] Generals Drury Lowe, Graham and Willis had the modest comforts of a railway carriage.

Percy Marling and his men finally got a ration of tea and bully-beef in the evening. Private Ebbs was buried at dusk in a hastily dug grave near the railway embankment. 'It was too dark to read the Burial Service, even if we'd had it' noted Marling, 'and I just said the Lord's Prayer over him'.[53]

Next morning, the sun rose high again and the bloated Egyptian dead began to smell. 'Beastly place Mahsamah,' wrote Graham in his diary. He was delighted to leave that afternoon and take possession of 'a nice little villa with verandah' by Kssassin Lock. The advance had been ordered by Wolseley on the previous night and seizure of the Lock was executed rather prematurely by Hugh McCalmont and some 4th Dragoons on the morning of the 26th after mounted infantry ran into some enemy fire in front of the place.

In his room at the governor's house at Ismailia, Wolseley sat and wrote letters to Childers and Louisa. In a long one to the War Minister he was able to assess what had happened in the past few days. 'Circumstances have pushed me forward sooner than I had intended,' admitted the general, 'and consequently the difficulty of feeding and forwarding camp equipment to the front has been very great'. What had been done would have been 'next to impossible' without Admiral Seymour's help with boats on the Sweetwater Canal. 'As usual transport has been our difficulty, and until we have an engine or two working on the line, I cannot move forward again.' It was an admission that the army had literally galloped ahead of its commissariat and transport services.

The general was not now so dismissive of the enemy:

> [The Egyptians] will not allow us to approach them – except perhaps in front – near enough to use the infantry ... Their works at Mahuta were well designed and very strong, but I shall always try to turn these great lines of works and take them in flank and rear.'

The Magfar and Mahuta dams, admitted Wolseley, 'were great works, remarkably well made ... The enemy's plan is not to cut the canals apparently, but to dam them ... As long as he has a force at Tel-el-Kebir, or anywhere along the line, he must have the Canal for supplying his own men with water.' The Egyptian artillery fire had also been 'very good ... Had they had shrapnel shells, we should have suffered severely.' The butcher's bill had been light – only 5 killed and 28 wounded, though there had been numerous cases of sunstroke. The troops were exhausted and Wolseley confessed that all his cavalry and artillery horses were 'well pumped out, so that I cannot use them again for some days'. General Willis had been 'knocked up ... the sun making him feel sick and faint. I am afraid he is not very strong.'[54]

To his wife Sir Garnet admitted that he had been through 'two very hard days', completing in just 48 hours what he had thought would take a week. A further advance was now impossible for ten to fourteen days. Privately, he knew that Tel-el-Mahuta had been a gamble, one that could have cost him the campaign or even his life. Had the Egyptians pressed their attack on the morning of the 24th the whole outcome might have been different. Now, on the 26th, he held the route to Kassassin, its Canal, telegraph and railway lines. Arabi's entrenchments at Tel-el-Kebir were just nine miles away. Time was still on his side; time to bring up his reserves from Alexandria and Ismailia, and to fix his transport problems and get more food and supplies to his troops, time to prepare for one decisive battle on a day and at an hour of his choosing. If only Arabi Pasha could be relied upon not to interfere with these plans.

8

# Kassassin I

*Household Cavalry, charge!*
Baker Creed Russell

On 26 August the commander-in-chief got a telegram from General Hamley at Alexandria. It began with a tetchy plea: 'Can you not tell me what you wish me to do?' It was the first indicator of the way things would soon go between the two generals. Wolseley poured a little more salt on Hamley's hurt feelings by keeping him waiting two days for a reply.

With eagerness Sir Edward had opened his sealed instructions early on 20 August. When he realised that, along with Alison and Wood, he had been duped, and the Abourkir attack was a sham, Hamley grew extremely annoyed. A brief note from Sir John Adye told him of 'the importance of silence and of keeping the enemy amused as long as possible'. Wolseley, at more length, after explaining his intended operations, pointed out that he had not told anyone in Britain of what was afoot and urged Sir Edward to tell no one of the letter's contents. He was urged to keep the enemy busy at Kafr-Dawar, and that he and his 1st Division would be brought to the front as soon as possible for the intended battle at Tel-el-Kebir, 'if Arabi will only in kindness stay and fight me there'.[1]

While there is no doubt that Wolseley's letter started the spat that would develop between the two it is also a disagreement misunderstood by some historians. Annoyed as he was by Sir Garnet's behaviour, Sir Edward appreciated both his superior's right to act in the way he did and, grudgingly perhaps, appreciated what a clever ruse was being played on the enemy. Any anger felt on reading Wolseley's instructions was small in comparison to that he felt a few weeks later when Hamley saw the Tel-el-Kebir despatches.

With a high domed forehead, oval face and receding hairline, Hamley looked every inch the intellectual soldier. From the outset he was not a typical officer. He read a lot, made few close friends and wrote magazine articles as a hobby (developing a special relationship with the Blackwood family, powerful publishers and owners of one of the most popular non-fiction magazines).

While stationed at Gibralter in the early 1850s a female acquaintance noted that 'Captain Hamley was very thin and angular, and looked much taller than he was ... a very reserved, quiet man, and though liked had few if any intimates ... Most people stood in awe of him, owing to his silent ways and stiff manner.'[2]

During the Crimean War, as a brave captain of artillery, Hamley was in the thick of action at the Alma, Balaklava and Inkerman. Twice he had horses shot from under him (on the second occasion he was trapped under the beast until a sergeant pulled him out). On his return from the war, now a major, he continued to shine, displaying in books like *The Story Of The Campaign Of Sebastopol*, and *The Operations Of War*, skill as a writer on military matters. The high point of his career came in the 1870s when as Commandant of the Staff College for seven years, the institution gained, as Spiers has written, 'prestige and credibility within the army'. Hamley was the judge in 1872 of the Wellington Prize Essay, a competition devoted to new military theory. The winning entry was by none other than Frederick Maurice (destined to be Hamley's sharpest critic) and one of the rejected essays was that written by Garnet Joseph Wolseley.

Reserved, shy, a bookish bachelor, Hamley had also grown by 1882 into an opinionated and somewhat fussy individual. He expected other officers 'to accept his deductions as well as his facts,' noted Evelyn Wood, who had also been a Staff College student.[3] William Butler, who disliked Hamley intensely, called him simply 'an autocrat'.

But Sir Edward had several endearing qualities too. In an age when soldiers smoked a lot of cigarettes Hamley did not and found the practice abominable. He also had a huge love of animals, especially cats and before leaving Alexandria he tried to set up a home for stray felines, while aides saw him in tears more than once at the sight of wounded camels and horses on the battlefield.

Within minutes of reading Wolseley's letter, Sir Edward ordered the dismissal of the troops who, since the previous evening, had been assembled for an attack on Kafr-Dawar. General Alison felt they should stage a late afternoon reconnaissance as he had done on 5 August. Hamley disagreed, finally opting for a small advance led by him personally during the day and a bigger one at dusk. The Egyptians fired many rockets and shells but for once they missed the range completely. The British returned to Ramleh at nightfall and Sir Edward felt the whole exercise had been futile and 'unsatisfactory'.

Each day small reconnaissances took place to keep the enemy on their toes. The most interesting of these had, in fact, been one led on the 19th by Evelyn Wood. He advanced within firing range of the Egyptians with two companies of the Berkshires when a shell hit a soldier 60 yards on Wood's left. An hour later, when retiring, he asked his adjutant to send a party to recover the man's body. To his astonishment Wood was told the man was 'not much hurt'. 'But I saw him struck by a shell; he was killed,' replied the general. His adjutant insisted otherwise adding that 'you must look at him only in front, sir!' As he got closer Sir Evelyn saw the joke too. The force of the shell, which had passed between the man's legs and exploded just behind him, had left his clothes on in front but incinerated the back of everything, 'so that from heels to belt he was absolutely naked'.[4] He was also bleeding from burns on his buttocks but otherwise was a remarkably lucky man.

'Shall I take any steps for embarkation?' Hamley asked Sir Garnet on 26 August. Later, Wood asked permission to use the Highland Brigade (1st Black Watch, 2nd Highland Light Infantry, 1st Gordons and 1st Cameron Highlanders) for an attack on the Egyptian lines. Wolseley, who must have been horrified when he read this impetuous suggestion, telegraphed a brusque reply: 'No; embark as soon as all ready; desire Sir E. W. to remain on the defensive and risk nothing.'[5]

In Cairo during August the situation had also changed within the nationalist government. A special war ministry, called the '*Majlis-al-Urfi*', was created on 3 August (Maurice is quite wrong when he claimed the War Council was made up of notables; it was mainly composed of army officers and bureaucrats). The most powerful person within the 29-strong ministry was Yaqub Sami, a civil servant who had been slightly injured by Arabi's supporters during the 1 February 1881 demonstration, but had later joined the nationalists, it was rumoured, because of an incident when his wife had been mistreated by Khedival officials. Despite war hysteria, coupled with all the domestic problems of trying to run an economy in wartime, the War Council coped remarkably well.

Arabi Pasha sent several telegrams to the Supreme Porte asking for support and was devastated when the Sultan confirmed Tewfik's dismissal of him. Abdul Hamid denounced the rising as 'against Allah, the Prophets and the Caliph'. The War Council wisely did not publish the Sultan's pronouncement and kept the information strictly to themselves. Perhaps the news would have made a difference but the country was gripped by a huge wave of patriotic support for Arabi and the Army. He was seen as the 'Protector of Islam'. The general also accepted this quasi-religious destiny and told one old friend that he could not let the people down and had a mission. By late August the War Council in Cairo were deciding policy, Arabi had enough on his plate dealing with more mundane military affairs, but his mystique among ordinary Egyptians as the popular nationalist figurehead was huge.

Hamley was finally allowed to embark on 28 August. That same day the Indian Contingent finally completed its concentration at Ismailia. Three days earlier General Wilkinson, who was in command of the 2nd (Indian) Cavalry Brigade, marched out of Suez heading across the desert for Ismailia, accompanied by his staff, one troop of the 6th Bengal Cavalry and one of the 13th Bengal Lancers. The Contingent's DAQMG, barely 23 years old, was James Grierson, a bright young man who had already written a *Gazetteer of Egypt* and would duly author a confidential report on the war for the Indian Government. 'Our column' he told his father in a letter, 'was rather a pretty sight, first the 6th Cavalry, with their Khaki uniform, then the 13th Lancers in blue with their red and blue pennons fluttering away; then long lines of mules with baggage and five days rations and forage.'[6]

Sir Garnet would denigrate the Indian troops in letters home (though never publicly), and the Indian high command had not sent the cream of its Army, wishing to retain them at home for security reasons, but the force that had been sent from India was a good mix of hardy regiments. The 7th Bengal Native Infantry had not seen active service since the Lushai Expedition ten years earlier. In their khaki uniforms with dark blue turbans striped in red, its 805 officers and men included a mix of Hindus, Muslims, Sikhs and Christians. The 27th and 29th Baluchis had served in the recent Afghan War. This was also true of the toughest infantry in Contingent – the 20th Punjabis. Known as 'Brownlow's Punjabis', after Sir Charles Brownlow who formed the regiment during the Mutiny, it was composed of battle-hardened North-West Frontier Pathans and led by a 50-year-old no-nonsense colonel, Robert Rogers. He had served in the 20th for more than two decades; holding back a great rush of ghazi swordsmen in fierce hand-to-hand combat at the Crag Picquet in the Umbeyla Campaign 1863; fighting Hazaris in 1868; Afridis in 1876–78; and Afghans in 1879. A later officer, Lionel Dunsterville (the model for Kipling's 'Stalky'), recalled the regiment's many idiosyncrasies, its irreverent attitude to footwear and uniforms, its cracked mess china and worn table centre-piece – an electro-plated design of a camel beneath a palm-tree, but the nuts supporting the animal had worked loose, 'and this enabled the camel to strike most unusual attitudes …' But the 20th Punjabis was not a regiment for pretty boys and chukkas of polo on the lawn. Its fighting qualities were epitomised by its senior Indian officer, Subedar-Major Mauladad Khan. A Kuki Khel Afridi from the Khyber Pass, Mauladad had joined the East India Company's Army back in 1847, fought in ten North-West Frontier expeditions prior to 1882 and had the scars of six wounds to prove it, along others caused by a British bullet and an Afridi knife, both acquired in his youth. Astonishingly, he had been awarded the Order of Merit, the sepoy's equivalent of the Victoria Cross, no less than three times. Dunsterville recalled that the old Subedar-Major 'could neither read nor write, and regarded these accomplishments with scorn'. His ethos was pure and simple: 'In the attack there is only one thing to remember, and that is, "Fix bayonets and charge".'[7]

The Indian Contingent was a constant source of irritation to Wolseley. Foisted on to him by HM Govt, the Indian troops did not sit well in his scheme of things. Indian Army officers on leave as well as civilian employees of the Raj who offered their services met with cool disdain from Sir Garnet. Things were no better for Macpherson's Staff; when Colonel Moore, Bombay Staff Corps, introduced himself to Wolseley as 'chief intelligence officer and interpreter of the Indian Division', the general coldly replied that 'there was only one Intelligence Branch for the Army in Egypt, the one formed in London; Colonel Moore's services, therefore, would not be required'. The colonel was terribly offended and later voiced the feelings of many officers of the Raj towards their British Army counterparts: 'How they hate the Indian Army!'[8]

While hurrying up British regiments to the front, Wolseley did nothing to hasten up the Indian Contingent. This so incensed Macpherson, and his senior commanders, that a telegram of complaint was sent to the Indian Government. Three days later the Indian soldiers were moved to Kassassin, so it seems likely that wires were exchanged between Simla and London on the subject. In another instance Langton Walsh, a civilian volunteer from the Indian Marine Postal Service, got himself attached to Baker Russell's cavalry brigade as Arabic interpreter. When Wolseley found out he swiftly refused to permit the appointment.

Sitting in his office at Ismailia on 27 August the British commander could feel pretty good about the successes of the past seven days. In addition to the guns and stores captured at Tel-el-Mahuta and Mahsama there had been an unexpected coup in the person of Mahmud Fehmy Pasha, chief engineer of the Egyptian Army. An early opponent of Tewfik, highly principled and technically bright, Fehmy had been supervising the new defences at Tel-el-Kebir. His seizure, recorded by many participants in the campaign, soon turned into myth. Whether he was arrested in disguise at Mahsama railway station or, as seems more likely, captured in the desert by a troop of the 1st Life Guards, then almost shot as a spy on Baker Russell's orders, is not really important. In a long tailed morning-coat and carrying an umbrella, the nervous Egyptian was eventually interviewed by Sir John Adye, the British chief-of-staff and Wolseley's second-in-command. 'Shoot me, if you please,' shouted Fehmy, but he begged not to be handed over to the Khedive's henchmen as they would torture him. Sir John replied that he would be treated as a prisoner of war and given a fair trial.

Wolseley now had a little time to gossip with Louisa. He told her how the Duke of Teck was already proving useless. 'He disappeared yesterday evening and took up his quarters at an hotel,' Sir Garnet told his wife, 'I have not time to look after him and he is just like a querulous child.' The Queen's son was another of Wolseley's grumbles. The Duke of Connaught, he told Louisa, 'has no stamina ... These princes have all been spoiled by their education; they have been made selfish by always having everyone give way to them and do everything for them. I wish they were all in Jericho.'[9]

On a more serious note the general wrote to say that he was 'very sorry' to leave Evelyn Wood, one of his best commanders, behind at Alexandria. He knew Wood would be 'furious' but, as the junior major-general commanding the junior brigade, 'it cannot, however, be helped. I shall never be able to face Lady Wood ... again.'[10]

Wolseley rode back to check on the situation at Tel-el-Mahuta and Mahsama on 27 August, the wind hitting his face like a furnace, while 'my poor old nose ... blossomed into a sort of half-cauliflower, half-fungus'. He had met with his old friend, Baker Russell, 'who had not shaved for three days, nor changed any of his things'. Russell had just got some tea, his first for a few days, and invited Wolseley to join him in a breakfast consisting of 'very dirty-looking rice boiled in an Egyptian pot and a little filthy treacle which he had found in the Egyptian camp'.[11]

Out in the desert the British troops were trying to cope with some tough conditions. 'Mahsama was enough to give anyone the cholera,' wrote a signaller in the Mounted Infantry, 'you could see Egyptians lying dead all over the place, and the stink was cruel.'[12] Innovation and a dry sense of humour served the Tommies very well. At Kassassin Lock, where the DCLI were part of Graham's small force, the men were so hungry by the 27th that they began stealing the beans provided to feed the mules. Thanks to the Navy, supply boats could get up the Canal as far as Magfar, much to the delight of the officers and men of the 4th Dragoons who were issued with coffee, tea and half-rations of tinned beef or mutton. One wheezing train also got to Mahsama. It was greeted with loud cheers from the troops. 'It was a grand thing to have a train at all,' wrote one participant.[13] Of the regimental carts sent from Ismailia with supplies on the 24th there was still no sign.

The notorious carts were just the tip of the iceberg insofar as commissariat and transport problems were concerned. The complaints and failures would increase to such an extent that, shortly after the war ended, a Royal Commission would be set up to investigate. But at this stage of the campaign it was already clear that several things were wrong: the carts were useless in desert conditions; 1,500 mules bought in ample time in Greece were refused shipment by the Turks, others purchased as far away as America would take almost a month to arrive; and there were too few commissariat troops at Ismailia for the huge task of unloading so many supplies and getting them to the front. Finally, to add insult to Sir Garnet's carefully laid plans, the infernal Indians arrived with better transport and a goodly supply of 2,500 mules.

Under a boiling sun a small army of men chipped away with picks and shovels at the two dams blocking the Sweetwater Canal. William Molyneux later said it was the hardest two days of manual labour in his life: 'We had no hoes and no baskets and when we tried our entrenching shovels on the wet sand and rushes it was like digging into a mattress.' He did, however, find it amusing to see the normally immaculate Guards 'with nothing on but helmets and shirts, in the water dragging out rushes and bailing away at the sand'.[14] Lieutenant King-Harman RN, whose bluejackets also dug away like beavers, called it 'a vile job'. The Tel-el-Mahuta dam turned out to be much easier to dislodge than the one at Magfar; composed only of sand this second dam was nevertheless 50 feet thick, rose 12 feet above the waterline and was 70 feet wide.

Camped at Tel-el-Mahuta were the Brigade of Guards, the King's Royal Rifle Corps, the 4th Dragoon Guards, 19th Hussars and four guns. Over the ridge a few miles away at Mahsama were the rest of the 1st Cavalry Brigade commanded by Sir Baker Russell along with the Royal Marines and six guns of the Royal Horse Artillery. In the forward position at Kassassin Lock, under General Graham, were the Duke of Cornwall's Light Infantry, the York and Lancaster Regiment, along with small detachments of the 4th and 7th Dragoons, 70 Mounted Infantry, and 40 officers and men of the RHA with two guns – a total of 1,895 officers and men.

Kassassin Lock lay in a low position, literally a valley, with the ground rising significantly to the north and west (in the direction of Tel-el-Kebir) in a series of hills. The situation resembled a natural amphitheatre with the Lock at its centre and was not so very different from the Tel-el-Mahuta position occupied by the British four days earlier that week.

Unbeknown to him, 28 August 1882 was destined to be a very special one for the commanding officer at Kassassin. A giant of a man, standing six feet four inches in his socks, broad and blue-eyed, with a smart grey moustache, Major-General Graham VC, Royal Engineers, was noted for his courage, though Wolseley, a life-long friend, admitted that he was also 'not exactly brilliant'. It was an age when qualities of leadership and bravery mattered most and no one ever denied that Graham had these in spades. He was about the same age as Wolseley and had won his Victoria Cross in an unsuccessful attack on the Redan in 1855. Garnet met him in the Crimea and was impressed by the way Graham refused to duck when the Russians took potshots at his big frame. A few years later the two met again during the China War, Garnet slapping Graham's leg with delight. 'Please don't slap that thigh. I've just got a bullet in there,' replied his friend calmly and, as Wolseley looked down at his hand he saw it was crimson with blood.[15] A soldier's soldier, who led from the front and thought nothing of sharing the privations of his men, Graham, as his commander once remarked, had 'the heart of a lion and the modesty of a young girl'.

A crimson sun rose on the morning of the 28th on a day that would see the thermometer reach 104 degrees. The men of the DCLI were still awaiting the arrival of their tents. Each soldier had thus created his own 'shanty'. Some had dug holes in the sand roofed over with palm leaves, others had simply stuck stakes in the ground and thrown their jackets over them. Most had slept fitfully as a result of hungry stomachs. Food was so scarce that a party of men were sent off at daybreak to the banks of the Sweetwater Canal 'to gather dirty brown biscuits, which in their haste the retreating enemy had thrown away in large quantities'.[16] One biscuit handed over to the quartermaster had to be shared between three men. 'Mouldy and dirty as they were, each man ate his square inch and longed for more,' recalled Corporal Philip. When some companies were sent to a nearby Arab village to scrounge for firewood (which the soldiers thought grimly funny in view of the lack of anything to cook), but several chickens were found, caught, quickly plucked, and found their way into a number of empty bellies.

Between noon and 1pm, if Philip is to be believed, Egyptian cavalry in large numbers began pouring over the hills about a mile from the camp. Enemy infantry and artillery were also spotted though at a greater distance. There was a hurried call to arms as the horsemen galloped down on Graham's men. 'Wheeling into line we marched out to meet the foe,' wrote Corporal Philip, 'when some 800 yards intervened we got the order to fire'.[17] Rifles flashed along the British line but the distance had been miscalculated and few Egyptians were hit. A second volley was more effective. Riders and horses rolled in the sand. For a few more seconds the Egyptians kept coming before swinging back to the hills again.

This account differs from General Graham's own despatch in which he recorded, probably accurately, that the enemy were first sighted at around 9.30am, his cavalry and mounted infantry watching them on the flanks until about 12 noon, when they opened fire with two guns. He completely omits Philip's description of a charge on his lines about this time, merely observing that after some artillery fire the enemy's 'attack seemed to languish, and about 3pm the officer commanding the mounted infantry reported the enemy retiring'.[18] It seems quite probable that Philip was being honest since he reported merely what he personally witnessed. During the morning Graham had heliographed to Drury Lowe to move up his cavalry and keep in touch by signals. The Egyptian artillery finally stopped shelling around 4pm.

The heat at noon had been tremendous. General Willis at Tel-el-Mahuta, alarmed by the distant sound of gunfire, sent Major Molyneux, DAA and QMG of the 1st Division, to investigate. Near Mahsama he met up with the main body of cavalry. They were all dismounted, 'most of them sitting under their horses to get some shade'.[19] He chatted with Baker Russell and Drury Lowe, the latter informing him that he intended to take the brigade back to Mahsama because in response to Graham's request they had spent the past few hours riding in the heat and not seen any of the enemy. Molyneux sent a fellow officer back to Willis with this news while he pressed on to the front. By the time Drury Lowe's cavalry got back to camp the horses were maddened with thirst, 'no sooner was the canal in sight than the horses took charge of their riders,' wrote an officer of the 7th Dragoons, 'and rushing down the muddy banks, plunged into the water girth-high, and drank as they had never drunk before'.[20]

Since the events of the day were now to be dominated by the cavalry it is worth examining Wolseley's senior cavalry officers. The Division was com-manded by 52-year-old Drury Lowe, an old school cavalry officer who, no doubt to the delight of the Duke of Cambridge, had spent almost his entire career in the 17th Lancers. With that regiment he had fought bravely in Central India in 1858–59, but it was the handling of his men during the Zulu War, notably in a charge at Ulundi, that did much to get him noticed. He was a popular officer and a modest one, not noted for shows of dash or impetuosity. His senior staff officer was Herbert Stewart; prematurely balding, with a droopy moustache, the son of a Hampshire clergyman, universally liked and with huge reserves of charm. Wolseley thought him 'always cheery, always prepared to take on any job, no matter how unpleasant it may be'.[21] A kind of renaissance man, Stewart's interests included architecture, engineering and legal affairs.

Commanding the 1st Cavalry Brigade was bulky, eccentric Sir Baker Creed Russell. To many who served under him Sir Baker was 'the beau ideal of a fighting leader'.[22] Russell bawled out his orders in a gravel voice that could wake the dead and did not suffer fools gladly but his magnetic larger-than-life personality led men to obey him without question. He had fought throughout the Mutiny in countless actions, organised a native regiment on special serv-ice in Ashanti and there made the friendship of Wolseley, who also used him in South Africa. Stories told about Russell during his years commanding the 13th Hussars – known in the Army as 'The Baker's Dozen' – were legendary. When a war office clerk rejected one of his expense forms for forage because the distance ought to have been shorter 'as the crow flies', Sir Baker sent the claim back with the words, 'I do not ride a crow – I ride a horse.' On another occasion a commissariat officer who had selected a bad camping ground made the mistake of jauntily inquiring of Russell if he was happy with the site? 'You sir, are only a civilian, that is evident by your dress,' replied the acerbic colonel, 'but by God if the commissariat officer should ever dare to show his damned nose within a mile of my camp, I should have him in arrest and shoved in the guard-room, not only as incompetent and unfit to be an officer, but as little better than a murderer.' On the parade ground woe betide any junior officer whose actions annoyed Sir Baker. Like an old wild boar (which, with his huge moustache he much resembled), he would gallop up to the unfortunate individual and give him a tongue-lashing. It was a temper 'short and quick and not malignant', noted Baden-Powell.[23] Those under him knew that Russell cared little for the drill-book, had an instinctive soldier's eye for where his men should be in a fight, and would have followed him to Hell if need be. In Egypt he had got his command over the objections of the Duke of Cambridge. It was another classic Wolseley Ring appointment. Russell was personally very grateful. He had just lost £5,000 (the better part of £500,000 by today's standards) in a bad business deal and he hoped the campaign would take his mind off such worries.

In the late afternoon sun things were peaceful at Kassassin. Corporal Philip and some of his chums were pursuing a few chickens that had escaped their earlier round-up when the call to arms was heard again. The Egyptians had returned and this time intended serious business. Left of the British camp lay the Canal, and slightly to the right, the embanked railway line. Close to the Canal, where the land was flat shingle, Graham positioned the Royal Marine Artillery, 800 yards east of them the DCL took up a position at right angles to the marines, the York and Lancaster's were echeloned upon the DCLI to form the right rear. With their rifles pointing to the hills of the north-west, now alive with white-uniforms, Graham extended three companies of the DCLI and two and a half companies of the York and Lancaster's into skirmishing order.

The British had plenty of time to get into position since the enemy were still a long way from the camp. Major Molyneux who had arrived only a short time before was just starting to eat his frugal lunch when a shell crashed into the sand nearby. Hastening over to General Graham he was ordered to ride quickly to Drury Lowe, ask for his battalion of marines, 'and to move the cavalry to the north-west to watch for an opportunity to attack the enemy's left flank'.[24] Bullets and shells started to whistle and screech all around him as Molyneux spurred on his thoroughbred across the soft desert towards Mahsama.

Two more guns had reached Graham that afternoon bringing his total to four. Unfortunately, an ammunition boat from Tel-el-Mahuta had not arrived, nor the regimental ammunition wagons. His gun crews were dependant entirely on their limber ammunition. Luckily, the marines, with splendid ingenuity, had managed to mount a captured Krupp on a railway truck. It was not long before the four guns exhausted their small supply of shells so the general was forced to send them back to Tel-el-Mahuta for more ammunition. Everything now depended on the single Krupp gun as the sole means of keeping the enemy at a distance. During the course of the battle, though they were fired upon by up to four enemy guns at a time, not a man among the Marines was killed as they blasted away with the Krupp's entire 93 rounds. By pushing the truck backwards and forwards on the railway track the Marines managed to keep the gun out of the enemy's range. 'The detachment seemed to bear a charmed life,' wrote *The Times* correspondent, 'In front of it, beside it, and behind it, fell shrapnel, bullets and ragged morsels of shell fired in salvoes by the Egyptian guns.'

When the Egyptians were within 900 yards the order to fire rang out. Instantly the Martini-Henry rifles flashed but the enemy fire was also telling as the men in red began to be struck, 'clutching vainly at the sand in their descent', as they rolled down the railway embankment.[25] In the gap between the Royal Marine Artillery and the DCLI the enemy made at least three attempts to break through. Each time, as they tried to cross the Sweetwater Canal, a small party of mounted infantry and 4th Dragoons hit them with a withering fire.

Medical officers worked as bullets and shells fell all around them. It was a frustratingly slow process for some of the men. Gunner Judge, wounded in the leg, was told to go to the rear, but instead went back to work with the Krupp since 'there were so many wounded in the hospital that they had better not be troubled by him also', (he was subsequently awarded the Conspicuous Gallantry Medal).[26] Surgeon-Major Shaw, who was attending to some of the DCLI, was shot through the head. Philip watched as the doctor 'clutched frantically at the air, and fell on his back dead.' The corporal also had a narrow shave when a bullet glanced off the chain on his helmet. The blow sent him rolling backwards down the embankment where he lay unconscious for a few minutes. Then, picking up his battered helmet, he went back up the slope. The men's shoulders were now getting bruised by the vicious recoil of their rifles. Philip estimated that by this time the men had each fired between 200 and 300 rounds and the weapons were blisteringly hot to touch. Several of the men took the huge risk of standing up on the railway line to get a clear view of the enemy rather than suffer the extra bruising inflicted from firing lying down. Skinny young Lieutenant Cunningham ran back and forth getting extra ammunition for the men even after a bullet smashed his right hand. It was not until he was hit in the leg that he agreed to visit the field hospital. Keeping his men in line, Sergeant-Major Carr, a tough disciplinarian admired and feared by the men, got hit by shrapnel that shattered his boot and foot, but he kept limping along, 'placing men here and there when he saw they were required'.[27]

Twenty-five minutes hard riding from Kassassin brought Major Molyneux to the British cavalry lines at Mahsama. The Royal Marines, with six 16-pounder guns, set off immediately to reinforce Graham, but Drury Lowe refused to hurry. After the morning's false alarm he thought it thoroughly 'inadvisable'. Stewart, an old Zulu War chum of Molyneux's, joked that they had had one 'scare already that day, and now their horses had their nose-bags full of the Khedive's best beans'.[28] Molyneux told him to listen to the sound of the guns. This was no scare, he insisted, but the real thing. After a short break he remounted and around 5.30pm set off for General Willis's camp at Tel-el-Mahuta.

Back at Kassassin the action was still going on, and to make matters worse the Egyptians started bringing up more troops by train. Graham, who clearly thought that reinforcements should have got to him by 5.30, must have assumed that Drury Lowe's cavalry were camped closer than was the case. He may not even have realised that after the morning's perambulations the whole brigade had gone back to Mahsama. He now despatched his extra aide-de-camp, Lieutenant Pirie of the 4th Dragoon Guards, with a verbal order to be conveyed to Drury Lowe. It was a stupid mistake on Graham's part not to write it down or order Pirie to do so (though the young officer must be censured for not making a written copy). Instead, General Graham told his aide to say to Drury Lowe: 'take the cavalry round by our right, under cover of the hill, and attack the left flank of the enemy's skirmishers'.[29]

In fast falling light the Egyptians tried a flank attack themselves on the British left. Corporal Philip was hugely impressed by one of the war correspondents (whom he does not name), who 'was the first to see the white-coated Egyptians creeping over the railway line'. The civilian sprang to his feet and with several soldiers helped to mow down the attackers as they tried to cross the tracks. He 'picked up a rifle, and, with his coat off, was blazing away'.[30] The Egyptians finally gave up the attack as darkness fell but the newspaper man was wounded by a bullet as he rose behind a wall and hit again as two soldiers dragged him out of the line of fire. It was so dark by 7.15 pm when the Royal Marines arrived from Mahsama, that it was thought inadvisable to expend the ammunition. The general had ordered a general advance about 6.45pm but the British walked forward very gingerly in the moonlight and some had 'narrow escapes in mistaking detached bodies of the enemy for British troops'.[31]

Drury-Lowe had left Mahsama just before 6pm. Sunset that night was beautiful as ever in the desert and over all too quickly. The 1st Cavalry Brigade found themselves riding under a full moon, 'an occasional order to trot, or to change direction alone breaking the silence', save the jingle of harness and the occasional snort of an excitable horse.[32] It was during this advance that Lieutenant Pirie found the cavalry commander. Poor Pirie had not had a good afternoon, pushing his horse too hard the beast had collapsed in the sand and he had to borrow another mount from one of the marine artillery batteries. Nervous of his responsibilities, lost and fretful in the darkness, he now was so overcome at finding Drury Lowe that he failed to convey Graham's message completely or accurately. He blurted out that the general was 'only just able to hold his own and wished General Drury-Lowe to attack the left of the enemy's infantry skirmishers'.

Mulling this over, the general continued his advance. In the far distance could now be seen the flash of rifle fire at Kassassin. The cavalry were about two-and-a-quarter miles north-west of Kassassin and about six from Mahsama, when the silence was broken 'by the boom of a gun, followed by the hissing of a shell which went far beyond us,' wrote Captain Talbot of the 1st Life Guards, 'and then in rapid succession were seen flashes from guns about 1,500 yards distant on the summit of the ridge along which we were advancing'.[33] The guns, on a slope above the cavalry, had been firing earlier down on the British camp. Now they had been turned around to face the cavalry. 'It was a wierd scene,' wrote Hugh McCalmont, riding in front with his friend, Baker Russell, and the latter's orderly, Lieutenant Henry Gribble. 'We were very close – closer than we knew – when the enemy opened on us from two corner-guns, and the infantry also. Being so near, the volleys went over us.'[34] Quickly the 7th Dragoon Guards moved to the rear as Drury-Lowe ordered up his guns to reply to the Egyptians. A few shots were exchanged while the Household Cavalry continued to advance at a walk to the right of the gunners.

Suddenly a white line of infantry became visible in the immediate front of the British horsemen. There was not a moment to lose. 'Front form in two lines' came the command. Riders quickly jostled their mounts as the order 'Draw swords' rang out. There was a steely sound as the blades slipped out of more than 450 scabbards. The Household Cavalry, its aristocratic and immensely wealthy officers, smart troopers and fine chargers, a unit that had not had one moment of glory in almost seven decades, prepared to do battle. Sir Baker Russell, fierce with his walrus moustache, unmistakable in his white jacket, sat high in the saddle and the stentorian voice thundered out the command: 'Household Cavalry, charge!'

The Egyptian soldiers had a chance to loose off a few more rounds before they turned into unwilling participants in a drama that had not been enacted since the day of Waterloo. Thundering towards them were hundreds of black stallions, their riders sabres glinting in the moonlight, as the rifles flashed 'like the lighting of some grand pyrotechnic display.' When the British were about 100 yards away the Egyptians stopped firing. A few seconds later, at 20 yards, they turned en masse to flee but by then it was too late. 'We rode them down in solid rank, but as they dispersed we opened out and pursued,' wrote Captain Talbot, 'they fell like nine pins, many of them unwounded, who fired and stabbed our horses as we galloped past them'. It was bloody work and the Egyptians did not die easily, but 'we could give no quarter, for they fired after they were wounded, as soon as one's back was turned'.[35] After 300 yards hard riding Lt-Colonel Ewart, 2nd Life Guards, called out 'Rally'. All gave a cheer. It was followed by a brief silence as officers and men took a few deep breaths before more Egyptians were cut down or troopers tried to regroup.

In the melee incidents occurred fast and furious. Baker Russell's horse was killed under him in the charge. The white-coated giant laid about him with his sabre. It had long been his motto that the duty of a cavalry officer was 'to look smart in time of peace and to get killed in war'.[36] Russell single-handedly despatched two or three of the enemy. One of the troopers named Lipscombe pursued a mounted Egyptian officer. Drawing level, the man raised his revolver and pre-pared to shoot at point-blank range. Lipscombe reached out, grabbed the gun by its muzzle, twisted it back on the officer and killed him. Hugh McCalmont rode so far that he got lost, one of several officers and men who were disorientated by the moonlight. Captain Sir Simon Lockhart of the 1st Life Guards galloped off towards the left front and ended up among the Egyptian artillery. He 'blazed away with his revolver' before galloping back. Lieutenant Gribble was less fortunate. Riding an excitable horse, Russell's aide went straight into the Egyptian lines and his mangled body was found on the sands a few days later.[37]

It was about 8.45pm when Graham got news of the moonlight charge from an officer of the 1st Life Guards who had lost his way. The Egyptian artillery had retreated and so, in the darkness, with the cavalry on outpost-duty, the army returned to camp.

Earlier in the evening, about ten minutes past six, Major Molyneux on an exhausted horse had reached Willis at Tel-el-Mahuta. Hearing of the attack on Kassassin he immediately sent off the King's Royal Rifle Corps. Heavy firing could be heard to the west and soon a trooper appeared who, like Pirie, gave a highly coloured version of events. Now quite alarmed, Willis sent an urgent message back to Wolseley at Ismailia, while at the same time ordering his whole force, except for a battery of artillery and half a battalion of the Guards, to march on Kassassin. Near Mahsama they halted while some of the staff, with a detach-ment of the 19th Hussars, cautiously rode on. One of them was Molyneux who quickly ran into several 1st Cavalry Brigade Staff 'carousing over an immense brass bowl full of boiling coffee'.[38] News of the victory was sent back to Willis who ordered his weary men to return to Tel-el-Mahuta. The Guards Brigade had all lain down on the sand and were fast asleep in ranks, 'the funniest sight I ever saw' wrote one of them.[39] On Willis's command they were woken up and trudged sullenly back to camp.

A railway truck was found for the hard-working Molyneux to get some sleep in, half full of lentils, but also crawling with bugs, fleas and mosquitoes. Next morning he was up at first light to view the scene of the charge. Bedouin were already there looting the bodies. They quickly rode off when the 19th Hussars arrived on the scene. Lt-Colonel Coghill, commanding the 19th, wrote to his wife that 'on going through the dead I came across a good many wounded. All of them reached out for their rifles to have a dying shot before being killed as they thought'. He was annoyed that they did not seem to understand they would be given medical assistance by the British, 'for they mutilate all our wounded whom they catch'.[40] Molyneux counted 58 Egyptian dead besides the many wounded (and it is likely many of these died later). Near Kassassin Lock, in front of the British camp and littering the Canal and railway line were hundreds more dead and wounded Egyptians. Once again, the British had got off comparatively lightly: a total of ten killed, eighty wounded and three missing of all ranks.

One of the missing was a trooper named Bennett. His charger bolted and Bennett had three sword wounds. Not long after he was captured by Bedouin who lassoed him out of the saddle and dragged him across the sands with a rope around his neck. Taken before Arabi Pasha the young soldier was given a stern lecture on his country's wrongdoings and taken in chains to Cairo. The locals spat and reviled him, yet otherwise unharmed, he was placed with Midshipmen De Chair in pleasant confinement.

# 9

# Kassassin II

*Got them within reach at last*
Gerald Graham

At Ismailia during the afternoon of 28 August the sound of very heavy firing coming from the direction of the advanced positions was heard with alarm by the troops camped there. 'I did not pay much attention to it,' Wolseley later wrote to his wife, 'especially as I knew we had plenty of troops to hold their own in front against any number the enemy could bring against us'.[1]

About 7pm the general got a telegram saying that Graham had been attacked, along with a 'very alarming' letter from Willis. One hour later came a telegram from Sir George which said: 'Enemy advancing on Mahsameh station, fear Graham has been defeated.'[2] Pondering this news, Wolseley ate his dinner, and then went to bed about 11pm, 'with orders to be called at 1am to start at 2am with enough grub for the day to enable me to spend the day and night out'. The general slept soundly, as he told Louisa, because:

> I could not and did not believe all this bad news which came tumbling in upon me every ten minutes before I went to bed. I have known Graham all my life. I have seen him under the heaviest fire as stolidly and ... as cool as if he were at a review. I felt as confident that he would never retreat before any number of Egyptians as I should myself.[3]

Wolseley was not totally sanguine, confessing to his wife that he started to worry what might happen if Graham had been killed, and 'with these sad ideas running through me head I went to bed in a most depressed condition'. His relief was great when Lagden, the *Daily Telegraph* correspondent arrived breathlessly with the latest news from Kassassin. He, in turn, just managed to beat Cameron of the *Standard*, whose horse had tripped during the fierce ride the two journalists made across the desert. 'Good news, sir. We have a brilliant success,' blurted out Lagden, before giving the general a detailed account.[4] An hour later Sir Garnet was in the saddle, 'thanking God to myself with a light heart'. He reached the forward camp early that morning of 29 August.

During the day, listening to various stories, Wolseley was able to get a clear picture of what had happened during the battle. He was delighted with the Household Cavalry, who 'can be laughed at no longer; I believe they will owe the continuance of their existence to my bringing them here and pushing them well to the front'.[5] Baker Russell had 'led them like a man'. General Willis got a severe ticking-off and Sir Garnet was even less pleased with the Duke of Teck and George Fitzgeorge (Cambridge's son), both of whom were so worn out that they returned to Ismailia in boats intended for the wounded, 'confound them'.

Critics quickly rounded on Graham for his loose orders to Drury Lowe, the poor disposition of his picquets and lack of artillery. The 1st Battle of Kassassin, as it became known after the war, had shown despite the coolness of British troops under fire, 'that the task they had undertaken was likely to prove more than a parade across the desert, and that the enemy was willing to come within range and hold his own for hours together'.[6] In retrospect it seems likely that the reconnaissance by the Egyptians on the morning of the 28th had been designed to probe the British position. Arabi may well have realised that the call to arms would keep his enemies out in the blazing sun for the rest of the day and a fatigued army was easier to beat than a fit one. Reports of the camp's weakness in artillery and lack of much cavalry probably encouraged the Egyptian general, who had recently arrived at Tel-el-Kebir, to try a full-scale assault. He came within a hair's breadth of defeating the infidels. Only the coming of darkness and the fact that so many of his soldiers were new recruits, unable to compete with well-trained British regulars in a close-quarter engagement, settled the outcome. Nevertheless, the foreign press and foreign military attaches enjoyed reporting that: 'It is probable that Sir G. Wolseley has under-rated his enemy.'[7] One of Graham's sternest critics was Melton Prior who wrote in his memoirs:

> It has been said that the handful of men at Kassassin were able to hold their own, but I am prepared to state from personal knowledge that had it not been for Drury Lowe's cavalry charge that small handful of men under General Graham was likely to have met with a similar fate to that which befell our men at Isandlwana.[8]

Montagu Gerard spoke for many military men when he called the battle 'a curiously mixed-up sort of business,' and bluntly accused Graham of having 'absolutely no proper outposts, and the consequence was that the cavalry were continually having to mount, and move out to check some reconnaissance or demonstration on the part of our opponents'.[9]

One writer of a leading article in a London newspaper accused General Graham of faulty dispositions and quoted the disaster at Isandlwana in Zululand as an example of entrusting commands to Engineer officers. The writer concluded that the general was guilty of errors 'which would have been discreditable to the youngest regimental officer'. Harsh words indeed. After the campaign was over General Sir Lintorn Simmons, Colonel-Commandant of the Royal Engineers, took the unusual step of defending Graham's action in a public speech:

> His force at first was very small, and, knowing that he might be attacked by very superior numbers, he was compelled to keep his men ready for any emergency, fresh and full of fight. It would probably have required nearly one-third of his force to cover his camp completely, and his men would have been worn out with fatigue, by excessive outpost duty ... it would have been an act of decidedly poor generalship if he had gone out to a distance to attack. What he did was to await the development of the enemy's attack, and then, having secured the co-operation of the cavalry, to make a counter-attack.[10]

The truth seems to be that Graham's disposition of picquets was poorly organised, the camp had been caught napping and he issued sloppy orders. It was not his fault that he had so few guns and little cavalry support. Wolseley, and circumstances in general, were also to blame. But, like the courageous fighting soldier he was, Graham rose to the challenge under fire.

Across the battlefield after the fight, burying parties found that many of the bodies had been 'shockingly mutilated' by the Bedouin. Circumcised persons were spared, but the uncircumcised of both armies had lopped-off feet, hands and genitals, ripped abdomens and gashes on their foreheads. Major Tulloch, accompanied by his intelligence assistant, Captain Charles Watson, examined the Egyptians and found 'several wounded men, some in a state of delirium, others very weak but still sensible'. Watson, in a letter home, contradicted his chief and stated that only five of Egyptians were found alive (in view of the Bedouin this seems quite likely). The gruesome sights were described by Tulloch thus:

> One poor fellow I tried to carry had his abdomen sliced open by a sword-cut. Fortunately the bowels had not been touched; but I had to put them back in their place before I moved the man. Another was a wounded officer – a huge fellow. As I lifted him, his head, badly cut and festering, fell on my shoulder; the broken bone of his left arm was protruding through the cloth of his coat ... All the time the enemy's cavalry pickets were watching me at some few hundred yards distance.[11]

The British wounded had all been sent down the Canal to Ismailia in flat-bottomed boats towed by steam launches. Bluejackets carefully made sure that each invalid had their water bottle full of cocoa or tea and palms were fixed above the soldiers to give them respite from the sun. One man recalled waking next morning 'in a spacious, lofty room, the ceiling most elaborately decorated and gilded, the floor formed of different coloured woods in mosaic and the walls … decorated with paintings of flowers alternating with magnificent mirrors.'[12] The Khedive's two-storey palace had been turned into a hospital.

Their comrades in the desert continued to make the best of a bad situation. Lieutenant Balfour of the Scots Guards spent the whole of 30 August wearing his goggles and green veil to ease the glare of the sun and keep off the 'awful' flies, yet he found the Canal water, 'though very muddy, is perfectly wholesome in spite of the dead bodies and horses which we have pulled out'. Four days later he wrote: 'We are quite comfortable now – as comfortable as one can be, that is, with all one's things covered with more or less dust and two or three flies in each eye, five or six up one's nose, and as to one's ears!'[13]

The 'hot winds and sand storms and flies and the cold at nights' were wearying to Sergeant Spriggs, also serving with the Scots Guards. On the night of 29 August he was excused outpost duty and dreamed: 'I was at home nursing my little girl, but I woke up frightened to find I was all alone.' Next day he got his first letter from home in more than a month. 'I could not help a few tears falling as I read it' Spriggs noted in his diary.[14]

Eustace Dawnay thought the Coldstreams all looked like 'brutes', but on 31 August he had 'a capital bath' utilising a hole in the sand with his waterproof sheet on top of it. Like every other officer, Eustace did not have a good word to say about the commissariat department: 'The transport is wretched … All the Crimean and Indian fellows say they never saw anything like it.' Dawnay was pleased that his elder brother, Guy, was staying with the Coldstreams and had finally been granted the status of war correspondent, but he didn't think he would have much to write about. 'They say we shall have a big fight at Tel-el-Kebir but I don't think they will stand anywhere,' he wrote to their sister, Victoria.[15] Guy was sleeping most nights on the sand outside his brother's tent. On the 31st he rode over to Kassassin from Mahsama picking his way among the many unexploded shells on the battlefield. The advance staff and cavalry officers were living in looted Egyptian tents and Dawnay thought most things were luxurious. This was not, however, the opinion of Lt-Colonel Kendal Coghill commanding the 19th Hussars, an old Indian Mutiny campaigner, who was unhappy with the climate, poor food, bad water and no transport. 'The filth we eat and drink here is horrible,' he told his wife in a letter.[16] At Mahsama, where his King's Royal Rifle Corps company was guarding the station, Percy Marling had a wonderful dinner on 30 August cooked by one of his men, a pudding made of bully beef and dates and:

> ... slept out in the sand on the platform. Sand flies, mosquitoes and bugs something awful. We none of us got a wink the whole night ... Had a bit of a skirmish and shot 2 Arabs the other side of the Canal before breakfast. A Bedouin got into the hospital with a knife last night and killed a wounded man.[17]

Delays in transport and supplies were frustrating but Wolseley tried to put a brave face on things. He wrote to Childers on 31 August and explained:

> We are getting on very well, our difficulty is our railway, as the engines from England have not yet arrived, and, at present, we have only one locomotive working on the line ... We shall have some heavy losses in our big fight when it comes off, but one cannot make omelettes without breaking eggs ... I shall want cavalry horses badly soon ... we have lost a good number ... To please the Navy, I have asked Seymour to form a Naval Brigade for shore work. I have ordered Hamley on here with the Highland Brigade ... Of course the newspapers will howl at any delay, and tell of our broken-down commissariat, etc, etc, but we cannot help that.[18]

The Press back home had made a big fuss over the transport problems and there were cries of 'Sloth'. *Punch* had even published a cartoon showing Wolseley studying his maps and despatches, with the caption, 'Veni, Vidi------'. Matters reached a head on 4 September when Sir Garnet spent the day thrashing out transport problems with Sir John Adye, Major-General Sir Edward Morris, Commissary-General, and Major Henry Reeves, Director of Transport. 'Adye is unsafe on such points and very ignorant of practical war,' wrote Wolseley in his diary. He was particularly unhappy with Adye's locally hired transport team, a 'collection of Levantine officials whom he calls drivers'.

It was to Louisa that the general confessed his fears and frustrations. 'I am not in good spirits for I am so delayed by the difficulties of getting my supplies to the front that despair seemed to come over me at times,' he told her on 3 September, 'the longer I delay the stronger will become Arabi's lines of entrenchments and they are already very strong. I have no doubt that I shall take them but with heavy loss ... I have my plans in my head for taking them with the least loss possible.' That same day Sir Garnet had written to the Queen, 'for the first time in my life' directly. He added, 'I telegraph her nearly every day, but whilst nothing is doing, it is not easy to send home interesting telegrams.'[19]

Louisa Wolseley wrote regularly to her husband on campaign and it was in reading and re-reading her gossipy and witty letters that he could forget the duties and stresses of command: 'Mr Childers told me you had telegraphed back for 25,000 lb of soap. He said they were in doubt at first if you meant soup but decided it must be soap. Is it to wash Arabi white?' She also told her husband how she had stood for an hour on a balcony in Bond Street to see the Zulu King Cetewayo: 'The crowd was so great that I was afraid to venture into the street … I saw him capitally. He *rolled* majestically across the pavement … A boy in the crowd said rather wisely, "His name ain't 'Getawayo'", which was quite true.'[20]

In addition to his military, political, private and Royal correspondence, Sir Garnet also kept a detailed pocket diary and a daily journal. The latter has been lost and Adrian Preston, editor of three of Wolseley's other journals, even disputed its existence. Yet he wrote to Louisa on 5 September: 'I enclose a bundle of my Journal which I imagine is duller than usual but you said you would like to see it. I did not send it before because I don't imagine you even read much of that which I sent you from South Africa.' He added, 'I think you may lookout for good news from me telegraphed on the 15th or 16th September. The latter was always the day I said at home would be Arabi's last, at least in command of an army' (he had indeed told the War Minister this at their last meeting in London).[21]

Always mindful of the privations of his men, Wolseley confided in his pocket diary on 30 August: 'The men in front are still exposed to great discomfits and I can really do nothing for them,' but noted proudly that 'I never saw men bear these trials better or in a less complaining spirit.'[22] Sir Garnet remained most pleased with the way his mounted infantry had behaved throughout the campaign. 'Upon this small handful of men has really devolved the hardest work and most serious fighting', he told Cambridge in a letter. He told his superior that Arabi was extending his formidable line of entrenchments 'to prevent my turning it, as I did on the 25th inst.' Turn it must but 'I cannot say by which flank I shall turn him' until Tel-el-Kebir had been reconnoitred.[23]

Escorted by a small body of cavalry, Major Tulloch set off on 31 August along the railway line towards Tel-el-Kebir. 'With two of my flankers I came across a small picket of the enemy's cavalry on the Canal bank … They opened fire, but my second shot with a carbine got the range – 700 yards.'[24] The Egyptians cantered away and Tulloch's group got close to the advanced entrenchment that stood before the main Tel-el-Kebir lines. The major was able to make some notes before a squadron of enemy cavalry chased the British away. Bedouin spies and conversations with Egyptian prisoners also helped Tulloch prepare a 'wonderfully accurate' report for Wolseley. The number of guns it listed, to the major's later delight, turned out to be 'exact to a single piece'.

After being in charge of intelligence for the entire campaign, and having drawn up various invasion plans beforehand, Tulloch was 'exceedingly disgusted' on 5 September to be replaced by Colonel Sir Redvers Buller, the last of Wolseley's Ring to take up his command. With his usual charm Sir Garnet got the major to agree to serve under the newcomer but he felt poorly treated. Burly, plain-speaking Buller had been on his honeymoon when a letter from Sir Garnet had arrived on 21 August inviting him to Egypt as a special service officer. 'Do not go near the Horse Guards nor mention this to anyone if you mean to come,' wrote the Chief. Buller could hardly refuse if he valued his career and the general's patronage.[25] Taking his bride of eleven days back to England from The Hague, he rushed about buying a campaign kit and within four more days was en route to Egypt. 'I confess,' he wrote to his sister, 'I never left England with so heavy a heart.'[26]

A few hours after getting to Kassassin the energetic Buller had digested Tulloch's information about Tel-el-Kebir but decided to undertake his own mapping and reconnaissance. He rode out that night with 60 cavalry, left 50 on a ridge, and rode on with the remainder. Blundering about in the dark, Buller nearly ran into an Egyptian picquet but luckily saw their camp fire in the nick of time. When the sun broke over the horizon he was just a mile from the centre of the enemy defences. Wolseley and Buller obviously had talked about the importance of noting everything at daybreak because he repeated this reconnaissance the next night and managed to sketch the Egyptian southern flank positions.

By 4 September Sir Garnet was able to write to Childers that he had sorted out his difficulties with Macpherson and the Indian brigade would be called a 'contingent'. He told the War Minister that he fully expected to have 'at least six hundred casualties' at Tel-el-Kebir, and also regretted very much leaving Wood's brigade at Alexandria, 'a reduction in force that has been occasioned by the circumstances attendant upon the bombardment', which he considered 'silly and criminal', as he confided to Louisa, 'which Lord Northbrook and the Admiralty concocted between them for the glorification of Sir B. Seymour and his fleet, regardless of the injury it would be to England ...'[27]

The Indian cavalry forming Drury Lowe's 2nd Brigade were all at Kassassin by September 7th and two days later Lieutenant Grierson could write: 'Received my baptism of fire.' Following reports that the Bedouins had attacked some of the outposts, Brigadier-General Wilkinson, commanding the 2nd Cavalry Brigade, started off at once with a troop of the 2nd Bengal Cavalry and one squadron of the 19th Hussars. They soon saw some action:

Before we had gone a mile we saw the Arabs on a ridge in front of us and the bullets began to fly thick about us. Holland of the 19th was struck three yards from me. The Bedouins fell back slowly firing from horseback as they went. However, on we went, dismounted a troop of the 19th and some Mounted Infantry who came up and gave them a few volleys chasing them from ridge to ridge. Then the affair came to a standstill and we returned to camp.[28]

The Indian Cavalry were soon the heroes of the British infantry. Tall, fine warriors with beards and turbans, they took no prisoners, always wounding or killing any Egyptians unlucky enough to face them. Veterans of countless actions, they numbered in their ranks such stalwart, warriors as Ressaldar Major Tahour Khan of the 6th Bengal, who wore with pride the Punniar Star of 1843 on his blue-uniformed breast, and Hussein Ali Khan, Ressaldar Major of the 13th Bengal Lancers, who had served with the loyal 7th Irregular Cavalry at the Siege of Delhi. 'Our cavalry seemed to glory in rusty stirrups and scabbards,' wrote Corporal Philip, 'while those of the Bengal Lancers glittered and sparkled in the bright light of the sun.' When the regiment rode out of camp, 'they presented a noble sight as they swept past in two solid lines, the pendants on their long lances floating in breeze, and the sun glancing from their burnished steel.'[29] The Indian cavalrymen also got along well with their British counterparts. Household Cavalrymen went into the Indian lines to have their swords sharpened by sikhligars and exchange clasp knives for chapatties. When some British cavalry asked if they could be helped with forage the Indian troopers pointed out a field of Egyptian millet nearby – then went and cut it down for them.

After the battles of the previous week, the desert between Ismailia and Kassassin was littered with discarded carts, piles of hay and other articles. Molyneux took out a wing of the 4th Dragoons on 2 September and recovered six carts, over 10,000 rounds of ammunition, cooking pots, shovels and all kinds of odds and ends. Locomotives were starting to get supplies up to the front and soon Ismailia and Kassassin were actually connected by telephone, 'the very first time it was used for military purposes in the field'.[30] The device had only been invented six years earlier. Molyneux thought the corps of signallers were 'no use at all'. The flat desert and mirages made signalling extremely difficult. He was also not much impressed with the Post Office Volunteers, composed of 2 volunteer officers, 10 NCO's and 94 men, all civilians, from the 24th Middlesex Rifle Volunteers. A detachment of these clerks-cum-soldiers were now at Kassassin, the men armed only with sword bayonets, the officers a sword and pistol each.

On the 7th Wolseley wrote to his wife and told her that on the next Tuesday or Wednesday he intended to attack Tel-el-Kebir. He confessed it was probably going to take a two day assault:

> I am so afraid that he may bolt after the first day's work that I may possibly push on to make only one day's work of it. As you may imagine, my little sandpiper, my thoughts are serious under the circumstances, although I don't think I allow others to know this. I do so long for a complete victory that may make the world feel that England has yet something left in her and that her soldiers have still strength and courage ... God grant me a complete success, that may end the war at one blow.[31]

A band nearby was playing a melancholy air, one of Sir Garnet's favourites, 'Believe Me Of All Those Endearing Young Charms'. The music put him in a reflective mood. Soon Englishmen would read in the newspapers of 'the disgusting butcher's bill, over which Mr John Bull rather gloats and thinks, when the list is a long one, that he has something for his money'. Turning to other matters, Sir Garnet told his wife that:

> I have four foreigners, representatives of France, Germany, Russia and the United States coming to live upon me, so I have ordered Teck to look after them: they are, I am sorry to say, to live at my expense ... but they won't dine at my table which will be a comfort. It would be unbearable to have a bundle of foreigners listening to all one said at every meal.[32]

To cheer Louisa up her husband told her that a few nights previously he had dined with Captain Beckett, 3rd Hussars, who commanded the mounted police. This officer had clipped his hair like everyone else, 'but the effect upon him has been more peculiar than upon most men, for having peculiarly prominent cheekbones his face resembles that of a puff adder'. Wolseley had managed to find a staff appointment for his brother George, (a Lieutenant-Colonel in the York and Lancaster Regiment), but feared he would be 'late for the ball and even for the supper'. Fitzgeorge, Cambridge's playboy son, 'is really useful as a messman. He manages my mess entirely and does it very well'. All Sir Garnet's staff had suffered from stomach ailments and the most useful of them was Swaine, his military secretary, 'very exact and very methodical and hard working'.[33]

As the general prepared to move his headquarters to Kassassin, and men and supplies went on up to the front, the war correspondents sensed that something big was about to happen. They were, as always, a disparate bunch and each man was fiercely loyal to his publication. The younger Adye recounted a story in his memoirs that Bennet Burleigh, one of the most famous of them, managed to prevent his rivals sending a despatch on one of the battles while he was still writing up his own account by giving the telegraph operator the first chapter of Genesis to send, thus hogging use of the machine. His new desk in London had the shock of reading 'In the beginning', etc., as it clicked off the teleprinter.

One man who seemed to be everywhere and noticed by everyone was not exactly a civilian or a serving officer. This was Lieutenant-General Sir Henry Havelock-Allan VC, reckoned to be the most eccentric officer in the British Army. The son of the distinguished Indian Mutiny general, Havelock-Allan (the Allan had been added in 1881 to satisfy a cousin's bequest), had retired from the Army two years before the Egyptian War. Courageous, but prone to erratic behaviour, Sir Henry had come out to Egypt on the spur of the moment and seemed to wander about dispensing advice. He sneaked up on Percy Marling and slapped him on the back: 'Turning round I saw a total stranger in mufti with a military helmet on,' wrote Marling, 'I said, "Who the devil are you?"'[34] Havelock replied that he had stayed with Percy's grandfather when standing for Parliament. Frederic Villiers met him in an hotel at Ismailia where the eccentric general whispered, 'Villiers, don't for goodness' sake, mention me in your despatches, for my wife thinks I am somewhere on the Riviera; but I could not resist coming on here to see the fun'.[35]

Wolseley knew Havelock-Allan from the Mutiny and the latter succeeded him as DAQMG in Canada. He was 'curiously mad', thought Sir Garnet, with a 'cross-grained temper', but he also lauded him as 'the first soldier of his time' and 'bravest Englishmen alive'. Sir Garnet once told another great military thinker, George Denison, that 'Havelock missed by about that much,' as he held up his finger and thumb together, 'of being the greatest soldier our army ever produced'.[36] Denison admired Sir Henry, a great army reformer, and thought him 'much misunderstood'. The problem with Havelock-Allan was that he feared nobody and did not know how to channel his reckless nature. Once, when a newspaper editor refused to see him, Sir Henry rode his horse upstairs to the man's room. A sergeant who also annoyed him while playing billiards was flattened with the cue, and his dislike of the Duke of Cambridge was so great that during an Aldershot parade Sir Henry handed his sword to an aide saying he could not trust himself with it.

Sir Garnet wanted no hasty or forced actions to upset his plans. He was, therefore, caught off-guard by the battle forced upon him on 9 September 1882. With hindsight, and a clearer understanding of Egyptian history, it is surprising that he did not see it coming. One year before to the day, the colonels had taken their grievances to the Khedive. That date had set the course of a tumultuous year for the Egyptian nationalist movement. Bedouin spies had reported (or deliberately mislead) Arabi into thinking the British camp at Kassassin was still weakly defended. A superstitious man, perhaps the Egyptian general saw the date as auspicious, the omens as good? Why not destroy the invaders on the anniversary of this great day and it would live in the nation's heart for ever.

Ali Fehmy Pasha was to command the Egyptian forces though Arabi was also present. He had replaced Rashid Pasha in chief command, probably due to his failure on 25 August. Now, on this anniversary of their great victory over the Khedive and his foreign advisers, both Ali Fehmy and Ahmed Arabi were determined to throw all they could at the enemy. The attack would consist of seventeen infantry battalions, several squadrons of cavalry, a few thousand Bedouin and be supported by thirty heavy guns.

The first British officer to run into the advancing Egyptians was Redvers Buller. He was on one of his early morning spying expeditions when, at about 4am, he got trapped with just one aide behind a large body of enemy cavalry. In his retreat back to camp Buller's horse, 'a brute of an Arab' threw him off over its head. In typical fashion he picked himself up, remounted and spurred on the beast clinging tightly to the reins. Back at camp he reported that the Egyptians were either making a strong reconnaissance or going to attack.

Fehmy and Arabi had planned a double-pronged assault with columns from Tel-el-Kebir in the west, and Es-Saihiyeh, across the desert to the north. The generals had cleverly marched them through the night and dawn was just breaking when four sowars of the 13th Bengal Lancers found themselves on the wrong side of advancing Egyptian cavalry that had moved past them in the dark. With cries, the Indian troopers rallied together and charged through the enemy. Luckily for them they were about to be relieved by other troops commanded by Lt-Colonel C. Richard Pennington, who was Field Officer for the day. He now rode up with about 50 men and saw to his horror that three squadrons of enemy cavalry were bearing towards him. The steam of several trains in the cool morning air indicated that the Egyptians were hurrying up more infantry. He quickly ordered two of his men to gallop with the news as fast as they could back to Kassassin. Then, cooly dismounting his sowars behind a ridge, he and his men opened fire with their carbines on the enemy. When completely surrounded Pennington barked out the command, 'Stand to your horses! Mount!' Back in their saddles and with lances lowered, the Bengal horsemen charged the massed Egyptians, spearing and scattering men in all directions, as they galloped back to camp.

Just about the same time that Pennington encountered the enemy on the British left, a small party of the King's Royal Rifle Corps were marching out of the right of the camp to seize ammunition abandoned in the desert some days earlier. Kendall Coghill had also decided to have a look at this when he was

> ... met by an officer of Rifles begging me to save his men by galloping to stop them falling into an ambuscade. I rode for a mile and overtook them, and then I rode to the top of the hill and found three regiments of enemy's infantry and two cavalry lining the crest. I raced back to camp for supports and found about 12,000 of the enemy drawn up in three lines, evidently placed there overnight for a morning surprise of our camp.[37]

It was an audacious Egyptian plan requiring much skill and their night march has been completely ignored while that of the British a few days later was lauded to the skies.

Coghill quickly reported what he had seen to General Willis. He, in turn, sent a message to the Duke of Connaught at Tel-el-Mahuta to attack the left flank of the Es-Salihiyeh troops and at 7.45am he ordered a general advance of the whole army. Gerald Graham, who had to dress hurriedly when news of the attack was brought to his tent, was elated that the enemy at last wanted to meet him in a pitched battle. Now he could redeem the smudges on his honour suffered twelve days earlier. As more Egyptians appeared he turned to an aide and exclaimed: 'Got them within reach at last.'[38]

'For the first hour they shelled us very hotly and with admirable precision', wrote Lt-Colonel Coghill to his wife. Hugh McCalmont estimated the Es-Salihiyeh column at about three squadrons of cavalry, some guns and three or four battalions of infantry. When the British Horse Artillery under Major Borradaile opened fire with deadly accuracy the column broke and was soon in disarray. 'We went very fast but we could not catch them,' wrote Coghill, 'as they are demons to bolt and hate close quarters ... They overlapped us by quite a mile ... with a dense mob of Bedouins in rear.'[39]

On the opposite bank of the Canal the DCLI advanced in skirmishing order. 'Yet we had no risk,' wrote Corporal Philip, 'as not a bullet or shell came near us. It was a grand sight ... Our infantry were steadily advancing as though engaged on an ordinary field-day parade.'[40] Percy Marling admitted that his men were 'either asleep, in their pyjamas, or washing in the (so-called) Sweetwater Canal' when the battle began.

One shell pitched close to my tent, but didn't burst. Wilkins, our Quartermaster, picked up a live shell which fell near his stores, and threw it into the Canal, a jolly plucky act. The alarm sounded, and we all dressed as quickly as possible and advanced to drive back the enemy. The firing, both rifle and gun, was quite hot for some time. One of our corporals near me was the first man hit, in the face.[41]

About 10am Major Molyneux was with some of the Royal Marines and KRRC when they came under close-range fire from some Egyptian guns. The troops began swearing a lot when they were told to lie down as the vicious case shot flew around them:

> The desert slope was undulating, and the Egyptians had got good cover, and our men could only see the muzzles, for the gunners could load the Krupps without getting off their knees. There was a good deal of noise, and an officer may have given the command and I not have heard it. All I know is that the men of two adjacent companies, Marines and Rifles, suddenly jumped to their feet, rushed three hundred yards to the front and captured three guns before you could wink. Perhaps rivalry did it; who knows?[42]

When the shelling began Melton Prior had been out in the desert to the left of the camp. He, in company with fellow war correspondent, John Cameron, was rather late returning on 'a very poor, slow pony.' Re-saddling a better horse near his tent a shell burst close by, 'a large fragment of which passed right through both sides and struck the saddle of my horse as I was tightening the girths' he wrote later, 'this so startled him that he plunged madly, and I was desperately afraid that he would get away, but I hung on like grim death, and then mounting him rode back through the camp under quite a warm fire'.[43]

Out in the desert Prior came across General Willis who was leaning across a captured Egyptian cannon eating some sandwiches. He invited the portly newspaper man to share his feast and the two were soon chatting when Prior suddenly saw a shell bounding towards them along the sand. It passed between an astonished Arab and his camels and Prior just had time to shout, 'Look out, sir!', as he rolled onto his side. The shell 'struck the wheel we had been leaning against, then sprang into the air, without bursting, thank goodness', he later recalled.[44]

All over the battlefield the Egyptian shells seemed to drop with deadly accuracy. One who got alarmed was Major Tulloch. He went across to the Naval Brigade, who were manning a 40-pounder Armstrong gun mounted on a railway truck, and urged their commander, Lieutenant Purvis RN, to try and silence the enemy artillery, even at the risk of firing directly over the heads of the advancing British soldiers. Shells were falling so hard all around the truck that at first Tulloch could not get close enough to be heard. He finally managed to shout across his suggestion and Purvis agreed to give it a try. His fire took the enemy's heat off the British infantry but, like angry wasps, the Egyptian gunners turned their attention even more on the Naval Brigade and Purvis was wounded so badly that his right foot had to be amputated that afternoon.

There was no general rout but as the Egyptians retreated and the Es-Salihiyeh column disintegrated, the British were able to turn their attentions entirely on the soldiers from Tel-el-Kebir. At one point Tulloch was with Gerald Graham and an aide when three shells struck the ground a few yards away. 'I think, general, we had better shove on a bit,' said the major, 'they have evidently seen who we are, and we shall have the other three shells of the battery here in a minute.' 'No' replied Graham, displaying his characteristic disregard for danger, 'I don't see why we should hurry.'[45]

Somewhere between 10 and 10.30am some of the cavalry got a chance to charge but the action was halted on Willis's orders. He felt their numbers were insufficient to risk pressing the attack. The infantry meanwhile continued to advance to within 5,000 yards of the enemy entrenchments. Some batteries opened fire on the British but the distance was too great for any harm to be done.

The infantry advance was well described by Percival Marling in a letter to his mother written the day after the battle:

> We gradually advanced by short rushes of from 50 to 100 yards, and then came under musketry fire, first of all a few stray bullets and then as we got nearer and nearer a perfect hailstorm of them. Some of them came most unpleasantly close and whistled past our ears or tore up the sand at one's feet, in a manner that would have rejoiced the heart of any insurance company from whom you derived an annuity.[46]

By 11am the Egyptians were in full retreat. To get away faster they even cut off their camel packs and dropped ammunition boxes in hundreds. A short time earlier the British had halted their advance. According to Marling:

> The heat was intense and several of the men had sunstroke. The Egyptian dead and wounded looked ghastly as we passed them … After they began to retire one fellow jumped up in front of us about 200 yards and ran right along in front of the whole line … it certainly took 30 or 40 shots before he was hit, I felt quite sorry for the poor beggar. It was quite like rabbit shooting.[47]

Riding with his men, Lt-Colonel Coghill saw the Egyptians eventual retreat as 'a panic'. He was forced to stay on the battlefield until 7pm, by which time most of the British were back in camp. 'So we had a hot and starving day without water,' he told his wife, 'I lost one officer and one man from sunstroke.' Feeling famished, Coghill prowled among the dead Egyptians and found some black biscuits and water, though he thought the precious liquid was 'sheer mud which you can't see the spoon through in a tumbler'.[48]

And Wolseley? That morning at Ismailia he had been alerted by a telegram from Willis saying the enemy were advancing to attack and that he had ordered up the Guards Brigade. 'I know Willis to be an alarmist, so I went on with my toilette to await another report which he said he would send me,' wrote the general. 'The 2nd was also of an alarming nature, so I put my vile body into a train at 9am.' Sir Garnet preferred to travel in an open cattle truck rather than the one stuffy and smelly carriage. On arrival he was met by Paul Methuen and with a small escort they rode the three-and-a-half miles to the front. Here he found Willis debating whether he should continue to attack the Tel-el-Kebir lines, stand his ground or retire back to Kassassin. Wolseley had 'no doubts whatever'. He ordered outposts to be stationed in the hills and the rest of the army to return to camp. 'If Willis had pushed on our losses would have been enormous,' he later told Louisa, 'we might have failed – probably should – and even if we had succeeded, his success would have ruined all my plans of saving Cairo by a forced march on that place.'[49]

The decision not to pursue the Egyptians that day annoyed some of the Army and newspapers back home. 'If an advance had been ordered, it seems to be generally believed that Arabi's troops would have made no stand,' asserted *The Times* correspondent. Wolseley, however, explained his reasons to his wife thus:

> I had little more than half the troops up with which I meant to fight Arabi, and to have attempted to strike him hard before I was fully ready to follow up my success – even assuming that I could obtain one with half my force – would have been most stupid.[50]

Putting aside Wolseley's ego and thirst for glory he was probably right in his estimate of the situation and correct to increase his army to maximum strength before assaulting Tel-el-Kebir. One Royal Marines officer later complained to his local newspaper in England that the men had fought and marched twelve miles that day, 'and that on an empty stomach is no joke'.[51]

During the afternoon the Guards Brigade dribbled into camp. Sir Garnet felt very sorry that they had needed to march through the heat of the day.

Now he though Connaught 'one of the most active Brigadiers I have and is very keen'.[52] Lieutenant Balfour of the Scots Guards felt 'nearly cooked' by the march. His constitution had not been improved by 'diarrhoea brought on by eating tinned lobster'. That night he slept 'with my 'martial cloak' around me in a trench (I always dig one to sleep in as a burrow).'[53]

British losses had been remarkably slight – 3 men killed and 77 wounded, but criticisms rumbled; 'Graham's neglect – repeated neglect – of proper outpost arrangements has been scandalous' wrote Guy Dawnay.[54] His opinion was supported by Marling who noted: 'I think our outpost and cavalry scouting must have been very slack'.[55] In the official American report on the war, Commander Goodrich commented that 'there appears to be little doubt that the British came near being surprised'.[56] The *Standard* correspondent wrote that the result was 'absolutely ridiculous in proportion to the number of men engaged and the weight of lead expended'.[57]

The Egyptians got off comparatively lightly with only 46 dead and wounded counted later along the line of the main British infantry advance. This raised the question of the accuracy of British shooting on that boiling hot mirage-filled day. It was the Royal Horse Artillery who inflicted the greatest Egyptian losses – their shells killed more than 70. One direct hit was seen to take away a dozen of the enemy and three carefully aimed shells accounted for a heap of 25 dead.

The British victory may have been helped by other factors which remain somewhat murky. Ali Fehmy Pasha and Rashid Pasha were both wounded in the battle which must have effected the morale of their men. The Egyptian battle plan also fell apart. According to Arabi, a third body of troops was going to sweep south of Kassassin in an arc and attack the British rear, but his plan was betrayed by the Bedouin leader, Ali Bey Yusuf Khunfis, who took the original sketch made by him to Wolseley. There is no reference to this in Sir Garnet's writings but it probably occurred. Information may have been conveyed to Tulloch or Watson both of whom spoke fluent Arabic. The failure of Mahmud Sami, commanding the Es-Salihiyeh column, to join up with the Tel-el-Kebir troops was Arabi's own view of why he lost the battle. Later, when in prison, Sir Charles Wilson brought him the plan and asked if it was in his own hand? 'Yes' replied the general. Wilson apparently replied, 'It is a good plan and you might have beaten us with it.'[58]

That night, in a tent at Kassassin, the British commander settled down on his bed to write to Louisa. He pulled the mosquito curtains closer, 'for the flies here beat any plague I have ever experienced'. The letter reveals a Wolseley shorn of all smugness and conceit, and shows that, contrary to the myth, he was far from sure of success and realised only too well that in war nothing is certain:

I have determined to move out from here on Tuesday night to attack the enemy's fortified position on Wednesday morning a little before daybreak. I am so weak that I cannot afford to indulge in any other plan and it requires the steadiest and the best troops … I know that I am doing a dangerous thing, but I cannot wait for reinforcements, to do so would kill the spirit of my troops. I hope I may never return home a defeated man. I would sooner leave my old bones here, to go home to be jeered at. I wish I could see you for five minutes, but then I know you would say, 'Don't risk anything.' Well, the die is cast, and I must stand by it … My plan depends upon the steadiness of my infantry – If they behave well and are steady in the dark – a very crucial trial for troops, I must succeed – If they are not steady I may fail all of this or may even at best achieve very little. You can fancy that the responsibility tells a little upon me, but I don't think any soul here thinks so. By this hour on Wednesday we shall know all. How inscrutable are the ways of God and how ignorant we are of what the next hour may bring.[59]

# 10

# Tel-el-Kebir

*It is there that I hope to measure swords with Mr Arabi*
Garnet Joseph Wolseley

Well before dawn on 12 September 1882, Sir Edward Bruce Hamley was in a
sweat. He had arrived at Kassassin less than 24 hours earlier and spent much of
the day arguing with Wolseley. Now, en route for a dawn rendezvous with the
general in the desert, he was hopelessly lost.

The conference was to be held at Ninth Hill, a sandy height so-called by
Sir Garnet since it was the centre of the fighting on 9 September. General Hamley
set off with Archibald Alison and one aide apiece, but their guide, Captain James of
the 2nd Dragoons, one of Willis's staff officers, got confused by the stars and took
his small party in the wrong direction. Then, crossing the railway embankment,
the officers and their horses got entangled in loose telegraph wires. Eventually
they stumbled on a picquet and found Wolseley and the other generals, colonels
of regiments and several staff waiting for them. It was about 4am.

Spurring on his horse the commander led this elite group across the desert
to within 800 yards of the Tel-el-Kebir lines. Only a few stars lit the sky and the
night was dark. Sir Garnet had personally reconnoitred the enemy defences on
the previous two mornings and knew exactly what he wanted to show his surbor-
dinates. For some time the whole group sat silently in the darkness. Then, as the
first streak of dawn showed itself, and Egyptian sentries could be seen dimly in the
distance, Wolseley exclaimed, 'Note the time.' It was 5.45am. 'Our attack must be
delivered before this hour, otherwise those vedettes will detect our presence.'[1]

Straining their eyes the officers could see the entrenchments 'fairly well' but,
as one of them later recalled, 'they did not seem to be very formidable, but of
course we could not see what sort of ditch there might be for us to cross'.[2]
Sir Garnet pointed out that no one knew for sure how many heavy guns the
Egyptians had, but he believed most of them were on the enemy's right near the
Canal. He surmised that the Egyptians could not be bothered to carry heavy
guns and ammunition way out in the desert to their left flank (an accurate

assessment). His attack would thus be by direct assault across open ground concentrating on the centre and left of the Egyptian lines. It would have to be prepared in darkness and the troops marched across the desert at night. This was a risky undertaking. Its success depended entirely on the element of surprise and how near the British army could reach the enemy lines undetected. The Indian Contingent was to advance on the left of the British, beyond the Canal, and to march directly on past Tel-el-Kebir and secure Zagazig, the important rail junction leading towards the capital. The assault, concluded the general, would be delivered that very night, with orders for the march and the attack being issued during the course of the day.

Each senior officer was given a simple plan that marked out the various parts of the army and their distances from one another during the march. Hamley and Willis, the two divisional generals, were told to 'form line of half battalion column and to attack directly we came upon the enemy's works'. Possibly Sir Garnet expected Gerald Graham's troops would do most of the work of the 1st Division because Willis later complained that 'he gave me very few instructions'.[3] To Hamley, now feeling more self-confident, Wolseley said: 'It will be a race between the Highland Brigade and Graham.' Sir Edward was warned that if, after taking the Egyptian trenches, he found the enemy's reserves massed for a defence of their camp, it was imperative to wait until the 1st Division had 'worked round its flank' before moving to attack. To all his senior officers Wolseley declared: 'Go straight in on them and then,' he added, stamping his foot on the sand, 'kill them all.' As the group murmured their assent Sir Garnet concluded by saying: 'Well, gentleman, don't talk about it until the orders are issued during the course of the day. I wish you all good luck.'[4] The officers saluted and Wolseley, the die now cast, set off back towards Kassassin.

Even before the campaign began Sir Garnet had maintained he would bring it to a successful conclusion by 15 or 16 September. His ability to keep within this timetable is one of the most remarkable aspects of the war. Several factors could have ruined his predictions but he had stuck somehow to the plan. Writing to his mother on 18 August from Alexandria he had advised her to examine a map and 'see a village marked Tel-el-Kebir about 28 or 30 miles east of Ismailia. It is there that I hope to measure swords with Mr Arabi. 'Tel' means a hill and on that hill, please God, I shall dispose of these rebels.' Remembering that he was writing to his mother, Sir Garnet concluded in a suitably religious vein: 'I hope I do not write in any swaggering manner: I feel very confident and have such a trust in God that I know I shall win.'[5]

There were plenty of people, especially in America and France, who were hoping such would not be the case. They wanted to see Great Britain humbled.

On 8 September the *New York Herald* crowed:

> Sir Garnet Wolseley went to Egypt, vaunting himself … that he would crush
> out the Egyptian resistance and be in London again by September 15. It is now
> evident that he will not keep that ridiculous promise, as to dates, and it is just pos-
> sible that he will not speedily fulfil even the first part of it … Indeed it is probable
> that the only warlike actions now on the carpet are manoeuvres.[6]

The same newspaper pointed out to its readers that the Egyptians

> … have artillery and know how to use it. They have a trained and disciplined
> infantry armed with modern rifles. They can perceive a line of defence and know
> how to strengthen and hold it.

On 10 September, the day after the 2nd Battle of Kassassin, a full Naval Brigade
had arrived with 15 officers, 199 sailors and 6 Gatling guns. Next day the Indian
infantry and 1st Battalion the Seaforth Highlanders had marched in to complete the Indian Contingent. Alison and Hamley also arrived that day with the
Highland Brigade of the 2nd Division.

The tents of the Headquarters Staff lay just across the Sweetwater from the
Highlanders and so Hamley had set off across a small pontoon bridge and found
Sir Garnet eating breakfast with some of his officers. A cheerful Wolseley invited
Sir Edward to join them. In a bad temper and acting like an irritated schoolmaster, Hamley began to lecture his superior about night marches, based upon, as
he later wrote: 'my experience, which might be useful for future guidance, that
when troops had to perform any part of a march in the night … it was better
to begin the march in the dark than to end it so.'[7] Wolseley, whose hairs must
have bristled at this lecture, replied that Hamley 'might have started later, and
so marched in a cooler period'. Not willing to agree, Sir Edward responded
by saying that the start of the march had been fixed by Wolseley's orders and
the men would have had no time to rest if it had begun any later. Now quite
irritated by Hamley's attitude, Sir Garnet snapped back that 'the men might have
had two hours rest which would have been quite enough'. Outside the tent
the two generals continued to bicker. Hamley was furious that he had been
forced to leave troops at Alexandria, and reminded Wolseley that he had been
promised Macpherson's troops as his 2nd Brigade. Sir Garnet, already aware that
Macpherson objected to serving under Hamley, now bluntly told Sir Edward
that since the Indian Contingent was going to operate on the other side of the
Canal from the British troops it could hardly be under his command.

Later that day a disgruntled Hamley voiced his complaints to Sir John Adye in his capacity as Chief-of-Staff. He asked why the 2nd Division had been stripped and his command treated so shamefully. It was not right that a lieutenant-general in command of a division should go into battle with just one brigade. The long-suffering Adye agreed to broach the subject with Sir Garnet again, but later had to tell Sir Edward, 'Wolseley says he has made his arrangements and won't alter them.' Hamley kept up the pressure and obstinately insisted that Adye should lobby for him to have a 2nd Brigade under the command of Cromer Ashburnham, composed of the King's Royal Rifle Corps and Duke of Cornwall's Light Infantry Battalions with the Naval Brigade in support. These troops could advance behind and in support of the Highlanders. The Brigade of Guards who, until this time, had been placed behind the Highland Brigade, would now support Graham's brigade. Thankfully, further unpleasantness was averted by Wolseley agreeing to the proposals. Riding back to camp on the morning of the 12th he let it be known that he had changed his earlier dispositions 'to please General Hamley'.

In public the Chief oozed confidence, but talking to Major Neville Lyttelton, one of Sir John Adye's aides that afternoon he was 'very frank'. He confided that he would win the battle but expected to lose 1,200 men. Lyttelton urged Sir Garnet to push the Guards Brigade into the assault but the general implied that he wanted to hold them well back. He failed to mention that the Guards were commanded by 'dear Arthur', and he could not, would not, risk the life of the Queen's favourite son.

The previous morning Connaught had joined Wolseley on a ride to the front. The commander had come across his general supervising the burial of dead men and horses lying near his advanced picquet. Guy Dawnay wrote the same day that the 'constant stumbling on dead Egyptians' was 'unpleasant', and the smell 'perfectly awful'. Lieutenant Eustace Dawnay had 'a shockingly bad night of it' on outpost duty near the dead bodies and came into the camp next morning looking 'seedy'. His brother described the British lines on the 12th as 'certainly very unpleasant as far as horrible smells went, and the water was undoubtedly really very unwholesome'.[8]

Despite the smells all agreed that the transport situation was now greatly improved. Sergeant Littlejohn of the 4th Dragoons recalled:

> Fresh beef in abundance ... compressed vegetables ... tea, coffee and sugar, were our daily rations, and occasionally potatoes and rum; it was even rumoured that a squadron of the Household Cavalry had actually revelled in the luxury of curried rice.'[9]

The great drawbacks seemed to be the lack of firewood and the bad Canal water. 'I dare say that "diluted Arab" is an acquired taste,' noted Littejohn.

Throughout the 'frightfully hot' day of 12 September aides scurried around the camp delivering sealed orders. Much of their time was spent in the tent of Lieutenant Wyatt Rawson, Wolseley's naval aide, who had been deputed to guide the Highland Brigade, very roughly in the centre of the British advance, towards the Egyptian defences. Less than a month past his 29th birthday, Rawson was immensely liked for his good-humoured ways. While barely out of his teens he had served in the Naval Brigade in the march to Coomassie in 1874, receiving a bullet wound in the thigh at the Battle of Amoaful. A year later, in an attempt to reach the North Pole, the youngster made an heroic trek across the ice to save a Danish dog-driver. Now much of the success – or failure – of the night march rested on his shoulders.

Trying to avoid the flies constantly crawling over everything, Lieutenant Balfour of the Scots Guards wrote on the eve of the battle: 'we have received orders to caution the men to be exceedingly careful of their water, as we may march soon (tonight for aught one knows) away from the Canal and on the following day attack.' He guessed it would be a flanking march of fifteen miles or more, done at night, 'as a march in the day with ater supply limited is not a prospect I look forward to'.[10] There had been clouds of dust on the horizon beyond the Egyptian positions on the 11th and loud rumbling in the night. Balfour thought it likely Arabi Pasha was 'bringing up trains of reinforcements'. The sound of trains shunting about also carried to the Coldstream Guards lines and Guy Dawnay wrote: 'I half expected Arabi would try and run a train down this way and drop a shot into us.'[11]

General Wolseley, his plans and preparations made, did his best not to feel too much the strain of his command. Luckily the arrival from India of his favourite brother, George, now hastily made an aide-de-camp, helped take the general's mind off more serious matters.

The plan he had outlined at dawn was a bold one. Wolseley also knew that it did not meet with the complete approval of his subordinates. Serious-minded old Adye thought it 'too bold', academic Maurice recalled how cackling geese at night had warned Romans of an attack on their city, and Buller 'could not recall a single campaign where Englishmen did not fire on Englishmen – in the daytime!'[12] Drury Lowe had memories of terrible panics by the men under bivouac in Zululand. Even Sir Garnet remembered how, during the Indian Mutiny, a soldier frightened by a snake crawling over his bed at night had instigated a riot; one colonel in terror fought a battle with a tree in the dark; another shot his own leg thinking it was part of a rebellious sepoy; while a general hopped around wildly brandishing Wolseley's sword.

Much has been made of the celebrated night march – for that was what it was – a march at night and a battle at dawn. Wolseley was not proposing a night battle. The Iron Duke had warned that 'night attacks upon good troops are seldom successful'. So Sir Garnet was intending, as Charles Callwell later wrote in his textbook on small wars, that a 'night march followed by an assault upon the hostile position at dawn is perhaps the most effectual means of carrying out a surprise'.[13] Wolseley knew that in the open desert between the British and Egyptian lines his force could encounter a stray animal, such as a camel whose sounds might rouse the enemy. In the cultivated wadi to his left, across the Canal, the Indian Contingent would meet animals, so 'the hour of the march of the Indian brigade was fixed accordingly'.[14]

In 1878, during the first phase of the 2nd Afghan War, a lofty ridge called the Peiwar Kotal had been taken by a night march and flank attack at dawn by troops under the command of Frederick Roberts, the man Wolseley saw as his chief rival in the Army. Perhaps in order to eclipse Roberts, he made his own dawn attack on the stronghold of Chief Sekukuni during his campaign against the Bapedi in November 1879. He may also have been influenced by the success, eight months prior to that action, by a similar attack on the mountain camp of Chief Morosi of the Basuto led by Colonel Charles Griffith of the Frontier Armed and Mounted Police.

The simple fact is that whatever lay in his mind, Wolseley knew he had very little option in defeating the Egyptians except by a direct assault at Tel-el-Kebir. He had known it since before the campaign began and it is why the potential loss of life weighed so heavily on his mind. The chief advantage he had on his side was surprise. A dawn assault in the cool of early morning would favour an adrenalin-high attacking force, especially one fighting mainly in heavy scarlet uniforms. Timed just as the sun was rising, the attack could disorientate a sleepy garrison and if successful, there was a full day ahead to cement the victory.

A few critics have wondered why Sir Garnet did not try and outflank the enemy, as Lieutenant Balfour had conjectured in his letter home. Fitzroy Hart, who wrote a report for him on the Egyptian defences after the battle, noted that the enemy right flank (as viewed from the Egyptian side), was 'secure from any turning movement on our part, for it rested on cultivated ground, where guns cannot pass, owing to the softness of the soil'. The enemy had prepared for a possible flanking manoeuvre on their left by placing nine gun batteries on hills commanding a clear view across the desert. Hart was adamant that 'the works could not have been turned, and that Sir Garnet's direct attack was the best possible'.[15]

Despite all the intelligence gathering by Tulloch and Buller it was impossible for Wolseley to be certain how many Egyptians might be waiting for him in the trenches at Tel-el-Kebir, how well they might fight, or what guns they had. It is, in fact, difficult to give an accurate estimate of the defenders. Sir Garnet reckoned there were 30,000 men opposing him, but the official ration return of the Tel-el-Kebir garrison for 12 September was 18,000 regulars and 7,000 irregulars – a total of 25,000 combatants. In his cavalry history Lord Anglesley accepts 8,500 well-disciplined regulars, including 2,000 cavalry, and an irregular rabble of 11,000, making a total of 19,500 men. According to Maurice in his official account, Arabi Pasha confirmed several months after the battle that he had 20,000 men. This seems an arbitrary number and cannot be taken as conclusive. A much higher figure came from the normally accurate Caspar Goodrich in his official American report. He listed eight Egyptian infantry regiments (24,000 men), two cavalry regiments (1,000 men), 1,000 artillerymen and 2,500 Bedouin – a total of 28,500. Under the circumstances the ration returns of 25,000 make sense and it seems that with the mounted desert Arabs there were some 28,000 enemy facing the British.

Arabi Pasha also later claimed to have 75 heavy guns at Tel-el-Kebir. Since he was writing to Maurice from exile in Ceylon it is a figure that must be suspect. Goodrich listed 60 cannon and the British captured 58 heavy guns on the battlefield. What is not in doubt is that the Egyptians had twenty gun batteries. Nine of these lay in a line that stretched more than four miles long from the Canal and into the desert. Facing the British by the Canal, where a dam had been made, was No 1 battery and the line extended to No 9 battery far out across the sands. Just slightly north of No 5 battery, and 1,100 yards closer to the British lines, was a small polygonal redoubt with a battery. Several of the batteries connected on rising ground to the remaining two miles of entrenchments built on the crests of hills in front of the Egyptian camp. Fitzroy Hart, examining them after the fight, wrote: 'The enemy's lines appear to me ably planned, for they secured his retreat either to the west or over the canal to the south.'[16] It is also sometimes forgotten that just across the desert on Arabi's left flank was another garrison at Es-Salihiyeh with 5,000 men ready to march at a moment's notice.

A parapet which in some places was as high as 6 feet ran along the defences. In front of it was a ditch from 8–12 feet wide and from 5–9 feet deep with vertical escarp and counterscarp. No obstacles stood in front of the defences to hinder an advancing enemy. This, as the Royal Engineers historian, Lt-Colonel Sandes wrote was: 'unfortunate for the Egyptians because much of their line was unfinished when attacked and it was too extended to be held properly'.[17]

Near the Canal dam were redoubts on either side with three guns apiece and two more guarded the railway line with one gun on either side of the track. Between the 1st and 5th batteries the defences were strong and well finished using a mixture of grass and sand with numerous shelters and slip-trenches. Further out in the desert, where Wolseley intended to concentrate his attack, the defences were more recent and done in haste.

Tel-el-Kebir – 'the great hill' – was a village with a railway station on the south side of the Canal with a small and unprotected bridge. The hill itself was part of two minor ranges which formed a tableland sloping northwards into the desert. An army barracks had been built many years before just west of the village. For months the engineer Mahmud Fehmy had worked to improve these defences. Now Arabi was in command, though field command had been given to Ali al-Rubi Pasha. A religious man who had fought bravely in the disastrous Abyssinian War and won his colonelcy there, Rubi Pasha had recently been in charge of Sudan affairs. Blunt described him as 'a very worthy but incompetent man ... one of Arabi's old companions of the early days of the National movement.'[18] General Arabi's two best local commanders, Ali Fehmy, his fellow 'colonel' and old friend, and Rashid Husni, the Khedive's brother-in-law, who had led the troops at the first Battle of Kassassin, were both injured on 9 September. Their loss was a serious blow. Many of the best regular soldiers were kicking their heels in Damietta, Kafr-Dawar and other garrisons including General Hilmi, also one of the original three colonels, who led a tough Sudanese regiment. Most of the soldiers at Tel-el-Kebir were raw recruits. One man captured at Kassassin told the British that he had only been in the army five days, another did not know to which unit he belonged or the names of his officers, while a third told Charles Watson that he had 'not learnt war' and 'did not like it'.

Sent into the trenches with barely any training, and a rifle thrust into their hands, these men were simply cannon fodder. Arabi must have realised that they would run at the first shot. The garrison's defence rested upon his Sudanese regulars and, as always, some excellent gunners. At least ammunition was plentiful and boxes of bullets, each containing 1,050 rounds, were placed all along the Egyptian lines at three or four yard intervals.

In his last days before the battle Ahmed Arabi spent much of his time in prayers and meditation. Aides brought cosy news of the British. On 12 September one report he received confirmed that five ships had left Egypt with British wounded – 'May Allah increase their confusion and weakness' – and the general himself wrote an account of the second Battle of Kassassin which was sent to a governor of Lower Egypt. It ran: 'The forces were great and the engagement lasted 12 hours ... The bullets from guns and rifles fell like rain all over the field of battle. We only lost 31 men killed with 150 wounded … It would seem the enemy lost about 2,500 killed.'[19]

Complacency had not totally descended on the Egyptian commanders. An additional 350 conscripted labourers were sent down to Tel-el-Kebir on the eve of the battle but the War Ministry admitted that others could not be coerced into going. It also appears, from an examination of captured Egyptian army telegrams, that empty ammunition boxes were not getting sent back quickly enough to Cairo, where there seems to have been a shortage.

In his famous book on the war Wilfred Blunt was adamant that treachery also played a part in the battle. Khedival agents managed to bribe two officers. Abdel el-Rahman Hassan, 'commander of the advanced guard of cavalry', who shifted his position on the night of the attack further out into the desert on the Egyptian left flank, so that his scouts would not encounter the advancing British, and Ali Bey Yusuf, commanding part of the central defences, who put out a lantern to help guide the British. It is hard to substantiate Blunt's claims but they seem most likely, and Arabi, an honourable man, certainly believed them to be true. Blunt insisted that Ali Bey Yusuf was paid £1,000 in gold before the battle and got a pension of £12 a month until his death. It is true that Khedival officials were working with British intelligence officers and both would have been grateful for help. But no British participant saw any lantern flickering in the enemy lines and it is doubtful if a scout could have got back to camp in time to raise an alarm. What really defeated the Egyptians at dawn on 13 September was a fierce rush of cold steel, a Martini-Henry rifle and a brave man behind it.

Wolseley's attack called for the 1st and 2nd Divisions to move on the enemy north of the Sweetwater Canal while the Indian Contingent did the same to the south. The Highland Brigade, led by Alison, would be 2,000 yards north of the railway line. On their right, at a distance of 1,200 yards, would be Graham's 2nd Brigade of the 1st Division. Supporting these men would be a second line. 1,000 yards in rear of the Highlanders would be Ashburnham's Brigade, while behind Graham's troops marched the Guards under Connaught. In the interval were massed General Goodenough's 42 heavy guns along with the Hedaquarters staff. On the extreme right of the British line would be the cavalry with 12 horse artillery guns. To the left rear would march the Naval Brigade following along the railway line with a 40-pounder gun mounted on a truck. The Seaforth Highlanders would lead the Indian Contingent south of the Canal with the Native Infantry as a second line. Escorting the Headquarters Staff would be Royal Marine Artillery and some of the 19th Hussars. The short straw had been drawn by the Royal West Kents who escorted the ammunition wagons and guarded the Kassassin camp and lines of communications. In total Wolseley was committing 634 officers and 16,767 other ranks, supported by 61 guns and 6 Gatling guns.

An advanced hospital had been set up at Kassassin with a dressing station for the wounded to be organised near the Canal on the battlefield. Deputy-Surgeon General Hanbury, Chief Medical Officer of the expedition, was not happy with this arrangement. He was only informed of Wolseley's plans by Adye on the morning of the 12th and to his surprise, was told that 'animal transport could *not* be provided for field hospitals and none would accompany the troops into action'.[20] The general's unorthodox plans meant that bearer companies and field hospitals be not be employed as normal behind each division.

In their tents the British soldiers cursed the blistering heat of that summer day and swatted flies as they wrote letters home. Those who were privy to Sir Garnet's plans were the most serious; the march could go awry, the fight might be a stiff one, and the butcher's bill could be high. Buller was terribly nervous that his intelligence might be faulty. With a new bride waiting at home he wrote to her warning: 'The Lord gave, the Lord taketh away ...'[21]

Tents were struck at dusk but fires were left burning to deceive the enemy. All valises were piled by the railway line. Each soldier had to carry 100 rounds of ammunition and enough provisions for three-and-a-half days. Water bottles, on the general's orders, were filled with weak tea. The first bivouac was planned two miles march from Kassassin. Colonel Richard Harrison, whose spying mission to Egypt ten months earlier had proved so useful, and his chief, Major-General Earle, set to work to ensure railways, telegraphs and other communications were ready to follow the attacking force. Just before dark 'C' Troop, Royal Engineers, headed off into the desert, the first men of Wolseley's army with a special job to do. Under the direction of Major Fraser R.E. they had to lay a line of telegraph poles as markers for over two miles across the sands. Later that night 'C' Troop would also lay a cable behind the left centre of the army, connected to another one laid by a mule telegraph train of engineers south of the Sweetwater so that Wolseley could communicate with Macpherson.

'Our last meal before the battle was eaten just as the swift darkness fell,' recalled Private Robert Tutt, Royal Marines Light Infantry, 'I am sure that the spirits of not a few sank with the sun, because the solemn thought came that for some of us the sun had set for ever.'[22] In the Black Watch the men of each company fell in around their captains eager to catch every word of command. In 'D' Company young Private John Gordon listened carefully as Captain Fox told him

> ... to march all night and at daybreak storm the trenches and take the enemy's
> position at the point of the bayonet. We are not to fire a shot till we have captured

their position. Be as quiet as possible. Don't speak above a whisper. Remember the striking of matches is absolutely forbidden.[23]

He concluded by warning that if the men kept close to the ground there was less chance of being hit.

Shortly after 6.15pm the men prepared to march to the first bivouac point on or near Ninth Hill. Thomas Archer described the scene thus:

From end to end the men were at work. Round the commissariat stores were parties of men from each regiment drawing their rations to be carried in the haversacks and by the regimental transports. Line by line the long rows of tents fell to the ground, and as fast as they did so they were rolled up, stowed away in their bags and carried down to the side of the railway.[24]

It was a dark night and as soon as the 1st and 2nd Divisions left the flickering lights of the camp the difficulties began. Finding the telegraph poles caused 'very great' difficulties. Bugle and trumpet calls had also been forbidden, making communications difficult. Corporal Philip in Hamley's hastily-conceived 2nd Brigade, marching behind the Highlanders, wrote of 'the darkness of the night' and the 'choking dust'. A mile from the camp things improved as hard desert gravel was reached and more stars appeared overhead. The Duke of Cornwall's Light Infantry was just one of several corps that had already started to deviate off course. In their case it was by 100 yards to the right, and so, for half an hour, the men stood at the rendezvous point while staff officers rode up and down checking positions and gradually putting each unit back into line. Somehow, by 11pm the various battalions and units had shuffled into position for the bivouac.

During the march, as the Royal Marines halted briefly on the north side of the railway track, the Chief rode up and spoke to the men, finishing with the words: 'the Highlanders said they would be in first'. This jest raised some laughs for there was a good natured rivalry between the regiments and divisions, especially the leading brigades. It was typical of Wolseley and a clever ploy because, as one Royal Marine officer wrote later: 'it raised the spirit of emulation to the highest pitch'.[25]

The men had been told to get some rest at the bivouac but it was not so easy. Tommies whispered to mates asking them to give messages to their loved ones if they were killed on the morrow, names and addresses of families and friends were exchanged on pencilled scraps of paper, but by midnight the men were told to be silent and get some sleep. 'Here and there rose a flash of a match as the soldiers lit their pipes,' noticed Thomas Archer, each flash being quickly followed by a stage-whispered command to extinguish it from their captains. The men in some regiments, such as the Black Watch, were given a tot of rum each, others sipped their refreshing cold tea.

When Sir Garnet reached Ninth Hill he ordered his aide, Lieutenant John Adye, to halt his mounted escort of 19th Hussars. Then, with some of his staff, he rode along the lines to inspect things. Adye was startled a short time afterwards to hear a loud babble of voices that died on the wind as soon it began. The dismounted escort stood by their horses wondering if an Egyptian attack was coming. Later Adye learned that as Wolseley, 'and the still rather large body of mounted men', reached the resting ranks of the Guards Brigade the startled men had jumped to their feet calling out to each other.[26] By a lucky chance no shots had been fired and the men soon calmed down and returned to their slumbers on the sands.

'For a while silence reigned in the desert' wrote a participant.[27] Even the Chief tried to snatch some sleep. At 1am the word to rise was passed softly around the ranks, men silently got to their feet and fell in. Everyone knew this was it. The big fight was now and there was the kind of tense silence which only excitement, expectation and fear can generate.

The desert terrain was flat and almost perfect for marching. Wyatt Rawson R.N. was piloting Alison's Brigade, while Buller, Hart and Captain Holbech, Brigade-Major, did the same for Graham's men and General Goodenough guided the artillery. It was an eerie night because the stars were now out yet it remained very dark. The Highlanders stopped briefly three-quarters of a mile beyond Ninth Hill. Three remaining telegraph poles could be seen in the dim light. Beyond was open desert and darkness. Rawson set off leading the Highland Brigade on horseback, a subaltern of the Cameron Highlanders following behind the horse's tail. 'The General and I rode in the interval between the two centre battalions,' wrote Captain Edward Hutton, Alison's aide, 'Rawson a few yards on our left, and rather in front, and thus we marched on, like spectres through the night.' Many officers, Alison and Hutton included, were at first 'more than sceptical as to the reliability of our guide', especially after the telegraph posts ended, 'and then we were dependant entirely on Rawson's knowledge of the stars'. The young naval officer seemed jauntily cool about the whole thing. Hutton asked him at one point how he seemed to know his way so well? Rawson simply pointed up to the sky and said: 'You see those two stars right in front of us, and a third almost directly below them – I am steering by them.' In fact, despite his calmness, it was no easy task because the British Army had no luminous compasses until the Nile Expedition in 1884 and so everything had to be done entirely by the stars. Clouds kept drifting across the sky and only the Little Bear and North Star were visible all night.[28]

Over on the right flank Generals Graham and Willis rode slightly to the left of the front troops of the 1st Division. The pace on the extreme left of the Brigade was faster than on the right. Before long the men of the Royal Irish, on the right of the line, started to drop behind. Major Hart felt increasingly frustrated as he tried to pilot the Division: 'Several times I advised the generals to halt the left and give the right the chance of getting up, but they were anxious to press on without any delay.'[29] Either Graham or Willis had chosen to ignore Wolseley's orders and the 1st Division moved in line of half-battalion quarter-columns to the left, 'perhaps because it was easier for the guides to see the next body towards the directing flank', thought William Molyneux.[30] Small connecting files led from the leading Brigade to the Guards marching behind them. It was Molyneux's job to make sure the leading troops did not run into or overlap the Highlanders on their left, or get too far away from the artillery with its guns on their left rear. The rumbling of the gun wheels seemed 'very loud' to Molyneux.

Elsewhere an impressive silence seemed to reign. Captain Stanier Waller R.E., an extra aide to Willis, had been permitted to join the march at the last minute. He found it 'a strangely weird business marching at night across the desert knowing there were so many thousand men all around us but being unable to see or hear them'.[31] Waller's sentiments are echoed by Quartermaster John Aislie of the Cameron Highlanders, who thought 'this low funeral-like march impressed me more than even the battle itself, for every minute I expected the enemy to open fire on us'. Private George Beedon in the Black Watch thought it 'was a grand sight', as the two lines advanced, 'they looked like walls moving'.[32]

Everyone was 'highly-strung and excited', wrote Private Tutt in Graham's Brigade. He later thought 'it is astonishing, considering the intense darkness and the excessive strain on everybody, that the army kept together as well as it did'. There was no talking in the ranks, but a 'hoarse excited whispering. Sometimes it would be a careless, jerky remark, accompanied by a snappy little laugh of nervousness – the kind of noise that people often make when they are afraid and ashamed to show their terror.' Tutt tried to keep his worst fears in check: 'You are afraid to breathe, for fear you should raise some mysterious alarm which would let loose every muzzle that you know is facing you, ready to blaze, and blast and sweep you off the face of the desert.'

'Bill', a hoarse voice creaked in the darkness. 'Hello', whispered back Tutt, 'What do you want?' It was his front rank man who had turned for a moment to face him. 'Bill, do you mind changing places with me? I've come over a bit queer.' Tutt knew the man had been suffering from dysentery for several days. 'All right, mate,' he shot back, 'I'll swap, but front or rear rank won't keep you from being shot, if its your luck to get a bullet.'[33]

Way behind the marines marched the Brigade of Guards. War correspondent Guy Dawnay was there with his officer brother Eustace and Coldstream Guards pals. He thought the march was 'nasty … going over a good more ground than the actual march demanded, though one might have slept once or twice fairly for an hour or so one never knew whether we were halting for an hour or two minutes …'[34] Sergeant Spriggs with the Scots Guards complained in his diary of the constant manoeuvring:'First we go to the right, then the left, then backwards and forward all through the night …'[35] Several hundred yards to Spriggs' left, in the 2nd Brigade of Hamley's Division, several men in the DCLI got sleepy because of the weary pace and needed a sharp shake from a mate to wake them up. One soldier during a rest period had a nightmare and shouted out. 'He was instantly seized and held firmly down,' recalled Corporal Philip, 'while some of his comrades placed their hands over his mouth, until he came to his proper senses'.[36]

The night's biggest scare was when a Highlander, apparently drunk on rum, laughed out loudly and hysterically (some accounts place him in the Camerons, others the Highland Light Infantry). Lt-Colonel Butler, riding by Wolseley's side, recalled 'the deep stillness' broken by this peal 'of wild and hilarious laughter'. Ever the philosopher, ruminating on all the armies and conquerors who had crossed this desert during Egypt's long history, Butler concluded:'What did our little night-march matter in that catalogue or context? Perhaps the poor hysterical Scottish soldier, whose weird laugh broke so rudely upon the desert silence … knew as much about it as the best of us.'[37]

The cavalry division, advancing on the extreme right, was led by Brigadier-General Wilkinson with the 13th Bengal Lancers and 6th Bengal Cavalry heading the advance. Behind them came 'N' Battery of 'A' Brigade and 'G' Battery of 'B' Brigade, Royal Horse Artillery with the mounted police following them. Earlier that day Wilkinson had positioned a flagstaff a mile due north of the camp but this marker proved almost impossible to find in the dark and it was not until 2.15am that the cavalry were finally able to advance properly. At least two of the officers rode refreshed and mildly drunk. On the morning of the 12th Baker Russell had sent his aide to Ismailia to buy a goodly supply of champagne which he and Hugh McCalmont now quaffed from a bucket as they rode through the night.

Several officers riding with the infantry experienced difficulties with their horses on the march. Neville Lyttelton, riding with the headquarters staff, found that his nervous Arab stallion neighed and whinnied so much that he could not sleep at any of the night's halts; Guy Dawnay complained of the same thing. Not far off, riding alone in the darkness to help guide the 1st Division, William Molyneux thought his horse would waken the dead. The blackness of that night was a confounded nuisance to some; Lieutenant John Adye, sent by the Chief to tell the Naval Brigade not to advance too quickly up the railway line, could not locate them in the darkness, while Lieutenant Brooks of the Gordon Highlanders mislaid his claymore during a halt, searched vainly and as his men chuckled, grabbed a pioneer's spade with the words: 'I'm going right in with this.'[38]

The Indian Contingent had deliberately set off one hour later than the rest of the army. Earlier that night they had been told to get some rest by the banks of the Canal. 'At about ten to twelve I awoke quite chilled but refreshed after 4 hours sleep,' noted Colonel Rogers, commanding the 20th Punjabis.[39] The Contingent, accompanied by 200 bluejackets under Captain Fitzroy of HMS *Orion*, moved off at 2am, 'but it was 3am before we got anywhere', according to Rogers. The advance was almost noiseless as there were no gun carriages to crunch over the ground. 'It was a most weird sight to see all the troops in khaki and almost invisible marching along the bank, and, below, the water, with the pontoons and boats for carrying off the wounded going with muffled oars along it,' wrote Lieutenant Grierson in a letter to his father.[40]

Several war correspondents intended on going into battle with the army but since the march was kept a closely-guarded secret until the last minute no one had seen fit to inform them. Frederic Villiers, the *Graphic* war artist, had gone to Ismailia to send home some sketches. He arrived back in camp at Kassasin expecting to dine with the Guards only to find 'piles of heavy baggage and nothing edible'. He set off towards Tel-el-Kebir on a nervous pony, the beast whinnying incessantly, and the desert haze 'chilling one with its moisture and preventing one from seeing more than a few yards in front'. After a time he noted a curious smell as a 'ghostly phosphorescent light dimly flickered along the sands'. Both rider and horse were appalled, the latter refusing to move as it began trembling. Digging in his spurs, Villiers pressed on a little closer until he saw that the luminous mass was a dead Egyptian killed on the 9th, the man's skull 'grinning up through the bluish vapour'. The thought occurred to him that unless he found the British Army soon a Bedouin's blade would ensure that he too would 'be found, one of these hazy nights, lighting the desert in the same indistinct and unsatisfactory manner'.[41] Finally, the sounds of his pony were answered by some braying commissariat mules and Villiers found out that he blundered into the rear of the King's Royal Rifle Corps in the 2nd Brigade of Hamley's Division.

The Chief had slept soundly during the halts, but in the saddle he kept constantly checking and re-checking the time on his repeater watch. 'It is only those to whom the lives of considerable forces and the honour of one's country have been entrusted who can really know what tension there is on every nerve at such a moment,' he wrote later to his wife, 'I fully realised the danger of the operations I had determined upon, and I knew that if I failed every wisea-cre in England would have said what a fool I was to have attempted a night attack.'[42] One of his worries was that contact with Macpherson by telegraph had been lost during the night. It left Sir Garnet praying that the 'damned' Indians would not get too far ahead and ruin the main show. The distance from the first bivouac at 1am to the Egyptian trenches had been estimated at three and three-quarter miles at a pace of one mile an hour including halts, so Wolseley expected to be at Tel-el-Kebir about 4.45 am, around an hour before sunrise. Extra halts as the army had changed positions in the night made the general aware that the minutes towards dawn were fast running out.

About 4am, Sir Garnet told William Butler, his AAG, along with his deputy Frederick Maurice, to ride ahead, find General Alison and tell him 'to move for-ward as rapidly as possible as ... daylight could not be far behind us'.[43] The pair had just reached the Highland Brigade when disaster almost struck. The order to rest had gone out from the centre of the Brigade but did not reach the flanks for a few more minutes. The result, as Butler wrote afterwards, 'was that the flank battalions wheeled inwards and lay down in a kind of half-circle'. When the advance began again the Highland Light Infantry on the left, and the Black Watch on the right, almost collided in 'a serious scrimmage'. It took almost half an hour to re-form the line.

Butler and Maurice rode back to the Chief trotting along besides Admirals Seymour and Hoskins and told him what had happened. Blackness was all around them but it was certain the Egyptian lines could not be far off. Quite cooly, Wolseley decided to dismount and await developments. Butler listened to the Chief's repeater watch strike 4.40, 4.45, then 4.50 minutes. Then, looking eastward, all saw as Butler described it, a 'large shaft of pale light, shaped like a sheaf of corn, and of the colour of pale gold ...' shoot straight up from the horizon into the sky.[44] Wolseley and his staff were at first mystified. Had they miscalculated the exact time of dawn? Then a fiery tail became visible behind the glow. Later it would be revealed as the Great Comet of 1882, but Sir Garnet cursed himself. The phenomenon would be seen in the Egyptian camp, maybe some might be roused early to look at it and discuss its portent. He vowed always to consult an almanac before planning his next battle.

Back in the saddle, Wolseley and his staff had ridden only a short distance further when the night's silence was finally broken by a single shot to their right front. 'It was quickly followed by the sound of two or three more shots,' then 'a thunderous roll of musketry, mixed with heavy gun fire, swelling from our right front far along the western desert on either side'.[45] The two forces had at last collided. It was 4.58am. The battle of Tel-el-Kebir had begun.

An Egyptian cavalry patrol almost ran smack into the left wing of Graham's Brigade. Lieutenant Field could later clearly recall how the fast approaching dawn 'made the nearest rise or wave of the brown desert visible against the still darkling sky' when a lone Arab horseman appeared over the sands in front of the Royal Irish. Several men raised their rifles to the 'ready' but officers told them not to fire. Heading on towards the Royal Marines the Arab, clearly more terrified than his horse, waved his hands in the air and made a desperate attempt not to get shot, calling out, 'Me Christian! Me Christian!' The front ranks parted to let him though and others behind pulled him off his steed. A small body of enemy cavalry on white horses came fast after him, were similarly surrounded, and pulled from their horses just as the opening salvo rang out.[46]

Everyone later recalled the opening shot. It seemed to come from a sharp-eyed sentry somewhere in the centre of the Egyptian lines. It is possible that the British centre were much closer than Maurice suggests. This, at least, was the opinion of Lieutenant Walter Churchward R.A. who wrote that same day: 'We had no idea we were so close … the bullet whizzed just over us. They had obviously seen the long line of batteries but not the infantry.'[47] In that awful half-light which precedes true dawn, when shapes can be dimly made out but not true forms, it would soon become apparent that the Highland Brigade had actually passed the Egyptian advanced redoubt and were within 350 yards of the trenches. Alison's right flank was also slightly overlapping the left of the British guns (which were parallel to the enemy). These mistakes had been caused, as Maurice explained, because the 'night sky was continually observed with clouds … It was therefore only possible to take up successive stars which appeared to be directly in front when the North Star was on the right hand.'[48] Since the stars set in a north-westerly direction Lieutenant Rawson had veered the Highlanders towards the right and so passed the Egyptian polygonal redoubt by almost 1,000 yards without the enemy hearing or seeing anything. It was a very lucky event. The original line of march would have taken the Brigade within 400 yards of the fort, involved heavy fighting and then meant a rush across 1,200 yards of exposed ground to assault the main trenches as the Egyptians blazed away.

'I never felt anything so solemn as that night march,' commented Archibald Alison in an address to the citizens of Glasgow one year later. Now he felt relief flooding over him as the enemy flashed a line of fire all along their front and he could see at last 'the swarthy faces of the Egyptians, surmounted by their red tarbooshes, lining the dark rampart before us.' Corporal Philip in Hamley's rear brigade later recalled a total of nine shots before, 'with the rapidity of a thunderbolt, the whole place for miles in front was lighted up by one blaze of fire, while the roar of cannon and din of musketry was terrific. Over our heads flew the bullets in a steady stream, with a sound as if sheets of iron were hurling through the air.'[49] Men around him reeled from their fusillade. Suddenly Colonel Richardson, commanding the DCLI, fell from his horse, his face shattered by a bullet that struck him in the mouth and passed out below his right ear. Until command was restored the men of the DCLI lay down on the sand 'and braced ourselves for the final charge which, even without instructions, we knew was close at hand'.

Along the British lines all eyes were dazzled at first by what Molyneux described as 'a perfect sheet of flame a mile long …'[50] Captain Waller, riding near General Willis, thought the sight was 'extremely pretty', while one of Wolseley's mounted escort felt 'as they opened fire the flash of their rifles and guns ran along the whole front, rather like one has seen the gas-jets light up at some circus entertainment'.[51] Sitting on his horse in the front rank of the artillery, not far off from the centre of the Egyptian lines, Lieutenant Churchward thought the fire was

> … tremendous … Perfect hail of bullets all around us and shells from the big guns bursting all over the place like squibs and crackers my eye! For about 10 minutes we were like statues under the fire of the whole line of trenches, it was just about as hot they make 'em.

He was proud that the troopers of the Royal Horse Artillery

> … sat their horses like bricks altho' dust knocked up every square yard in bullets. My mare got one in the shoulder and another just grazed the edge of my helmet just over my left ear, nice convenient place but it made me jump a bit.'[52]

One of the first shells screamed into the sand very close to where Sir Garnet was watching the action with his brother, George. The pair had dismounted and were using field-glasses to see what the leading brigades were doing. Luckily for them the enemy cannonade did not include shrapnel or canister, which would have caused ghastly injuries, and many shells buried themselves harmlessly in the sand.

Further back, among the Guards Brigade, an order had gone out for the Scots to lie down as the Coldstreams and Grenadiers extended themselves. 'The order had hardly been given when, Crack! Crack! Crack! Crack! and the horizon was lit up with flashes like summer lightning,' wrote Lieutenant Balfour, 'with a continuous crackle like the rumpling of several *Times* newspapers. We were kneeling and sitting down when it began, and about the third crack came Boom! and a shell swished over our heads.'[53] Guy Dawnay, with the Coldstreams, thought it burst 150 yards behind him. It was followed by another, much closer than the first, which terrified the battalion's interpreter. Then came the first Egyptian fusillade. 'It was a magnificent sight – magnificent', wrote Dawnay, 'it was still dark enough to see each flash of rifle and spit of fire, while the big guns blazed like meteors amongst the stars, and all along the line, except where an intervening ridge lit their works, the same fireworks lit up the horizon.'[54] Two companies of the Coldstreams were ordered up to the front line. Dawnay set off with the right company commanded by Major John Sterling and with the Hon. Alan Charteris and Guy's brother, Eustace, as his lieutenants. As they hurried forward shells streamed over them.

Sitting on the ground behind the Coldstreams listening to the battle, Charles Balfour 'felt a sense of pleasurable excitement' because, without needing to duck, 'I knew that once a shell is over one's head one is all right.'[55] The missiles landed from 100 to 300 yards behind where he was sitting, but Corporal Henry Porter, also with the Scots Guards, watched in horror as one of them burst in the middle of a cavalry troop to his left wounding some officers. Sergeant Ridout, also with the Scots, recalled the Duke of Connaught, riding along the lines saying: 'Now, my boys, be ready for them.' It was Ridout's first experience of being under fire and unlike the cool Balfour, he found it distinctly unnerving. 'Both in front and rear of us men were falling down', he wrote afterwards, 'I saw one of my own men fall down. He was shot in the head, but was only wounded, thank God!' Since Wolseley had decreed that the Egyptian trenches would be taken at the point of the bayonet the British artillery had still not opened fire, which 'we were all praying for them to do' said Ridout.[56]

Trying to remain unafraid behind the Guards Brigade were several Royal Engineers under the command of a recent hero of the Afghan and Zulu wars named Bindon Blood. Their carts included one loaded with dynamite and the engineers found themselves to be just at the range of the enemy guns. Major Blood later recalled the experience as 'lively', with 'shells falling all around us'.[57]

Now, as the Egyptians began to pepper their enemy, General Alison gave the command to fix bayonets. There was a sharp click as thousands of these steel instruments of death, 21.5 inches long, were slipped into their sockets. A few brief words of command were shouted out. Colonel Macpherson, who had marched with the Black Watch in Ashanti, rode down the line. The Colonel's voice was clear and firm: 'Men, not a shot is to be fired! All work must be done wi cauld steel! Forty-twa will advance!'[58] A lone bugle call rang out that was heard by just enough of the Highlanders to begin a cheer that ripped along the lines of kilted men. To the wail of the bagpipes and with a tremendous roar a vast wave of Highlanders rushed at the Egyptian trenches.

The Highland Light Infantry on the left of the line, and the Black Watch on the extreme right, were both delayed by stout resistance from strongly defended redoubts. The attack thus took on an apex formation as the centre battalions of Gordon and Cameron Highlanders charged spearlike at the trenches held by men of Ali Fehmy's celebrated 1st Guards Regiment. It was a distance of 150 yards but so hot was the fire that nearly 200 men went down in the charge. If the light had been better or the nervous Egyptian fire was lower, many more would have been killed or wounded. 'Come on 79th', yelled Colonel Leith, leading the Camerons. Pipe-Major Grant struck up: 'The March of the Cameron Men', the regimental quick-march. The first man to reach the enemy lines may have been Private Donald Cameron who, it was alleged: 'was the first man to mount the parapet and the second to fall'.[59] The first fatality was Wyatt Rawson who, riding ahead of the Brigade on his horse, was a perfect sitting target. Spencer Ewart, a young officer in the Camerons, wrote home that:

> ... we all ran cheering as hard as we could towards the earthworks, stumbling into holes in the darkness ... I was dead beat when I fell into their trench, a great deep place. I opened fire with my revolver to clear the way. It was a fearful sight, the Camerons bayoneted everyone.[60]

The charge 'was the finest sight I ever saw in my life' claimed a Camerons NCO writing to his local Elgin newspaper. 'We were like a lot of mad dogs let loose. We charged right up to the trench, into it, and right into their own ground without firing.'[61]

The fight was just as tough for the Gordon Highlanders who lost five dead (and one missing, presumed killed), along with 29 officers and men wounded, two of whom died later. Perhaps the most poignant loss was 23-year-old Harvey Brooks. He was found 20 yards beyond the first trench, lying on his back, with four bullet wounds and his hands still clutching the spade he had picked up in the desert, but now dented and bent in the struggle. His missing claymore was found on the sands the next day.

It was the Highland Light Infantry who had the biggest fatalities. Attacking one redoubt protected by an exceptionally wide, deep and steep ditch they lost 17 killed and 57 wounded, a grim tally of 74 men in what once had been the 74th Foot. Their commanding officer, Lt-Colonel Abel Straghan, wrote to his mother in Hereford that he had 'no time to think of dismounting or of the absurdity of charging a redoubt on horseback. The greatest thing was to get the men on.'[62] One of the first to rush the battery along this section of the defences was Lieutenant William Edwards, a Norfolkman, who 'killed the artillery officer in charge, and was himself knocked down by a gunner with a rammer, and only rescued by the timely arrival of three men of his regiment'. His courage earned Edwards the only Victoria Cross awarded during the battle.

The Black Watch also had a tough fight on the Brigade's right flank. Private John Gordon rushed forward cheering as loud as his lungs would allow. Quickly he noticed the Egyptian aim was too high, 'for as our rear rank sloped arms, the bullets rattled on steel bayonets like a shower of hail on a tin roof'.[63] Some of the bayonets were even bent out of shape by the fusillade. The men were in line of double companies at the charge, but reached the trenches 'in one line of four deep'. Jumping across, Gordon landed on hard sand and pulled himself to the top of the parapet. Captain Fox, his company commander, took on three Egyptians at once; swinging his claymore he decapitated one and pushed the point into another before the third man shot him in the thigh. Fox was rescued by Private Gordon and some comrades who helped him to a dressing-station. 'The 42nd charged over the last 50 yards like tigers,' wrote a sergeant of the Black Watch, describing the bullets as 'whirring, whizzing and pinging like as many bees'.[64] Some two dozen men were wounded in the advance and confronted by some of the deepest trenches in the fortifications and an embankment 14 feet high in places. Men fell or were shot in the trench, others died trying to scale the parapet. One who fell into the pit was Captain Andy Wauchope leading a rush of men. The lanky officer picked himself up and somehow clambered up and out, a bullet through his helmet, and another in his scabbard. Eventually the NCOs and men cut steps in the compressed sand with their bayonets. Leading the way forward was Lieutenant Lord Kennedy, 'splitting them at a terrific pace', followed by 'swarms, wheeling to right and left, bayoneting and shooting every man'.[65] Young Lieutenant Graham-Stirling had half his head blown away by a bullet. Sergeant-Major John McNeill, a giant of a man and every inch a senior NCO, ran his sword through six Egyptians in succession before getting plugged in the thigh. A sergeant with a revolver shot the assailant:

> McNeill fell, but rose and led on for a minute, but got shot again in the stomach and groin, and fell fatally wounded. We charged on at a six gun battery which was mowing down the 72nd Highlanders, bayoneted over 100 men, who defended themselves well, three minutes did it all.[66]

'The bayonet was the only thing we used, and we used it right well,' wrote Private Lachlan McLean. In the crushing melee there was no space or time for men to aim a rifle. 'It was horrible work, and a horrible sight when it was done' noted McLean. Private James Judson, thought the sights were: 'Heartrending ...

an old man here, a young lad there, or a riderless horse galloping madly on in confusion.'[67]

Early on, during the heaviest part of the close-quarter fighting, the Egyptians seemed to hold or check the Highland Brigade's advance. It seemed that for a moment the Camerons and Gordons at the apex might have fallen back. It was later said that there were a few cries of 'Retire' uttered by Glasgow Irishmen with Fenian sympathies. But officers urged the men on and General Alison, a hero to all, and oblivious of the dangers, strode about waving a pistol in his only hand. General Hamley described the enemy fire as 'extraordinarily brisk and rapid – the air was alive with bullets and shells.'[68] The Camerons and Gordons found themselves fired on by three sides. It was, according to Hamley, 'a very ticklish moment'. He reinforced them from the second line and the Highlanders moved forward again. Amid the dust and smoke, Sir Edward could not see Ashburnham's troops and both of his aides had their horses shot from under them. He loaned one of them his stallion and ordered him to hurry up the 2nd Brigade.

'The history of the seizure of the works, for the first ten minutes to a quarter of an hour of the fight, is the history of the advance of the Highland Brigade,' wrote Maurice in the Official History.[69] The British right flank, led by Graham's brigade, began the battle much further away from the enemy. Depending on whom you believe this was something between 500 and 1,200 yards away. The brigade had also been marching at the wrong angle. Fitzroy Hart had noticed the faulty alignment some time earlier and just started to get the Royal Marines, who were marching on the left flank of the Brigade, to wheel more to the left (west) when the enemy fusillade began. 'The Marines wheeled regularly into the new line' he wrote, 'and I galloped along the Brigade, directing the other three battalions ... This was done in an orderly manner. Fortunately for us a slight rise of ground sheltered us from the enemy's fire.'[70]

Below this hillock the front line of Graham's men got ready to attack. The air above 'literally hissed with bullets'. Hart rode across to the 18th Royal Irish, on the right flank and decided to try and assist their advance. The whole Brigade moved forward, according to him, 'at the double and in a series of rushes ... With a terrific cheer the 18th rushed forward at the line of flame. I rode with them, cheering with all my might.'[71] Just as the Royal Irish got ready to jump the parapet their white coated enemies turned and ran. Pipers playing, the Royal Irish jumped into 'a shallow unfinished ditch' and fired on the retreating foes. But Egyptians in the redoubt on the regiment's left were made of sterner stuff and began to pepper them. Lieutenant Chichester led a storming party. Two of his men stood back-to-back, 'tackled six Nubians and accounted for them all,' though their gallant officer and some of the other men were hit.

Chichester later recalled a reservist who lay where he had fallen. 'He had eight bullet holes in his body,' said the officer, 'when the men came to attend him on the battlefield he said, "Don't mind me; look after others, worse hit".'[72] Two gallant Irishmen, Lance-Corporal Devine and Private Milligan, rushed over the first defences and could be seen for a time fighting bravely against impossible odds right in the middle of the Egyptian rear lines before both were killed.

In a single rush the York and Lancaster Regiment, in the right-centre of the Brigade, helped their Royal Irish comrades take the 3-gun battery. One of its officers ran off with Fitzroy Hart in pursuit. The Egyptian had a rifle but Hart wished to spare the man his life: 'I waved my revolver downwards and signed as best as I could to him to drop his rifle,' he wrote later, 'instead of doing so he seized my revolver by the muzzle and … tried to drag it out of my hand or me off my horse. In an instant I shot him full in the chest while he still held the barrel of my revolver.'[73] As the York and Lancaster's pressed on into the trenches 'we shot them down like rain falling,' noted Private Edward Brown from Sheffield.[74] The Royal Irish Fusilers, fighting in the space between the Royal Marines and York and Lancaster Regiment, had only arrived at Kassassin on the afternoon of the 12th, yet they fought gallantly and mainly in support of the latter regiment.

The stiffest fighting encountered by the Brigade was its left flank manned by the Royal Marines. 'It was a furious rush', said Private Tutt, to earthworks that 'were not much to speak of'. Night was now rapidly turning into day. The vanishing blackness also allowed the Egyptians to see their targets at close range. Running and cheering Tutt reached the parapet in a state of frenzy:

> I looked up and saw against the sky a white-clad Egyptian with a short brass-hilted sword. He must have been a bugler, for he had a bugle hanging from his shoulder … He was about four feet above me, fighting downward, and slashing at me savagely. I drove my bayonet swiftly upward, and the weapon went through his chest. He tumbled down upon me as I drew it out, and we rolled to the ground together.[75]

Tutt quickly got to his feet and moved on. 'It was all so swift, so bewildering, and yet there was such a clean and splendid sweep of everything' he wrote later. Finding that the breech-block of his Martini-Henry was clogged with sand, Tutt realised that: 'now I had to rely entirely on steel' to press on with the attack.

'There was to be no surprise visit on our part,' was the feeling of Lieutenant Cyril Field before the charge. Bullets 'in thousands' buzzed and hissed overhead, or rebounded on the hard sand, 'and men began to drop fast'.[76] The regiment had formed into four companies as a firing line and four in support, moving towards the trenches in short rushes, and lying down to shoot. To everyone's relief a bugle finally sounded 'Charge' and, as Field recorded: 'The whole line, every man burning to get at the Egyptians, rushed forward at the double, with a continuous shout or roar rather than a cheer.' Major Strong was shot dead in the act of dismounting from his horse near the parapet and Captain Wardell was killed as he crossed the summit. Crazy with fury, his subaltern Lieutenant Luke, almost decapitated the assailant. Thirty-nine-year-old John Wardell had been a popular officer and the second member of his family to die in action within four years (his elder brother George was killed at Isandlwana). In total the regiment lost 5 killed and 54 wounded.

Lt-Colonel Jones, commanding the Royal Marines, was one of those who scrambled to get out of the trench, using his sword as a lever. When he did so he viewed a scene of stiff hand-to-hand fighting, 'in which our bayonets played an important part'. Choosing his words carefully, Jones later wrote: 'It took me a long time to get the men in hand again.'[77] The truth was that the mens' blood lust was up and they bayoneted every remaining Egyptian. Later, he caused a spat by insisting his regiment beat the Highlanders to the trenches. Arabi Pasha gave this opinion substance when he said: 'the attack on the Egyptian left was delivered before the Highland attack on their centre'.[78] Maurice disagreed and the accounts of those present support his contention that while Graham's men, in most cases, were able to rush at unfinished or weakly defended earthworks, the Highlanders had a tougher time of it. In other words, they found it harder to press home the full weight of the Brigade, but nonetheless reached the Egyptians ahead of the 1st Division.

Across the battlefield other incidents were played out. Within five minutes of the opening cannonade a shell 'came smack into us', wrote Lieutenant Henry Earle, aide to his uncle, General Earle. 'The Gen's horse and my horse were hit and we galloped to the left to a hollow to change horses.'[79] In the confusion Richard Harrison lost sight of his chief, 'and I edged away a little to the right where I was behind the Black Watch'.[80] He gingerly led his horse into and over the trench and followed the pipers of the Gordons, who were acting as a rallying point for the Brigade, on into the Tel-el-Kebir lines.

Poor old General Willis, who had got sunstroke at Tel-el-Mahuta and almost been hit by a shell at Kassassin, was talking quietly with William Molyneux when

... slap came a bullet to his left shoulder; it cut through his tunic and shirt, making a scar four inches long, fell onto the top of his field-glass, and thence onto the sand, where he secured it as a memento. It was a very narrow escape, for though the ball was spent, a touch on his spine would have paralysed my chief. As it was, he was black and blue for a fortnight.'[81]

All battles mean scrapes and there were these aplenty. The Duke of Connaught had a near shave when his bugler was hit. Shortly after the battle began the Headquarters Staff scattered so as not to draw attention to General Wolseley. At one point a body of enemy cavalry from the advanced redoubt galloped towards him. 'Sir Garnet will be cut off!' yelled Tulloch but danger was quickly averted by Butler sending a squadron of the general's escort to chase them away.

When the battle began the cavalry division were about 2,000 yards from the nearest Egyptian lines. Maurice wrote that they were trotting slowly, but Littlejohn and McCalmont, both of whom were there, disagree with the official historian and said that the men were dismounted and, in many cases, asleep. A shell came screaming over the scene of more than 2,000 horses 'with their noses almost resting on their riders' heads'.[82] Sir Baker Russell shouted out: 'We shall be under fire in three minutes.' Sergeant Littlejohn kicked some of his fellow dragoons awake and men hurriedly got into their saddles. 'Trot', barked out Russell, and the division was off. McCalmont admitted to having been 'lying in the sand by my horse much too cold to sleep' when the first shell woke up the whole division.[83] Battery 9 on the Egyptian extreme desert flank now opened up on the cavalry but it was engaged and silenced by the Horse Artillery who also dealt with a field battery in the rear of the same fortification. Quickly, Drury Lowe's men, riding in line of squadron columns, swept past the entrenchments and began to swing round the rear of the Egyptian lines. Within 30 minutes the cavalry were 'well to the west of the northern redoubt and about level with it,' and soon 'moving south at considerable speed'.[84] The cloud of dust they raised was so large that British gunners in front of the entrenchments were warned not to fire towards the north-west in case they hit any of the cavalry.

At the opposite end of the advancing British front, on the other side of the Sweetwater Canal, the night had gone well for the Indian Contingent. They were not noticed by the enemy until about seven minutes after the fighting began north of the Canal. According to Lieutenant Grierson:

The first shell or two fell short but the third we heard whizzing towards us. Nearer and nearer it came till with a crash and a roar it buried itself in the ground in the middle of the Staff not two yards from my horse's head. My beast reared straight on end, most of the others did so likewise, and not a few fellows measured their length on the ground.

Grierson was sent to hurry up the native troops as the Seaforths in front extended themselves. 'It was the most unpleasant ride I ever had,' he recalled, 'it was still very dark, the road was ... full of holes and swamps, and blocked by ammunition mules and dhoolie bearers and the shells were plumping into the column but doing wonderfully little damage.'[85] While the Seaforth Highlanders prepared for a frontal assault, the 20th Punjab Native Infantry, supported by the other Indian regiments, tried to get through some maize fields to outflank the enemy. Surgeon Gimlette wrote that: 'the shells came screaming down, just overhead and on each side of the narrow column, falling so close as to scatter mud and dust over the men. The noise of the cannonade by this time was hideous.' Told to march at the double the men were soon within rifle range 'and had the pleasant sensation of bullets whistling about our ears in addition to the shells overhead. Soon the rush came; the Seaforths who were in front ... drove the Egyptians out of their battery with their bayonets, capturing twelve guns.'[86]

The maize was so tall that Colonel Rogers, mounted on his horse and leading the 20th Punjabis, could not see his way. He led his men out of the fields and found the Seaforths hard at work in the battery. Macpherson now ordered him to take the nearby village, some 150 yards away, by a bayonet charge. This the Indian troops did 'in splendid style', yelling as 'the Egyptians ran like hares'.[87] Bedouin on hills to the south threatened to ride down and loot the extended column, so the 29th Bombay Native Infantry kept up a hot fire, expending some 1,800 rounds, to keep them at bay.

The Naval Brigade had hauled its Gatlings along cursing much of the way but they too were in range of the Egyptian guns near the railway line. 'Round whirred the Gatlings, "rrrr rum, rrrr rum, rrrr rum!", that hellish noise the soldier so much detests in action,' wrote a correspondent. 'The parapets are swept. The embrasures are literally plugged with bullets ... The Egyptian fire is silenced. With a cheer the Bluejackets dash over the parapet, only just in time to find the enemy in full retreat.'[88]

Light was coming up fast across the whole skyline by 5.15am, at which point fighting was taking place along the whole battlefront, an incredible sight of red and white coated men in vast masses locked in a life and death struggle as smoke and noise surrounded them. It was about this time that Brigadier-General Goodenough ordered his artillery, who dismounted and stood by their guns, to advance. What happened next would never be forgotten by Lieutenant Churchward:

> The R.A. advanced at a smart trot, and then we had a regular race as to who would be the first over the parapet; no joke for a gun and team of horses to jump. My No 1 gun and self went at it a hell of a pace and we got over in the most

248

extraordinary way, but had two men and two horses shot in a few minutes as we were again under a hot fire from enemy's second line of trenches. We all got over in a few minutes, then away we went on the open, straight for the top of the hill, came into action and blazed away, taking enemy's left flank in reverse.[89]

Around 5.20am, Major Lugard, one of Hamley's staff officers, found an entrance into the battery that had delayed the Black Watch. With ten Highlanders he sneaked in and killed the gunners. The Black Watch, supported by the King's Royal Rifle Corps, surged forward. Percy Marling reached the trench and saw it was full of Highlanders. A helping hand lifted him up onto the parapet. With drawn sword he ran forward – and fell flat on his face over the body of a dead Egyptian. Picking himself up, Percy got on with the task of killing. 'The black Sudanese regiments fought like blazes', he noted in his diary, 'most of it was bayonet work'. Private Wilson of 'D' Company, KRRC, added graphically: 'we dropped them down like rotten sheep'.[90]

Goodenough urged on Major Brancker to drag and push his guns through a gap just south of the recently captured battery. One 16-pounder, damaged during this manoeuvre, led to N/2 RA being known as the 'Broken Wheel Battery'. Brancker's remaining five guns did savage work among the enemy. As the Highlanders surged forward the Scottish divisional battery rode past them and saluted their comrades, shouting: 'Scotland Forever'. Viscount Fielding, who had been riding with the broken gun battery, left it 'every single spoke being broken' and galloped after the enemy with his remaining guns, letting loose a shell every 300–400 yards. 'It was a most exciting chevy' he wrote home afterwards, 'as we were quite by ourselves, going down one side of a long line of entrenchments, which we were able to enfilade. We drove the enemy out of two or three redoubts … We went on like this down the whole of the line, nearly two miles.'[91]

The clear turning point of the battle came about 5.35am. The British artillery were in the trenches and causing havoc, on the British right flank Graham's Brigade moved forward again and five minutes later the Highland Light Infantry on the left flank, assisted by the Duke of Cornwall's Light Infantry, succeeded in pushing the Sudanese who had so stubbornly resisted them. In the meantime the Camerons and Gordons were finding that the enemy in the second line of trenches on their sector were not running but resisting and dying at every turn of the parapet, embrasure and traverse. It was not until 6am that this sector was finally secured.

In the ranks just behind the Highland Light Infantry in their rush forward came Corporal Philip and his DCLI chums. Ahead of him, men were bayoneting and clubbing one another. 'The moment we leapt over the broad ditch into the pile of soft sand beneath' he wrote, 'this giving way under our feet, many were precipitated back into the trench'.[92] The dead and wounded lay in hundreds, many with awful bayonet wounds or shot at point-blank range. Others rolled in agony as their clothes and flesh slowly burned. When Lieutenant Sales La Terriere, one of Wolseley's escort, rode through the lines his first impression 'was an appalling smell of roast mutton! ... It wasn't nice'.[93]

Hamley rode up to his most advanced troops and placed himself at their head. Alison declined a horse and walked on with his men. The way was over hilly ground sloping gradually downwards to the Egyptian camp that lay on flat desert near the Canal. From the hill everyone could see that the 'tents were all standing, with pots on the fire for breakfast'.[94] Some trains were under steam in the station. The whole plain beyond was dotted with thousands of retreating enemy, like scurrying ants, along with the ghastly sight of hundreds of dead and wounded animals. Near the camp a huge body of enemy cavalry moved forward as if to block the advance but then melted away. An officer carrying a white flag rode up to Richard Harrison. He turned out to be the commissary-general of the army. Harrison accepted his surrender and agreed to get him safely to Headquarters. In return, the officer promised to ensure that Harrison was not shot by one of the roving bands of Egyptian cavalry who continued to fight on until almost completely surrounded.

Wolseley entered the Egyptian lines in the wake of the Highland Light Infantry and DCLI men accompanied by Butler, who recalled that the large advanced so narrowly missed on the march was still firing as they advanced, but all the other enemy batteries had been silenced, (it was finally silenced with two well-aimed shots from Lt-Colonel Schreiber's guns). Butler described the scene thus:

> To the right one could see the First Division moving quickly in regular formation across the desert. Portions of the Second Division were still in our front, descending the slopes towards the railway station of Tel-el-Kebir, and to our left, where the desert sloped to the railway and canal, the wrecks of Arabi's late army were strewn in all directions. Down the slopes, through the camps, over the railway, and across the canal, the white-clad fugitives were flying south and west in dots, in dozens, in hundreds.[95]

Another one of the general's escort, Alexander Tulloch, recalled: 'so many dead and wounded Gippies were lying about that I could hardly get my pony through without treading on them'. On his way into the village Sir Garnet stopped to offer sympathies to a few British wounded including one officer shot in the throat and not expected to live.

On the British right flank and mounted on his horse, Fitzroy Hart urged on the Royal Marines double-quick, but with brief stops, so the men might catch their breath. 'We fired volley after volley at short rangle into the enemy's back' he wrote, 'until at last it was clear that Arabi's army had melted away'.[96] Private Tutt now had time to try and see how his comrades had fared in the battle. He discovered that the front-rank man who exchanged places with him on the march had been shot in the left arm. Since this would mean a war pension, Tutt considered it 'a nice bit of luck for him'.

Walter Churchward led his gun battery down from the hills towards Tel-el-Kebir and noted that they 'could have killed hundreds ... Only I wanted to bag the trains and engines at the Railway, but they were too sharp.'[97] Others had, in fact, beaten him to it. A first train carrying Arabi left early in the battle. It was followed by one with two engines that narrowly evaded capture by scouts of Wilkinson's Indian cavalry, one of whom was hit as the occupants exchanged shots with the troopers. Before the train got very far it was hit by Viscount Fielding's battery on the ridge. He noted that his men 'blew it to blazes' and yelled with glee. A third train was brought to a standstill when the driver and stoker were both wounded and a clever sowar killed a camel crossing the line thereby effectively blocking it. The occupants leapt out of the carriages and jumped into the canal rather than be captured. In the distance a fourth train approaching from the direction of Cairo screamed on its brakes and reversed down the line.

Behind the main body of troops the Guards Brigade had lost only one man killed but 23 had been wounded by bullets almost spent. During the advance, Major Sterling, leading the small group which included the Dawnay brothers, had a lucky escape when a bullet struck the field-glasses hanging from his belt, leapt to the revolver, ran along it and smashed his hand, the force knocking him down. Entering the lines within ten yards of troops still blazing away, Guy Dawnay spotted Drury-Lowe and some of the cavalry staff and went over to them. Certain that the battle was won and further resistance futile, Drury-Lowe urged Dawnay to tell any Egyptians who would listen to thrown down their arms and go home to their villages, or have their wounds treated at one of the field hospitals.

An order had already been issued by Drury-Lowe that all Egyptians laying down their arms were to be spared by his cavalry. Initially they had deliberately cut down the fleeing enemy, 'as rumour had it that they would otherwise lie down and hamstring the horses ... Or shoot our troops in the back'[98] recalled Lieutenant Steele, riding with the 2nd Bengal Cavalry. Several eyewitnesses wrote of the cold-blooded ruthlessness of Wilkinson's elite Indian horsemen. 'They cut heads off as if they were cabbages and the head fell in many cases eight foot away from the body' recalled an anonymous trooper in the 7th Dragoon Guards. But he admitted:

I could not help cutting some down because they fired on us up to the last. One of the enemy was laid on his face, and as a man of the 4th Dragoon Guards rode past him he rose up and fired at him, and I just caught him as he galloped by and cut him from his shoulder to the middle of his back.[99]

The speedy flight of the enemy repeated south of the canal. In the fields, amid the crushed maize, the advancing Indian Contingent found scores of hastily discarded Egyptian uniforms and weapons. The latter were smashed up as friendly Arabs soon began to appear offering water and fruit to the soldiers. One even cheerfully admitted to Colonel Rogers of the 20th Punjabis that 'they had all been at Tel-el-Kebir'.[100]

War correspondents like Guy Dawnay were not the only civilians who fought in the battle. Langton Walsh, recently sacked from the Indian Political Service, entered the lines with Mubarek, his huge manservant. Both men were armed with revolvers, which they used, 'at close quarters with great effect,' and Mubarek was also expert with his Somali quarter-staff. Walsh propped up a dying Highland NCO who asked: 'Are we in sir?' 'Yes', he replied, as the man died 'with a smile on his face'.[101] Mubarek was near Colonel Richardson of the DCLI when he was hit and helped to get him medical assistance.

England's most eccentric general, Sir Henry Havelock-Allan VC was there too He charged the lines with the Highland Brigade on a chestnut hunter that slid down the trench and toppled him off. One legend records that he was armed only with a hunting crop (though it is hard to believe, even of Havelock-Allan).

Frederic Villiers was another civilian who *walked* into the Tel-el-Kebir lines. His pony bolted during the shelling taking with it his sketch book, glasses and water bottle (luckily the beast was found later). He recalled seeing the dying Graham-Stirling and never forgot the tender moment as a small drummer boy of the Black Watch placed a handkerchief over the face of his stricken officer.

The Egyptian Army was in full retreat by 6.20am when Wolseley reached the little bridge close by the village of Tel-el-Kebir. The only man still fighting was a 'pathetic old Arab lying on his stomach and firing wildly into the blue air at imaginary foes. On disarming him, he was found to be totally blind.'[102] A few hundred Highlanders along with a squadron of cavalry and other mounted troops had just arrived. Dismounting, Sir Garnet sat down on the low parapet of the stone bridge and chatted with Macpherson and Drury Lowe. He ordered the Indian Contingent to march straight on to Zagazig, the main railway terminus in the direction of Cairo, cut off rail communication by the enemy and prevent them from making a stand there, while the Cavalry Brigade was to move swiftly on the capital.

Puffing at his cigars, Wolseley began issuing despatches to the Queen and other dignitaries back home. These were sent by telegraph from the battlefield, (in fact so swift did the information get back and so early that the main evening newspapers that same day were able to carry reports of the victory). The bridge had been designated a rendezvous point by Sir Garnet before the battle. Hamley, who had lost a little time by mistaking Willis on a hill north of the station for Wolseley, and stopped along the way to tell soldiers not to shoot the poor camels, now rode up as the Chief talked with Alison. What happened next is described by Hamley in his diary:

> Sir G. Wolseley looking, not in my face, but towards my breast, muttered what sounded like, 'Oh Hamley, is that you?' and turning from me, began to write on a paper placed on the parapet of the bridge. I cannot describe the astonishment which this reception caused me, when I had come to him expecting welcome and approval after leading the attack which had won the battle (and made his fortune).[103]

It appears that Wolseley's only question was to ask Hamley the extent of his division's losses. Sir Edward defended the exploits of his men and made it plain, before riding away, that he felt slighted. From now on the gloves would be off as both generals added fuel to what was to become a celebrated feud.

When Sir Garnet got up to leave, his horse could not be found. It had become a victim of the looting that was taking place all over the battlefield, (later it was found by Arthur Creagh among the Highlanders, though how a cheeky Scottish subaltern justified acquiring an English saddle with the initials 'G. J. W.' was never divulged). The general soon got the military police to restore order but it seemed for a time that officers as well as men were obsessed with grabbing all they could lay their hands on. Even the Duke of Connaught 'acquired' some carpets and was seen by Walter Churchward riding through the camp, 'smoking a cigarette and with a silver coffeepot in his hand which he had just looted'.[104] Wolseley helped himself to a brace of Arabi's pistols and a small copy of the Koran found in his tent.

One of the first to enter the Egyptian commander's quarters found that it was actually three tents linked by canvas passages: a large one for receptions,

> … with beautiful carpets, tables, chairs and sofas; a smaller contained several excellent French bedsteads, and the smallest a lavatory. Stuck in the sand outside the entrance was the lance of a man of the 13th Bengal Lancers killed on the 9th, probably passed off by Arabi as a captured standard.[105]

253

There were sweetmeats, biscuits and rice cakes but no water. An envelope from an English supporter, (possibly Blunt), lay on a writing table with old Armstrong shell cases as paperweights.

Waving their helmets on the top of their bayonets the cheery Tommies passed through the deserted Egyptian camp and ransacked every tent they could enter. Boxes and mirrors were smashed, cushions slit, everything done in a vain search for gold or precious gems, or the sheer joy of wanton destruction. Corporal Philip admitted 'gathering curiosities, looting provisions, of which there was an enormous quantity, picking out only the very best'.[106] He also saw nothing wrong in stealing chickens and goats from the villagers but it was this very act that got Major Tulloch to complain to the provost-marshal.

Occasionally shouts would eddy around groups of men as rumours abounded that Arabi had been caught hiding in a tent, but in reality, there was no sign of the Egyptian commander. His flight early in the battle was seen as cowardice by many observers and even Wilfrid Blunt thought it less than honourable. Ahmed Arabi saw things differently. His first thought was to continue the war and to do so meant escaping from a battle he knew he could not win. He argued later that his reserves fled the minute they saw the British cavalry on the horizon. Quickly General Arabi rode towards Zagazig from where he telegraphed: 'Send me a special train and take me to Cairo with my cavalry.' He made it out of the station just in time, travelling in the guard's van. Abdul Rahman, the bimbashi at Zagazig, was ordered not to leave but to 'take up a good position to stop the enemy'. Arabi promised: 'I will reinforce you immediately from Cairo and Salahie'. Conflicting orders came from the War Council in Cairo: 'Make known to citizens that they are not to leave their homes and to fear nothing. Should the English troops appear receive them with all honour and respect.' On his way towards the capital Arabi telegraphed the es-Salihiyeh commander 'to come at once with your force via Massoora'. He also wired ahead with instructions to 'collect at once all the troops that are at Cairo so as to defend the city'. He complained that his men had 'made a feeble defence, left the fortifications and fled,' (an unfair slur on many brave Egyptians who died that day), and concluded with the order: 'Take care of the city and our honour.' It seems clear that regardless of the huge defeat at Tel-el-Kebir and the confusion and uncertainty it engendered, Ahmed Arabi still wanted to continue the war.[107]

Gradually as the morning wore on and the sun blazed overhead the full horror of war began to seem apparent to some of the officers and men. Thinking of the slaughter, eight inches of a blood-stained sword protruding from his broken scabbard, Captain Andy Wauchope of the Black Watch remarked: 'What brutes we men are!' The sights were pitiful indeed. An NCO recalled the wounded Highlanders 'burying their heads in the sand to cool them and all who were able crying for water', though men who made it to banks of the Sweetwater gulped a foul liquid, 'you would not wash the door-step with, as it was thick with blood and mud...'[108]

Chaplains began to try and alleviate the sufferings of many, last rites were given to the dying, and even wounded Egyptians were given succour where possible. Inside one of the trenches Chaplain Male counted 50 of the enemy lying dead in an area of 20 paces. Examining the bodies more closely he was struck by the way fair-skinned Circassians had fought and been killed alongside black Nubians. The tops of the parapets presented the awesomely horrible spectacle of mile upon mile of white-coated Egyptian dead, kneeling and lying in countless shapes, their bodies interspersed here and there with those of red coated and often kilted British soldiers.

Across the sands, on the hills, in the trenches and along the parapets lay 58 British killed, 401 wounded, with 15 missing, but a 'precise number was never officially published, as owing to the immediate advance which took place the returns were not regularly made out, and several days elapsed before Sir Garnet Wolseley received and sent in regimental returns'.[109] Yet it was the vast numbers of Egyptian dead, more than 2,000 of them, that most shocked observers. How many fellahin slunk homewards with wounds is unrecorded, but 534 were treated at Tel-el-Kebir by British doctors during the four days after the battle and 27 major operations were performed.

It is true that Wolseley's losses were much lower than he had ever dared to hope, but taken on the scale of Victorian colonial warfare the blood-drenched sands of Egypt made Tel-el-Kebir a major battle. The British dead seem light in comparison to those in many other fights such as Isandlwana or Hlobane, but it is worth remembering that the numbers of wounded in this one Egyptian battle were considerably more than in all the *combined* battles of the Zulu War (indeed full wounded casualties for the campaign are about two-and-a-half times greater). Tel-el-Kebir was a short battle but it was no mere walkover.

British officers seem to have had more sympathy for the unfortunate Egyptians than most Tommies. William Butler heard an officer ask a Highlander, who was filling his canteen at the canal, to give a drink to a gasping Egyptian trooper. 'I wadna wet his lips,' was the indignant reply. It seems there had been several instances where enemy wounded had been given water by Tommies only to shoot their benefactors in the back. Corporal Philip recalled seeing just such an act and Dr Shaw of the Marines was shot by his Egyptian patient (a nearby orderly quickly bayoneted the man). Captain Charles Watson, R.E. was so moved by the plight of the wounded enemy that he gave them all his water and cigarettes. 'We afterwards heard stories of how the wounded Egyptians tried to shoot those who came to assist them' he wrote later, 'but this was quite opposed to my own experience'.[110]

So worn out that he could hardly stand, 'having not had a morsel, except a little muddy water since noon the day before', Walter Churchward was told to accompany General Goodenough in a tour of the battlefield to count the the captured guns. He described the sights as

> ... awful ... Our own wounded were just being brought in, while the dead Highlanders lay face down all round the parapets ... The Egyptians were lying so thick that we had to pick our way with the horses very carefully and we must have counted a good 2,000 and then did not see those caught by the Cavalry and R.H.A. on the right.[111]

A ranker later recalled:

> The artillery had wrought fearful havoc. I remember one heap of 24 corpses, some blown absolutely to fragments, others headless, others with limbs lopped off. Some of the dead Egyptians were roasting slowly as they lay; their clothing had been ignited and was still smouldering. A man of the Rifles came along, drew his pipe from his pocket, and lit it at one of those bodies, remarking somewhat brutally, it struck me; 'By --- I never thought I should live to use a dead Egyptian for a light to my pipe!'[112]

In the outer trenches the British dead lay more thickly than the Egyptians but beyond 'for one man of ours there were certainly ten Egyptians'. Corporal Porter, Scots Guards, was so horrified by the dead Egyptians, 'literally smashed to bits', that he wrote in his diary, 'the sights I saw are too bad to put in this book'. Guy Dawnay saw thirteen of the enemy lying around two Krupp guns and in another place sixteen dead lying together in a long line. 'As one approached the big work at the end of the flanking trench the dead lay thicker still,' he wrote, 'and amongst them lay wounded men motioning for water, poor old camels still writhing on the ground, with no one to think of putting them out of their misery.'[113]

Those who had expected the Egyptians to all turn tail at the first shot had been mistaken. It was true that the reserves and even some officers had run for their lives but large numbers had stayed on, fighting and dying to the last.

The Sudanese in particular had refused to yield, while the artillerymen stuck grimly to their guns. One-armed Archibald Alison, a longtime campaigner, paid them a great compliment when he said: 'I never saw men fight more steadily.'

At crowded field hospitals doctors with shirt sleeves turned up were hard at their bloody, sweaty work trying to save lives as swarms of flies buzzed around them. Outside the tents, sitting still, the wounded waited their turn. Nearby the bodies of the British dead were being collected by stretcher parties and laid out in neat rows. Burials began that evening. Samaritans that day included Captain Walker R.A. and his friend, Veterinary-Surgeon Boulter, who walked over the battlefield trying to moisten the lips of as many injured as possible. Next day they returned with a water-cart and left a bottle with every man. Colonel the Hon. Paul Methuen, Scots Guards, took a water cart out himself on the 13th, assisted by Major Francis Grenfell, King's Royal Rifle Corps. In the Egyptian trenches Grenfell recalled: 'the sun beating down on their ghastly wounds, and though the sufferings must have been great, they were calm and collected, grateful for water and begging for cigarettes.'[114]

Some of the Egyptians seem to have survived horrendous injuries. Fitzroy Hart, an officer well used to the horrors of war, was astounded by an Egyptian who had lost both his eyes and much of his face – 'nose, cheeks, lips and chin had totally disappeared' – yet was somehow alive. Hart did all he could for the poor man. Luckily his teeth and tongue were not affected and his brain seemed okay and the last Hart saw of him the man was sitting up in a hospital bed eating boiled meat and drinking coffee.

It seems that several Egyptian women had been in the trenches, possibly visiting loved ones, when the attack began. Major Hart was moved by the sight of a young woman 'of comely features and short black hair' in the blue dress of a peasant, lying beside the body of 'an old man with very grey hair' who might have been her father.[115] Chaplain Male witnessed 'a young handsome creature' at a dressing station who had fiercely attacked a Tommy when her husband fell and been bayoneted for her pains. Amid the dead and dying by the bridge Lt-Colonel Butler was impressed by a female camp follower washing her child in the canal 'as though to steady her thoughts'.[116]

As the morning wore on towards noon and it got even hotter, the excited soldiers were gradually brought to order by their officers and the military police. Slowly men who had been firing their rifles (one almost shot Guy Dawnay by accident), or stampeding around on captured Arab ponies, or examining the looted tents, calmed down. On the hill above the camp the band of the Guards Brigade played favourite marches and cheers resounded from time to time as one of the senior generals – Alison, Graham, Hamley or Willis – rode through the camp.

Away from the bustle and noise, Sir Garnet sat in a smelly tent and jotted down in his diary: 'Our loss has not been as heavy as I had anticipated.'[117] It was true. His night march had been a success and a crushing surprise had been inflicted on an enemy armed with modern weapons. Three thousand prisoners had been taken too. It was all quite splendid and according to plan. But real success, as Wolseley knew, depended on two things: would Cairo resist a British advance? And was it also likely that Arabi, who had escaped, might rally Egyptian garrisons in other parts of the country? Sir Garnet knew that speed, especially a rapid advance on the the capital, was vital if the war was to be ended swiftly – and in war nothing is ever certain.

# 11

# Trial

*I have only one word to say in my defence – I am an Egyptian*
Ali Fehmy

There was no time to lose. Under Wolseley's orders and Macpherson's command, the Indian Contingent pressed on to Zagazig, eighteen miles closer to
Cairo. A squadron of the 6th Bengal Cavalry rode ahead and broke into a gallop
five miles before the town. Macpherson, who took part in the ride, described
it as 'something like a hunt'. Tired by the loose sand, most of the horses were
too exhausted to keep up the gruelling pace for long and only one sowar was
with Lieutenant Burn-Murdoch R.E. when he reached the railway station well
ahead of the rest of the army. Two days later he wrote:

> It was very rough on old 'Rocket', but he went in rare style, and we got in, tear-
> ing along as hard as we could, at about four o'clock. When in sight of the station,
> which is a great big junction, we saw some 6 engines under steam, getting ready
> to be off. One of them did get off before we got in, but we nailed all the rest,
> although three of them were actually on the move.[1]

In fact when the leading train refused to stop, Burn-Murdoch shot the driver,
jumped onto the foot-plate and applied the brake himself. The resourceful young
officer then went back down the line and picked up the Seaforth Highlanders.

There were no train rides for the rest of the Indian troops, just more foot-
slogging over Africa. Colonel Robert Rogers, 20th Punjabis, called it 'a devil of
a march'.[2] Later he would write to his sons:

> I have had longer, but taking heat, dust, flies etc. etc. never a more tiring one
> – and not even one of our followers fell out … glad was I on searching the rail-
> way refreshment room to get a bottle of beer … gladder was I when I had seen
> to the men and to lie down on a wooden bench with my helmet as a pillow and
> sleep as soundly as fighting horses and cursing Britishers would allow.[3]

Having missed the plunder and much of the battle left a feeling of resentment among several rank and file in the Indian force. Veterans of the celebrated march from Kabul to Kandahar in the recent Afghan War, one Seaforth Highlander complained that Tel-el-Kebir was 'about the shortest fight that ever I had, and as cheap a medal that any army got'.[4] An old Sikh officer thought it also a poor show: 'Call this war! No fighting, no slaughter – not even loot!'[5]

The cavalry division had moved off from Tel-el-Kebir along the north bank of the Sweetwater, later crossing to the canal's south side, where a running fight ensued for several miles leaving 20–30 Egyptian troopers dead as the remainder scattered out across the desert. By the time the men and horses reached Belbeis at 11.30am, they had ridden more than 30 miles, 'the last seventeen being through very heavy sand'.[6] Here they rested until 2am on the 14th with Drury Lowe riding with the advanced guard.

Late afternoon saw the British just two miles north-east of the outskirts of Cairo near the Abbasieh Barracks, 'round which we could see thousands of Egyptian soldiers swarming and looking just like ants whose ant-hill has been disturbed,' wrote Captain Charles Watson R.E.[7] Earlier that day the War Council had decided, it seems on the urging of Arabi Pasha, to try and defend the city. Digging some new defences had just begun when the British cavalry were spotted in the distance.

Playing for high stakes, Drury Lowe ordered Lt-Colonel Herbert Stewart to take 50 men, along with Hugh McCalmont, Charles Watson and two Khedival officers on a reconnaissance mission. They were met by a squadron of Egyptian cavalry. Watson noted with a sigh of relief that 'every man of whom had a white flag, or something that represented a white flag, tied to his carbine'.[8] It was, he felt, a dramatic scene with Cairo and its domes and minarets silhouetted in the distance by the fiery radiance of a big red sun sinking on the eastern horizon. Quickly the small body of British officers accepted the surrender of the Abbasieh men. When the news reached the British and Indian troopers a ringing cheer rent the air.

A wise old fox, Drury Lowe quartered only a small body of British cavalry at the barracks, so as not to reveal the size of his force, and sent in squadrons to be fed and watered before they were returned to camp in the desert. When the city's governor and commandant both visited him to surrender, Drury Lowe ordered them to go back into the city and fetch Arabi Pasha. The Egyptians urged him not to try and occupy the citadel, but Watson counselled quite the opposite view. At the last minute Drury Lowe decided to retain Stewart by his side and so the honour of capturing the citadel fell to Charles Watson. His small escort consisted of 5 officers and 84 non-commissioned officers and men of the 4th Dragoons under Captain Darley and 4 officers and 54 other ranks of the mounted infantry under Captain Lawrence. Watson also decided to take one Khedival officer along with three Egyptians from Abbasieh but he warned them 'that their future in life depended on doing exactly as I told them'.[9]

Surprise was to be the element that night. At 8pm, Watson led his escort by the old desert road towards the citadel. Sergeant Littlejohn later recalled floundering 'in the most broken ground it was ever my lot to ride over' before a hard pavement gave fresh life to the horses who, at a smart trot, swept through a gateway and into an outer courtyard of the fortress.[10] Here the men dismounted to await events. The senior Egyptian officer was roused from his bed and curtly told by Watson that the garrison must surrender and march out that night. With no knowledge of just how many soldiers might be at the Englishman's back the citadel's commander had little option but to agree. The keys of the ancient fortress were presented to him as the Egyptian soldiers began to depart by the Bab-el-Azab gate (the narrow defile where Muhammad Ali had massacred the Mamelukes 71 years earlier). Watson wisely kept his troopers hidden on a different road so that the enemy had no idea of the true size of his small force. The British officer's luck still held when, debating how to secure the capture of the fort on the Mokattam Heights that overlooked the city, he hailed 'an intelligent-looking Egyptian officer ... and said that I would be much obliged if he would go up to the fort, send the garrison to the Kasr-en-Nil, lock the gate and bring me the keys. He thought for a moment, then said: "'Hadir, ya Sidi" (all right, sir), and went off at once ... he came back in two hours with the keys.'[11] By their prompt actions and without firing a shot Drury Lowe and Watson had stolen the city, and taken the surrender of more than 10,000 armed men, a remarkable achievement.

Excitement at the citadel was not quite over. Hearing the garrison depart, the prisoners now rioted in a vain attempt to escape. Next morning the British made a tour of the dungeons and saw, as one officer related:

> ... some of the most horrible sights I have ever witnessed. Nearly all the prison-
> ers had at one time or another been victims of the bastinado, some had had their
> eyes gouged out with hot irons, and many were chained by their legs together in
> couples with a big cannon-ball attached between them.[12] [The next day the chief
> torturer was made to enjoy his own leg-irons].

Everywhere was 'chaos and indescribable filth'. There were two prisons in the citadel, one for common criminals, who were badly ill-treated, and another for wealthier citizens and political prisoners. Later that same day Midshipman de Chair and Corporal Bennett, the only two British prisoners taken by the Arabists, were released healthy and unharmed from their confinement.

By this time the final act of Egyptian humiliation had taken place. Around 10pm on the 14th a message was received by Montagu Gerard, Stewart's deputy, that someone had arrived who wished to speak urgently with General Drury Lowe. 'Going out I found a neat brougham, whence issued two Egyptian officers' wrote Gerard, 'the first of whom, through his friend, who spoke French, announced that he was Arabi Pasha, and that to save further trouble he had come to surrender'. In Arabi's presence Drury Lowe was polite but firm: 'Tell him that I give him no terms at all, and that he surrenders unconditionally.' Arabi bowed to this demand and accepted his fate, adding merely that he had never wanted to fight the British and only acted in defence after they attacked Egypt. Drury Lowe coldly replied that he had nothing to do with politics and was only there to carry out his orders. Arabi bowed courteously and asked if his servants could accompany him? 'Tell him,' added the British general, 'that he may have them, but that the guard will shoot him if there is any attempt at a rescue'. Throughout the interview Arabi was neither 'cringing or arrogant, but acted like a well-bred gentleman' noted Lt-Colonel Gerard, 'and produced the most favourable impression on us all'.[13]

Arabi's surrender brought a memorable 48 hours to a close. Earlier on the 14th General Wolseley had woken in a 'most stinking' tent on the battlefield. One of the first things he did that morning was write to his beloved wife: 'Thank God all has gone well with me. I had a very nervous time of it, for I was trying a new thing I may say in our military annals ... I hope the English people will be pleased ... Arabi has bolted I know not where.' He told his daughter, Frances, that: 'I have not been able to obtain the tip of his nose' for her, but was sending home 'one of his visting cards which was found in his tent'.[14]

One of Wolseley's more sombre duties on the afternoon of the 13th had been to see the dying Wyatt Rawson. 'He was a fine plucky fellow' wrote Sir Garnet, 'When I found him yesterday he was in a large tent ... which was so full of of wounded, some of whom were dying, that I had difficulty in getting to him. The sight was horrible.'[15] The young naval aide, who had guided the army so well and been one of the first to be shot, was racked with pain, but managed to mutter: 'General, did I not lead them straight?' Wolseley, who was genuinely moved, grasped Rawson's hand. 'Yes,' he replied, 'I know you were well to the front all the time, old fellow'. (The young officer lingered in great pain and finally died eight days later.)

The stench of the battlefield and its grisly sights were not easily forgotten by those who were there on 14 September 1882. Lt-Colonel Coghill of the 19th Hussars recalled 'about 2,000 wounded screaming for water or a doctor'. He loathed especially the Bedouins: 'terrible villains and murder the wounded for their clothes'. On the morning of the 14th, in the company of the regimental doctor and a water cart, Coghill like many other British officers toured the battlefield trying to ease the suffering. The Bedouins, he noted, were 'crazy for pillage, so I don't spare them … I drove in several hundred prisoners who are engaged in burying their dead.'[16]

Some things probably happened on the battlefield that did not find their way into the official histories. Sergeant Ridout, Scots Guards, wrote in his diary of the Egyptian wounded: 'some you could see moving and the order was given to some Regiments to stab them to put them out of their pain. Some was brought to camp wounded. Those that they thought would not live was taken and shot.'[17] An English stretcher bearer with one of the field hospitals wrote how on the 13th: 'I was carrying wounded men all day, and up early the next morning fetching in wounded Arabs, and yesterday it was like a butcher's shop here, cutting off arms and legs by the dozen.'[18] Surrounded by so much death soldiers remembered a grim morsel of humour. When one guardsman protested loudly: 'Oh doctor, my arm! I shall die!' an Irish medic, (probably Surgeon O'Dwyer) replied, 'Be aisy wid yer noise now; sure ye're makin' more noise than that poor chap wid his head cut off!'[19]

All the wounded were in tents by the 15th, but across the sands there still lay plenty of swollen and disfigured corpses. Molyneux was put in charge of this burial work. There was also a huge stock of enemy weapons that needed to be destroyed. Remington rifles were smashed at the lock and these, along with tons of small arms ammunition, were thrown into several mass graves with the Egyptian dead on top. The Bedouins, who continually tried to dig up the bodies, were shot whenever Coghill and his 19th Hussars could find them.

With reasonable speed the British troops prepared to move on to Cairo. Wolseley, his staff and the Highlanders were at Zagazig by the night of the 14th. The officers had to sleep on the platform and Sir Garnet's aide, Captain John Adye, recalled the mosquitoes as 'simply murderous'. It was unfortunate that Sir Edward Hamley had been put in charge of Zagazig because Wolseley blamed him for various train delays and mishaps on the line. Then, near Benha, officers and men were thrown to the floor when the commander-in-chief's train ran into the back of one carrying Hamley and Alison. Poor Sir Edward was now told he must remain at Benha while lesser generals went on to Cairo. He decided to remonstrate with Wolseley; 'Where do you want to go?' asked the Chief. 'I should like to go with you to Cairo' replied Hamley. 'Thank you' came the sharp reply as Wolseley swept past him, 'you had better remain with your own troops.' It was a further humiliation for Hamley whose anger and bitterness would soon demand revenge.

A train steamed into Zagazig at 5am and took Sir Garnet onto Cairo. He could write that day to Louisa from the 'cool luxury' of the Abdin Palace: 'Yesterday living on filth, today having iced champagne.' So complete was his success that Wolseley had been able to telegraph Childers that the war was now over, though it 'remains to be seen how long we shall have to stay here'. A letter arrived from Louisa, who had been told by the Prince of Wales that her husband had 'rather under-rated' the Egyptians. She was furious and Wolseley, equally incensed, commented: 'Let him stick to tailoring, that is his province.' When Gladstone sent his congratulations and the offer of a barony the Wolseleys began carping at the thought that Beauchamp Seymour would be similarly treated. 'All he has done has been to bombard and destroy Alexandria which he did living comfortably on board his ship and risking next to nothing', grumbled Sir Garnet, 'Seymour destroyed Alexandria. I saved Cairo ... Tel-el-Kebir has been worth millions to Gladstone's administration and if they behave shabbily to me I shall show them up.'[20]

Within a few days, a victorious Evelyn Wood had received the surrender of the coastal garrisons and General Hilmi, one of the original trio of nationalist colonels, presented his sword personally at Damietta. The one town where trouble seemed most likely was Tanta, scene of the ugly massacre of foreigners after the bombardment. A large gathering of soldiers were dispersed by the ever cool Archibald Alison supported by three companies of the Gordons. Slowly at first, and then in increasing numbers, the Egyptian soldiers, part of the Es-Salihiyeh force that had fought at Kassassin, surrendered their arms and dispersed.

On 25 September, in a great display of pomp, the Khedive returned to his capital. A little after three in the afternoon Tewfik's train drew into the station, the Brigade of Guards presented arms, a gun was fired and the band struck up not the Khedival hymn but, perhaps as a sign of new times, 'God Save The Queen'. Ulema in chocolate-coloured robes and golden turbans jostled with notables to kiss their sovereign's hand. *The Times* correspondent thought that Tewfik's face held shadow of loathing and contempt as he recognized so many men 'who had prostituted themselves and then cringed to Arabi'.[21] In a ceremony at the palace Wolseley was decorated with the Order of the Osmanieh, 1st Class, Egypt's highest honour, and thought the Khedive was 'much affected' by his reception. Fireworks lit the sky that night. The Arabist Revolution was truly at an end.

The occupying British troops now had time to relax, take donkey rides through the bazaars, climb the pyramids and act like normal tourists. The Scots Guards had been the first regiment to arrive and marched up to the citadel from the railway station followed by thousands of 'very noisy' Arabs. Officers and men both agreed that the citadel barracks was 'very dirty and full of vermin and funny insects'. Most of the regiment chose to sleep outside on the parade ground but Sergeant Spriggs constructed a hammock to keep free of the bugs. It broke, giving him 'a good lump' and making all the drummer boys laugh. Exploring some rooms, Spriggs found a batch of Arab shirts, hats and robes and he and his friends enjoyed dressing up in them. 'We can see the Pyramids from our room,' he noted delightedly in his diary.

Irrepressible Lieutenant Churchward R.A. thought Cairo was 'the very best of places, like a small Paris. Best of iced drinks, champagne to any amount and excellent dinners at the hotels.' Colonel Macpherson took his Black Watch to the pyramids and treated the men to a picnic. Private Gordon recalled racing up and down the steps and enjoying a 'glorious' day out. Even Wolseley was encouraged by William Butler to tour the sights. From the top of a pyramid the chief signalling officer excitedly signalled 'Forty centuries salute you!' This lofty praise was too much, even for Wolseley. He shot back a message: 'Don't be a fool! Come down!'[22]

All the barracks in the city were found to be so unsanitary that officers and men recalled their experiences with equal distaste and preferred to sleep outside. The 2nd Brigade was moved across the iron bridge to ground near the Ghezireh Palace on Bulak Island. Soon a city had grown up with its own infrastructure of Arab, Greek and Maltese traders. 'Acres and acres were covered with neat rows of white tents and soldiers in thousands strolled about the environs of Cairo.'[23]

Favouritism was part of Wolseley's personality, along with a rather petty desire to punish those who annoyed him. Both Generals Hamley and Willis, his two least favourite commanders, were given no help at all in finding quarters in the city. Hamley, for instance, was assigned to the 'filthy and unwholesome' citadel and refused permission to take up quarters elsewhere. Later, while headquarters staff and other favourites were allowed to stay in palaces both Hamley and Willis were allotted stone huts near the camp on Ghezireh Island. The huts had been used by local farmers to store vegetables now gone mouldy due to the damp. Hamley found his bed 'drenched in moisture' each morning and took to sleeping in a tent. Such a billet seems inexcusable when contrasted with that given to Ring member Hugh McCalmont (a mere Lieutenant Colonel), who wrote home that 'we live in the most magnificent of palaces ... I wish the business had gone on longer.'[24]

Still complaining about his proposed honours, Sir Garnet wrote to Louisa that: 'I certainly have no reason for loving any of our Royal Family and yet strange to say I do not know a more loyal man than I am.' Three days later, on 28 September, those loyalties were put under strain by a letter he got from the Queen – 'the only one she has ever honoured me with' – which the general thought 'as cold-blooded an effusion as you have ever read'. The feeling, rightly or wrongly, that he was being shabbily treated by the Establishment stayed with him for days. On 1 October he confessed: 'I have always been ambitious' but added that 'to see England great is my highest aspiration, and to lead in contributing to that greatness is my only real ambition.' He admitted that his down-to-earth wife might think such philosophizing was 'twaddle', but he was expressing his innermost thoughts – 'I am not writing for the public.'[25]

Wolseley's remarks and fears, like so many of his private utterings, were rather unjustified. His victory at Tel-el-Kebir and speedy conclusion of the war had made him, for the time at least, hugely popular within all classes of Society. The telegraph wires between Balmoral, the War Office and Downing Street almost hummed with congratulatory messages. The Queen told her cousin George that she was 'indeed thankful' at 'darling Arthur's safety', but grieved for her troops. The Duke of Cambridge, in turn, was 'thoroughly delighted' with the outcome, not least Wolseley's thoughtfulness in sending his son home with the victorious despatches, a singular honour which, by tradition, resulted in a monetary reward. Childers wrote to say that Tel-el-Kebir was 'the most perfect military achievement that England has seen for many a long year,' adding: 'Abroad we have quite regained our military reputation ... We owe this to your skill and energy, and to the valour of the Army.'[26]

Sir Garnet's loudest supporter was none other than the Queen's soldier son. Prince Arthur told his mother: 'Sir Garnet has been most kind to me all the time I have been under his orders, and I don't wish to serve under a pleasanter chief, or one in whom one feels greater confidence. He is the least fussy General I have ever served under, and his orders are short and clear; he never interferes with one and always gives one credit for what one does.'[27] Now a hardened campaigner, Arthur felt entitled to tell the Royal George a thing or two: 'The clothing supplied to the men – viz red serges and blue serge trousers – was thoroughly inappropriate to this climate and the men suffered terribly.' Clearly a reformer, the Duke of Connaught argued that

... khaki is the only sensible fighting dress for our men ... At the present moment the clothes of the troops from England are in such a state that you would be horrified to see them, whereas the troops from India look just as clean today as when they disembarked.[28]

The only real excitement during the Cairo occupation occurred on 28 September when there was a fire at the railway station. William Molyneux, racing to the station, found that 'shells and small-arm ammunition were going off all over the place'.[29] Several buildings were alight including one full of exploding Chicago beef tins. Riding up to the station Guy Dawnay saw a lump of shell burst near his knee and realised that some of the blazing lines of trucks were packed full of British and Egyptian ammunition. With Commissary-General Morris in tow, Dawnay tried to move some of the trucks as shells exploded all around them and 'white spits' in the fire splattered Remington bullets in all directions. Gradually, more troops, some of them led personally by Connaught who, as Commandant of Cairo, took his duties seriously, helped to control the blaze. Several senior officers got involved. Major Ardagh moved trucks and trains all through the night, even driving some locomotives himself, while Bindon Blood recalled the intense heat and risks:

> For example in one place I found two of my sappers carrying live shells out of one end of a luggage compartment, while the other end and the floor were burning, and it blew up a couple of minutes after I cleaned them out![30]

The blaze took two days to extinguish and the cause was never ascertained for sure, though arson was strongly suspected.

Two days a later a grand review was held, with the Khedive and Sir Garnet inspecting all the British troops in a march past at the Abdin Palace. Seventeen thousand officers and men stepped out smartly but, as Guy Dawnay noted: 'the Guards company was sadly diminished in strength. The Grenadiers have 180 sick as well as the Coldstreams ... There is a great deal of opthalmia also at the Ghezireh camp.'[31] At Tanta, where the Gordons remained for twelve days, five officers and 140 men fell sick. Diarrhoea, dysentery and opthalmia began to take their toll, all waterborne diseases that days of living in filth and drinking the not very aptly named Sweetwater had stimulated. Only six men died from heatstroke on the campaign proper but now the army was to have nearly 3,300 cases of opthalmia.

Each day the health of the troops continued to deteriorate. The Sweetwater, though unhealthy, was not a source of typhoid, but the dirty and damp conditions of the Cairo camps, along with the close proximity to the Nile, led to the first case on 30 September, fifteen days after the British entered the city. The disease normally has a gestation period of between seven and fourteen days. During October and November it would decimate the British garrison. One of those in hospital on the day of the khedival review was Sergeant Charles Spriggs. The hospital did not have enough beds and soldiers like Spriggs were forced to lay on the floor writhing with diarrhoea and severe stomach cramps. Luckily for him and many others, a prescription of castor oil and opium with quinine tablets three times a day, washed down with warm cocoa and a little rice, did the trick.

The ennui of life at Cairo, not made any better by the sickness among the troops, soon began a major move to get the men home. In his diary on 3 October Sir Garnet wrote: 'Teck left … He insists upon going home with the Life Gds and they don't want to have him.'[32] On the 11th Hamley and Willis left. 'Glad to get rid of them' was Wolseley's caustic comment in his private diary.[33] Both divisional generals had received identical letters on 7 October saying that a telegram requested the Chief to send them home. This was, according to a furious General Willis, 'a deliberate lie. Wolseley had recommended that we should be sent home and he raised orders to do so that morning.'[34] By now Sir Garnet had made enemies with both his senior commanders.

He hardly cared. What Wolseley wanted was to get back to his 'snipe' and 'see a good English shower of rain'. The climate had given him a touch of fever, the constant flies were 'vexatious' and the hot wind every afternoon was 'trying and unpleasant'. Personally he felt 'uglier than ever, with a growing stomach'.[35] Cairo, the general told his wife, was 'charming', but that when he went to the bazaar to buy her some carpets, 'I have to pay half as much again as others which is unfortunate.'[36]

Within Cairo, as life returned to the coffee shops and the hotels, the main topic of conversation was what would happen to Arabi and the other ringleaders? The popular press, in Egypt as well as England, bayed for blood. Even the Queen told Childers that 'if Arabi and the other principal rebels are not severely punished, revolution and rebellion will be greatly encouraged'. Wolseley was all for a court-martial and a quick hanging. Like his Sovereign, he felt that: 'One cannot afford to trifle with rebellion; it is too serious a crime to be treated lightly.'[37]

Not all officers agreed with the Chief and there was one lone rebel prepared to speak out. William Butler warned Gladstone that Arabi's execution would be a 'national crime'. Butler argued, in direct opposition to Wolseley, that

… leniency towards men who have been in rebellion has seldom been thrown away in history; the wounds inflicted in war, no matter how deep they may be, soon heal compared to those which are left in the memory of a people by the work of the scaffold'.[38]

Officers who saw Arabi in his cell were singularly impressed by his demeanor. Lieutenant Eustace Dawnay was in charge of the guard for a time and wrote home: 'I think they are treating Arabi rather hastily in putting him here. He treated de Chair very well.'[39] Frederic Villiers was permitted to sketch the Egyptian commander in his cell and, though he spoke no Arabic, was similarly charmed. He confessed: 'I was one of those Englishmen who had considerable sympathy with the Egyptian patriot' adding: 'I rather admired him for the good fighting he had put up.'[40]

Arabi most certainly expected to die. His arch-enemy, Tewfik, had by now arrested more than 1,200 men he considered opponents or nationalist sympathisers. He wanted the ringleaders dead. Circassians like Nubar Pasha suggested that Arabi should be beaten to death in the presence of Bedouin sheikhs.

The first obstacle to summary justice appeared in the shape of a 46-year-old officer of the Royal Engineers. His name was Lt-Colonel Sir Charles Wilson and, as a distinguished orientalist and intelligence department spy, he had been appointed as liaison with the expected Turkish troops. Now that the war was over, and with time on his hands, Wilson seemed the perfect man to look after the prisoners. It is to his credit then that he was determined to take his responsibilities seriously, regardless of the caprices of the Khedive or whims of HM Govt. Within five days of his arrest, Arabi found that this unlikely champion had managed to stop khedival officials looting his property, placed sentries to guard the homes of the other nationalist prisoners and told the authorities bluntly that such behaviour would not be tolerated. Wilson spent several hours talking in Arabic to Ahmed Arabi and found himself sympathising with him. He decided that if at all possible, his prisoner would get a fair trial.

One man was determined to make this happen – at any price. Wilfrid Scawen Blunt had watched helplessly as the war unfolded, painfully aware that there was nothing he could do. Arabi's premature departure from Tel-el-Kebir had also not impressed him, but he thought the man, even if he lacked physical courage 'had moral courage to a high degree'.[41] The same day that Wilson at Cairo saved Arabi's furniture, Blunt in London was asking an eminent lawyer, Alexander Broadley, to go out to Egypt and lead the defence of the nationalist prisoners. It was a clever move. Broadley was known to be a smart attorney, fluent in Arabic, who had acted as European advisor to the Bey of Tunis after the French invasion.

At first the British Consul-General was not helpful to the English defence team of Broadley, assisted by Mark Napier, another lawyer, and the solicitor Richard

Eve. He put them in touch with Borelli Bey, a sly Frenchman who headed the prosecution and cheerfully informed Broadley that under Egyptian law he would not be allowed to speak of politics before the court. It was not until the defenders met Charles Wilson that their rights to see their clients were fully respected.

The prisoners were held at the Daira Sariya, a large building near the Opera that had once been a depot for theatrical properties and lumber and was now a hastily white-washed makeshift gaol. Each cell was 'about twelve or fourteen feet square and sufficiently lofty' with two narrow windows. The only furniture in Arabi's room was 'a handsome shiraz rug, a mosquito-curtain, a mattress, and some pillows, an embroidered prayer-carpet, a divan and some brass and earthenware vessels'. Arabi wore a pair of undress military trousers with a white shirt and jacket. Nervously holding his prayer beads he read a letter of introduction from Blunt. The contents, noted Broadley, made him smile and he 'raised his hand to his forehead in token of gratitude and acquiesance'. Heartily he agreed to appoint the Englishmen as his defence team.[42]

During the next few days the lawyers managed to acquire Arabi's personal papers, a lucky find since the contents of his home had been trashed and the building converted into a hospital for sick soldiers. They also met their other clients. Ali Fehmy impressed Broadley the most. He described him as 'a spare, intelligent looking, dark-complexioned man of about 40. His expression is pleasing and he welcomed us very heartily.'[43] Dressed in a military topcoat and limping from his wound at Kassassin, Broadley rightly surmised that Fehmy was fiercely loyal to Arabi Pasha. He never tried to excuse his actions by blaming others and was more worried about a brother who had been arrested than he was for himself (Malet obtained a release). Quite different in looks and personality was Abd-el-Al Hilmi, the bluff and noisy general who 'greeted us almost boisterously and declared he feared nothing now'. Hilmi was almost moved to tears when Broadley arranged for his young son to visit him in prison.

Eventually the English defence team found themselves with a mixed bag of clients. In addition to the 'three colonels' they included Sheikh Abdu, an old friend of the Blunt's, who had edited the official Arabist newspaper; Toulba Pasha, 'a timorous mortal, short of stature, pallid from anxiety and chronic asthma' who had commanded the artillery at Kafr-Dawar; tearful, almost mentally unhinged Yacoub Sami, one-time head of the War Council; and Mahmud Sami al-Barudi, the poet-nationalist (and Circassian) who had for a time been the country's first minister. A later client was the brilliant engineer, Mahmud Fehmy, who had been captured near Kassassin. With 'merry black eyes', Broadley found him to be 'clever, honest, cheerful,' a man who 'never flinched in his profession of political faith...'

The official hardline had also crumbled in Britain. One of Blunt's admirers, Algernon Bourke, 'persuaded' the editor of *The Times* to announce that Arabi would not be executed without the consent of HM Govt and a defence fund was now publicly supported by such eminent persons as General Gordon and Lord Randolph Churchill. In the corridors of Whitehall a mood of clemency began to take shape. On 13 October the Foreign Secretary told Malet that HM Govt 'are of the opinion that Arabi should be defended by counsel of his own choice, whether native or foreign, who should be allowed free access to him; that interpreters should be provided and that the trial should be conducted in public.' Wanting to please the Khedive, Sir Edward wired back that the publicity and probable length of such a trial was causing the Egyptian Government 'the greatest anxiety'. By now the Cabinet had met and decided to make the trial as open as possible. Malet was curtly told that HM Govt now thought the Egyptian penal code 'inconsistent with the conditions of a fair trial'. When Tewfik suggested a military court martial as an alternative, or a public trial with the Egyptian Government as the accusers, Granville rejected both suggestions. The Khedive and Cherif Pasha (who was leading the government) threw in the towel on 19 October. Two days later the British Consul-General also got a letter from a very unlikely defender of Arabi; Auckland Colvin, arch-pragmatist, told his protégé that 'clemency is the true policy ... I would not even shoot Arabi or Sami or any of the ringleaders unless murder was brought home to them. Colvin explained his simple reasoning: 'Whatever is done should, I think, be done *quickly*.'[44]

On the same day that Colvin was writing to Malet, a fast ship steamed out of the harbour at Alexandria carrying home the conquering hero. The new peer, to be styled: 'Lord Wolseley of Cairo, and Wolseley in the County of Stafford' arrived back at Charing Cross on 28 October to be met by an immense crowd. Lady Wolseley, who was there, saw Gladstone 'gasping for breath' as the 'poor old gentleman was sadly pushed and pummelled in the crowd'. It was an ecstatic welcome:

> I saw Mrs Childers disappear in a whirlpool of people double her height; I heard Lord Granville say to me, 'This is your Tel-el-Kebir,' and I should have liked to say 'Dawdling won't do here' but in the struggle for life, I don't think I said much to anyone. The bulk of Royalty (George and Mary) was very useful, and the Duke cleared the way beautifully for us, indeed without him we should never got into the carriage at all.[45]

Outside the station an even bigger and more boisterous crowd threatened to crush the brougham like a shell. 'Ten dirty hands thrust in on each side to be shaken' wrote Louisa, 'and the owners not to be got rid of without a shake'.[46] Policemen ran manfully on each side of the carriage until halfway up St James Street, where the incline left the crowd falling behind as it picked up speed. A small group of well-wishers also waited outside the Wolseley residence in Mayfair, one of whom was an old soldier whom Sir Garnet had carried wounded out of an action many years before. He had come to welcome home 'my little general'.

Next day Wolseley set off for Balmoral where he made pleasant remarks about the Duke of Connaught and found the Queen 'very gracious'. As he was leaving, her servant, John Brown 'gave a present, so I must be rising in R.I. favour'.[47] Gifts and honours, celebratory dinners and rousing speeches seemed to be the order of the day. Sir Garnet gave the Duke of Cambridge three guns found in Arabi's tent. For his 'little snipe' there was a special gift. Wolseley carefully removed the diamonds from a ceremonial sword given to him by the citizens of Cairo and presented them to his wife. Each sick soldier got tobacco and pipes courtesy of Messrs Rothchilds so they could have a hearty smoke in bed. Most regiments held a dinner for their returning heroes. The Scots Guards banquet included: 'Mashed Potatoes ala Arabi' with pie, followed by 'Tel-el-Kebir Puddings with Kassassin Sauce', 'Cairo Creams' and 'Egyptian Jelly'. At one dinner, held just before leaving Egypt, Colonel Ashburnham, old warrior of numerous wars, got shakily to his feet and amid much cheering made a little speech: 'I have been in the Rifles for 30 years, and owe everything to the Regiment. I never wore a red coat. I was never on the Staff, I hate the Staff, damn them!'[48] Then, to much laughter and clapping he dropped drunkenly under the table unconscious.

The most popular general besides Wolseley was Archibald Alison. His courage at the head of the Highland Brigade during the battle, and little Gaelic touches, like wearing a sprig of heather on his chest during the khedival review, were public relations gems. When, in a final address to his men, the old one-armed soldier spoke of how 'had my older chief, Sir Colin Campbell, risen from his grave, he would have been proud of you'.[49] This reference to the great Indian Mutiny general sent a thrill of pride through many Scottish hearts. Madame Tussauds paid him the ultimate compliment – a wax statue standing next to that of the new peer.

The popular newspapers vied in reports of the battles, denunciations of Arabi and a surfeit of bad poetry. 'A Wreath Of Song' by Kynnesley Lewis, dedicated to Wolseley, praised how:

The flower of Britain was placed within they hands,
To bear the blast of guns on Egypt's scorching sands;
And many a mother, many a wife,
Will bless thee for the loved one's life.

Wolseley must have been tickled to read 'A Few Lines On The War In Egypt' by Thomas Adams, who extolled Connaught:

> Always forward to be in the fight
> He, with the gallant Duke of Teck,
> Proved that in Royal blood was the true pluck
> Of true heroes on victory bent.

One poet, T. J. Macartney, managed an epic that ran to 22 pages ('price six-pence') but perhaps the worst was a fifteen stanza poem from the Scottish bard, William McGonagall, it began:

> Ye sons of Great Britain, come join with me,
> And sing in praise of Sir Garnet Wolseley;
> Sound drums and trumpets cheerfully,
> For he has acted most heroically.

It got worse:

> Arabi's army was about seventy thousand in all,
> And, virtually speaking, it wasn't very small,
> But if they had been as numerous again,
> The Irish and Highland brigades would have beaten them, it is plain.

Taking up the mood of a people joyful that their troops were home, ready also to show clemency to a fallen enemy, a doggerel in one of the pictorial newspapers had the benefit, at least, of being witty:

> John Bull is enraptured
> Now Arabi's captured,
> And Garnet will soon be a peer;
> In a year and a day, O
> Like King Cetewayo,
> Will Arabi come over here?
>
> For a while p'raps a prison
> Abroad will be his'n
> Till Time has healed over the sore;
> Unless we have from his

Own lips a strong promise
He'll never go wrong anymore.

His chains will be undone,
They'll bring him to London,
And give him a house near a park;
All snugly and rightly
Refurnished by Whiteley
And there he'll receive men of mark.

His lot we shall pity,
In West-end and City,
We shall think him the nicest of chaps;
If from Tewfik we sever
And Arabi's clever,
He may go back a Khedive perhaps.[50]

Amid all the jubilation a sombre note was struck by the grisly discovery on 24 October at a lonely spot in the desert of the remains of two Europeans – 'a skull, jaw-bone, numerous ribs and broken bones, much gnawed by wild beasts, a truss of a very small man, supposed to be Professor Palmer; two socks marked W. G. (W. Gill); with the feet still in them.'[51] These were clear signs that the British spies sent by HM Govt to bribe the Bedouin tribes in July had been murdered. It did not take Colonel Charles Warren, a fellow Royal Engineer like Gill, very long to find the culprits. The entire Palmer Expedition, it transpired, including another Englishman, Lieutenant Charrington, had been marked out for slaughter as soon it was known that they were carrying large sums of money. Months earlier, on 11 August, stripped almost naked and made to walk to a lonely ravine, Palmer had been shot prematurely and his companions cut down as they tried to escape. Five of the murderers were publicly executed at Zagazig as a sheikh, and two Bedouin from every tribe in Lower Egypt, were forced to look on. The remains of the Englishmen were brought back to London and given an honourable burial in the crypt of St Paul's Cathedral.

A dense white frost fog hung over the imperial capital when Queen Victoria reviewed the Egyptian War troops on 17 November 1882. Eight thousand officers and men, representing all branches involved in the war, marched past their Sovereign as she sat in a carriage on Horse Guards Parade. Some in the crowds noticed tears in the eyes of Her Majesty when Prince Arthur, at the head of the Brigade of Guards, stepped smartly past. The Queen felt moved by the occasion, as her favourite boy 'looked so like his beloved father I felt quite overcome'. Victoria was most taken by the handsome and beautifully dressed Indian Army officers and men brought to London to meet their Queen-Empress. The entire Indian Contingent were feted everywhere, including a special performance of the hit pantomime 'Robin Hood', though what the old Punjabi and Sikh soldiers made of this traditional British entertainment, complete with a funny man dressed as a dame and a principal boy played by a girl was anyone's guess. Queen Victoria went to Netley Hospital to see her wounded war heroes. 'I gave the Egyptian medal to a number of them' she wrote in her Journal, 'it was very touching to bend over the beds of these brave, noble, uncomplaining men and pin medals on their shirts. Took good care to prick no one.'[52]

Wolseley had even patched things up with Evelyn Wood – 'What a good fellow he is when his vanity is not over-excited' – and things looked rosy between him, the Queen and Cambridge. The sky fell in, however, with the publication of an article by Hamley called 'The Second Division at Tel-el-Kebir'. In it Sir Edward accentuated the hard fighting done by his troops along with his role. Many officers were irritated by this article. For instance, when Hamley claimed that the Egyptians at the back of the defences 'were taken in reverse, and shot down, both in the ditches and behind the parapets', General Willis wrote on his copy: 'As a matter of fact, these were old works, thrown up for practice in former years ... The profile was weak ... It was never held by the Egyptians and no dead were found along it.'[53] Willis also took umbrage to Hamley's insistence that the 1st Division had attacked at 1,200 yards distance, insisting that his men were only 500 yards from the trenches. The article, thought Wolseley, was written by Hamley

> to glorify himself and make out that no one but he did anything in Egypt. It is too flagrant and untruthful not to do him harm in the long run, though it will afford my enemies to heap venom on me.[54]

Just three days after reading the article the two bickering generals met at a reception and Lord Wolseley lectured Sir Edward, rather bluntly, on his 'want of generosity to others'.[55]

While the country celebrated the successful little war, termed by Wolseley his 'tidiest', HM Govt were left wondering how long the occupation of Egypt was going to last? Many within Gladstone's Liberal Party agreed with Granville that Britain should 'get out of it as soon as we could possibly do so'.[56] At Cabinet meetings the general view, as expressed later by Joe Chamberlain, was that 'we were all desirous of a speedy evacuation and believed that the conditions we had laid down would be accomplished in a year or two at the outside'.[57] The radicals within Parliament were calling for an 'Egypt for the Egyptians', while the Liberal hawks, notably Hartington and Northbrook, argued for strong khedival rule assisted by a single British financial controller. To try and resolve the dilemma of what to do with Egypt, HM Govt asked Lord Dufferin, a smooth diplomat who had lately been British ambassador at Constantinople, to visit the country and make a report.

A major problem was that a get-out-quick policy and self-government for the Egyptians, in whole or in part, depended upon the country being entirely at peace. Even with the Egyptian Army broken up and the nationalist leaders in gaol, discontent rumbled below the surface. In the countryside, as Malet told HM Govt, 'ill-feeling against Europeans has not abated' and was 'rather on the increase', while in Cairo there had been several cases of 'gross insults'. The Consul-General blamed the damned trial of Arabi which, Broadley had threatened, might last eight or nine months and involve more than 420 defence witnesses alone. Malet thought that Arabi's advocates would try and 'bespatter the Khedive and Government with scandalous evidence'. On 31 October he told Granville officially that:

> The fellaheen, having given their faith to Arabi, continue to believe that he is still in power. In outlying districts they refuse to pay their debts to Europeans on the ground that they were told by Arabi that such debts were cancelled.

When Dufferin arrived in Egypt on 7 November, a mob in front of the prison mistook the new Greek Consul for the British envoy who, it was whispered, was 'coming by order of the Sultan to liberate Arabi'.[58]

With public opinion at home and abroad now conciliatory towards the Egyptian patriots, and agitation still upsetting the locals, HM Govt needed the Arabi trial to take place quickly. By the 18th Dufferin and Malet had convinced Tewfik it was 'very unlikely that sufficient proof would be forthcoming to authorize the execution of Arabi and the political prisoners'. They suggested deportation. Tewfik, sitting uneasily on his throne but ever the survivor of events, readily agreed.

News that the prisoners were going to be deported in return for a guilty plea soon became the worst-kept secret in Cairo. When Arabi walked into court on the morning of Sunday 3 December, an observer noted that he looked 'crushed by his misfortunes, yet there was still a dignity of bearing which compared favourably with the judges'.[59] In front of a bench of fat and medal-bedecked pashas, General Ahmed Arabi pleaded guilty to rebellion. There was then a recess of a few hours before the court reassembled and Arabi was told the sentence – which was death. For a moment there was complete silence before a clerk rose and declared that: 'The penalty of death pronounced against Ahmed Arabi is commuted to perpetual exile from Egypt and its dependencies.'[60] The judges rose and the court erupted in excitement. Mrs Napier, wife of Arabi's counsel, rushed forward and handed him a bouquet of roses which he held 'looking very foolish'. The first thing the pasha did on returning to his cell was go down on his knees and give thanks to Allah. Then he rose and thanked his lawyers 'in very touching terms' and settled down to write a long letter to Wilfrid Blunt.

In the days preceding the trial, Alexander Broadley and Lord Dufferin had met several times and found that they had much in common. Meanwhile Blunt had been badgering away for a country with a Muslim population as a place of exile for Arabi and the other prisoners. It was thus through Blunt's persistence and Broadley's persuasive talents that Dufferin recommended Ceylon. When Broadley, armed with an atlas, showed Arabi where he was going his face broke, for once, into a broad smile and he said:

> This is really too much honour … My adversaries seem actually bent on sending me to Paradise … after being driven out of Eden our common father went to Ceylon, since called the 'Paradise of Adam' … Nothing could be more just.[61]

Six others were to join Arabi in exile – Ali Fehmy, Mahmud Fehmy, Abd-el-Al Hilmi, Mahmoud Sami, Yacoub Sami and Toulba Pasha. The Khedive and his supporters, disappointed not to execute the Arabists, still got a little revenge. The original document allowing a sufficient number of wives and servants to go with the patriots was reduced and on 15 December a decree declared them 'civilly dead and incapable of inheritance'. Later that day, all their homes were broken into by khedival guards including the harems. The prisoners tried to be as cheerful as possible. At 9pm on 25 December, from a siding at the Kasr-el-Nil Barracks and under a full moon, Broadley and a few others waved them off.

Dufferin, Malet and Wilson now put their heads together to get as many other prisoners held without trial since Tel-el-Kebir set free. In a handful of cases, such as Ahmed Rifat – the brilliant Circassian secretary to the War Council – this meant banishment for a few years, but most captives were allowed to return to their homes. Finally, on 2 January 1883, the Khedive issued a general amnesty. The future of Egypt looked brighter.

In the final weeks of 1882, Wolseley and the Army had sat to examine the many complaints, partly fuelled by newspaper reports, that the Medical Department had not performed its duties satisfactorily during the recent campaign. A report of the committee, chaired by Lord Morley, recommended a reorganization of the Army Hospital Corps and better training facilities. The evidence presented against Deputy-Surgeon-General Hanbury and his team was 'conflicting', one member of the committee thought the complaints 'greatly exaggerated' and most senior officers like General Sir John Adye, expressed themselves 'very much satisfied' by the work of the medical services. Dissenters to this view included Colonel Knox, Scots Guards, who called the hospital arrangements at Cairo 'lamentable'; General Drury Lowe told the committee that one principal medical officer supplied to the Cavalry Division was 'worth nothing' and castigated the Army Hospital Corps; Surgeon-Major Hume-Spry said that his field-hospital at Mahsama was created from 'four most wonderfully equipped' Egyptian hospitals, due to a lack of British medical supplies at the front.

Lord Wolseley answered the committee's questions on 12 December, immediately after Sir John Adye, who he thought, had given 'a most *coleur de rose* view' which was 'dangerous to the future of the Army'.[62] Always outspoken, Wolseley had a field day at the medical department's expense: the hospital at Ismailia had been 'discreditable' and he 'never saw a field-hospital properly equipped during the whole war'; the sick were given bad bread; had no mosquito nets; and the Army Hospital Corps men were such 'bad nurses' that the troops got better treatment from their regimental doctors. The general recalled the anger he had felt when he saw his soldiers 'lying on the ground and lying in those filthy, dirty clothes that they had fought the campaign in' at the Cairo hospital.[63] The ophthalmic cases had been kept in a garden tent, covered by 'myriads and myriads' of flies. When a doctor said there was no money to buy fly whisks Wolseley had angrily told him: 'I will pay for them.'

On the last day of the year, while the SS *Marriott* headed for Colombo across the sparkling blue expanse of the Indian Ocean with Arabi and his compatriots aboard, Garnet Joseph Wolseley wrote the final lines in his pocket diary for 1882: 'God has been good to me this year ... my constant prayer is that he will not, or rather may not punish me in this world by defeat.'[64]

Nineteen days later, deep in the scorching wastes of the Sudan, the garrison of Obeid, a starving fraternity of local families, Egyptians, Shiagi militiamen and Nubian slave-soldiers surrendered to the dervish army of the self-styled 'Mahdi' or 'expected one'. Six thousand Remington rifles fell into the hands of the religious warrior who had proclaimed jihad against all non-believers.

One man, one dream of conquest, one mission; Muhammad Ahmed had no way of knowing that he would help to ensure that the British stayed on in Cairo, and a hundred other towns across the land, for seven more decades. Wolseley, too, had no inkling that his tidy little war was but the first act in a drama that would lead him back to Egypt and disaster and humiliation in the Sudan, along with the deaths of many brave men who had fought at Tel-el-Kebir, a final legacy of his brilliantly planned invasion.

# Epilogue

*He will live for centuries in the people*
Charles George Gordon

Fast forward seven decades to 31 March 1956. Dustily, bloodily, yet proud as always, the men of the Grenadier Guards and Life Guards, with 'Tel-el-Kebir' on their battle honours, prepare to leave Egypt. They were the last British regiments on Egyptian soil. 'Their departure' wrote *The Times* correspondent, 'was almost as silent and devoid of ceremony as presumably was the nocturnal disembarkation of General Wolseley's forces which captured Port Said 74 years ago.'

The 1956 Suez War was an ill-conceived blunder that had more than a whiff of Wolseley about it. The Prime Minister, Anthony Eden, had stood in the shadow of Churchill and listened to his rhetoric so long that he had quite forgotten the great war leader had also been the architect of the Gallipoli debacle. The Suez Canal, old Tories in the shires fumed, must not be allowed to fall into unfriendly hands, the ruler of Egypt was seen as a nationalist demagogue who would strangle the imperial lifeline that the waterway represented. So began for the British, and their French Allies (who did not want to be left out this time) a short, sharp war and a humiliating withdrawal. It was, noted one historian 'a cruel parody of the British Imperial style'.[1]

Gamal Abdul Nasser, Egypt's fiery new leader, had some superficial similarities with Ahmed Arabi as well as several differences. Both were village boys from relatively poor families, though from opposite ends of the country. Both became famous as colonels and had a strong physical presence. When Clarissa Eden met Nasser she thought he gave 'a great impression of health and strength – terrifically broad and booming'.[2] It was a description that also fitted Arabi perfectly. Nasser was 38 at the time of Suez, Arabi Pasha was 41 in 1882. They had each read Napoleon, but Nasser was also a student of many other writers including Ceasar, Gandhi and Rousseau. Both patriots wanted to see a united, strong and independent Egypt. Nasser had also studied Arabi and the other nationalists. He was no simple popular demagogue or religiously-inspired soldier, but a man with a vision and a strategy to cleanse Egypt's social and political ills.

Back in 1882, although Lord Dufferin's compromise solution was well-intentioned, it was, as one MP said, 'a perfect sham of Constitutional government.' The Anglo-French dual control was declared officially dead (it had actually died the day Freycinet refused to mount a joint invasion with the British). Now a new Consul-General would rule what became known as 'the veiled Protectorate'. The man chosen to replace Malet was Evelyn Baring, soon to be better known as Lord Cromer. He would remould Egypt into an Imperial dominion (in all but name) and hardly answerable to anyone as a pro-consul of the Empire for the next 24 years.

Whether the British or Egyptians realised it or not this new form of rule was the natural effect of power abhorring a vacuum. With the nationalists crushed Egypt's only real alternative was a return to strong Khedival authority, but Tewfik found himself sidelined after Tel-el-Kebir, no longer trusted completely by the people he ruled nor by those who gave him back his throne. Increasingly he was seen for what he really was – a puppet of the British. There were rumours that the Turks or British poisoned him when he died suddenly on 7 January 1892. His doctor's report listed influenza, double pneumonia and an inflammation of the kidneys; he was only 39 years old. Obituaries were generally kind. He was, one suspects, far more cunning than any gave him credit.

Malet left Egypt for milder climes as ambassador at Brussels and did achieve his ultimate ambition to fill the same post at Berlin. In later years he grew increasingly neurotic and sensitive to slurs that he had not been wholly impartial when in Egypt. The publication in 1907 of Blunt's *Secret History Of The English Occupation Of Egypt*, full of gossip and innuendo disguised as facts, hurt him deeply. He was working on a riposte to this book when he died in 1908 (the work was re-edited and privately published in the following year).

The British Empire's leading foe, Wilfrid Blunt, moved away from Egyptian nationalism and took up the cause of the down-trodden Irish. His enthusiasm landed him in Galway Gaol for two months in 1888. Undaunted, he returned to Society, still championing anti-Imperialist causes. He wrote on 31 December 1900: 'I bid goodbye to the old century, may it rest in peace as it has lived in war. Of the new century I prophesy nothing except that it will see the decline of the British Empire. Other worse Empires will rise perhaps in its place.'[3] He died in 1922.

Of the principal Americans in the drama, Charles Pomeroy Stone, the immensely loyal Egyptian Army chief of staff to both Ismail and Tewfik returned to America and was made engineer in charge of erecting the Statue of Liberty. One of his assistants on the project was hot-blooded James Morgan who had once galloped over an Egyptian train. When the Statue was dedicated on 28 October 1886, General Stone was given the honour of being grand marshal. He caught a chill and died on 24 January 1887 (less than a month after his comrade, one-armed William Loring). Morgan retired to his beloved Louisiana plantation and died in 1928. Charles Chaille-Long, one of the first men to enter the burning Alexandria, continued to despise the British and tried to set up a hare-brained scheme to crush the Mahdi with a Franco-Abyssinian force that would make the Sudan a French protectorate. He later married but died childless in 1917.

The security of Egypt was one of the reasons the British stayed on. With the war drums of the Mahdi growing louder in 1883, the Egyptian Government sent a British-led expedition to crush the insurgency. It was destroyed spectacularly by the dervishes in the forest of Shaykan and the new rulers of Egypt found themselves drawn into a war across the country's southern frontiers. When Garnet Wolseley's old friend, Charles Gordon, got besieged at Khartoum it seemed perfectly natural that 'England's only general' would rescue him. It all started off gloriously and went badly awry. More than a handful of those who had fought in the 1882 Egyptian War lost their lives within three years to Mahdist spears or bullets. Morice Bey, who had proved so brave during the Alexandria Riots, died at the First Battle of El Teb; John Cameron, the tough war correspondent, was instantly killed by a bullet as he handed his servant a tin of sardines at Abu Kru; General Earle, who had been at Tel-el-Kebir, got shot at Kirbekan; and Herbert Stewart was similarly struck at Abu Klea. Hearing the news that his friend was badly wounded Lord Wolseley wrote: 'If he dies I lose a friend, England her most promising General, better in my opinion than Buller.' Later, after Stewart's death was announced, he called him 'the best of soldiers, most gallant of leaders and warmest of friends'.[4]

Most of Wolseley's Ring re-assembled for the Sudan War – Buller, Butler, Graham, Lyttelton and others. Percy Marling was there and got a Victoria Cross for saving the life of a private soldier at Tamaii. The rest of Marling's life – although it included service in the Boer War – was not so spectacular. He continued to record it all, with great humour and honesty, in his diary. One incident more frightening than all his days and nights under fire happened when, as a senior officer, he was providing an escort for the aged Queen-Empress. His horse, trotting very closely by the Sovereign's open carriage, suddenly sneezed, showering Her Majesty in snot. Luckily she was veiled but Marling quailed as Victoria shot him a look like thunder. Next day a Court circular demanded that in future escorts must keep their distance from the Royal carriage.

Both Melton Prior and Frederic Villiers were once again in the thick of action in the Sudan. A tablet in St Paul's Cathedral commemorates several of their colleagues, including Cameron, who were not so lucky. Prior reported on nine more campaigns ending with the Russo-Japanese War in 1905. Villiers was around for the First World War. The old journalist, who had experienced the very stuff of high adventure, even visited Hollywood and witnessed a new world of make-believe derring-do.

Wolseley's generals went on to greater or lesser glory. Some, like Macpherson, who died in 1886, went suddenly. Others such as Adye, Alison and Willis, became venerated old soldiers in ceremonial roles. The same was true of Gerald Graham, later Colonel-Commandant of the Royal Engineers, though he had a tough fight on his hands along the Red Sea coast of the Sudan against a wily dervish leader called Osman Digna. In retirement he once told a friend that he had cherished every 'little bit of sunshine' in his life. Going out to get a news-paper with the latest Boer War news Sir Gerald caught a chill. It hastened his death on 17 December 1899. He is buried in the pretty churchyard of Bideford in Devon.

The South African War wrecked the life of another Devon man. Redvers Buller was sent out to command the Natal Field Force. The sharp-eyed intel-ligence chief of the Egyptian War, now grown fat and prematurely aged, was accused of being an ineffective commander though, to be fair to him, he had not wanted the job. He died in 1908, just six years after the war's end. By then Frederick Roberts had proved himself to be 'England's only other general', much to the chagrin of the Ring, and the huge campaign, dwarfing all other colonial wars, had been brought to a close by none other than Herbert Kitchener, the young intelligence officer in 1882 who rose to avenge Gordon's death in 1898, destroy the dervishes and become in turn a legendary field-marshal.

Hardly any of Wolseley's warriors came out of the South African War with enhanced reputations. One of the few was Neville Lyttelton, Gladstone's nephew, who fared better than most. Fitzroy Hart, so courageous at Tel-el-Kebir, got command of the Irish Brigade but, sad to relate, his impetuous nature led them to bloody and foolhardy massacre at Colenso. Maurice, 'whose brain never seems to rest', as Wolseley once said, wrote an excellent though dry Official History of the Egyptian War and co-authored a similarly dull one on the Boer War.[5]

Before then Maurice had defended his old Chief against a final attack from Hamley – delivered from beyond the grave. Sir Edward died ten years after Tel-el-Kebir, but in 1895 many of his documents, including letters and diaries, were printed in a book by Alexander Innes Shand, a writer of military biogra-phies. The long accounts of the battle accused Wolseley of suppressing Hamley's despatches and of bias in favour of the 1st Division. The book was, said one reviewer, 'as much an indictment of Lord Wolseley, as a eulogy of General Hamley'.[6] Maurice was particularly incensed because he had come into conflict with Sir Edward while writing his Egyptian War book. 'I want to know whether you are responsible for this thing?' asked Hamley, addressing Maurice 'like a slave-driver to a slave'. In a spirit of conciliation Maurice had altered his text to suit the general, but now he went into an attack, though one suspects Wolseley was orchestrating the piece. It was revealed that before the battle Sir Garnet had concluded that Hamley 'had completely lost touch of the practical working of large bodies of men, and that he was always so full of his own importance that he could not be trusted to carry out orders he received without the cavilling which shakes confidence.' Wolseley's comment to Hamley: 'Alison will be with his brigade. You go where you please', made it plain that the Chief's orders 'would go direct to the brigades and they did'. Sir Edward was 'cranky' and 'useless in the field'. On the celebrated night of 12 September 1882, wrote a sarcastic Maurice, Hamley was 'wrapped in swaddling and nursed across a march'. After the battle 'no soldiers took any notice of him, but when he subsequently appeared with Alison the cheers rent the air'.

A few critics in the military press defended Hamley but the majority were won over by Maurice's steam roller. One writer summed up the problem with Sir Edward very well: 'The trouble was that the public is apt to look on a man with a grievance as a bore … And so Hamley found it. He alienated sympathy by the persistency and vociferation of his complaints.'[7]

The Egyptian War's numerous commissariat and transport problems were scrutinised by a committee in 1884. Its vast 874 page report contained more information on mules, the conveyance of hay and tinned meats, maltese carts and flour than any sane person might want to read in a lifetime. Wolseley tried to learn from mistakes made in 1882 when planning his Sudan campaign. One witness who tried to be exempted from giving evidence was Lt-Colonel Tulloch. His testimony touched on several aspects of his intelligence work and at least has the merit of being interesting along with showing him to be very egocentric. He retired to South Wales and published his memoirs in 1903.

Among the less celebrated players in the Egyptian War it is worth mentioning perhaps that Private Gordon of the Black Watch fought in the Sudan and then emigrated to Boston, USA. Corporal Philip of the Duke of Cornwall's Light Infantry, whose recollections are the best we have from the ranks, later became an Aberdeen policeman. Curiously, Lieutenant Pirie, the subaltern whose confusion about his orders was one of the incidents during the First Battle of Kassassin, also left the Army and became an MP for the same city.

George, Duke of Cambridge, arch conservative and admirer of Wellington, went to the great parade ground in the sky aged 85 years in 1903. His wastrel son George, who had been Wolseley's aide in Egypt and brought back the Tel-el-Kebir despatches, found himself cut out of his father's will. Among senior officers the last to die was probably Bindon Blood. The hero of the Zulu, Afghan and Egyptian wars became a great fighting general on the North-West Frontier of India in the 1890s where he watched over the services of a young scamp (and friend of Wilfrid Blunt's) called Winston Churchill. Full of honours he died at the ripe old age of 97 years on 16 May 1940.

Most of the naval officers encountered in these pages, such as Lieutenant Field and Cadet Chambers, rose to the rank of admiral. Beresford and Fisher became bitter foes over naval reform yet died as much revered men. Beauchamp Seymour told a friend that he found his peerage an embarrassment – 'I would give £500 to get off. I have only accepted it because I consider it an honour conferred on the service and not on me individually.'[8] Honours and medals given out after the war provoked a good deal of grumbling in the Services. One outraged private citizen wrote to Seymour, now Lord Alcester, saying that

> … it is really quite sickening and *highly annoying* to educated people to read you and Sir Garnet Wolseley so constantly recommending one another … and for what? For doing your duty? Are you not all well and over-paid for doing what you were sent to do!!

Admiral Lord Alcester had a bad accident in 1883 when he was hit by a hansom cab but continued to enjoy good food and wine right up to death in 1895. His namesake, Captain Edward Seymour, who had kept order at Port Said, also became an admiral and was given command of the Peking Relief Force during the Boxer Rebellion in 1900. He was blamed for failing to relieve the city quickly enough and had an ignominious subsequent career.

Garnet Wolseley, now a peer, tried an audacious gamble in 1884 to relieve Khartoum. He over-reached himself with a scheme that involved Canadian boatmen, Australian troops and a mounted corps of camel riders alongside regular British infantry. It was all too ambitious and the man who had the ill luck to reach Khartoum too late to save Gordon was Charles Wilson, the quiet orientalist who had been Arabi Pasha's fair-minded gaoler. He was made the scapegoat by the Ring for the Sudan Expedition's failure. Wolseley was genuinely distraught. 'May God have mercy on me, but this is enough to drive most men mad' is the entry in his recently discovered pocket diary on the day he got the sad news of Gordon's death.[9] It is difficult not to see Wolseley's subsequent career as a disappointment. It certainly was to him despite being made Commander-in-Chief in succession to Cambridge. Many of the mistakes made in 1899 when the Boer War broke out, not least the appointment of Buller to command in South Africa, were laid, perhaps unfairly, at Wolseley's door.

In later years he grew less opinionated and more philosophical. In 1902 he admitted: 'I am a vulgar, prejudiced fellow who expects everyone to have the same habits that I have.'[10] He died in 1913, sadly estranged from his daughter, though still much loved by his 'snipe'. Memory loss had begun six or seven years earlier. Wolseley had never intended that his acid remarks would be published and they certainly reveal all his failings. Yet he was greatly admired and fiercely defended by his ring of friends and worked tirelessly to improve the Victorian Army. His place in History as the greatest exponent of the 'small war' is assured.

By then, Arabi Pasha and his compatriots were also dead. When they stepped down from the gangplank in Ceylon on 10 January 1883 more than 32,000 local Muslims were waiting to honour them. For a time the group found themselves to be superstars, their dress and even methods of praying being carefully studied and copied. Over the years every celebrity visiting the island wanted to see only two sights at Colombo – an ancient tortoise and Arabi Pasha. Drunken sailors often threw bottles at his house and taunted him as a coward. Arabi wrote to the authorities begging for help. On the day an officer went to investigate he found three carriages of rowdy tourists causing trouble, and recommended that a constable should guard the house, but nothing was done. Eventually Arabi was allowed to move inland to Kandy. His home on Hallloluwa Road is today a small museum dedicated to his memory.

For years the exiles begged for an increase in their meagre allowances. An investigation found Ali Fehmy's house, for instance, 'absolutely destitute of furniture'. Finally, in 1886, the allowance was raised to £435 a year with Arabi, the poorest of the lot, getting an extra £20 per month. Envy now set in among some of the others who were also desperate to return home. Only Mahmud Fehmy, the engineer with the twinkling eyes, remained cheerful. He was the first to die, without warning in 1890. Two years later General Hilmi succumbed to a brain clot. By the end of the decade a depressed Yacoub Sami had also passed away.

Arabi's pardon came in May, 1901. The Egyptian Government arranged free passage for him and his family – four wives, fifteen children, one nephew, four Sinhalese female servants and five others. The new generation of nationalist politicians had, in the interim, dubbed him a traitor who had made possible the British occupation. Half-blind and no longer interested in politics it was enough for Arabi to be back in his beloved homeland. He bore no hatred towards the English. They had, he would tell anyone who would listen, been kind to him. Egypt, he thought, was an infinitely better place in 1901 than it had been nineteen years earlier. He died of cancer in his small house at Helwan on the edge of the desert in 1911.

In prison before his trial Arabi had been befriended by Charles Wilson who thought him a poor man of action, badly educated, with no administrative talent. He was, said Wilson, 'a religious enthusiast and a dreamer,' sincere in his aims to help the fellahin, but 'lost in a whirl' despite great gifts as a speaker.[11] Absolutely free of corruption, Arabi Pasha was a poor man when he started in politics and a poor man when his life ended. 'Probably few characters in themselves so insignificant have ever so largely influenced the history of our times' wrote *The Times* in its obituary. For a brief spell, glorious to the Egyptian people, Arabi had galvanised the country in a way not seen for centuries. In this sense he truly was the father of modern Egypt and the natural parent of Gamal Abdul Nasser and his later successful revolution. Wolseley would have been surprised and angered if he had known that one of Arabi Pasha's greatest admirers was his own hero, Gordon of Khartoum. He wrote to Wilfrid Blunt during the Egyptian War with great perception: 'As for Arabi, whatever may become of him, he will live for centuries in the people, they will never be your "obedient servants" again.'[12]

# Notes

## Prologue

1 Loring, *A Confederate Soldier In Egypt.*
2 Duff-Gordon, *Letters From Egypt 1863–65.*
3 Duff-Gordon, *Last Letters From Egypt.*
4 Green, *Armies Of God.*
5 Blake, *Disraeli.*

## Mutiny

1 Manthorpe, *Children Of The Empire.*
2 Loring.
3 Morgan, *Recollections Of A Rebel Reefer.*
4 Ibid.
5 Scholch, *Egypt For The Egyptians.*
6 Blunt, *Secret History Of The English Occupation Of Egypt.*
7 Scholch.
8 Mansfield, *The British In Egypt.*
9 Scholch
10 Blunt.
11 Ibid.
12 Mansfield.
13 Sanderson, *Egypt 1879–1883 By The Right Honourable Sir Edward Malet Bart; GCB.*
14 Scholch.
15 Sanderson.
16 Blunt.
17 Ibid.
18 Ibid.
19 Sanderson.
20 Broadley, *How We Defended Arabi And His Friends.*
21 Broadley, *The Last Punic War.*
22 Pakenham, *The Scramble For Africa.*

23 Hanotaux, *Historie Des Colonies Francaises Et De L'Expansion De La France*.
24 Scholch.
25 Parliamentary Papers Egypt 1882 Nos 1–20 hereafter referred to as P. P.
26 Cromer, *Modern Egypt*.
27 Ibid.
28 Sanderson.
29 P. P
30 Scholch.
31 Blunt
32 Ibid.
33 P. P.
34 Bell, *Khedives And Pashas*.
35 P. P.
36 Blunt
37 P. P.

# Riot

1 Cromer.
2 Sanderson.
3 Ibid.
4 P. P.
5 Ibid.
6 Robinson, Gallagher and Denny, *Africa And The Victorians*.
7 Ibid.
8 Marlowe, *Anglo-Egyptian Relations 1800–1953*.
9 Morley, *Fortnightly Review, July 1882*.
10 Blunt.
11 Cromer.
12 Ibid.
13 Sanderson.
14 Blunt.
15 Al-Sayyid, *Egypt And Cromer*.
16 Sanderson.
17 Robinson, Gallagher and Denny.
18 Sanderson.
19 Scholch.
20 Blunt.
21 P. P.
22 Sanderson.
23 P. P.
24 Ibid.

25 Scholch.

26 Sanderson

27 National Maritime Museum, Seymour Papers, hereafter referred to as NMM.

28 Scholch.

29 Ibid.

30 NMM.

31 Ibid.

32 Goodall, *Warm Corners In Egypt.*

33 Kusel, *An Englishman's Recollections Of Egypt 1863 To 1887.*

34 Ibid.

35 Ibid.

36 Scudamore, *A Sheaf Of Memories.*

37 Farman, *Egypt And Its Betrayal.*

38 P. P.

39 Sanderson.

40 Fortescue, *Looking Back.*

41 P. P.

42 Royle, *The Egyptian Campaigns 1882 To 1885.*

43 Kusel.

44 Ibid.

45 Cole, *Colonialism And Revolution In The Middle East.*

# Bombardment

1 Goodall.

2 P. P.

3 Chamberrs, *Salt Junk.*

4 Scholch.

5 P. P.

6 NMM.

7 Pearsall, *The Worm In The Bud.*

8 Brett, *Journals And Letters Of Viscount Esher.*

9 Robinson, Gallagher and Denny.

10 Royle.

11 Robinson, Gallagher and Denny.

12 Karsh and Karsh, quoting Foreign Office 79 vol 3397.

13 Beresford, *Memoirs.*

14 Malet, *Shifting Scenes.*

15 Sanderson.

16 Tulloch, *Recollections Of Forty Years Service.*

17 NMM.

18  Sanderson.

19  Tulloch.

20  Ibid.

21  Robinson, Gallagher and Denny.

22  P. P.

23  Meyer, *The Farther Frontier.*

24  NMM.

25  Rodgers, *Mariners Mirror, 1975.*

26  NMM.

27  P. P.

28  Robinson, Gallagher and Denny.

29  NMM.

30  Al-Sayyid.

31  Freycinet, *La Question D'Egypte.*

32  P. P.

33  Villiers, Villiers.

34  NMM.

35  Robinson, Gallagher and Denny.

36  Ibid.

37  P. P.

38  Blunt.

39  Pakenham.

40  NMM.

41  Blunt.

42  P. P.

43  Ibid.

44  Blunt

45  NMM.

46  Massie, *Dreadnought.*

47  Lowis, *Fabulous Admirals.*

48  Padfield, *Rule Britannia.*

49  Childers, *The Life And Correspondence Of The Right Hon Hugh C.E. Childers.*

50  Gordon, *The Rules Of The Game.*

51  Morris, *Pax Britannica.*

52  Lowis.

53  Gordon.

54  Willis, *The Royal Navy As I Saw It.*

55  Massie.

56  Rodgers

57  NMM.

58  Rodgers.

59  Gordon.

60 Massie.

61 Beresford.

62 Fortescue.

63 NMM.

64 Bacon, *The Life Of Lord Fisher Of Kilverstone*.

65 Villiers.

66 Chambers.

67 Childers.

68 Goodrich, *Report On The British Military And Naval Operations In Egypt 1882*.

69 Chaille-Long, *My Life In Four Continents*.

70 White, *Mariners Mirror, 1980*.

71 Tulloch.

72 Beresford.

73 NMM – Field Papers.

74 Chambers.

75 Ibid.

76 NMM.

77 Hough, *First Sea Lord*.

78 Bacon, *The Life Of Lord Fisher Of Kilverstone*.

79 Massie.

80 Gordon.

81 Marder, *Fear God And Dread Nought*.

82 Ibid.

83 Ibid.

84 NMM.

85 Wilson, *Ironclads In Action*.

86 Bradford, *Life Of Admiral Of The Fleet Sir Arthur Knyvet Wilson*.

87 Tulloch.

88 NMM.

89 Ibid.

90 Tulloch.

91 NMM – from official recommendation for the Victoria Cross.

92 White.

93 Prior, *Campaigns Of A War Correspondent*.

94 NMM.

95 Ibid.

96 Ibid.

97 Beresford.

98 Chambers.

99 NMM.

100 Ibid.

101 Chambers.

102 Tulloch.
103 Kusel.
104 Scudamore.
105 NMM.
106 Mackay, *Fisher Of Kilverstone.*
107 Ibid.
108 Grant, *Cassell's History Of The War In The Soudan.*

# Invasion

1 Stone, Century Magazine June 1884.
2 Duckers, *Egypt 1882.*
3 Broadley, *How We Defended Arabi And His Friends.*
4 Scott.
5 Ibid.
6 Chaille-Long.
7 Ibid.
8 Villiers, Villiers.
9 Ibid.
10 Royle.
11 Broadley, *How We Defended Arabi And His Friends.*
12 NMM.
13 Marder.
14 Bacon, *The Life Of Lord Fisher of Kilverstone.*
15 *The Times* – 17 July 1882.
16 Kusel.
17 Prior.
18 Ibid.
19 Beresford.
20 NMM.
21 Goodall.
22 Chambers.
23 Gerard, *Leaves From The Diaries Of A Soldier And Sportsman During Twenty-Five Years Service In India, Afghanistan And Other Countries.*
24 Johnson, *Spying For Empire.*
25 Harrison, *Recollections Of A Life In The British Army.*
26 Low Parks Museum, *Wolseley Diaries,* hereafter referred to as LPM
27 Tulloch.
28 Hove Public Library, hereafter referred to as HPL.
29 Childers.
30 Lyttelton, *Eighty Years.*

31 Childers.

32 Davis and Huttenback, *Mammon And The Pursuit Of Empire*.

33 British Museum – Gill Diary.

34 Verner and Parker, *The Military Life Of HRH George, Duke Of Cambridge*.

35 Childers.

36 Maurice, *Military History Of The Campaign Of 1882 In Egypt*.

37 Butler, *Sir William Butler*.

38 Adye, *Soldiers And Others I Have Known*.

39 Butler.

40 Wood, *Winnowed Memories*.

41 Harris, *My Life And Loves*.

42 Lehmann, *All Sir Garnet*.

43 Wolseley, *The Soldier's Pocket Book For Field Service*.

44 HPL.

45 Harris.

46 Lehmann, *All Sir Garnet*.

47 Preston, *The South African Diaries Of Sir Garnet Wolseley*.

48 Wolseley, *The Story Of A Soldier's Life*.

49 Ibid.

50 Farwell, *For Queen And Country*.

51 Settle, *Anecdotes Of Old Soldiers*.

52 Farwell, *For Queen And Country*.

53 Ibid.

54 Blood, *For Score Years And Ten*.

55 Gleichen, *A Guardsman's Memories*.

56 Ibid.

57 Spiers, *The Late Victorian Army 1868–1902*.

58 HPL.

59 Manthorpe.

60 Lehmann, *All Sir Garnet*.

61 Middleton, *Records And Reactions*.

62 Alexander, *The True Blue*.

63 Robertson, *From Private To Field-Marshal*.

64 Menzies, *Reminiscences Of An Old Soldier*.

65 Buckle, *The Letters Of Queen Victoria*.

66 HPL.

67 Gwynn and Tuckwell, *The Life Of Sir Charles W. Dilke*.

68 HPL.

69 Royal Archives, Cambridge Papers.

70 St Aubyn, *The Royal George*.

71 Ibid.

72 Farwell, *For Queen And Country*.

73 Ternan, *Some Experiences Of An Old Bromsgrovian*.
74 St Aubyn.
75 Maurice.
76 Robson, *Roberts In India*.
77 Fitzmaurice, *Life Of Granville*.
78 P. P.
79 Gladstone, *Nineteenth Century 1877*.
80 Ronison, Gallaher and Denny.
81 Blunt.
82 P. P.
83 Royal Archives.
84 Robinson, Gallagher and Denny.
85 Buckle.

# Kafr Dawar

1 Beresford.
2 Brooks, *The Long Arm Of Empire*.
3 Beresford.
4 Bacon, *The Life Of Lord Fisher Of Kilverstone*.
5 Scholch.
6 Ibid.
7 Chaille-Long.
8 Stone.
9 Ibid.
10 Ibid.
11 Ibid.
12 Gleichen.
13 Gerard.
14 Ibid.
15 Ibid.
16 Ibid.
17 Marling, *Rifleman And Hussar*.
18 Philip, *Reminiscences Of Gibralter, Egypt And The Egyptian War, 1882*.
19 Marling.
20 Gerard.
21 Holland, *The Life Of Spencer Compton*.
22 Davis and Huttenback.
23 Spiers, *The Late Victorian Army 1868–1902*.
24 Lehmann, *All Sir Garnet*.
25 Ibid.
26 Harris.

27 Aston, *His Royal Highness The Duke Of Connaught And Strathnearn.*

28 Repington, *Vestigia.*

29 NMM.

30 HPL.

31 Male, *Through The Battle Smoke.*

32 Featherstone, *Tel-El-Kebir 1882.*

33 Male.

34 Marling.

35 Bradford.

36 Bacon, *The Life Of Lord Fisher Of Kilverstone.*

37 Stone.

38 Marling.

39 P. P.

40 Bradford.

41 NAM.

42 Philip.

43 Hart-Synnot, *Letters Of Major-General Fitzroy Hart-Synnot.*

44 Grant.

45 Fortescue-Brickdale, *Sir Henry Hallam Parr.*

46 Gerard.

47 Mackay.

# Ismailia

1 LPM.

2 Lehmann, *All Sir Garnet.*

3 LPM.

4 HPL.

5 Ibid.

6 Ibid.

7 Shand.

8 HPL.

9 Ibid.

10 Shand.

11 Philip.

12 Bradford.

13 Goodrich.

14 Vetch, Life, *Letters And Diaries Of Lieut.-General Sir Gerald Graham.*

15 Clowes.

16 NAM.

17 Spiers, *The Scottish Soldier And Empire 1854–1902.*

18 NAM.
19 Ward, JSAHR 1973.
20 Gordon.
21 Dawnay Letters.
22 Beresford.
23 Bradford.
24 Ibid.
25 Fortescue–Brickdale.
26 Karsh and Karsh.
27 HPL.
28 P. P.
29 HPL.
30 Childers.
31 HPL.
32 Grenfell, *Memoirs*.
33 HPL.
34 Ibid.
35 Ibid.
36 Ibid.
37 Tulloch.
38 Vetch.
39 Shand.
40 LPM.
41 Molyneux, *Campaigning In South Africa And Egypt*.
42 Philip.
43 Grant.
44 Scott.
45 Childers.
46 Dawnay, *Campaigns*.
47 Brooks.
48 Molyneux.
49 Bacon, *The Life Of Lord Fisher Of Kilverstone*.
50 Marling.
51 Royle.
52 Bradford.
53 Dawnay.
54 Blunt.

# Mahsama

1 Marling.
2 HPL.

3 Molyneux.

4 Male.

5 Bond, 'Victorian Military Campaigns' – essay by M.J.Williams.

6 Childers.

7 Featherstone, *Tel-El-Kebir.*

8 Featherstone, *Victoria's Enemies.*

9 Ibid.

10 Butler, *Sir William Butler.*

11 Hart–Synnot

12 Wood, *Life And Adventure In Peace And War.*

13 Sandes, *The Royal Engineers In Egypt And The Sudan.*

14 Philip.

15 Maurice.

16 Butler, *Sir William Butler.*

17 Ibid.

18 Fortescue-Brickdale.

19 Ibid.

20 Prior.

21 Butler.

22 Household Cavalry Museum – Talbot Letters.

23 Butler.

24 Philip.

25 Butler.

26 Philip.

27 Maxwell, *The Ashanti Ring.*

28 Ibid.

29 Household Cavalary Museum – Talbot Letters.

30 NAM.

31 Dawnay Letters.

32 Molyneux.

33 Small, *Told From The Ranks.*

34 Philip.

35 Dawnay.

36 NAM.

37 Male.

38 Lehmann, *All Sir Garnet.*

39 Philip.

40 Butler.

41 Maurice, Fortnightly Review, July 1888.

42 Household Cavalry Museum, Talbot Letters.

43 Callwell, *The Memoirs Of Major-General Sir Hugh McCalmont.*

44 Male.

45 Philip.
46 Ibid.
47 Marling.
48 Ibid.
49 Littlejohn, 4/7th Dragoon Guards Regimental Magazine, Sept–Dec 1931.
50 Ward.
51 NAM.
52 Molyneux.
53 Marling..
54 HPL.

# Kassassin I

1 Shand.
2 Ibid.
3 Farwell, *Queen Victoria's Little Wars.*
4 Wood, *From Midshipman To Field Marshal.*
5 Maurice.
6 Macdiarmid, *The Life Of Lieut.General Sir James Moncrieff Grierson.*
7 Dunsterville, *Stalky' Reminiscences.*
8 Walsh, *Under The Flag.*
9 HPL.
10 Ibid.
11 Ibid.
12 Emery, *Marching Over Africa.*
13 Littlejohn.
14 Molyneux.
15 Harris.
16 Philip.
17 Ibid.
18 Ibid.
19 Molyneux.
20 Thompson, *Seventh (Princess Royal's) Dragoon Guards.*
21 Arthur, *The Letters Of Lord And Lady Wolseley 1870–1911.*
22 Baden-Powell, *Indian Memories.*
23 Ibid.
24 Molyneux.
25 Philip.
26 Duckers.
27 Philip.
28 Molyneux.

29 Maurice.
30 Philip.
31 Royle.
32 Household Cavalry Museum – Talbot papers.
33 Ibid.
34 Callwell, *The Memoirs Of Major-General Sir Hugh McCalmont.*
35 Household Cavalry Museum – Talbot papers.
36 Baden-Powell.
37 Household Cavalry Museum – Talbot papers.
38 Molyneux.
39 Ward.
40 NAM.

# Kassassin II

1 HPL.
2 Ibid.
3 Ibid.
4 Ibid.
5 Ibid.
6 Goodrich.
7 Vogt, *The Egyptian War Of 1882.*
8 Prior.
9 Gerard.
10 Sandes.
11 Tulloch.
12 Littlejohn.
13 Ward.
14 NAM.
15 Dawnay Letters.
16 NAM.
17 Marling.
18 Childers.
19 HPL.
20 Ibid.
21 Ibid
22 Ibid.
23 Verner and Parker.
24 Tulloch.
25 Powell, *Buller – A Scapegoat?*
26 Melville, *Life Of General The Right Hon. Redvers Buller VC; GCB; GCMG.*

27 HPL.
28 Macdiarmid.
29 Philip.
30 Sandes.
31 HPL.
32 Ibid.
33 Ibid.
34 Marling.
35 Villiers.
36 Denison, *Soldiering In Canada*.
37 NAM.
38 Vetch.
39 NAM.
40 Philip.
41 Marling.
42 Molyneux.
43 Prior.
44 Ibid.
45 Tulloch.
46 Marling.
47 Ibid.
48 NAM.
49 HLP.
50 Ibid.
51 Emery.
52 HPL.
53 Ward.
54 Dawnay.
55 Marling.
56 Goodrich.
57 Grant.
58 Blunt.
59 HPL.

# Tel-el-Kebir

1 Callwell, *The Memoirs Of Major-General Sir Hugh McCalmont*.
2 Lyttelton.
3 Notes in Author's possession.
4 Callwell, *The Memoirs Of Major-General Sir Hugh McCalmont*.
5 NAM.
6 *New York Herald,* September 1882.

7 Shand.

8 Dawnay.

9 Littlejohn.

10 Ward.

11 Dawnay.

12 Lehmann, *All Sir Garnet.*

13 Callwell, *Small Wars.*

14 Maurice.

15 Hart–Synnot.

16 Ibid.

17 Sandes.

18 Blunt.

19 NAM.

20 Cantlie, *A History Of The Army Medical Department.*

21 Melville.

22 Knight, *Marching To The Drums.*

23 Gordon.

24 Archer, *The War In Egypt And The Soudan.*

25 Field, *Britain's Sea Soldiers.*

26 Adye.

27 Archer.

28 Rawson.

29 Hart–Synnot.

30 Molyneux.

31 NAM.

32 Spiers, *The Scottish Soldier And Empire 1854–1902.*

33 Knight.

34 Dawnay.

35 NAM.

36 Philip.

37 Butler.

38 Male.

39 Rogers Papers in Author's possession.

40 Macdiarmid.

41 Villiers.

42 HPL.

43 Butler.

44 Ibid.

45 Ibid.

46 Field.

47 NAM.

48 Maurice.

49 Philip.
50 Molyneux.
51 Sales La Terriere, *Days That Are Gone.*
52 NAM.
53 Ward.
54 Dawnay.
55 Ward.
56 NAM.
57 Blood.
58 Villiers.
59 Inscription on Cameron's gravestone in Moulin churchyard near Blair Atholl.
60 Emery.
61 Spiers, *The Scottish Soldier And Empire 1854–1902.*
62 Ibid
63 Gordon.
64 Spiers, *The Scottish Soldier And Empire 1854–1902.*
65 Emery.
66 Spiers, *The Scottish Soldier And Empire 1854–1902.*
67 Emery.
68 Shand.
69 Maurice.
70 Hart-Synnot.
71 Ibid.
72 Gretton, *The Campaigns And History Of The Royal Irish Regiment.*
73 Hart-Synnot.
74 Emery.
75 Knight, *Marching To The Drums.*
76 Field.
77 Emery.
78 Blunt.
79 NAM.
80 Harrison.
81 Molyneux.
82 Littlejohn.
83 Callwell, *Memoirs Of Major-General Sir Hugh McCalmont.*
84 Anglesey, *A History Of The British Cavalry 1872–1898.*
85 Macdiarmid.
86 Rawlinson, *The History Of The 3rd Battalion, 7th Rajput Regiment.*
87 Rogers Papers in Author's possession.
88 *Army & Navy Gazette,* 14 October 1882.
89 NAM.
90 Ibid.

91  *The Times*, 7 October 1882.
92  Philip.
93  Sales La Terriere.
94  Harrison.
95  Butler.
96  Hart–Synnot.
97  NAM.
98  Whitworth, *A History Of The 2nd Lancers (Gardner's Horse)*.
99  Emery.
100  Rogers Papers in Author's possession.
101  Walsh.
102  Lehmann, *All Sir Garnet*.
103  Shand.
104  NAM.
105  Molyneux.
106  Philip.
107  NAM.
108  Spiers, *The Scottish Soldier And Empire 1854–1902*.
109  Archer.
110  Lane-Poole, Watson Pasha.
111  NAM.
112  Palmer, *Nineteenth Century*, March 1890.
113  Dawnay.
114  Grenfell.
115  Hart–Synnot.
116  Butler.
117  LPM.

# Trial

1  Sandes.
2  Rogers Papers in Author's possession.
3  Ibid.
4  Spiers, *The Scottish Soldier And Empire 1854–1902*.
5  McLeod Innes, *The Life And Times Of General Sir James Browne RE. KCB. KCSI.* (Buster Browne).
6  Grierson, *Precis Of The Arrangements Connected With The Despatch Of The Indian Contingent To Egypt And Of Its Operations In That Country.*
7  Lane-Poole.
8  Ibid.
9  Ibid.
10  Littlejohn.

11  Lane-Poole.

12  Dawson, *A Soldier-Diplomat.*

13  Gerard.

14  HPL.

15  Ibid.

16  NAM.

17  Ibid.

18  Emery.

19  Settle.

20  HPL.

21  *The Times*, September 1882.

22  Settle.

23  Philip.

24  Callwell, *Memoirs Of Major-General Sir Hugh McCalmont.*

25  HPL.

26  Childers.

27  HPL.

28  Verner and Parker.

29  Molyneux.

30  Blood.

31  Dawnay.

32  NAM.

33  LPM.

34  Notes in the Author's possession.

35  HPL.

36  LPM.

37  Childers.

38  Butler.

39  Dawnay Letters.

40  Villiers.

41  Blunt.

42  Broadley, *How We Defended Arabi And His Friends.*

43  Ibid.

44  Sanderson.

45  HPL.

46  Ibid.

47  Ibid.

48  Maxwell.

49  Spiers, *The Scottish Soldier And Empire, 1854–1902.*

50  HPL.

51  Haynes, *Man-Hunting In The Desert.*

52  Longford, *Victoria R.I.*

53  Notes in the Author's possession.
54  HPL.
55  LPM.
56  Fitzmaurice.
57  Robinson, Gallagher and Denny.
58  Sanderson.
59  Ibid.
60  Male.
61  Broadley, *How We Defended Arabi and His Friends*.
62  LPM.
63  Parliamentary Papers, Morley Committee Report.
64  LPM

# Epilogue

1  Morris, *Farewell The Trumpets*.
2  Sandbrook, *Never Had It So Good*.
3  Longford, *A Pilgrimage Of Passion*.
4  LPM.
5  HPL.
6  *Army & Navy Gazette*.
7  Naval and Military Record.
8  NMM.
9  LPM.
10  Ibid.
11  Watson, *The Life Of Major-General Sir Charles William Wilson*.
12  Blunt.

# Select Bibliography

## Original Documents

*British Museum, London*
Diary of Captain William Gill, Royal Engineers.

*Household Cavalry Museum, Windsor*
Papers of Lt-Colonel Reginald Talbot, 1st Life Guards.

*Gwent Record Office, Cwmbran*
Papers of Major-General Sir Alexander Tulloch, Welsh Regiment.

*Low Parks Museum, Hamilton*
Private diaries of Field-Marshal Lord Wolseley 1877–1906.

*National Archives, Kew*
Foreign Office Egypt files 1870–82.
Cabinet Papers 1881–82.

*National Army Museum, London*
19th Hussars – papers of Lt-Colonel K. Coghill
Scots Guards – diaries and papers of Surgeon F. Baker, Sergeants J. Ridout and
    G. Spriggs, Corporal H. Porter.
York and Lancaster Regiment – papers of Captain W. Kirkpatrick.
King's Royal Rifle Corps – papers of Private Wilson.
Royal Artillery – papers of Lieutenants R. Churchward and P. Enthoven.
Royal Engineers – papers of Captain S. Waller.
Post Office Rifles – papers of J. Boon.
Papers of Lieutenant H. Earle, King's Own Yorkshire Light Infantry, aide to General
    Earle commanding lines of communication.
Letter of General Sir G. Wolseley to his mother.
Original Egyptian Army telegrams seized and translated by the Indian Contingent.

## National Maritime Museum, Greenwich
Papers of Admiral Sir Beauchamp Seymour, Admiral Sir Berkeley Milne, Admiral
George Field and Captain Tynte Hammill.
Logs of HMS *Monarch*, HMS *Northumberland* and HMS *Superb*.

## Public Library, Hove
The Wolseley Collection – letters of Sir Garnet and Lady Louisa Wolseley, friends
and associates 1882, unpublished sections of an autobiography, scrapbooks and
ephemera.

## Royal Archives, Windsor
Papers of HRH the Duke of Connaught and Strathearn.
Papers of HRH the Duke of Cambridge.

## University Library, Nottingham
Ephemera of Major-General Sir D. Drury Lowe.

## Private Manuscripts
Coldstream Guards – letters of Colonel A. Lambton, Captain R. Follett and
Lieutenant E. Dawnay (in the possession of Peter Metcalfe Esq.).
20th Punjab Native Infantry – campaign letters and documents of Colonel R.
Rogers and Notes made by Lt-General Sir George Willis, commanding the First
Division (in possession of the Author).

# Printed Works

## Official Publications
Clarke, Capt. G. *Report On The Defences Of Alexandria*. London 1883.
Goodrich, Lt-Comm. C. *Report On The British Naval And Military Operations In
Egypt, 1882*. Washington 1883.
Grierson, Lt. J. *Precis Of The Arrangements Connected With The Despatch Of The Indian
Contingent To Egypt And Of Its Operations In That Country, 1882*. Simla 1883.
Maurice, Col. J. *Military History Of The Campaign Of 1882 In Egypt*. London 1887.
Parliamentary Papers *–Egypt Nos 1–20*. London 1882.
*Report Of A Committee Appointed By The Secretary Of State For War, To Inquire Into The
Organization Of The Army Hospital Corps, Hospital Management And Nursing In The
Field, And The Sea Transport Of Sick And Wounded*. London 1883.
*Report From The Select Committee On Commissariat And Transport Services (Egyptian
Campaign)*. London 1884.

## Other Books

Adye, Gen. Sir J. *Recollections Of A Military Life.* London 1895.

_____ *Soldiers And Others I Have Known.* London 1925.

Ahmed, Maj-Gen. R. *History Of The Baloch Regiment 1820–1939.* Abottabad 1998.

Aldridge, J. *Cairo.* Boston 1969.

Alexander, M. *The True Blue.* London 1957.

Al-Sayyid, A. *Egypt And Cromer.* London 1968.

Anglesey, Marquess of. *A History Of The British Cavalry 1872–1898.* London 1982.

Anon. *History Of The 20th (Duke Of Cambridge's Own) Infantry, Brownlow's Punjabis.* Devonport 1909.

Archer, T. *The War In Egypt And The Soudan.* London 1887.

Arthur, Sir G. ed. *The Letters Of Lord And Lady Wolseley 1870–1911.* London 1923.

Aston, Maj-Gen. Sir G. *His Royal Highness The Duke Of Connaught And Strathearn.* London 1929.

Bacon, Adm. Sir R. *A Naval Scrapbook 1877–1900.* London 1925.

_____ *The Life Of Lord Fisher of Kilverstone.* London 1929.

Baden-Powell, R. *Indian Memories.* London 1915.

Bahlmann, D. ed. *The Diary Of Sir Edward Walter Hamilton.* Oxford 1972.

Barthorp, M. *War On The Nile.* Poole 1984.

_____ and Turner, P. *The British Army On Campaign 1856–1902.* London 1988.

Beatty, C. *De Lesseps Of Suez.* New York 1956.

Beckett, I. *The Victorians At War.* London 2003.

Belich, J. *The New Zealand Wars.* Auckland 1986.

Bell, M. *Khedives And Pashas.* London 1884.

Bennett, G., *Charlie B.* London 1968.

Beresford, Adm. Lord C. *Memoirs.* London 1914.

Blake, R. *Disraeli.* London 1966.

Blaxland, G. *Objective Egypt.* London 1966.

Blood, Gen. Sir B. *Four Score Years And Ten.* London 1933.

Blunt, W. *Secret History Of The English Occupation Of Egypt.* London 1907.

Bond, B. ed. *Victorian Military Campaigns.* London 1967.

Bonnett, S. *The Price Of Admiralty.* London 1968.

Brackenbury, Gen. Sir H. *Some Memories Of My Spare Time.* Edinburgh 1909.

Bradford, Adm. Sir E. *Life Of Admiral Of The Fleet Sir Arthur Knyvet Wilson.* London 1923.

Brett, M. ed. *Journals And Letters Of Viscount Esher.* London 1934.

Broadley, A. *The Last Punic War.* London 1882.

_____ *How We Defended Arabi And His Friends.* London 1884.

Brooks, R. *The Long Arm Of Empire.* London 1999.

Buckle, G. ed. *The Letters Of Queen Victoria.* London 1930.

Burnett, J. *A History Of The Cost Of Living.* London 1969.

Butler, A. *Court Life In Egypt.* London 1887.

Butler, E. *Autobiography.* London 1912.

Butler, Lt-Gen. Sir W. *Sir William Butler.* London 1911.

Callwell, C. *Small Wars.* London 1899.

_____ ed. *The Memoirs Of Major-General Sir Hugh McCalmont.* London 1924.

Cameron, D. *Egypt In The Nineteenth Century.* London 1898.

Cantlie, Lt-Gen. Sir N. *A History Of The Army Medical Department.* Edinburgh 1974.

Cavendish, A. ed. *Cyprus 1878.* Nicosia 1991.

Chaille-Long , Col.. *My Life In Four Continents.* London 1912.

Chambers, Adm B.. *Salt Junk.* London 1927.

Chaplin, Lt-Col. *The Queen's Own Royal West Kent Regiment 1881–1914.*
Maidstone 1959.

Childers, Lt-Col. S. *The Life And Correspondence Of The Right Hon. Hugh C. E.
Childers.* London 1901.

Clowes, Sir W. *The Royal Navy.* London 1903.

Cole, J. *Colonialism And Revolution In The Middle East.* Princeton 1993.

Colomb, Vice-Adm. P. *Memoirs Of Admiral The Right Hon. Sir Astley Cooper Key.*
London 1898.

Colvin, A. *The Making Of Modern Egypt.* London 1906.

Cowan, J. *The New Zealand Wars.* Wellington 1922.

Crabites, P. *Ismail – The Maligned Khedive.* London 1933.

Creagh, Sir O and Humphries, E. *The Victoria Cross 1856–1920.* Polstead 1985.

Cromer, Earl of. *Modern Egypt.* London 1908.

Curtin, P. *Disease And Empire.* Cambridge 1998.

Davis, L. and Huttenback, R. *Mammon And The Pursuit Of Empire.* Cambridge 1988.

Dawnay, G. *Campaigns: Zulu 1879, Egypt 1882, Suakim 1885.* Cambridge 1989.

Dawson, Brig-Gen. Sir D. *A Soldier-Diplomat.* London 1927.

Denison, Lt-Col. G. *Soldiering In Canada.* Toronto 1900.

Douglas, Sir G. *The Life Of Major-General Wauchope CB; CMG; LL.D.* London 1904.

Douin, G. ed. *Une Mission Militaire Francaise Aupres De Mohammed Aly.* Cairo 1923.

_____ *Regne Du Khedive Ismail.* Cairo 1933–38.

Duckers, P. ed. *Egypt 1882.* London 2001.

Duff-Gordon, L. *Letters From Egypt 1863–65.* London 1875.

_____ *Last Letters From Egypt.* London 1902.

Dunsterville, Maj-Gen. L. *Stalky's Reminiscences.* London 1928.

Emery, F. ed. *Marching Over Africa.* London 1986.

Farman, E. *Egypt And Its Betrayal.* New York 1908.

Farwell, B. *Queen Victoria's Little Wars.* London 1972.

_____ *For Queen And Country.* London 1981.

_____ *Eminent Victorian Soldiers.* London 1986.

Featherstone, D. *Victoria's Enemies.* London 1989.

_____ *Tel-El-Kebir 1882.* London 1993.

Field, Col. C. *Britain's Sea Soldiers.* Liverpool 1924.

Fitzmaurice, E. *The Life Of Granville.* London 1905.

Fortescue, Capt. S. *Looking Back.* London 1920.

Fortescue-Brickdale, Sir C. ed. *Major-General Sir Henry Hallam Parr.* London 1917.

Fraser, J. *Sixty Years In Uniform.* London 1939.

Freycinet, C. *La Question D'Egypte.* Paris 1904.

Fuller, J. *The Army In My Time.* London 1935.

Gardyne, Lt-Col. C. *The Life Of A Regiment 1816–1898.* London 1929.

Gerard, Lt-Gen. Sir M. *Leaves From The Diaries Of A Soldier And Sportsman During Twenty-Five Years Service In India, Afghanistan, Egypt And Other Countries 1865–1885.* London 1903.

Ghorbal, S. *The Beginnings Of The Eastern Question And The Rise Of Mehemet Ali.* London 1928.

Gleichen, Maj-Gen. Lord E. *A Guardsman's Memories.* Edinburgh 1932.

Goodall, W. *Warm Corners In Egypt.* London 1886.

Gordon, A. *The Rules Of The Game.* London 1996.

Gordon, J. *My Six Years With The Black Watch 1881–1887.* Boston 1929.

Grant, J. *Cassell's History Of The War In The Soudan.* London nd (c. 1886).

Greaves, A. and Knight, I. *The Who's Who Of The Anglo-Zulu War.* Barnsley 2006.

Green, D. *Armies Of God.* London 2007.

Greene, J and Massignani, A. *Ironclads At War.* Conshocken 1998.

Gregg, P. *A Social And Economic History Of Britain 1760–1965.* London 1965.

Grenfell, F.M. Lord. *Memoirs.* London 1925.

Gretton, Lt-Col. G. *The Campaigns And History Of The Royal Irish Regiment.* Edinburgh 1911.

Gwynn, S. and Tuckwell, G. *The Life Of Sir Charles W. Dilke.* London 1917.

Hanotaux, G. *Historie Des Colonies Francaises Et De L'Expansion De La France.* Paris 1929–33.

Hare, Maj-Gen. Sir S. *The Annals Of The King's Royal Rifle Corps.* London 1929.

Harris, F. *My Life And Loves.* London 1964.

Harrison, Gen. Sir R. *Recollections Of A Life In The British Army.* London 1908.

Harrison, R. *Gladstone's Imperialism In Egypt.* Westport 1995.

Hart-Synnot, B. ed. *Letters Of Major-General Fitzroy Hart-Synnot.* London 1912.

Haynes, M. *Man-Hunting In The Desert.* London 1884.

Holland, B. *The Life Of Spencer Compton.* London 1911.

Holt, P. ed. *Political And Social Change In Modern Egypt.* London 1968.

Hough, R. *First Sea Lord.* London 1969.

Hourani, A. *Arabic Thought In The Liberal Age 1798–1939.* Cambridge 1983.

Humble, R. *Before The Dreadnought.* London 1976.

Johnson, P. *Front Line Artists.* London 1978.

Johnson, R. *Spying For Empire.* London 2006.

Karabell, Z. *Parting The Desert.* London 2003.

Karsh, E. and Karsh, I. *Empires Of The Sand.* Harvard 1999.

Knight, I. *Queen Victoria's Enemies*. London 1989.

———— ed. *Marching To The Drums*. London 1999.

Kochanski, H. *Sir Garnet Wolseley*. London 1999.

Kusel, Baron de. *An Englishman's Recollections Of Egypt 1863 To 1887*. London 1915.

Laband, J. *The Transvaal Rebellion*. London 2005.

Lane, E. *Modern Egyptians*. London 1890.

Lane-Poole, S. *Watson Pasha*. London 1919.

Lehmann, J. *All Sir Garnet*. London 1964.

———— *The First Boer War*. London 1972.

Lesseps, F. de *Recollections Of Forty Years*. London1887.

Longford, E. *Victoria R.I.* London 1964.

———— *A Pilgrimage Of Passion*. London1979.

Loring, W. *A Confederate Soldier In Egypt*. New York 1884.

Low, C. *General Lord Wolseley*. London 1883.

Lowis, Comm. G. *Fabulous Admirals*. London 1957.

Lyttelton, Gen. Sir N. *Eighty Years*. London nd (c. 1927.).

Macdiarmid, D. *The Life Of Lieut. General Sir James Moncrieff Grierson*. London 1923.

Macdonald, Brig-Gen. J. *Fifty Years Of It*. Edinburgh 1909.

Mackay, R. *Fisher Of Kilverstone*. Oxford 1973.

Magnus, P. *Kitchener*. New York 1959.

Male, A. *Scenes Through The Battle Smoke*. London nd (c. 1885.).

Malet, E. *Shifting Scenes*. London 1901.

Malmesbury, Countess of. *The Life Of Major-General Sir John Ardagh*. London 1909.

Manning, S. *Evelyn Wood VC*. Barnsley 2007.

Mansfield, P. *The British In Egypt*. London 1971.

Manthorpe, V. *Children Of The Empire*. London 1996.

Marder, A. *Fear God And Dread Nought*. London 1952.

Marling, Col. Sir P. *Rifleman And Hussar*. London 1931.

Marlowe, J. *Anglo-Egyptian Relations 1800–1953*. London 1954.

———— *Spoiling The Egyptians*. London 1974.

Massie, R. *Dreadnought*. London 1992.

Maurice, Maj-Gen. Sir F and Arthur, Sir G. *The Life Of Lord Wolseley*. London 1924.

Maxwell, L. *The Ashanti Ring*. London 1985.

McLeod Innes, Gen. *The Life And Times Of General Sir James Browne R.E. K.C.B. K.C.S.I. (Buster Browne)*. London 1905.

Melville, Col. G. *Life Of General The Right Hon. Redvers Buller VC; GCB; GCMG*. London 1923.

Menzies, Sgt. J. *Reminiscences Of An Old Soldier*. Edinburgh 1883.

Meyer, L. *The Farther Frontier*. Selinsgrove 1992.

Middleton, Earl of. *Records And Reactions*. London 1939.

Molyneux, Maj-Gen. W. *Campaigning In South Africa And Egypt*. London 1896.

Moneypenny, W. and Buckle, G. *The Life Of Benjamin Disraeli*. London 1910–20.

Moorehead, A. *The White Nile*. London 1960.

_____ *The Blue Nile*. London 1962.

Morgan, J. *Recollections Of A Rebel Reefer*. Boston 1917.

Morley, J. *The Life Of William Ewart Gladstone*. London 1903.

Morris, J. *Pax Britannica*. London 1968.

_____ *Heaven's Command*. London 1973.

_____ *Farewell The Trumpets*. London 1978.

Murray, Col. Sir W. *A Varied Life*. Winchester 1975.

Nicoll, F. *The Sword Of The Prophet*. Thrupp 2004.

Padfield, P. *Rule Britannia*. London 1981.

Pakenham, T. *The Scramble For Africa*. London 1991.

Parkes, O. *British Battleships*. London 1966.

Pearsall, R. *The Worm In The Bud*. London 1969.

Philip, Sgt. J. *Reminiscences Of Gibralter, Egypt And The Egyptian War 1882*. Aberdeen 1893.

Powell, G. *Buller: A Scapegoat?* London 1994.

Preston, A. ed. *In Relief Of Gordon*. London 1967.

_____ *The South African Diaries Of Sir Garnet Wosleley 1875*. Cape Town 1971.

Rawlinson, H. *The History Of The 3rd Battalion 7th Rajput Regiment*. London 1941.

Rawson, Lt. G. *Life Of Admiral Sir Harry Rawson*. London 1914.

Reid, M. *No Complaint Or Failure*. Southam 2004.

Repington, C. *Vestigia*. London 1919.

Robertson, Sir W. *From Private To Field-Marshal*. London 1921.

Robinson, R, Gallagher, J. and Denny, A. *Africa And The Victorians*. London 1961.

Robson, B. ed. *Roberts In India*. Thrupp 1993.

Royle, C. *The Egyptian Campaigns 1882 To 1885*. London 1900.

Sales La Terriere, Col. B. de. *Days That Are Gone*. London 1925.

Sandbrook,.D. *Never Had It So Good*. London 2005.

Sanderson, Lord. ed. *Egypt 1879–1883 By The Right Honourable Sir Edward Malet, Bart; GCB*. London 1909.

Sandes, Lt-Col. E. *The Royal Engineers In Egypt And The Sudan*. Chatham 1937.

Scholch, A. *Egypt For The Egyptians*. London 1981.

Scott, Adm. Sir P. *Fifty Years In The Royal Navy*. London 1919.

Scudamore, F. *A Sheaf Of Memories*. London 1925.

Settle, J. *Anecdotes Of Soldiers*. London 1905.

Seward, D. *Eugenie*. Thrupp 2004.

Seymour, Adm. Sir E. *My Naval Career*. London 1911.

Shand, A. *The Life Of General Sir Edward Bruce Hamley*. Edinburgh 1895.

Sheppard, E. *George Duke Of Cambridge*. London 1907.

Simkin, R. *The War In Egypt*. London 1883.

Sims, G. *The Bitter Cry Of Outcast London*. London 1883.

Small, M. ed. *Told From The Ranks*. London 1897.

Smith-Dorrien, Gen. Sir H. *Memories Of Forty-Eight Years Service*. London 1925.

Spiers, E. *The Late Victorian Army 1868–1902*. Manchester 1992.

———— *The Scottish Soldier And Empire, 1854–1902*. Edinburgh 2006.

St Aubyn, G. *The Royal George*. London 1963.

Steegmuller, F. ed. *Flaubert In Egypt*. Boston 1972.

Strachey, L. *Eminent Victorians*. London 1920.

Stuart, V. *Egypt After The War*. London 1883.

Ternan, Brig-Gen. T. *Some Experiences Of An Old Bromsgrovian*. Birmingham 1930.

Thompson, Col. C. *Seventh (Princess Royal's) Dragoon Guards*. Liverpool 1913.

Thornton, Dep-Surg-Gen. J. *Memories Of Seven Campaigns*. London 1895.

Toomey, T. *Heroes Of The Victoria Cross*. London 1895.

Tulloch, Maj-Gen. Sir A. *Recollections Of Forty Years Service*. Edinburgh 1903.

Tylden, G. *The Rise Of The Basuto*. Cape Town 1950.

Urabi, A. *Mudhakkirat Urabi*. Cairo 1953.

Verner, Col. W. and Parker, Capt. E. *The Military Life Of H.R.H. George, Duke Of Cambridge*. London 1905.

Vetch, Col. R. *Life, Letters And Diaries Of Lieut.-General Sir Gerald Graham*. Edinburgh 1901.

Villiers, F. *Peaceful Personalities And Warriors Bold*. London 1907.

———— *Villiers*. New York 1920.

Vogt, Lt-Col. H. *The Egyptian War Of 1882*. London 1883.

Wade, S. *Spies In The Empire*. London 2007.

Walsh, L. *Under The Flag*. London nd (c. 1920.).

Watson, Col. Sir C. *The Life Of Major-General Sir Charles William Wilson*. London 1909.

Wheeler, Capt. O. *The War Office Past And Present*. London 1914.

Whitworth, Capt. D. *A History Of The 2nd Lancers (Gardner's Horse)*. London 1924.

Wilkinson-Latham, R. *From Our Special Correspondent*. London 1979.

Willis, Capt. G. *The Royal Navy As I Saw It*. London 1924.

Wilson, C. *Ironclads In Action*. London 1895.

Wilson, R. *Chapters From My Official Life*. London 1916.

Wolseley, F. M. Visc. G. *The Soldier's Pocket-Book For Field Service*. London 1868.

———— *The Story Of A Soldier's Life*. London 1903.

Wood, Maj-Gen. Sir E. *Life And Adventure In Peace And War*. London 1924.

Wood, F. M. Sir E. *From Midshipman To Field Marshal*. London 1906.

———— *Winnowed Memories*. London 1918.

## Articles

Bond, B. 'The Effect Of The Cardwell Reforms In Army Organization 1874–1904' in *Journal Of The Royal United Service Institution* (November 1960).

Cox, F. 'Arabi And Stone' in *Cahiers D'Historie Egyptienne VIII* (1956).

Dilke, C. 'Sir Charles Dilke And 'How We Went Into Egypt'' in *Manchester Guardian* (27 June 1907).

Exelby, J. 'The Secret Service Major And The Invasion Of Egypt' in *History Today* (November 2006).

Gladstone, W. 'Aggression On Egypt And Freedom In The East' in *Nineteenth Century* (August 1877).

Holloway, Col. E. 'Egypt 1882' in *Journal Of The Duke Of Cornwall's Light Infantry Vol 1, No 3* (November 1930).

Littlejohn, Sgt. 'From Ismailia To Cairo With The 4th Royal Irish Dragoon Guards' in *4/7th Dragoon Guards Regimental Magazine* (September–December 1931).

Loring, Gen. W. 'The Egyptian War' in *New York Herald* (8 September 1882).

Maurice, Sir J. 'Critics And Campaigns' in *Fortnightly Review* (July 1888).

McLaughlin, Lt G. 'The Lines Of Kafr Dwar' in *Journal Of The Royal Artillery Vol XII* (1885–1886).

Morley, J. in *Fortnightly Review* (July 1882).

Palmer, A. 'A Battle Described From The Ranks' in *Nineteenth Century* (March 1890).

Raugh, H. 'Vignettes Of Victoria's Generals: General Sir Archibald Alison' in *Soldiers Of The Queen No 117* (June 2004).

Rodgers, N. 'The Dark Ages Of The Admiralty 1869–1885' in *Mariners Mirror* (1975–76).

Smith, P. 'Tel-El-Kebir' in *Army Quarterly* (October 1980–January 1981).

Stone, F. 'Diary Of An American Girl In Cairo During The War Of 1882' in *Century Magazine* (June 1884).

Tylden (Maj G.). 'Tel-El-Kebir, 13th September, 1882' in *Journal Of The Society For Army Historical Research Vol 31* (1953).

Ward, S. ed. 'The Scots Guards In Egypt, 1882' in *Journal Of The Society For Army Historical Research Vol 51* (1973).

White, C. 'The Bombardment Of Alexandria 1882' in *Mariners Mirror* (1980).

Wright, W. 'Tel-El-Kebir' in *Soldiers Of The Queen No 31* (December 1982).

## Magazines and Newspapers

*Army and Navy Gazette*
*The Graphic*
*Illustrated London News*
*Manchester Guardian*
*National Observer*
*Naval & Military Record*
*New York Herald*
*Pictorial World*
*Punch*
*The Review Of Reviews*
*The Times*

# Index

Abbat, Hotel, 53, 107

Abaid, Muhammad, 25

Abbas Pasha, 10, 22

Abdin Palace, 25, 31, 33, 34, 35, 36, 153, 178, 264, 267

Abdul Hamid II, Sultan of Turkey, 13, 36, 43, 47, 48, 49, 63, 66, 134, 165, 193

Aboukir Bay, 118, 145, 160, 161, 165, 167, 168, 169, 171,

Ada, Fort, 85, 86, 98

Adjemi Fort, 85, 105

Adye, General Sir John, 135, 278

Adye, Captain John, 125, 263

Afghan War (1878–80), 6, 72, 119, 123, 126, 146, 194, 228, 260

Al Hilmi, Colonel (later General) Abdul, 24–25, 34, 46, 50, 230, 264, 270, 277, 286

Alexandria (harbour), 84–85

Bombardment of, 71–75, 84–104

riots, 52–66

Alison, Major-General Sir Archibald, 141–142, 83, 115, 134, 135, 138, 141–145, 152, 154, 156, 157, 160, 161, 165, 167, 169, 191, 192, 223, 225, 234, 238, 239, 241, 243, 249, 253, 256, 257, 263, 264, 272, 283–284, 315

Arabi Pasha, 9, 22, 52, 65, 67, 75, 86, 103, 106, 108, 110–111, 135–136, 139, 141, 152–153, 161, 167–168, 190, 193, 205, 227, 229, 246, 260, 262,

career, 19, 26–27

views, 28–29

loyalty to Sultan, 49–50

tent, 253

at Tek, 254

trial, 269–271, 276–277

death, 286–287

importance of, 287

Ardagh, Lt-Colonel John, 141–142, 166

Armoured Train, 152, 154, 156–157, 162–163

Ashburnham, Colonel Cromer, 144, 153, 154, 185, 186, 226, 231, 244, 272

Ashanti War (1873–74), 86, 89, 127, 147, 148

Balfour, Lt. Charles, 162, 184, 188, 209, 220, 227–228, 240–241

Baring, Evelyn, 40, 116, 129, 281

Bedouins, 62, 114, 153, 162, 181, 212–213, 217, 263,

atrocities, 208

Bell, Moberley, 86, 98

Beresford, Commander Lord Charles, 62, 87, 145

Blood, Major Bindon, 127, 241, 267, 285

Blunt, Wilfred, 29, 33, 35, 40, 43, 45, 60, 74–75, 120, 174, 231

Bright, John, 42, 71, 73, 135

British Army, 6, 116, 121, 122, 125, 129, 133, 141, 215, 234, 237

Army Life 127–128 (officers), 130–131 (ranks),

equipment, 18, 127, 151–152, 171, 177, 187, 189

Intelligence Department, 7, 116–117, 120, 142–143, 148, 160, 176, 269

Regiments (1882 Egypt):

1st Life Guards, 183, 195, 203–204

2nd Life Guards, 179, 204

Royal Horse Guards, 125, 129–130, 212, 274

4th Dragoon Guards, 187, 188, 197, 202, 251

7th Dragoon Guards, 184, 186, 203, 251,

19th Hussars, 178, 185, 197, 204–205, 209, 212, 231, 233, 263

Grenadier Guards, 127, 130, 280

Goldstream Guards, 9, 163, 173, 227, 308

Scots Guards, 150, 160, 162, 184, 188, 209, 220, 227, 236, 241, 256, 257, 263, 265, 272, 278, 307

18th Royal Irish, 244

32nd/46th Duke of Cornwalls Light Infantry, 144, 154, 173, 180, 183, 188, 197, 226, 233, 249, 284, 315

38th/80th South Staffordshires, 154–156

42nd/73rd The Black Watch, 126, 162, 232, 233, 235, 238, 241–243, 246, 248, 252, 254, 284

49th/66th Berkshires, 150, 192

50th/97th West Kents, 231

60th King's Royal Rifle Corps, 127, 144, 155, 197, 204, 210, 217, 226, 237, 248, 257, 307,

65th/84th York and Lancasters, 176, 178, 180, 197, 214, 244–245, 307

71st/74th Highland Light Infantry, 150, 193, 236, 238, 241, 242, 249–250,

72nd/78th Sea Forth Highlanders, 172, 225, 231, 247, 259, 260

75th The Cameron Highlanders, 193, 234–235, 241

87th/89th Royal Irish Fusiliers, 150, 245

Royal Artillery, 116, 125, 185, 307, 315

Royal Engineers, 101, 116, 120, 122, 143–145, 197, 208, 229, 232, 241, 269, 283, 298, 307, 313

Royal Marines, 111, 114–115, 134, 153–154, 156, 178, 180, 197, 202, 218, 220, 232–233, 239, 244–246, 250

Post Office Volunteers, 213

Staff Officers, 6, 34, 145, 147, 168, 178, 180, 223, 233, 248

Traditions, 125–128

Uniforms, 18, 82, 87, 99, 125, 127, 150, 150, 156, 162, 194, 200, 228, 252

Weapons, 18, 77, 127, 177, 178, 201, 252, 258, 263

Bennett, Corporal, 261

Buller, Colonel Sir Redvers, 148–149, 166, 212, 216, 227–228, 232, 234, 282–283, 286, 300

Burleigh, Bennet, 86, 215

Butler, Lt-Colonel William, 148, 166, 178, 180, 183, 192, 238, 255, 265, 268, 294

Burmese War (1852–54), 77, 125

Cairo, 10, 12, 15–17, 19–21, 23–27, 31, 17–38, 41–53, 74, 85, 104, 117, 122, 138–141, 159–161, 168, 171, 173, 193, 205, 231, 252, 254, 258, 260, 263–267, 271, 276, 278, 279

Cameron, John, 86, 109, 112, 168, 218, 282

Cambridge, Hrh Prince George, Duke of, 119, 121, 123, 128, 130, 135, 141–142, 147, 149, 167, 199–200, 215, 266, 272, 285

Cardwell, Edwards, 116, 124, 129, 130–131, 133, 150, 314

Cetewayo, Zulu Chief 211, 211, 273

Ceylon, 229, 277, 286

Chaille-Long, Colonel Charles, 70, 86, 108–109, 114, 139, 282,

Chair, Midshipman Dudley De, 205

Chambers, Cadet B, 88–89, 92, 99, 115, 285

Chamberlain, Joseph, 73, 120, 136, 275

Cherif Pasha, 15, 19, 22, 36, 38, 41–45, 271

Childers, Hugh, 23, 81, 84, 118

China War (1858–60), 68, 128, 197

Churchward, Lt. Walter, 239–240, 248, 251, 253, 256, 265

Coghill, Lt-Colonel Kendal, 185, 205, 209, 217, 219–220, 263

Colvin, Auckland, 23, 32, 35–36, 44, 76, 112, 271

Connaught, HRH Prince Arthur, Duke of, 128, 149–150, 157, 166, 184, 196, 217, 241, 246, 253, 266, 272

Conrad, Rear-Admiral, 49

Cookson, Charles, 32, 35, 56, 62

Corbett, Private Frederick, 155–156

Cornish, John, 143

Courcel, Baron Alphonse De, 30

Crimean War (1854–56), 7, 100, 125, 128–129, 147, 149, 192

Cyprus, 30, 69, 115, 121, 124, 132, 134–135, 142, 147, 158, 310

Dawnay, Lt. Eustace, 163

Dawnay, Guy, 171, 173, 185, 221, 226–227, 235–236, 240, 251–252, 256–257, 267

Dervish Pasha, 62–63, 75

Dilke, Charles, 9, 42, 60, 314

Disraeli, Benjamin, 13, 312

Drury-Lowe, Major-General Sir Drury, 148, 202–203, 251

Dufferin, Lord, 66, 165, 276–277, 281

Earle, Major General William, 172, 232, 246, 282, 307
Edwards, Lt. William, 242
Egypt,
Chamber of Notables, 12, 40–41, 43
population, 20–21
State of Country (1881), 15, 18–21
Egyptian Army,
weapons and equipment, 176–178
dispositions at Kassassin, 215–216
bravery at Tek, 256
Esbekiah Square, 15, 16
Egyptians,
anti-European sentiment, 45, 49, 104
women at Tek, 257

Fehmy, Ali, 24–25, 29, 31–34, 50, 178, 216, 221, 242, 259
Fehmy, Colonel (later General) Mahmud, 195, 230, 270, 277, 286
Field, Lt. George, 89, 308
Fisher, Captain John, 90, 162
Fitzgeorge, Major George, 149, 207, 214
Freycinet, Charles De, 44

Gambetta, Leon, 38
Gerard, Lt-Colonel Montagu, 143, 156, 164, 207, 262
Gill, Captain William, 120, 307
Gladstone, William, 22, 38, 42, 44, 46, 65–66, 71–73, 101, 103, 118–119, 129, 131–134
Gleichen, Lt. Lord Edward, 127, 142, 294–295, 311
Goodall, Walter, 51, 67, 114
Goodenough, Brigadier-General William, 231, 234, 248–249, 256
Goodrich, Commander Caspar, 101, 110, 161, 221, 229
Gordon, Private John, 162, 232, 242
Graham, Major-General Sir Gerald, 149, 161, 169, 180, 206, 217, 219, 224, 283
career, 197–198
criticism of action at Kassassin, 207–208
defence of, 208
criticism of action at 2nd battle at Kassassin, 221
Granville, Lord, 35, 38, 43–44, 62, 134, 271
Grenfell, Major Francis, 149, 167, 257
Gribble, Lt. Henry, 203–204
Grierson, Lt. J., 194, 212, 237, 247

Halim, Prince, 49
Hamley, Lt-General Sir Edward, 147, 263
career, 191–192
Harding, Gunner Israel, 96
Hallam-Parr, Major Henry, 149, 155
Hardy, Midshipman, 156
Harris, Frank, 123–124
Harrison, Colonel Richard, 116, 149, 172, 232, 246, 250
Hartington, Lord, 40, 146
Havelock-Allan, Lt-General Sir Henry, 215, 252
Helwan Society, 22, 29
Heeage, Captain Algernon, 78, 271
Hewett, Rear-Admiral Sir William, 153, 170–172
HMS *Alexandra*, 50–51, 67, 69, 82, 87, 89, 93–96, 101, 103, 114, 118, 153
HMS *Beacon*, 91, 172
HMS *Carys* Fort, 171
HMS *Condor*, 62, 72, 87–88, 91, 97–98, 111
HMS *Coquette*, 50, 171
HMS *Hecla*, 93–94, 101, 138, 163, 173
HMS *Helicon*, 62, 87, 91, 106, 164, 166, 173
HMS *Inflexible*, 51, 79, 83, 87–88, 90–91, 93, 98, 105, 111, 143
HMS *Invincible*, 50, 52, 59, 62, 68–69, 73, 80, 83, 85–86, 88, 92–100, 109, 137
HMS *Iris*, 64, 73, 75, 86, 122, 129, 131, 134, 142, 148–150, 152, 171
HMS *Monarch*, 50, 62–63, 86, 88–89, 92, 97, 100, 115, 171
HMS *Northumberland*, 88, 115, 171, 308
HMS *Orion*, 171, 183, 237
HMS *Penelope*, 74, 88
HMS *Salamis*, 166
HMS *Sultan*, 89, 95
HMS *Superb*, 89, 162
HMS *Temeraire*, 87
Hoskins, Rear-Admiral Sir Anthony, 112, 121, 166, 170–172, 238
Hotham, Captain Charles, 89
Hardy, Midshipman, 156
Hospitals, 59, 232, 251, 257, 263, 278

Indian Army, 195, 275
2nd Bengal Cavalry, 212, 251
6th Bengal Cavalry, 194, 236, 259
13th Bengal Lancers, 194, 213, 216, 236
7th Bengal Native Infantry, 194

20th Punjab Native Infantry, 194
27th/29th Baluch Regiment, 194
Indian Contingent, 146, 150, 167, 172, 177, 184, 193, 195, 224–225, 228, 231, 237, 247, 252, 259, 275
Indian Mutiny (1857–59), 128, 199
Invasion, Plans, 212
Ismail Pasha, 10–11, 19, 27
Ismailia, 5, 7, 121–122, 134, 158–159, 160–167, 169, 171–176, 185, 188–190, 196, 206, 209
Isandlawana, Battle of, 73, 132, 149, 207–208, 246, 255,
Ismat, General Tulbah, 47

Joint Note, 30, 41–44, 50, 66
Jones, Lt-Colonel Howard, 246

Kafr-Dawar,
   action at, 154–157
Kassassin ,
   1st battle, 197–208
   2nd battle, 216–221
Key, Admiral Sir Astley, 70
Kimberley, Lord, 120
Kitchener, Lt. Herbert, 69, 100, 283
Kusel, Baron Samuel De, 21, 51, 53–55, 58, 74, 92, 99, 112
Khan, Subedar-Major Mauladad, 194–195

Lambton, Commander Hedworth, 58, 84, 88, 92, 99, 105–106, 156
Lancaster, USS, 70, 73, 86, 139
Lesseps, Ferdwand De, 10, 66, 71, 166–168, 172–175
Littlejohn, Sergeant, 188, 226, 247
Loring, Brigadier-General William, 16–17, 22, 27, 32, 282
Lyttelton, Major Neville, 148, 226, 236, 283
Lyons, Lord, 41, 43, 71

Macpherson, Major-General Sir Herbert, 8, 146, 195, 212, 225, 232, 238, 241, 248, 252, 259, 265
   career, 146
Magfar, 176, 178–181, 189, 196–197
Mahsama, 7, 175–190, 177, 195–199, 202–204, 209
Male, Padre Arthur, 150–151
Malet, Sir Edward, 43, 165, 288, 313
Marling, Lt. Percival, 144, 152, 188, 219

Malta, 49, 51, 79, 82, 93, 121, 134, 146, 160
Marabout Fort, 84–85, 97, 113
Mareotis, Lake, 84, 138, 143, 152, 164
Maurice, Major John, 6, 7
McCalmont, Lt-Colonel Hugh, 127–128, 148, 187, 189, 203–204, 217, 236, 247, 260, 266
Methuen, Colonel Paul, 166, 168–169, 171, 220, 257
Mex Fort, 74, 85, 87–88, 92–93, 97, 99, 105, 163
Molyneux, Captain Richard, 52, 54–55, 59, 89, 92, 95, 149, 158, 169, 172, 185, 189, 197, 199, 200, 202
Molyneux, Major William, 119, 149, 158, 175, 197, 235–236, 246, 267
Morgan, Captain James, 17–18, 282
Morice Bey, 54–55, 59, 282
Morris, Major-General Sir Edward, 210
Morrison, Lt. W, 62, 66, 106
Muhammad Ali Pasha, 10, 19, 21, 28, 46, 52–55, 57, 70, 84, 103, 109, 112, 114, 175, 261

Naval Brigade, 7, 73, 76–77, 88, 153–154, 156–157, 162–163, 210, 218–219, 225, 236
Nefiche, 160, 167, 171, 176, 178, 180
Nicholson, Rear-Admiral, 70, 86, 90, 109, 139
Northbrook, Lord, 7, 64–66, 70–72, 108, 116, 120, 129, 134, 159, 212, 276
Nubar Pasha, 21, 269

Palmer, Professor Edward, 120
Pas-El-Tin Palace, 69, 75, 84–85, 87, 93, 95, 99–100, 108, 110, 138
Pharos Fort, 53, 85, 87, 99, 105, 108
Philip, Corporal John, 144
Pibworth, Lt. James, 54
Pirie, Lt. A., 202–203, 284
Place Muhammad Ali, 21, 52–57, 70, 103, 109
Port Said, 169, 170–174, 176, 280, 285
Porter, Corporal Henry, 150, 241
Prior, Melton, 86, 89, 96, 112, 169, 182, 207, 218, 283
Pennington, Lt-Colonel C., 216–217
Purvis, Lt., 218–219

Quinnebaug, Uss, 86, 108

Ramleh, 52–54, 68, 105–106, 110, 118, 138, 144–145, 152–153, 157, 161–163, 168–169
Rushid Pasha, General, 178, 183, 216, 221
Rawson, Captain Harry, 166, 170, 313
Rawson, Lt. Wyatt, 227, 234, 242, 262
Riaz Pasha, 15, 22, 24, 32
Ribton, Herbert,, 58
Richardson, Lt-Colonel W., 58, 180, 240, 252
Rifky, Osman, 22, 24–26, 47
Ring, Baron De, 25
Roberts, Major-General Sir Frederick, 123, 228, 283
Rogers, Lt-Colonel Robert, 9, 194
Ross, John, 109, 112
Royal Navy, 81–82, 90–92, 95, 101, 107, 147, 163
Russell, Colones Sir Baker, 148, 184, 187, 196–197, 199–200, 203–204, 207, 236, 247
  eccentricities, 199–200

Said Pasha, 10, 19, 26–27
Sami-El-Barudi, Mahmud, 26, 29, 45, 270
Sami, Colones Suliman, 59, 106
Sami, Yacoub, 270, 277, 286
Schreiber, Lt-Colonel B., 185, 250
Scott, Lt. Percy, 79, 106, 170
Scudamore, Frank, 53–57
Sekukuni, Chief, 132, 228
Seymour, Captain Edward, 75, 171, 285
Seymour, Admiral Sir Frederick,
  background and career, 75–77, 81–83
  opinions, 78, 81
  death, 285
Silsileh Fort, 72, 73, 75, 85, 87
Smith-Dorrien, Lt. Henry, 73, 164
Spriggs, Sergeant Charles, 162, 268
Spying, 68–69, 73, 116, 120, 216, 232
Stewart, General Sir Donald, 134, 146
Stewart, Lt-Colonel Herbert, 148, 158, 199, 260, 282
Stockwell, Lt-Colones C., 172
Stone, General Charles, 74, 85
Stone, Fanny, 140–141
Stone, Mrs. (mother of Fanny), 140–141
Suez Canal, 30, 65–66, 69, 71, 117–120, 134–135, 142, 147, 153, 159, 174–176, 280
Sultan Pasha, 36, 50
Swaine, Major Leopold, 166, 173, 214

Talbot, Captain Reginald, 183
Tanjore, P+O Ship, 57, 67, 74, 85, 99, 114
Teck, HRH Duke of, 207
Tel-El-Kebir, 6, 8–9, 61, 118, 126, 160, 177, 191, 211–214, 257, 264, 266, 285
  battle, 238–258
  fortifications, 228–230
  night march, 228, 232–238
Tewfik, Khedive, 36
Timsha, Lake, 167, 175
Toulba Pasha, 70–71, 103, 105, 110, 270, 277
Tulloch, Major Alexander, 94, 250
Tunisia, 30–31, 38, 47, 120
Turco-Circassians, 18–19, 27, 45–46
Tutt, Private Robert, 232

Vernoni, Alessandro, 38, 57
Victoria, HRH Queen, 13, 22, 124, 126, 274–275, 294, 309
Villiers, Frederic, 83, 86–88, 109, 215, 237, 252, 269, 283

Walsh, Langton, 195, 252
War Correspondents, 72, 85–86, 109, 112, 123, 134, 166, 168, 202, 214, 237, 252
War Council (Majlis-Al-Urfi), 193
Watson, Captain Charles, 208, 230, 255, 260
Wauchope, Captain Andrew, 243, 254
Wilkinson, Brigadier-General H., 193, 212, 236, 251
Willis, Lt-General George, 9, 147
Wilson, Captain Arthur, 152, 163
Wilson, Lt-Colonel Sir Charles, 116, 221, 269, 270, 285, 287
Wolseley, Lt-General Sir Garnet, 6, 83, 117, 121, 124, 130, 135, 142, 255, 273, 294
  career, 125–133, 285–286
  personality, 122–124, 221–222
  strategy, 159–161, 165–170, 214, 220, 222, 224, 227–228
  hatred of Royalty, 149, 195–196
  transport delay, 210
  journal, 211
Wolseley, Lady Louisa, 128–129
Wood, Captain Elliott, 126–127, 143
Wood, Major-General Sir Evelyn, 123, 126–127, 148, 192, 196, 264, 275

Zagazig, 26, 118, 122, 124, 252, 254, 259, 263
Zulus, 132, 155